CIMA

TUDY TEXT

OPERATIONAL

PAPER E1

ENTERPRISE OPERATIONS

Our text is designed to help you study **effectively** and **efficiently**.

In this edition we:

- **Highlight** the **most important elements** in the syllabus and the **key skills** you will need

- **Signpost** how each chapter links to the syllabus and the learning outcomes

- **Provide** lots of **exam alerts** explaining how what you're learning may be tested

- **Include examples** and **questions** to help you apply what you've learnt

- **Emphasise key points** in **section summaries**

- **Test your knowledge** of what you've studied in **quick quizzes**

- **Examine your understanding** in our **exam question bank**

- **Reference all the important topics** in the **full index**

FOR EXAMS IN NOVEMBER 2011 AND MAY 2012

LEARNING MEDIA

First edition 2009
Third edition June 2011

ISBN 9780 7517 9475 5
(Previous ISBN 9780 7517 8457 2)

e-Book ISBN 9780 7517 9602 5

British Library Cataloguing-in-Publication Data
A catalogue record for this book
is available from the British Library

Published by

BPP Learning Media Ltd
BPP House, Aldine Place
London W12 8AA

www.bpp.com/learningmedia

Printed in the United Kingdom

Your learning materials, published by BPP
Learning Media Ltd, are printed on paper sourced
from sustainable, managed forests.

We are grateful to the Chartered Institute of
Management Accountants for permission to
reproduce past examination questions. The
suggested solutions in the exam answer bank have
been prepared by BPP Learning Media Ltd.

Contents

How our Study Text can help you pass

Streamlined studying	• We show you the best ways to study efficiently
	• Our Text has been designed to ensure you can easily and quickly navigate through it
	• The different features in our Text emphasise important knowledge and techniques
Exam expertise	• **Studying E1** on page xiv introduces the key themes of the syllabus and summarises how to pass
	• We highlight throughout our Text how topics may be tested and what you'll have to do in the exam
	• We help you see the complete picture of the syllabus, so that you can answer questions that range across the whole syllabus
	• Our Text covers the syllabus content – no more, no less
Regular review	• We frequently summarise the key knowledge you need
	• We test what you've learnt by providing questions and quizzes throughout our Text

Our other products

BPP Learning Media also offers these products for the E1 exam:

Practice and Revision Kit	Providing lots more question practice and helpful guidance on how to pass the exam
Passcards	Summarising what you should know in visual, easy to remember, form
Success CDs	Covering the vital elements of the E1 syllabus in less than 90 minutes and also containing exam hints to help you fine tune your strategy
i-Pass	Providing computer-based testing in a variety of formats, ideal for self-assessment
Interactive Passcards	Allowing you to learn actively with a clear visual format summarising what you must know

You can purchase these products by visiting www.bpp.com/mybpp

CIMA Distance Learning

BPP's distance learning packages provide flexibility and convenience, allowing you to study effectively, at a pace that suits you, where and when you choose. There are four great distance learning packages available.

Online classroom	Bringing the classroom experience to you via the web and offering you great flexibility, with the quality for which BPP classroom courses are renowned
Basics Plus	Combining the paper-based and e-learning approaches of our Basics and Basics Online distance learning packages
Basics	Consisting of high quality BPP Learning Media study materials and access to BPP Professional Education subject experts
Basics Online	Including the best online learning and practice

You can find out more about these packages by visiting http://www.bpp.com/courses/examination-courses/accounting--finance/cima-2011/ways-to-study.aspx

Features in our Study Text

 Section Introductions explain how the section fits into the chapter

 Key Terms are the core vocabulary you need to learn

KEY TERM

 Key Points are points that you have to know, ideas or calculations that will be the foundations of your answers

KEY POINT

 Exam Alerts show you how subjects are likely to be tested

 Exam Skills are the key skills you will need to demonstrate in the exam, linked to question requirements

 Formulae To Learn are formulae you must remember in the exam

LEARN

 Exam Formulae are formulae you will be given in the exam

EXAM

 Examples show how theory is put into practice

 Questions give you the practice you need to test your understanding of what you've learnt

 Case Studies link what you've learnt with the real-world business environment

CASE STUDY

 Links show how the syllabus overlaps with other parts of the qualification, including Knowledge Brought Forward that you need to remember from previous exams

 Website References link to material that will enhance your understanding of what you're studying

 Further Reading will give you a wider perspective on the subjects you're covering

 Section Summaries allow you to review each section

Streamlined studying

What you should do	In order to
Read the Chapter and Section Introductions	See why topics need to be studied and map your way through the chapter
Go quickly through the explanations	Gain the depth of knowledge and understanding that you'll need
Highlight the Key Points, Key Terms and Formulae To Learn	Make sure you know the basics that you can't do without in the exam
Focus on the Exam Skills and Exam Alerts	Know how you'll be tested and what you'll have to do
Work through the Examples and Case Studies	See how what you've learnt applies in practice
Prepare Answers to the Questions	See if you can apply what you've learnt in practice
Revisit the Section Summaries in the Chapter Roundup	Remind you of, and reinforce, what you've learnt
Answer the Quick Quiz	Find out if there are any gaps in your knowledge
Answer the Question(s) in the Exam Question Bank	Practise what you've learnt in depth

Should I take notes?

Brief notes may help you remember what you're learning. You should use the notes format that's most helpful to you (lists, diagrams, mindmaps).

Further help

BPP Learning Media's *Learning to Learn Accountancy* provides lots more helpful guidance on studying. It is designed to be used both at the outset of your CIMA studies and throughout the process of learning accountancy. It can help you **focus your studies on the subject and exam**, enabling you to **acquire knowledge**, **practise and revise efficiently and effectively**.

Syllabus and learning outcomes

Paper E1 Enterprise Operations

The syllabus comprises:

Topic and Study Weighting

		%
A	The Global Business Environment	20
B	Information Systems	20
C	Operations Management	20
D	Marketing	20
E	Managing Human Capital	20

Learning Outcomes		
Lead	**Component**	**Syllabus content**
A	**The Global Business Environment**	
1 Explain the social, political and economic context of business.	(a) Explain the emergence of major economies in Asia and Latin America	• Cross-cultural management and different forms of business organisation.
	(b) Explain the emergence and importance of outsourcing and offshoring	• Emerging market multinationals.
		• Liberalisation and economic nationalism.
	(c) Explain the impact of international macroeconomic developments (eg long-term shifts in trade balances), on the organisation's competitive environment.	• Outsourcing and offshoring.
		• Major economic systems including US, European and transition economies.
		• National account balances (especially from international trade), monetary policy and their impact on markets.
2 Analyse the relationship between the internal governance of the firm and external sources of governance and regulation.	(a) Explain the principles and purpose of corporate social responsibility and the principles of good corporate governance in an international context	• Corporate governance, including stakeholders and the role of government.
		• Principles of corporate social responsibility and the scope for international variation, eg between developed and developing economies.
	(b) Analyse relationships among business, society and government in national and regional contexts	• Business-government relations in developed and developing economies.
	(c) Apply tools of country and political risk analysis	• Regulation in the national and international context and its impact on the firm.
	(d) Discuss the nature of regulation and its impact on the firm.	• Role of institutions and governance in economic growth.
		• Corporate political activity in developed and developing markets.
		• Country and political risk.

Learning Outcomes			
Lead		**Component**	**Syllabus content**
B	**Information Systems**		
1	Discuss the wider business context within which information systems operate.	(a) Identify the value of information and information systems organisations (b) Discuss the reasons for organisations' increased dependence on information systems (c) Discuss the transformation of organisations through technology	• The role of information systems in organisations. • Emerging information system trends in organisations (eg Enterprise-wide systems; knowledge management systems; customer relationship management systems, eg E-business, Web 2.0 tools). • Information technology enabled transformation; the emergence of new forms of organisation. • Geographically dispersed (virtual) teams; role of information systems in virtual teams and challenges for virtual collaboration.
2	Analyse how information systems can be implemented in support of the organisation's strategy.	(a) Discuss ways for overcoming problems in information system implementation (b) Discuss ways of organising and managing information system activities in the context of the wider organisation.	• Assessing the costs and benefits of information systems; criteria for evaluating information systems. • Privacy and security. • System changeover methods (i.e. direct, parallel, pilot and phased). • Information system implementation as a change management process; avoiding problems of non-usage and resistance. • Information system outsourcing (different types of sourcing strategies; client-vendor relationships). • Aligning information systems with business strategy (eg strategic importance of information systems; information systems for competitive advantage; information systems for competitive necessity).

Learning Outcomes		
Lead	**Component**	**Syllabus content**
C **Operations management**		
1 Explain the relationship of operations management to other aspects of the organisation's operations.	(a) Explain the shift from price-based to relational procurement and operations (b) Explain the relationship of operations and supply management to the competitiveness of the firm (c) Explain the particular issues surrounding operations management in services (d) Explain the importance of sustainability in operations management.	• Supply chain management as a strategic process. • An overview of operations strategy and its importance to the firm. • Supply chains in competition with each other; role of supply networks; demand networks as an evolution of supply chains. • Design of products/services and processes and how this relates to operations and supply. • The concept of sustainability in operations management.
2 Apply tools and techniques of operations management.	(a) Apply contemporary thinking in quality management (b) Explain process design (c) Apply tools and concepts of lean management (d) Illustrate a plan for the implementation of a quality programme (e) Describe ways to manage relationships with suppliers.	• Different methods of quality measurement (eg Servqual). • Approaches to quality management, including Total Quality Management (TQM), various British and European Union systems as well as statistical control processes. • External quality standards. • Systems used in operations management: Manufacturing Resource Planning II (MRPII); Optimized Production Techniques (OPT) and Enterprise Resource Planning (ERP). • Use of process maps to present the flow of information and product across supply chains and networks. • Methods for managing inventory, including continuous inventory systems (eg Economic Order Quantity, EOQ), periodic inventory systems and the ABC system (Note: ABC is not an acronym; A refers to high value, B to medium and C to low value inventory). • Methods of managing operational capacity in product and service delivery (eg use of queuing theory, forecasting, flexible manufacturing systems).

Learning Outcomes		
Lead	**Component**	**Syllabus content**
		• Application of lean techniques to services.
		• Practices of continuous improvement (e.g. Quality circles, Kaizen, 5S, 6 Sigma).
		• The characteristics of lean production.
		• Criticisms and limitations of lean production.
		• Developing relationships with suppliers, including the use of supply portfolios.
D	**Marketing**	
1 Explain developments in marketing.	(a) Explain the marketing concept, and the alternatives to it	• The marketing concept as a business philosophy.
	(b) Describe the marketing environment of a range of organisations	• The marketing environment, including societal, economic, technological, political and legal factors affecting marketing.
	(c) Explain marketing in a not-for-profit context	• Marketing in not-for-profit organisations (ie charities, non-governmental organisations; the public sector).
	(d) Explain the social context of marketing behaviour	
	(e) Describe theories of consumer behaviour.	• Theories of consumer behaviour (e.g. social interaction theory), as well as factors affecting buying decisions, types of buying behaviour and stages in the buying process.
		• Social marketing and corporate social responsibility.
2 Apply tools and techniques used in support of the organisation's marketing.	(a) Explain the relationships between market research, market segmentation, targeting and positioning	• Market research, including data gathering techniques and methods of analysis.
	(b) Apply tools within each area of the marketing mix	• Segmentation and targeting of markets, and positioning of products within markets.
	(c) Describe the business contexts within which marketing principles can be applied	• How business to business (B2B) marketing differs from business to consumer (B2C) marketing in its different forms (ie consumer marketing, services marketing, direct marketing, interactive marketing, e-marketing, internal marketing).
	(d) Describe the market planning process	
	(e) Explain the role of branding and brand equity.	• Promotional tools and the promotion mix.
		• The 'service extension' to the marketing mix.

Learning Outcomes				
Lead		**Component**		**Syllabus content**
			•	Devising and implementing a pricing strategy.
			•	Experiential marketing.
			•	Marketing communications, including viral, guerrilla and other indirect forms of marketing.
			•	Distribution channels and methods for marketing campaigns.
			•	The role of marketing in the business plan of the organisation.
			•	Brand image and brand value.
			•	Product development and product/service life-cycles.
			•	Internal marketing as the process of training and motivating employees so as to support the organisation's external marketing activities.
			•	The differences and similarities in the marketing of products, services and experiences.
			•	Product portfolios and the product mix.
E	**Managing human capital**			
1	Explain the relationship of Human Resources (HR) to the organisation's operations.	(a)	Explain how HR theories and activities can contribute to the success of the organisation	•	Theories of Human Resource Management relating to ability, motivation and opportunity.
		(b)	Explain the importance of ethical behaviour in business generally and for the line manager and their activities.	•	The psychological contract and its importance to retention.
				•	The relationship of the employee to other elements of the business.
				•	Personal business ethics and the fundamental principles (Part A) of the CIMA Code of Ethics for Professional Accountants.
2	Discuss the activities associated with the management of human capital.	(a)	Explain the HR activities associated with developing the ability of employees	•	Practices associated with recruiting and developing appropriate abilities including recruitment and selection of staff using different recruitment channels (ie interviews, assessment centres, intelligence tests, aptitude tests, psychometric tests).
		(b)	Discuss the HR activities associated with the motivation of employees		
		(c)	Describe the HR activities associated with improving the opportunities for employees to contribute to the firm	•	Issues relating to fair and legal employment practices (eg recruitment, dismissal, redundancy, and ways of managing these).

Learning Outcomes		
Lead	**Component**	**Syllabus content**
	(d) Discuss the importance of the line manager in the implementation of HR practices	• The distinction between development and training and the tools available to develop and train staff.
	(e) Prepare an HR plan appropriate to a team.	• The design and implementation of induction programmes.
		• Practices related to motivation including issues in the design of reward systems (e.g. the role of incentives, the utility of performance-related pay, arrangements for knowledge workers, flexible work arrangements).
		• The importance of appraisals, their conduct and their relationship to the reward system.
		• Practices related to the creation of opportunities for employees to contribute to the organisation including job design, communications, involvement procedures and appropriate elements of negotiating and bargaining.
		• Problems in implementing an HR plan appropriate to a team and ways to manage this.
		• HR in different organisational forms (eg project based, virtual or networked firms) and different organisational contexts.
		• Preparation of an HR plan (eg forecasting personnel requirements; retention, absence and leave, wastage).

Old and new syllabuses

The syllabus for the E1 *Enterprise Operations* paper is similar to the syllabus for the old syllabus paper P4 *Organisational Management and Information Systems*. Four of the five syllabus areas are the same for both the old and new syllabus exams – however there have been some changes to syllabus content as well as changes in study weightings.

One old syllabus area, change management, has been replaced with the new area of the global business environment. That said, some aspects of change management have been kept and they form part of the information systems syllabus area in respect of implementing new information systems.

The information systems area itself now focuses on the role of information systems, types of information systems and the strategic implications of information systems. Much of the old syllabus concentrated on how information systems are developed and the various types of hardware and software.

Process mapping is now included in the operations management syllabus area as a method of presenting the flow of information over supply chains and networks.

Compared to old syllabus P4, the following topics have been added, with references to the chapter in which they are covered:

- The social, political and economic context of global business (1)

- Governance and the regulation of economies, markets and organisations (2)

- Emerging information system trends (enterprise-wide, knowledge management and customer relationship management systems, e-commerce and Web 2.0) (3)

- Aligning information systems with business strategy (4)

- Demand networks, supply portfolios and sustainability in operations management (5)

- Servqual as a measurement of quality (6)

- Product development, product portfolios and the product mix, promotional tools and the promotion mix, branding, direct/indirect/interactive marketing, guerrilla/viral/ experimental marketing (9)

- Marketing not-for-profit organisations and corporate internal marketing. Coverage of corporate social responsibility and marketing has been extended (10)

- Maximising employee contribution to the organisation (11/12)

Studying E1

1 What's E1 about

E1 explores several discrete subjects which all affect how organisations operate. However, please note that exam questions are likely to cover more than one of these subjects. You should therefore appreciate the various links between them.

1.1 The global business environment

In Chapter 1 we introduce the setting within which all organisations compete – the **global economy**. We begin by looking at the main influences on the **international environment** including the major **economic systems** of the world, and how **nations develop their economy and industry**. Following on from this we shall study the different **types of businesses** and the **cultural considerations** multinational companies have to think about when managing business units in several countries.

The focus of Chapter 2 is on how governments affect their economies through **economic policy** and **regulation**. The chapter also looks at non-legal regulation, in the form of **corporate governance** and **corporate social responsibility,** which are becoming increasingly important to all business organisations.

1.2 Information systems

You are not expected to become an information systems (IS) expert, but the syllabus does require you to appreciate the **role IS plays in organisations**. This includes the various **types of system** and the role systems play in **transforming how organisations operate** and the **types of business** they do. These areas are all covered in Chapter 3.

Chapter 4 is primarily concerned with how organisations **implement new systems**. However, you should also understand the importance of organisations **aligning** their **information systems** with their **overall business strategy**.

1.3 Operations management

Operations are the main activities of an organisation. They are **'what it does'**, and it is the subject of Chapters 5, 6 and 7.

We begin by studying how operations develop around a **value chain** and how organisations join together to form **supply chains** and networks. **Quality** is an important issue for all businesses, whether in terms of products or services, and we shall see how quality can be **measured** and **managed** to ensure the customer is satisfied. Finally, we shall find out how organisations can **balance** their **inputs** (inventory) and **outputs** (products and services) with **changing demand levels**.

1.4 Marketing

Marketing is about **communicating** the organisation's **sales messages** to the customer. It forms a major part of its business strategy and is the subject of Chapters 8, 9 and 10. We shall firstly study the **marketing environment** and see how a **marketing strategy** and **plan** are put together. Following on from this, our study looks into how the **marketing message is communicated** to the customer and the important issue of **corporate branding**.

The syllabus also covers several smaller areas of marketing. These include; **consumer behaviour**, marketing **not-for-profit organisations**, marketing an organisation's message to its employees (**internal marketing**) and how **corporate social responsibility** affects how an organisation markets its products and services. We shall cover all these areas in full as well.

1.5 Managing human capital

Many believe that an organisation's **employees** are its main asset and they should be **carefully managed** to get the best out of them. The E1 syllabus looks at all aspects of managing employees to **maximise their potential**. Motivation, remuneration, appraisals and various types of working arrangement are all important to this end and are covered in Chapters 11 and 12. We shall also look into what constitutes good **HR practice** and the importance of employees acting **ethically**.

2 What's required

You will face a **variety of questions** in the E1 exam. Each type of question tests a different skill and you must be confident in answering each of them.

20% of the marks are for **objective test questions**, such as those requiring a short written answer or the selection of one correct answer from a choice of four. These questions test your ability to make **quick decisions** and **write succinctly**.

When answering multiple choice questions try to **eliminate any obviously wrong answers first** before considering the others.

A further 30% of the marks are available for answering **five short answer questions** which are based around a **single scenario**. These test your ability to **assimilate information quickly** and either **apply theoretical knowledge** or provide a **brief analysis** or **evaluation**.

It is always a good idea to list a few **bullet points** as a plan for each question, covering what you want to say. This helps to focus your mind on the subject and your answers on the question.

The final 50% of the marks are awarded for answering **one or two compulsory questions**, each of which may be related to a **scenario.** These scenarios will not necessarily be any longer than those in the short answer questions, but your **answers must be in more depth** to earn the majority of the marks available.

Always produce an **answer plan**, including any models or theory that you need to mention. A good tip for answering questions that require you to, for example,' explain five advantages of...' is to produce a bullet list which you then use to provide the **headings** in your answer. Add some good explanation to this and you'll be well on your way to passing.

What the examiner means

The table below has been prepared by CIMA to help you interpret the syllabus and learning outcomes and the meaning of exam questions.

You will see that there are 5 levels of Learning objective, ranging from Knowledge to Evaluation, reflecting the level of skill you will be expected to demonstrate. CIMA Certificate subjects were constrained to levels 1 to 3, but in CIMA's Professional qualification the entire hierarchy will be used.

At the start of each chapter in your study text is a topic list relating the coverage in the chapter to the level of skill you may be called on to demonstrate in the exam.

Learning objectives	Verbs used	Definition
1 Knowledge What are you expected to know	• List • State • Define	• Make a list of • Express, fully or clearly, the details of/facts of • Give the exact meaning of
2 Comprehension What you are expected to understand	• Describe • Distinguish • Explain • Identify • Illustrate	• Communicate the key features of • Highlight the differences between • Make clear or intelligible/state the meaning of • Recognise, establish or select after consideration • Use an example to describe or explain something
3 Application How you are expected to apply your knowledge	• Apply • Calculate/ compute • Demonstrate • Prepare • Reconcile • Solve • Tabulate	• Put to practical use • Ascertain or reckon mathematically • Prove with certainty or to exhibit by practical means • Make or get ready for use • Make or prove consistent/compatible • Find an answer to • Arrange in a table
4 Analysis How you are expected to analyse the detail of what you have learned	• Analyse • Categorise • Compare and contrast • Construct • Discuss • Interpret • Prioritise • Produce	• Examine in detail the structure of • Place into a defined class or division • Show the similarities and/or differences between • Build up or compile • Examine in detail by argument • Translate into intelligible or familiar terms • Place in order of priority or sequence for action • Create or bring into existence
5 Evaluation How you are expected to use your learning to evaluate, make decisions or recommendations	• Advise • Evaluate • Recommend	• Counsel, inform or notify • Appraise or assess the value of • Propose a course of action

3 How to pass

3.1 Study the whole syllabus

You need to be comfortable with **all areas of the syllabus**, as questions will often span a number of syllabus areas. For example, question four in the Specimen Paper tested training (from the Managing Human Capital syllabus area) in the context of systems implementation (from the Information Systems syllabus area). A little wider reading will help you keep up to date with the global environment and new technologies.

3.2 Lots of question practice

You can **develop analysis and application skills** by attempting questions in the Exam Question Bank and later on questions in the BPP Practice and Revision Kit.

3.3 Analysing questions

For E1 it's particularly important to **consider the question requirements carefully** so that you understand exactly what the question is asking. It is easy to misread multiple choice questions and therefore choose the wrong answer.

Section C questions will often require you to produce an answer in the context of the scenario. Always read the question carefully and answer the question set, not the question you hoped would be set!

3.4 Answering questions

Well-judged, clear recommendations grounded in the scenario will always score well as markers for this paper look to reward good answers. Lists of points memorised from texts and reproduced without any thought won't score well – you must always relate your knowledge to the specific question that you are facing. Additionally, only include scenario information or detailed theory in your answer if it supports the points you're making.

3.5 Exam technique

The following points of exam technique are particularly relevant to this paper.

- Answers with **answer plans** attached tend to score better and don't repeat the same material in different question parts.

- You should consider in advance how you are going to use the **20 minute reading time** as it can help reduce time pressure. It is suggested that a good use of this time is to **begin answering the multiple choice questions** by marking the question paper. Your answers can be transferred to your answer book when writing time commences. **Do not mark your answer book until you are permitted to do so.**

- **Read the question carefully**. A question that may appear on first glance to be about the product lifecycle, may not require you to state the main stages of the cycle, but discuss how the model is used or the principles behind it.

- Leave time to **check your answers** at the end to identify and correct any silly mistakes.

4 Brought forward knowledge

CIMA has stated that syllabus material covered by any of the papers within the CIMA Certificate in Business Accounting qualification may be relevant for assessment purposes in related subjects.

5 Links with other Operations level exams

The Operations level syllabus is wide and covers a number of different syllabus areas. The E1 syllabus alone covers five significant syllabus areas, giving the examiner more than enough on which to base the E1 exam. Therefore, it is unlikely that an E1 examination question would require knowledge from the other operations level papers (F1 and P1).

The exam paper

Format of the paper

		Number of marks
Section A:	Ten **compulsory** objective test questions, each worth between 2 marks. Mini scenarios may be given to which a group of questions relate.	20
Section B:	Six **compulsory** short answer questions, each worth 5 marks. A short scenario may be given, to which some questions relate.	30
Section C:	Two **compulsory** written questions. Scenarios may be given, to which questions relate	50
		100

Time allowed: 3 hours, plus 20 minutes reading time

CIMA guidance

CIMA has stated that credit will be given for focusing on the right principles and making practical evaluations and recommendations. Plausible alternative answers could be given to many questions, so model answers should not be regarded as all-inclusive.

Numerical content

Questions in this paper usually require written answers. These involve applying theory or explaining key concepts, so do not expect many calculations. However you should bring a calculator with you to the exam just in case.

Breadth of question coverage

Questions in *all* sections of the paper may cover more than one syllabus area.

Knowledge from other syllabuses

Operations level papers can be taken independently and do not require knowledge from other syllabuses.

May 2011 exam paper

Section A

1   Ten multiple-choice questions covering the whole syllabus

Section B

2   Six short written questions covering a wide range of syllabus areas

Section C *(two longer scenario questions worth 25 marks each)*

3   ISO 9000, remuneration and reward packages, performance measures

4   Branding, product and place mix, HR activities

November 2010 exam paper

Section A

1   Ten multiple-choice questions covering the whole syllabus

Section B

2   Six short written questions covering a wide range of syllabus areas

Section C *(two longer scenario questions worth 25 marks each)*

3   HR Practices, HR \ workforce plan, e-HR

4   Ethics and CSR, marketing mix and branding, Internet marketing

May 2010 exam paper

Section A

1   Ten multiple-choice questions covering the whole syllabus

Section B

2   Six short written questions covering a wide range of syllabus areas

Section C *(two longer scenario questions worth 25 marks each)*

3   Emerging economies (BRIC), off-shoring; HR and redundancy

4   Supply chain management, process design, code of ethics

Specimen exam paper

Section A

1   Ten multiple-choice questions covering the whole syllabus

Section B

2   Six short written questions covering a wide range of syllabus areas

Section C *(two longer scenario questions worth 25 marks each)*

3   Marketing, market segmentation, promotional activity and ethics

4   Information system implementation problems and training provision

THE GLOBAL BUSINESS ENVIRONMENT

Part A

THE SOCIAL, POLITICAL AND ECONOMIC CONTEXT

We start our E1 studies by looking at the **wider environment** that organisations operate in. This consists of the global economy and the nations which participate in it.

Once we have set the global context for business we shall turn our attention to looking at **how nations** develop and then apply our knowledge to the recently **emerging economies** of Asia and Latin America.

Finally, we consider the **different types of organisation** and the important **cultural issues** that face businesses who operate globally.

topic list	learning outcomes	syllabus references	ability required
1 The global business environment	A1(a)	A1(ii)	comprehension
2 International environmental influences	A1(a), A1(b) A2(c)	A1(ii) , A2(vi), A2(vii)	application
3 Economic context	A1(a), A1(b)	A1(iii), A1(v)	comprehension
4 Emerging economies	A1(a), A1(b)	A1(ii), A1(iv)	comprehension
5 Different types of organisation	A1(a), A1(b)	A1(i), A1(ii)	comprehension
6 Culture and the global organisation	A1(a), A1(b)	A1(i)	comprehension

1 The global business environment

Introduction

Today, **international trade** is truly global. In this section we consider the factors which led to the globalisation of world trade.

1.1 Globalisation   05/11

KEY TERM

GLOBALISATION refers to the growing interdependence of countries worldwide through increased trade, increased capital flows and the rapid diffusion of technology.
Adapted from an IMF definition

Features of globalisation include:

(a)   The ability of individuals to enter into transactions with individuals and organisations based in other countries.

(b)   The increased importance of global economic policy relative to domestic policy.

(c)   The rise of globally linked and dependant financial markets.

(d)   The reduction in importance of local manufacturing.

(e)   Reduced transaction costs through developments in communications and transport.

(f)   The rise of emerging, newly industrialised nations (covered later in this chapter).

On an organisational level, global production implies that an organisation's production planning is considered on a global scale.

(a)   **Global manufacture**. A company can **manufacture** components for a product in a number of different countries. China is becoming the workshop of the world.

(b)   **Global sourcing**. Sub-components may be purchased from countries overseas.

1.2 Factors encouraging the globalisation of world trade

(a)   **Financial factors** such as Third World debt. Often, lenders require the initiation of economic reforms as a condition of the loan.

(b)   **Country/continent** alliances, such as the European Union, which foster trade and other phenomena such as tourism.

(c)   **Legal factors** such as patents and trade marks, which encourage the development of technology and design.

(d)   **Markets** trading in international commodities. Commodities are not physically exchanged, only the rights to ownership. A buyer can, thanks to efficient systems of trading and communications, buy a commodity in its country of origin for delivery to a specific port.

Section summary

Global production involves manufacturing and sourcing on a global scale.

World trade has been encouraged by **financial factors**, **trade alliances**, **legal factors** and **international markets**.

2   International environmental influences

Introduction

The **global business environment** can be analysed against a number of factors, such as **political**, **economic**, **social/cultural** and **technological**. This is known as **PEST** analysis. There will be differences between different countries.

2.1 Political and legal

2.1.1 Political - corporate political activity

KEY POINTS

Political risk is the risk of an organisation incurring losses due to **non-market factors**. These factors are usually related to government policy, for example trade rules, investment incentives and the tax regime.

Political risk is also related to **financial factors** such as currency controls and the economy, and **stability factors** such as rioting and civil war.

Corporate Political Activity (CPA) refers to the involvement of companies in the political process with the aim of influencing policies towards their preferences.

Organisations may need to **deal with governments** and perhaps make their policy preferences known in a number of situations. Examples include:

(a)   **Multinational companies** from developed countries may negotiate terms for their investment in that country. For example finance, taxation and export agreements.

(b)   **Multinationals** may **lobby governments** to **provide conditions** in the economy that benefit them. For example reducing restrictions or controls over labour such as working hours and minimum wages. The MNC may threaten to withdraw its investment if the government fails to agree.

(c)   **New industries** in **developing nations** may **seek protection** from their government, for example import restrictions.

(d)   **Developing industries** may seek **government support** such as subsidies or tax breaks to help them compete in the global market.

Corporate political activities can be classified into two types, **buffering** and **bridging**.

(a)   **Buffering** refers to proactive actions such as warning the government about the impact of legislation while it's being considered, in an attempt to **influence** the content.

(b)   **Bridging** is more reactive and focuses more on ensuring the firm is aware of and meets required standards of behaviour, for example ensuring the company is aware of proposed new legislation and **complies** with it when it is passed.

2.1.2 Country risk

KEY POINT

Country risk is similar to political risk although it is usually restricted to risks relevant to the **business environment** (including market factors) **in a specific country**.

It is important that organisations analyse the political and country risk of a nation before investing or trading with it to minimise the risk of losses.

2.1.3 Analysing political and country risk

Analysis of political and country risk is difficult. Some elements of risk, such as financial factors, can be **quantified**, however some factors such as the risk of civil war are based on assumptions and judgements.

Macro-political risks are general risks that affect all foreign firms in the same way. The risk of the seizure of all overseas owned business assets is an example of a macro political risk. Risks relevant to particular organisations or sectors are referred to as micro-political risks. Industry specific regulation is an example of a micro political risk.

Many organisations employ a **third party** to carry out a risk assessment for them.

Rugman and *Hodgetts* summarised different aspects of political risk as shown in the following tables.

Sources of political risk	
Changing economic conditions	Social unrest and upheaval
Religious competition and disputes	Local business people vested interests
New international alliances	Increased nationalism

Groups that generate political risk	
The government and its agencies	Foreign governments that have influence
International organisations (eg World Bank, United Nations)	Terrorist groups
Organised interest and protest groups (eg students)	Political opposition groups

Effects of political risk	
Expropriation (seizing) of assets, with or without compensation	Influence on government by non-government groups
Disruption and / or damage from terrorist activity	Restrictions on ways of operating
Increased taxes and / or other financial penalties	Cancellation or revision of contracts
Restrictions on foreign ownership and / or the favouring of local firms (indigenisation laws)	

2.1.4 Weighing up political and country risk

Once the risks have been identified, the organisation needs to weigh up the **probability of the risk** occurring and the **consequences to the organisation** should the event occur. *Jennings and Wattam* (1998) devised the following model to weigh up political risk.

Impact of risk

		Low	High
Probability of risk	**High**	A	B
	Low	C	D

The model is used to **classify** the probability of the risk and impact of the risk as low or high. Four possible situations will result:

(a)   **Situation A – High probability of risk, low impact**. There is a good chance of the risk occurring, although if it does it will not have a significant impact on the organisation. The company should accept the risk but take action to manage it. If the cost of risk management is too high, the organisation may decide to simply accept the risk (if it has a very low impact).

(b)   **Situation B – High probability of risk, high impact**. Due to the high risk and potential impact on the organisation, investing or dealing with the country should only go ahead if the risk can be managed and contingency plans put in place. The potential benefits of the deal must outweigh the costs of managing the risk.

(c)   **Situation C – Low probability of risk, low impact**. The probability of the risk is low and the potential impact on the organisation is also low. This is the ideal situation as the costs of managing the risk will be low. The organisation may decide that risks classified in this quadrant can be accepted with minimal or no additional risk management actions.

(d)   **Situation D – Low probability of risk, high impact**. It can be difficult to decide what action is appropriate in this situation because although the probability of risk is low, the damage it can inflict on the organisation is high. If the organisation chooses to go ahead, then it must take action to minimise the chance of the risk occurring and the potential impact it will have (for example, an insurance policy). If this cannot be achieved in a cost-effective manner then the organisation should consider abandoning its plans.

2.1.5 Managing country and political risk

KEY TERM

RISK MANAGEMENT involves reducing the probability of the risk occurring and minimising the impact on the organisation that it will cause.

The following table contains examples of **how businesses can minimise the probability and impact of risk**.

Minimising probability of risk	Minimising impact of risk
Postponing/abandoning of project until the level of risk is reduced	Continually monitor the environment and be prepared to react quickly
Develop links with relevant government departments to help shape policy	Develop contingency plans
Abandon the project	Take out country/political risk insurance

You will revisit risk management when you study P3.

2.1.6 Legal

The **system of courts and the law** will differ from country to country although many share similar characteristics. The **rule of law** and **independent judiciaries** may be strong in one country but absent in another. Rules relating to corporate status, property, the regulation of business and to financial reporting may all be very different.

2.2 Economy and economic development

Various **economic factors** specific to a country may affect international trade:

*   Is there **growth** or is the economy stagnating?
*   Is the **exchange rate** stable?
*   How does the **interest rate** compare with other countries? Is it stable?
*   What is the rate of **inflation**? What is the government's policy? Is it realistic?

Economic factors affect the **demand** for, and the **ability to acquire**, goods and services. As countries develop, demand increases for more and more sophisticated products and services. Countries generally have larger **agricultural** sectors in the early stages of economic development. As the economy develops, the **manufacturing** sector increases.

PEST analysis can also be used as a tool to identify the risks **within an economy**. In this case, potential risks are generated for each of the four headings.

Factor	Example of risk
Political	Unstable government
Economic	Economic slowdown
Social	High crime rates, risk of civil war
Technological	Lack of technological infrastructure – poor telecommunications network

2.2.1 Level of economic development

Generally each country can be classified under one of five headings. Note that **gross domestic product (GDP)** is the value of the goods and services produced by an economy in a given period.

KEY TERMS

LESSER DEVELOPED COUNTRY (LDC). Relies heavily on primary industries (mining, agriculture, forestry, fishing). Low GDP and poorly developed infrastructure.

EARLY DEVELOPED COUNTRY (EDC). Largely primary industry based but with developing secondary (manufacturing) industrial sector. Low but growing GDP, developing infrastructure.

SEMI-DEVELOPED COUNTRY (SDC). Significant secondary sector still growing. Rising affluence and education with the emergence of a 'middle class'. Developed infrastructure.

FULLY DEVELOPED COUNTRY (FDC). Primary sector accounts for little of the economy. Secondary sector still dominates, but major growth in tertiary (service) sector. Sophisticated infrastructure.

TRANSITIONAL ECONOMIES (TEs). These are countries which used to be part of the planned economy of the Soviet Union but which are now in various stages of transition towards a market economy.

2.3 Social/cultural

A country's culture consists of a number of factors such as **beliefs**, **morals** and **how citizens behave**. A nation's culture is very difficult to change and if change does occur it will take place very slowly.

National culture is important to businesses because it influences the perceptions and behaviour of consumers as well as employees and managers. The national way of doing things pervades society. Business practice is part of the **structure of society** and therefore subject to cultural influences.

Language is another important aspect of culture. While English is fast becoming the international language of business, there are many areas where it is not commonly understood, sometimes as a matter of local pride. Mistaken use of a foreign language can have a detrimental affect on a business.

2.4 Technology

Technology is the **key driver** of **global economic activity**. It is an enabler, allowing new types of business and organisational structure. It has had other impacts, such as:

(a)   Protection of **intellectual property.** Patents, trademarks and copyright are particularly important in international operations. Can they be protected? Similarly, in manufacturing, can trade secrets be protected, perhaps by importing part-completed assemblies? Some countries require local ownership of relevant patents before production can proceed in that country.

(b)   If advanced technology is involved, it will be necessary to consider local **standards of education and technical infrastructure**.

(c)   Reliance on **'e' methods** for marketing communications and product delivery (eg information or music downloads) depends on potentially differing levels of infrastructure (eg availability of broadband Internet connections) and adoption (eg mobile phone ownership).

(d)   Ease of **communication** with overseas markets (eg via email and e-commerce) creating potential **fulfilment/delivery** problems (given distance and infrastructure).

You can use PEST analysis to analyse many aspects of an organisation's environment so expect to apply it in your future exams, up to and including TOPCIMA.

We shall apply PEST again in Chapter 3, in connection with gathering information about an organisation's environment, and in Chapter 8 in relation to the marketing environment.

PEST analysis is also sometimes known as PESTEL analysis. This is the same as PEST, but considers ecological factors and at legal factors separately from political factors.

Section summary

The **global business environment** can be analysed into **political**, **economic**, **social** and **technological** factors, this is known as **PEST** analysis.

3 Economic context

Introduction

Free trade is not a new concept, but free trade on a global scale has grown massively in recent decades. There are arguments for and against free trade.

In the global business environment a number of **regional trading arrangements** exist. These regional trading groups take three forms, **free trade areas**, **customs unions** and **economic unions/common markets**.

Another feature of the global environment is the increasing number of **transition economies** which are becoming more outward looking and competitive.

3.1 Free trade v protectionism

KEY TERM

FREE TRADE encourages easy movement of goods, services labour and capital between different countries. Free trade involves an absence of quotas, tariffs, subsidies and discriminatory taxation or other barriers that may hinder trade.

Free trade is sometimes referred to as **liberalisation** or liberal trade policies.

Arguments for free trade
Conflict is less likely between countries that trade and communicate with each other
Facilitates specialisation by countries in the production of the goods and services they are best suited to producing
Enables countries to develop and invest in resources leading to more efficient production
Encourages entrepreneurship and economic growth

Arguments for free trade
Encourages all countries to export
Leads to better quality goods and a better quality of life

Arguments against free trade
Countries become dependent upon a single product or type of product (eg the oil exporting countries of the Middle East)
Less developed countries become dependent upon other countries for some products (eg high tech products)
Can undermine local culture (eg the Americanisation of Europe)
Increases consumer expectations and encourages inefficiencies (eg air-freighting fruit to areas it is out of season)
Free trade can prevent new industries developing and becoming established

KEY TERM

PROTECTIONISM aims to restrict trade with one or more other country to protect home country producers from overseas suppliers.

Protectionism is sometimes referred to as **economic nationalism**.

Protective trade measures
Quotas - restricting the quantity able to be imported
Tariffs and/or customs duty - effectively taxing imports making them more expensive
Subsidies - helping local producers giving them an advantage over overseas competitors
Campaigns - encouraging citizens to buy locally produced goods
Technical barriers - implementing strict quality, environmental, health and safety and / or packaging regulations that effectively restrict imports

3.2 The move towards free trade

From the industrial revolution in the nineteenth century until the middle of the twentieth century, nations held a **nationalist view of their economy** – in other words governments were only interested in protecting and developing their own industries.

However, in the mid to late twentieth century **economic liberalisation** took place. Governments moved away from the single minded view of looking after their own economies, towards working with others in groups for the common good of all members.

Three forms of trading group developed during this period, **free trade areas**, **customs unions** and **economic unions/common markets**.

3.3 Free trade areas

Members in these arrangements agree to lower barriers to trade amongst themselves. They enable free movement of **goods** and **services**, but not always the factors of production such as materials and labour.

3.4 Customs unions

Customs unions provide the advantages of free trade areas and agree a common policy on tariff and non-tariff barriers to **external countries**. They attempt to harmonise tariffs, taxes and duties amongst members.

3.5 Economic unions/common markets

In an economic union or common market, members become one for **economic purposes**. There is free movement of the factors of production. The European Union (EU) has economic union as an aim, although not all members, including the UK, necessarily see this goal as desirable. The EU has a 'rich' market of over 500 million people and could provide an economic counterweight to countries such as the USA and Japan.

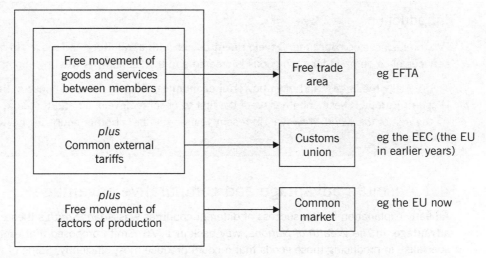

The major **regional trade organisations** are as follows.

(a)   North American Free Trade Agreement (**NAFTA**) – US, Canada and Mexico.

(b)   European Free Trade Association (**EFTA**) – Norway, Switzerland, Iceland, Liechtenstein.

(c)   European Union (**EU**) – Ireland, United Kingdom, France, Germany, Italy, Spain, Portugal, Finland, Sweden, Denmark, Luxembourg, Belgium, the Netherlands, Austria, Greece, Bulgaria, Cyprus, Czech Republic, Estonia, Hungary, Latvia, Lithuania, Malta, Poland, Romania, Slovakia, Slovenia.

(d)   Asean Free Trade Area (**AFTA**) – Brunei, Indonesia, Malaysia, the Philippines, Singapore, Thailand.

(e)   Asia-Pacific Economic Co-operation (**APEC**) – Australia, Brunei, Malaysia, Singapore, Thailand, New Zealand, Papua New Guinea, Indonesia, the Philippines, Taiwan, Hong Kong, Japan, South Korea, China, Canada, US, Mexico, Chile.

(f)   **Mercosur** – Brazil, Argentina, Paraguay and Uruguay (Chile is an associate).

(g)   Southern African Development Community (**SADC**); Angola, Botswana, Lesotho, Malawi, Mozambique, Mauritius, Namibia, South Africa, Swaziland, Tanzania, Swaziland, Zimbabwe.

(h)   West African Economic and Monetary Union (**UEMOA**) – Ivory Cost, Burkina Faso, Niger, Togo, Senegal, Benin and Mali.

(i)   South Asian Association for Regional Co-operation (**SAARC**) – India, Pakistan, Sri Lanka, Bangladesh, the Maldives, Bhutan and Nepal.

(j)   **Andean Pact** – Venezuela, Colombia, Ecuador, Peru and Bolivia.

(k)   Association of Southeast Asian Nations (**ASEAN**) – Indonesia, Malaysia, Philippines, Singapore and Thailand.

Section summary

Economic nationalism is a nation's view that it should protect its own economy and industries.

Economic liberalisation involves nations moving away from economic nationalism towards working with others in a group to benefit all member economies and industries.

Free trade areas, **customs unions** and **economic unions/common markets** are all types of economic system designed to provide members with a trade advantage.

4 Emerging economies   11/10

Introduction

Economies develop over time. **Development** begins with **agriculture** and moves to **manufacturing** and **services** once demand for such goods is created and the economy is wealthy enough to afford them.

Traditionally the largest and most **powerful economies** of the world were those of the **US**, **Japan** and **Western Europe**. These countries were the first to become developed and therefore they had a 'head start' on the rest of the world. However, in recent years a number of **other countries** have begun to **compete** with them.

4.1 Absolute advantage and comparative advantage

An early explanation for the success of different countries was *Adam Smith*'s theory of **absolute advantage**. In *The Wealth of Nations*, way back in 1776, Smith proposed that each nation should specialise in producing those goods that it could produce most efficiently. Some of these would be exported to pay for the imports of goods that could be produced more efficiently elsewhere.

Smith's theory of absolute advantage is based on the assumption that the nation is more efficient at production of certain goods than are its trading partners, and that nations would gain from trade.

Smith's theory was refined by *David Ricardo* (around 1817) and in the 1930s by *Hecksher* and *Olin* to become the theory of **comparative advantage**. This held that relative opportunity costs were most relevant when considering economic activities in relation to other countries. Even if a country is able to produce all its goods at lower costs than another country can, trade would benefit both countries.

4.2 Competitive advantage - Porter's diamond

Michael Porter argues that comparative advantage is too general a concept to explain national sources of competitive advantage. His **The Competitive Advantage Of Nations** (1992), suggests that some nations' industries are more internationally competitive than others.

Porter believes the conditions within a country affects the ability of organisations and industries based in that country to compete with organisations based in other countries. He identifies **four principal factors**, that impact on the competitiveness of organisations as shown in the following diagram - the **diamond**. Governments can **intervene** in their economy to **support each factor** and as a result can influence the competitiveness of its organisations.

Porter's diamond

```
                    ┌──────────────────┐
                    │  Firm strategy,  │
                    │ structure, rivalry│
                    └──────────────────┘

┌──────────────┐                        ┌──────────────┐
│    Factor    │◄──────────────────────►│    Demand    │
│  conditions  │                        │  conditions  │
└──────────────┘                        └──────────────┘

                    ┌──────────────────┐
                    │   Related and    │
                    │supporting industries│
                    └──────────────────┘
```

4.2.1 Factor conditions

Factor conditions relate to those factors used as inputs in the production of goods and services.

- **Human resources** (skills, price, motivation, industrial relations)
- **Physical resources** (land, minerals, climate, location relative to other nations)
- **Knowledge** (scientific and technical know-how, educational institutions)
- **Capital** (amounts available for investment, how it is deployed)
- **Infrastructure** (transport, communications, housing)

Porter distinguishes between **basic** and **advanced** factors.

(a)   **Basic factors** are natural resources, climate, semiskilled and unskilled labour. They are inherent, or at best their creation involves little investment. They are **unsustainable** as a source of national competitive advantage, since they are widely available. For example, the wages of unskilled workers in industrial countries are undermined by even lower wages elsewhere.

(b)   **Advanced factors** are associated with a well-developed scientific and technological infrastructure and include modern digital communications networks, highly educated people (eg computer scientists), university research laboratories and so on. They are necessary to achieve high order competitive advantages such as differentiated products and proprietary production technology.

An abundance of factors is not enough. It is the efficiency with which they are deployed that matters. The former Soviet Union had an abundance of natural resources and a fairly well educated workforce, but was an economic catastrophe.

Porter also notes that **generalised factors**, such as transport infrastructure are not significant in establishing competitive advantage as **specialised factors**. Specialised factors are relevant to a limited range of industries, such as knowledge bases in particular fields and logistic systems developed for particular goods or raw materials. Such factors are integral to innovation and very difficult to move to other countries.

4.2.2 Demand conditions: the home market

The **home market determines how organisations perceive, interpret and respond to buyer needs.** This information puts pressure on organisations to innovate and provides a launch pad for global ambitions.

Important home market considerations include:

(a)   There are **no cultural impediments** to communication.

(b)   **Segmentation** of the home market shapes an organisation's priorities. Companies will be successful globally in segments which are similar to the home market.

(c) **Sophisticated and demanding buyers at home encourage high quality standards.**

(d) **Anticipation of buyer needs**. If consumer needs are expressed in the home market earlier than in the world market, the organisation benefits from experience.

(e) The **rate of growth**. Slow growing home markets do not encourage the adoption of state of the art technology.

(f) **Early saturation** of the home market will encourage an organisation to export.

4.2.3 Related and supporting industries

Competitive success in one industry is linked to success in related industries. Local suppliers may be preferable to overseas suppliers if continuing close co-operation and co-ordination is important. The process of innovation is also enhanced when innovative organisations in related industries are based close to each other. For example, many innovative high-tech businesses are based in "Silicon Valley", California.

4.2.4 Firm strategy, structure and rivalry

Management style and industrial structure. Nations are likely to display competitive advantage in industries that are culturally suited to their normal management practices and industrial structures. For example, German managers tend to have a strong bias towards engineering and are best at products demanding careful development and complex manufacturing processes. They are less successful in industries based on intangibles such as fashion and entertainment.

Strategy. Industries in different countries have different **time horizons**, funding needs and so forth.

(a) **National capital markets** set different goals for performance. In Germany and Switzerland, banks are the main source of capital, not equity shareholders. Short-term fluctuations in share prices are not regarded as of great importance as funds are invested for the long term. In the USA, most shares are held by financial institutions whose own performance indicators emphasise short-term earnings growth.

(b) National attitudes to **wealth** are important. The egalitarian Swedes (as a generalisation) may be less motivated to pursue success in industries that have the potential to create individual fortunes but depend on new start-ups.

(c) **National culture** affects industrial priorities through the relative prestige it allots to various industries and their leaders. Italy values fashion and furnishings, for instance, while in Israel the most prestigious industries are agriculture and those related to defence.

Domestic rivalry is important for several reasons.

- All rivals are working under the same domestic conditions
- With little domestic rivalry, organisations may be happy to rely on the home market.
- Tough domestic rivals teach an organisation about competitive success.
- Domestic rivalry forces organisations to compete on grounds other than basic factors.
- Each rival can try a different strategic approach.

The promotion of one or two '**national champions**' who can reap major economies of scale in the domestic market is undermined by the vigorous domestic competition among high-performing companies. Examples are the Swiss pharmaceutical industry and the US IT industry.

 Porter's diamond is a key theory which you will use again in the future, for example in paper E2.

4.3 Influencing the diamond

A nation's competitive industries tend to be **clustered**. *Porter* believes clustering to be a key to national competitive advantage. A cluster is a linking of industries through relationships which are either vertical (buyer-supplier) or horizontal (common customers, technology, skills). For example, the UK financial services industry is clustered in London.

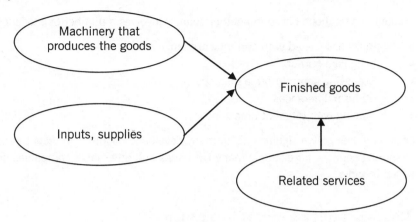

4.3.1 Government intervention

How does a country create a diamond of competitive advantage? Governments cannot compete, only organisations can do that. Governments can influence the **context** in which an industry operates and can create opportunities and pressures for innovation.

(a)   **Factors of production** provide the seeds for development. A large endowment of easily mined iron ore would suggest metal-working industries.

(b)   **Related and supporting industries** can also be a foundation, if the competences within them can be configured in a new way.

(c)   **Government policy** should support cluster development and promote high standards of education, research and commercially relevant technologies.

(d)   **Extraordinary demand in the home market** based on national peculiarities and conditions can set the demand conditions determinant in the diamond.

It must be remembered that the creation of competitive advantage can take **many years**.

Individual organisations will be more likely to succeed internationally if there is a **supporting cluster.** Businesses should be prepared to invest in co-operative ventures in such fields as training, infrastructure and research. However, the cluster approach is not guaranteed to be successful.

4.4 Offshoring and outsourcing   11/10

Two relatively recent techniques organisations may decide to utilise are offshoring and outsourcing. Cost reduction is often the primary reason for offshoring and outsourcing.

KEY TERMS

OFFSHORING is the relocation of some part of an organisation's activities to another country.

OUTSOURCING involves an organisation sub-contracting business activities to external providers. These providers may be in the same country as the organisation, or based overseas.

Developments in technology have made offshoring and outsourcing feasible in many situations. These technological advances permit business processes to be split up and performed in several locations. Communication devices such as smartphones and computers allow people in various locations to work together and to share information.

4.4.1 Offshoring   05/10

Offshoring could involve locating a department or subsidiary in another country, or using an external company based in another country (referred to as 'offshore outsourcing').

The most common motivation for offshoring is to make cost savings by taking advantage of lower labour and / or other costs.

Managing operations based in another country involves a number of challenges:

- Risks associated with currency exchange rates
- Language barrier
- Exercising control from a distance
- Cultural differences
- Dealing with different time zones

Offshoring has grown significantly in many developed countries in recent years. India is one popular offshoring country, for example many UK banks and other large companies now have service centres based in India.

4.4.2 Outsourcing - what to outsource?   05/11

Generally speaking, outsourcing is appropriate for **peripheral, non-core activities**. To outsource strategic or **core competences** could lead to loss of competitive advantage and risk the collapse of the whole organisation.

Outsourcing of non-core activities is widely acknowledged as having the potential to achieve important cost savings. However, it can be difficult to distinguish between core and non-core competences.

Cox categorises competences into three groups.

Cox's types of competence
Core competences are those that result in competitive advantage. They should not be outsourced. Product design is an example.
Complementary competences aren't core themselves, but are connected or essential to core competences. These may be outsourced, but only to trusted key suppliers with whom a strategic relationship is formed. In many industries and organisations, the IT function is a complementary competence.
Residual competences aren't in any way core and are suitable for outsourcing. The payroll function is an example.

Quinn and Hilmer identified three tests to establish whether an activity should be outsourced.

Quinn and Hilmer's tests to establish whether an activity should be outsourced
Potential for competitive advantage. The lower the potential for competitive advantage, the more suitable an activity is for outsourcing.
Risk of market failure. What impact does the activity have on the organisation's ability to deliver its goods and / or services to market? The lower the risk, the more suitable the activity is for outsourcing.
Potential to reduce risk. Can steps be taken with suppliers that reduce the risks of outsourcing? The greater the protection, the more attractive the outsourcing.

4.4.3 Advantages and disadvantages of outsourcing

The **advantages** of outsourcing are as follows.

(a)   Outsourcing can remove uncertainty about cost, as there is often a long-term contract where services are specified in advance for a fixed price.

(b) Long-term contracts (maybe up to ten years) encourage planning for the future.

(c) It can save on costs by making use of a suppliers' economies of scale.

(d) It can increase effectiveness where the supplier deploys higher levels of expertise.

(e) Access to specialist knowledge and innovations in technology is made easier. A specialist company can share staff with specific expertise between several clients.

(f) Flexibility (contract permitting). Resources may be able to be scaled up or down depending upon demand.

Some possible **disadvantages** are outlined below.

(a) Difficulties negotiating and managing a Service Level Agreement that meets the organisation's needs.

(b) It can lead to loss of control, particularly over quality.

(c) It means giving up an area of threshold competence that may be difficult to reacquire. The organisation may become out-of-touch with new developments resulting in a lack of in-house knowledge.

(d) The same outsourcing service is likely to be available to competitors.

Question 1.1	Offshoring and outsourcing

Learning outcome A1(iv)

Explain the differences between offshoring and outsourcing.   **(4 marks)**

4.5 Newly industrialising and emerging nations   05/10

Newly industrialising and **emerging** nations (**NIEs**) are countries which are grouped together by virtue of the fact that their economies have grown significantly in recent years and they are becoming increasingly important in the world economy.

NIEs are often (but not always) located in Asia and Latin America and include the BRIC nations (Brazil, Russia, India and China - see below) and other countries such as Argentina, Mexico, South Korea, Taiwan, and Singapore.

4.5.1 The BRIC economies

Brazil, **R**ussia, **I**ndia and **C**hina have all experienced rapid economic growth in recent years. When combined, the BRICs have a bigger share of world trade than the USA.

China has attracted most attention. China is now the second largest economy in the world (behind the US), having recently overtaken Japan.

The BRIC countries have experienced the emergence of a relatively wealthy middle-class living in urban areas and fuelling economic growth through consumer spending. They also have large rural regions and populations that have been largely excluded from the changes and benefits resulting from economic growth. This has led to increased economic disparity between rich and poor.

It is hoped that growth will filter from urban areas to rural areas, increasing the purchasing power of the population as a whole and providing even larger potential markets for both domestic and overseas producers.

4.5.2 Second tier emerging nations

Many other nations are often referred to as 'emerging nations'. Examples include Vietnam, Indonesia, Columbia and the Ukraine (which is also a transition economy - see later in this section). We now take a brief look at three other emerging nations - South Korea, Taiwan and Mexico.

In **South Korea** since the 1980s the government has reduced the amount of control it held over industry and allowed more foreign investment. Controls over the financial system were removed and the previously controlled exchange rate was left to market forces.

This liberalisation saw the Korean government abandon many of the principles that had brought previous economic growth, but was necessary for the country to integrate into the global economy – which is seen as essential for long-term prosperity.

Taiwan's government initially focussed on the development of certain industries such as plastic, fibreglass and textiles. Like South Korea, import-substitution policies were introduced for protection. This development created an industrial base that could be built on.

The government was able to steer private investment away from industries which already produced a surplus, or which operated in a non-growth market, into products that could be exported.

As a result of government intervention and operational efficiency, Taiwan has moved from a textiles based economy to one which now produces hi-tech electrical goods.

Mexico suffered an economic crisis caused by its level of international debt and the oil price crash of 1981. After the economic crisis Mexico followed protectionist policies while it tried to stabilise itself. This was followed by reform and more liberal trade and economic policies. The country formed an association with the USA and Canada (NAFTA) and entered into a trade agreement with the European Union. These measures led to an opening up of the economy to global business and helped to drive investment in the economy to record levels.

4.6 Transition economies

The term 'transition economy' has been applied to the countries that **abandoned the Soviet-type political and economic system** at the end of the twentieth century. Often quoted examples include the Russian Federation, Poland, Hungary, Romania, the Czech Republic, Ukraine, Kazakhstan, the Slovak Republic, Bulgaria and Belarus. A number of these countries have completed their transition to a market economy and have become members of the European Union.

The term is sometimes used with a wider meaning, referring to any country emerging from a socialist-type economy towards a market-based economy (eg China). This means that in general usage, there is **overlap between transition economies and emerging economies**.

4.7 Industrialisation strategies

Successful emerging nations follow **three main strategies**.

- Export of natural commodities
- Import-substitution
- Export-led industrialisation

4.7.1 Export of natural commodities

Countries are endowed with **natural resources** in various degrees. For example, oil, precious metals such as gold, and fertile agricultural land. The first stage of industrialisation is to simply sell natural resources to foreign countries. This generates **income** for the country which can be used to invest in infrastructure (such as education and technology) and develop the economy. However the country must import products that it cannot produce domestically.

4.7.2 Import-substitution

Once the economy has created wealth through exporting natural resources it begins to invest in **new industries** which produce the more advanced products that it needs. Historically, to **protect** these fledgling industries so that they can be developed and to reduce the country's dependence on foreign imports, protectionist measures were used (eg import tariffs and quotas).

4.7.3 Export-led industrialisation

Protecting and developing new industries was the only perceived method of creating an industrial base up until the 1960s. However, with the **liberalisation of economic systems** came an alternative – an export-centred, outward looking strategy.

Governments realised that the key to rapid economic growth was to **increase exports** – and that by doing so the wealth of the country would be substantially improved.

4.7.4 Foreign Direct Investment (FDI)   11/10

Many emerging and / or transition economies have benefited from **Foreign Direct Investment (FDI)**. For example, the growth of the Russian economy has been stimulated by multinational companies such as Coca-Cola establishing bases in the country. In China, foreign investment has largely funded the growth in the manufacturing sector.

FDI is now global in nature, with investment flows becoming more multi-directional. The BRIC nations are now making and well as receiving foreign investments. For example, Ford sold its Jaguar and Land Rover operations to India's Tata Group in 2008.

Section summary

Porter identifies **four principal factors** that influence the competitiveness of an economy. These **are factor conditions**, **demand conditions**, **related and supporting industries** and **firm strategy, structure and rivalry**.

Governments can influence the **context** in which an industry operates and can create opportunities and pressures for investment.

Offshoring is the relocation of an organisation's business activities (such as manufacturing) from one country to another. **Outsourcing** involves an organisation sub-contracting business activities to external providers.

Newly industrialising and **emerging** nations (**NIEs**) are countries which are grouped together by virtue of the fact that their economies have grown significantly in recent years and they are becoming increasingly important in world politics.

The term **transition economy** has been applied to the countries that abandoned the Soviet-type political and economic system at the end of the twentieth century.

5   Different types of organisation

Introduction

Economies contain **different types of organisation** and the economy itself can be divided into the **public** and **private sectors**.

In this section we consider the different types of organisation found in each sector.

5.1 The public and private sectors

The economy of a developed country can usually be divided into two sectors – **public** and **private**. Private sector organisations, also called businesses, are owned and operated by private individuals or institutions, while organisations in the public sector are usually owned by the state.

5.2 Private sector organisations

Private sector organisations are of two main types – those that **seek profit** for their owners and those that have **other objectives**. The latter are known as non-profit making or not-for-profit organisations. However, the majority of organisations in the private sector are businesses which aim to make profits for their owners (shareholders).

5.2.1 Not-for-profit organisations

This terminology is a little misleading, in that 'not-for-profit' organisations often engage in profitable trade and they are not able to run consistently at a loss. The essence of their status is not that they seek to avoid generating a surplus of funds, but that the generation of wealth for their owners is **not the primary purpose** of their existence.

Such organisations still aim to operate as **efficiently** as possible, but their primary objective is to provide a service rather than to maximise profit. Not-for-profit organisations include co-operatives, charities and unincorporated clubs, societies and associations.

Not-for-profit organisations use the surplus they generate to further their other objectives. Clubs and associations exist to provide some kind of benefit to their members. **Charities** and **voluntary organisations** generally exist to provide some kind of benefit to society at large.

Although not-for-profit organisations are not profit seekers, they still use economic factors of production to produce goods or services. Therefore they need to be **efficiently** managed so that their resources are used **effectively** to meet the objectives of the organisation whilst not making a financial loss.

5.2.2 Mutual organisations

Mutual organisations are a special type of non-for-profit organisation in the private sector. The essence of their nature is that they are commercial operations **owned by their customers**, rather than having capital and associated shareholders for whom they have to earn profit. This means that their customers benefit both from the **services** the mutuals provide to them and from the **trading surplus** they make by doing so.

It is also possible for the managers of mutuals to pursue **purposes other than maximise their trading surplus**. These can include a high level of charitable giving, the promotion of community interests and a high quality of service. Mutuals therefore resemble both not-for-profit organisations and profit-seeking companies, but as they don't produce profit for shareholders, strictly speaking are not-for-profit organisations.

5.2.3 Profit seeking organisations

The economy is mostly driven by the profit-seeking part of the private sector. It is businesses that undertake the most enterprising aspects of economic activity. They provide the bulk of employment opportunities and tax revenue and create the growth needed to enhance economic welfare. Businesses are of two main types, distinguished by the extent to which the owners are liable for the debts of the undertaking.

(a) An individual may set up business on their own account as a **sole trader** or in **partnership** with others. In either case, the law will not distinguish between the private assets and liabilities of the owners and those of the enterprise. The owners have **unlimited liability** for the debts of their businesses.

(b) This degree of risk is unattractive to many potential investors, so to enable them to invest and therefore release more funds for wealth-producing enterprise, the legal systems of most countries provide for some form of **limited liability** enterprise. Such businesses are referred to as corporations or **companies**.

In the UK, there are two forms of **limited liability company**. They both limit the liability of investors to the nominal value of their share holdings but they differ in the extent to which they are permitted to solicit investment from the general public.

KEY POINT

Private limited companies may not offer their securities to the public – public limited companies (plcs) may.

When the shares of plcs are regularly bought and sold on a stock exchange, they may be referred to as **quoted companies**, because the current price of their shares will be quoted in a journal of record.

Exam skills

Remember that not all public limited companies are quoted companies.

5.2.4 Multinational corporations

The largest businesses may develop into **multinational corporations** (MNC's). These organisations have the capacity to produce in more than one country, usually with a centrally located head office. MNC's are estimated to account for a quarter of the world's economic output (*Campbell and Craig*, 2005; *Worthington and Britton*, 2006).

The **growth of MNCs** can be attributed to

- Innovation in communications technology
- Improved transport and infrastructure
- Market homogenisation (eg the world's needs and wants have become increasingly similar)
- Political stability
- Increased merger activity

Due to these factors and especially **Internet** improvements and **political changes** such as the opening of trading borders, some organisations, although they are still small, are actually 'born global' now .

MNC's have many opportunities because they are able to identify countries in which they are able to **maximise their competences** and make the most of the variances in the business environment.

Many UK based **IT companies** are now retaining their sales divisions in the UK, but moving their system development activities to India where there is a large pool of newly qualified system development specialists who can be employed at a cheaper rate than in the UK. This is an example of offshoring that we explained earlier.

MNC's also benefit from being able to **spread their risk** over many businesses in many countries. Companies such as **Proctor & Gamble**, **Pepsi co**, **Philips** and **Nestle** for example, have large portfolio's of businesses and brands which are located in many countries.

The **legal** and **tax differences** between countries in which they operate also means that MNC's, through the process of internal transfer pricing, can reduce their overall tax burden and significantly increase profits.

Many **emerging nations** have made use of **MNCs** by attracting their investment through subsidies and low labour costs. We have already seen that (for some organisations) it no longer really matters where an organisation is based. This type of organisation has been the key to **export-led industrialisation**.

5.3 Public sector organisations

Public sector organisations used to be divided into **two main groups** – those that **provide public services** (such as hospitals, schools, the police and the armed forces) and **state owned industries**. This distinction has become less clear over the last quarter-century as governments have privatised state-owned industries and sought to **reform the public sector** by involving private companies in the provision of public services. The objective has been to **curb waste** of public money and **improve efficiency** by importing the disciplined cost control found in the private sector.

In the UK, many providers of public services such as hospitals and schools, and formerly state owned industries such as London Underground, are now involved in different forms of **public-private partnership**. In such partnerships, the private sector provides funds for public sector purposes such as education. For example the Private Funding Initiative (PFI) for schools seeks private partners to fund and manage school buildings in return for an agreed fee. Some services in the UK such as the National Health Service (NHS) are provided by self-governing trusts. These trusts sell their services to the NHS.

Public sector bodies are all, ultimately, **responsible to government** for their activities, and their purposes are defined in the laws that establish them. They have a range aims and objectives but rarely will they set out to trade at a profit. Nevertheless, their managers will be expected to exercise **good stewardship** and **prevent waste of resources**. Public sector bodies' objectives will usually be defined in terms of the **provision of a service** that is deemed to be beneficial to society.

An important feature of **public sector bodies** is that they have little control over their income. This is because they depend upon government for the funds they need to operate. The funds they receive will be influenced by a large number of factors, including current public opinion, government aspirations, the skill of their leaders in negotiation, the current state of the public finances overall and the current economic climate.

Alongside public sector organisations there are also **quasi autonomous non-governmental organisations** (QUANGOs), which are private organisations independent of the government but to which governments have devolved the authority for running public services.

Section summary

The economy of a developed country can usually be divided into two sectors – **public** and **private**.

Private sector organisations are of two main types – those that **seek profit** for their owners and those that have **other objectives**.

Examples of **not-for-profit organisations** include **charities** and **voluntary or mutual organisations**.

Examples of **profit making organisations** include **sole traders**, **partnerships** and **companies**.

Multinational companies have the capacity to produce in more than one country, usually with a centrally located head office.

Public sector organisations provide services to the general public such as **hospitals** and **schools**.

6 Culture and the global organisation

Introduction

We have already discussed **culture in a society** as a factor of an organisation's environment. The issue of corporate culture is important for **multinational businesses** because culture influences how things are done.

KEY TERM

CULTURE embodies the common set of values: 'the way things are done around here'.

Culture is embodied in **rituals** and **behaviour**.

Culture is an important filter of **information** and an **interpreter** of it. For example, an organisation might have a cultural predisposition against embarking on risky ventures. Existing behaviour patterns may make a proposed strategy incompatible with the culture and so impossible to implement.

An **organisation's culture** is influenced by many factors.

(a)   The organisation's **founder**. A strong set of values and assumptions may have been established by the organisation's founder. Even after they have retired, these values have their own momentum.

(b)   The organisation's **history.** The effect of history can be determined by stories, rituals and symbolic behaviour. They legitimise behaviour and promote priorities.

(c)   **Leadership and management style**. An organisation with a strong culture recruits managers who naturally conform to it.

(d)   **Structure and systems** affect culture as well as strategy.

(e)   The **industry** (eg computer software organisations in the 'silicon valley' had a reputation for being laid back on office dress).

(f)   **Location of head office** – and its acquired culture

6.1 Management culture

A factor which has an impact on the culture of transnational organisations, or organisations competing in global markets, is **management culture**. This is the view about managing held by managers, their shared educational experiences, and the 'way business is done'. Obviously, this reflects wider cultural differences between countries, but national cultures can sometimes be subordinated to the corporate culture of the organisation (eg the efforts to ensure that staff of Euro Disney are as enthusiastic as their American counterparts).

KEY TERM

MANAGEMENT CULTURE is a part of overall organisational culture and relates to the prevailing view within management about how to do its job.

6.2 Managing across borders

There are often severe cultural differences as to what constitutes 'management' in the first place. Are **management** principles universally applicable? Organisations need an awareness of effective management approaches in different cultures.

6.2.1 Hofstede   05/11

Geert Hofstede analysed the role of national culture within organisations based on a large scale investigation of the cultural attitudes of the employees of IBM in the 1960s and 70s. *Hofstede* identified a number of dimensions that contributed to cross-cultural differences in beliefs and values.

Dimension	Comment
Power – distance	This refers to how far society and organisations tolerate an unequal distribution of power. In high power-distance cultures (eg India) and organisations, power tends to be concentrated at the top and managers exert their status and power over subordinates.
Uncertainty avoidance	This measures the extent to which people are able to tolerate ambiguity and uncertainty. For example whether individuals wait until they are completely sure of all details before acting.
Individualism versus collectivism	This measures the extent to which people see themselves in individual terms as opposed to being members of a group - be it family, company, caste, class or even simply a sporting club.
Masculinity versus femininity	This is about the degree to which a culture encourages one set of qualities (the 'masculine' ones such as competitiveness and assertiveness) as opposed to another set (the so-called 'feminine' ones such as concern for others, attention to quality of life or to the environment).
Confucian dynamism	The extent to which conformity based on position influences behaviour and relationships between individuals. This is typically seen as being high in China and Japan.

LEARNING MEDIA

Hofstede subsequently added another dimension – long term orientation (versus short term orientation). This was based on observing the extent to which people are driven by immediate concerns (as distinct from attention to the longer term future), and the effects on organisational culture and operational

Hofestede's work has its critics. The following points must be considered.

(a)   *Hofestede*'s study is based on data that is now thirty years old. International attitudes have changed significantly in that time – many people in the middle 1970s had hardly travelled away from their home country. Today we have global organisations and markets, and the consequent movement of people across the world.

(b)   People's experience of other cultures has therefore changed, and so has their own self image and behaviour.

CASE STUDY

McDonalds – national cultures and global organisations

The 'golden arches' logo of McDonalds is now the most recognised symbol in the world. Alongside the logo, McDonalds have developed a business format that is successful and established in 130 countries of the world.

This success has occurred even in places where there has been 'cultural resistance', for example France and Spain where there is a very distinctive (perceived and real) attitude to food as a key aspect of national and regional culture.

Countries have absorbed the influences of McDonalds and have grown familiar with the nature of the brand and what it has to offer. McDonalds have absorbed the influences of the communities in which they locate, by offering differentiated and localised meals and foods according to location.

6.2.2 Other models

Trompenaars and Hampden Turner (1997) developed a **Seven Dimensions of Culture** model.

Five of their dimensions relate to how people deal with each other.

1   **Universalism versus particularism**. In universalistic cultures, rules are more important than personal relationships. For example, high value is placed on written contracts.

2   **Individualism versus collectivism** (or communitarianism). Does the culture value and encourage self-orientation and decision making or group orientation and decision making?

3   **Neutral versus emotional** (or effective). In neutral cultures, emotions aren't expressed openly.

4   **Specific versus diffuse**. This refers to whether people change the way they act and relate to each other in specific situations (specific) or whether behaviour and relationships are consistent (diffuse). For example, in a culture that favoured specific behaviour people may relate to each other differently outside the workplace than at work.

5   **Achievement versus ascription**. Is status based on achievement, or on other factors such as age and years of experience?

The sixth dimension refers to how different societies view the concept of time.

6   **Sequential versus synchronic**. Do individuals work on one thing at a time (sequential) or on several things at once (synchronic)?

The seventh and final dimension looks at how culture views the effect of the general environment.

7   **Internal or high context versus external or low context**. High context behaviour includes tradition and ritual, the environment controls behaviour. Low context behaviour is controlled by individuals rather than the environment.

Ronen and Shenkar (1985) identified **four key characteristics** of national culture.

- The importance placed on work goals
- The role of job satisfaction
- The impact of organisational and managerial factors
- The impact of work roles and interpersonal relationships

They identified groups of nations that displayed shared characteristics.

Models provide a framework that enables managers to consider what management structure and style may work best in different countries. Managers need to be **flexible** enough to adapt to cultural differences and are able to ride what *Ronen and Shenkar* refer to as 'the waves of culture'.

6.3 Management structure

Local conditions and the **scale of operations** will influence the organisational structure of companies operating internationally. Very large and complex companies may be organised as a **heterarchy**.

A heterarchy is a rather **organic structure** with significant local control.

(a) **Some headquarters functions are diffused geographically**. For example, R&D might be based in the UK, marketing based in the US. Or certain products made in one country and others elsewhere (motor manufacturers do not make every model of car at each factory.) Some central functions might be split up – many organisations are experimenting with having several centres for R&D.

(b) **Subsidiary managers have a strategic role for the corporation as a whole** (eg through bargaining and coalition forming).

(c) **Co-ordination is achieved through corporate culture and shared values** rather than a formal hierarchy. Experienced employees might have worked in a number of different product divisions.

(d) **Alliances** can be formed with other parts of the company and with other businesses, perhaps in joint ventures or consortia.

6.4 Influences on structure and methods

A variety of **factors influence management methods** in an international setting. These factors pull in different directions and it may be that **compromise** is necessary. As always, a consideration of objectives is a good starting point. A company merely seeking to expand sales volume while concentrating on its home market will use very different methods from one seeking to operate in truly global markets such as energy and telecommunications.

Central control may be appropriate if the volume of international business or the company's experience in international operations is low. Centralisation is seen as promoting efficiency and prevents duplication of effort between regions. Even when operations are on a limited scale, when conformity with demanding technical standards is required, **functional representation** in international management may be necessary. For example, a largely autonomous international subsidiary may have to accept supervision of its quality assurance or financial reporting functions.

If business is done globally, a form of **regional organisation** may be appropriate if there is some measure of social and economic integration within regions. The need for rapid response to local opportunities and threats may be served by a significant measure of **decentralisation**. National political and cultural sensitivities may reinforce this, but a shortage of local talent may limit it.

As far as **management processes and decision making** are concerned, typical problems include:

(a) **Poor information systems and communications**. However, the rapidly falling costs of telecommunications and the development of e-mail and video-conferencing facilities mean this is now less likely to be a problem.

(b)   **Interpretation of information**. Culture affects how information is interpreted and can also determine the priorities of the planners. By **failing to allow for diversity** or to understand local culture, planners based elsewhere can make marketing on the ground more difficult.

     (i)   Managing a local market in a large country with a rural population would be different from marketing to a small country with most people living in cities.

     (ii)   High tech products may not be suitable for a country with a poorly developed educational and technological infrastructure.

     (iii)   Consumers and managers in countries with very high rates of inflation will have different priorities to those in countries with low inflation. Managers' may need to minimise holdings of local currency, by converting it into a harder currency or into tangible assets.

(c)   **Meetings** can become difficult and expensive when a company expands internationally. Air travel and hotel costs can be significant. Video-conferencing is emerging as an alternative to face-to-face meetings.

You will study organisational culture further in paper E2.

6.5 Human resource management

The **balance between local and expatriate staff** must be managed. There are a number of influences.

- The availability of technical skills such as financial management
- The need for control
- The importance of product and company experience
- The need to provide promotion opportunities
- Costs associated with expatriates such as travel and higher salaries
- Cultural factors

6.5.1 Expatriates or locals?

For an **international company**, which has to think globally as well as act locally, there are a number of problems.

- Does it employ mainly **expatriate staff** to control local operations?
- Does it employ **local managers** with the possible loss of central control?
- Is there such a thing as the **global manager**, equally at home in different cultures?

Expatriate staff are sometimes **favoured over local staff**.

(a)   Poor **educational opportunities** in the market may require the import of skilled technicians and managers. For example, expatriates have been needed in many western business operations in Russia and Eastern Europe, simply because they understand the importance of profit.

(b)   Some senior managers believe that a business run by expatriates is easier to **control** than one run by local staff.

(c)   Expatriates might be better able than locals to **communicate** with the corporate centre.

(d)   The expatriate may **know more about the organisation** overall, which is especially important if they are fronting a sales office.

The use of **expatriates** in overseas markets has certain **disadvantages**.

(a)   They **cost** more (eg subsidised housing, school fees).

(b)   **Culture shock**. The expatriate may fail to adjust to the culture (eg by associating only with other expatriates). This is likely to lead to poor management effectiveness, especially if the business requires personal contact.

(c)   A **substantial training programme** might be needed.

   (i)   **Basic facts** about the country will be given with basic language training and some briefings about cultural differences.

   (ii)   **Immersion training** involves detailed language and cultural training and simulation of social and business experiences. This is necessary to obtain an understanding and awareness of the culture.

Employing **local managers** raises the following issues.

(a)   A **glass ceiling** might exist in some companies. Local managers may not make it to board level if, as in many Japanese organisations, most members of the board are drawn from one country.

(b)   In some cases, it may be hard for locals to assimilate into the **corporate culture**, and this might led to communication problems.

(c)   They will have **greater local knowledge** but may not be trained to understand the wider corporate picture, but this is true of most management at operational level.

Question 1.2	Setting up overseas

Learning outcome A1(i)

Identify four issues which may affect an organisation that wishes to set up an overseas subsidiary.

(4 marks)

Section summary

Culture embodies the common set of values: 'the way things are done around here'.

Organisations need an awareness of **effective management approaches in different cultures**.

Local conditions and the **scale of operations** will influence the **organisational structure** of companies trading internationally.

The **balance between local and expatriate staff** must be managed.

Chapter Roundup

✓   **Global production** involves manufacturing and sourcing on a global scale.

✓   **World trade** has been encouraged by **financial factors**, **trade alliances**, **legal factors** and **international markets**.

✓   The **global business environment** can be analysed into **political**, **economic**, **social** and **technological** factors, this is known as **PEST** analysis.

✓   **Economic nationalism** is a nation's view that it should protect its own economy and industries.

✓   **Economic liberalisation** involves nations moving away from economic nationalism towards working with others in a group to benefit all member economies and industries.

✓   **Free trade areas**, **customs unions** and **economic unions/common markets** are all types of economic system designed to provide members with a trade advantage.

✓   *Porter* identifies **four principal factors** that influence the competitiveness of an economy. These **are factor conditions, demand conditions, related and supporting industries** and **firm strategy, structure and rivalry**.

✓   Governments can influence the **context** in which an industry operates and can create opportunities and pressures for investment.

✓   **Offshoring** is the relocation of an organisation's business activities (such as manufacturing) from one country to another.

✓   **Outsourcing** involves an organisation sub-contracting business activities to external providers.

✓   **Newly industrialising** and **emerging** nations (**NIEs**) are countries which are grouped together by virtue of the fact that their economies have grown significantly in recent years and they are becoming increasingly

✓   The term **transition economy** has been applied to the countries that abandoned the Soviet-type political and economic system at the end of the twentieth century

✓   The economy of a developed country can usually be divided into two sectors – **public** and **private**.

✓   **Private sector organisations** are of two main types – those that **seek profit** for their owners and those that have **other objectives**.

✓   Examples of **not-for-profit organisations** include **charities and voluntary or mutual organisations**.

✓   Examples of **profit making organisations** include **sole traders, partnerships** and **companies**.

✓   **Multinational companies** have the capacity to produce in more than one country, usually with a centrally located head office.

✓   **Public sector organisations** provide services to the general public such as **hospitals** and **schools**.

✓   **Culture** embodies the common set of values: 'the way things are done around here'.

✓   Organisations need an awareness of **effective management approaches in different cultures**.

✓   **Local conditions** and the **scale of operations** will influence the **organisational structure** of companies trading internationally.

✓   The **balance between local and expatriate staff** must be managed.

Quick Quiz

1   Which type of country is described below?

'Largely primary industry based, but with a developing secondary (manufacturing) industrial sector. Low but growing GDP, developing infrastructure.'

A   Lesser developed country
B   Early developed country
C   Semi-developed country
D   Fully developed country

2   Which of the following is not classed as a transitional economy?

A   Poland
B   Romania
C   Japan
D   Belarus

3   Which of the following cannot be described as a newly industrialised emerging economy?

A   China
B   Singapore
C   South Korea
D   Hungary

4   Briefly explain the main reason why organisations choose to offshore or outsource their operations.

5   Which of the following is a public sector organisation?

A   A school
B   A charity
C   A public limited company
D   A partnership

Answers to Quick Quiz

1 B The text describes an early developed country.

2 C Transitional economies include those countries which have recently emerged from the planned economy of the Soviet Union and are moving towards a free market economy.

3 D NIEs are mainly located in Asia and Latin America and include nations such as Brazil, Argentina, Mexico, India, South Korea, Taiwan, Singapore and China.

4   Cost reduction is the primary reason for offshoring and outsourcing. Organisations will locate production units where production costs are lowest and then move completed units around the world for sale.

5 A Public sector organisations provide services for the general public. Charities are part of the private sector as not-for-profit organisations. Companies and partnerships are examples of profit seeking organisations in the private sector.

Answers to Questions

1.1 Offshoring and outsourcing

Offshoring is the relocation of part of an organisation's business activities from one country to another.

Outsourcing involves an organisation sub-contracting business activities to external providers.

Two key differences are:

Outsourcing often involves the activity remaining in the same country, using an outsourcing partner based in the home country.

Offshoring always involves the relocation of some activity outside the home country, and usually means the activity remains within the organisation.

1.2 Setting up overseas

Four issues which may affect an organisation that wishes to set up an overseas subsidiary include:

Educational constraints – poorly educated employees will result in poor management and decision making.

Sociological constraints – the employees of some countries may have a greater work ethic than others.

Legal and political constraints – legal or other regulations may restrict the subsidiary's working practices.

Economic constraints – factors such as inflation will affect the subsidiary's cost base and profitability.

Now try this question from the Exam Question Bank	Number	Level	Marks	Time
	1	Examination	25	45 mins

GOVERNANCE AND REGULATION

 Governments have a key role to play in the economy and development of a nation.

The decisions they make and the policies they establish all have an effect on an organisation's business environment.

Government influence is usually associated with **economic policy**, but as we shall see, governments also affect a market through **regulation**.

Later in this chapter we consider the impact of two topical areas - **corporate governance** and **corporate social responsibility**.

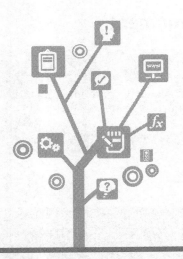

topic list	learning outcomes	syllabus references	ability required
1 Government intervention in business	A2(b)	A2(iii), A2(iv)	analysis
2 Government and the macroeconomic environment	A1(c), A2(b)	A1(vi), A2(iii), A2(v)	analysis
3 Market regulation	A2(d)	A2(iii), A2(iv), A2(v)	analysis
4 Corporate governance	A2(a)	A2(i), A2(ii)	comprehension
5 Corporate social responsibility	A2(a)	A2(i), A2(ii)	comprehension

1 Government intervention in business

Introduction

In the previous chapter we focussed on the emergence of newly industrialised nations in the global economy. In this chapter we consider how governments influence their economies and the competitive environment of organisations.

A country's **government** has a major role to play in the success or failure of its economy. We have already seen how it can influence a number of factors related to competitive advantage and foreign investment but these are only part of the story.

Governments can **influence** a number of other areas:

*   The macroeconomic environment
*   Legal and market regulation
*   Corporate governance and social responsibility

Section summary

Government influence over business extends to the **macroeconomic environment**, **legal** and **market regulations**, **corporate governance** and **social responsibility**.

2 Government and the macroeconomic environment

Introduction

The **macroeconomic environment** is concerned with factors in the **overall economy**, for example interest rates, exchange rates and levels of demand and supply.

Microeconomics is concerned with economic circumstances of individual industries or companies.

2.1 The balance of trade

KEY POINT

A country's **balance of trade** is the difference, in financial terms between the value of its imports and exports. If a country imports more than it exports there is a **trade deficit**, if it exports more than it imports there is a **trade surplus**.

National account balances measure the production, income and expenditure levels within an economy. The balance of trade forms part of the **current account** of a nation's national account balances.

2.1.1 Factors affecting the balance of trade

A number of factors influence a country's balance of trade.

Factor	Influence
Availability, price and quality of goods produced by local producers	If local producers are able to supply the home market with high-quality, competitively priced goods, it will be difficult for overseas producers to export to that market.

Factor	Influence
Inflation	If a nation's inflation rate is higher than its competitors, producers in that country will face higher costs which will cause the price of their products to rise.
Exchange rates	If a nation's currency weakens against those which export to it, then the goods it imports become more expensive. We shall look at exchange rates again later on.
Trade agreements	Trade agreements affect the volume of imports and exports between nations. Nations are more likely to be able to export competitively to nations they are on an 'even playing field' with.
Taxes, tariffs and trade measures	Taxes and tariffs increase the price of imports, making them less attractive to buy. Governments may attempt to help home producers with subsidies, although free trade agreements mean this may be difficult (or lead to tit-for-tat retaliation).
The business cycle	Nations looking for export-led growth require sufficient demand in overseas markets for their products.

If producers in one country are able to produce something cheaper than producers in other countries, it is likely they will export it. This improves the balance of trade in the country in which the producers are based.

On the other hand, if overseas suppliers are able to supply something cheaper than domestic producers can, demand for imports will increase.

Most countries expect to import some goods and services and export others. For example New Zealand produces lamb for export, far more is produced than the home market could consume. Many countries import oil as they lack their own supply.

The volume of imports and exports, and the price levels of the products and services imported and exported, **affect the balance of trade**.

2.1.2 National accounts

Like businesses, nations produce accounts that show their financial performance. The format of each country's accounts will differ, however they are usually based around four elements.

(a)   **Current account**. This is made up of three sub-accounts.

   (i)   **Production accounts** – the value of the nation's output less the value of the goods and services used to create it. The difference is the nation's gross domestic product (GDP).

   (ii) **Income accounts** – the total income generated by production less government redistribution of tax and social security benefits. The difference is the nation's disposable income.

   (iii) **Expenditure accounts** – this records how the nation's disposable income is either spent or saved.

(b)   **Capital account**. This records the total accumulation of the nation's non-financial assets and how they were financed. The difference is the nation's net borrowing or lending.

(c)   **Financial account**. This records the nation's net acquisition of financial assets and liabilities. The difference between them is the change in the nation's financial position.

(d)   **Balance sheet**. This records the nation's financial and non-financial assets and liabilities. The difference between them is the nation's net worth.

2.1.3 Effect of balance of trade on national account balances

A nation's **balance of trade** forms part of its **national account balance**. National outputs and the resources used to produce them will be reflected in the production account. A nation's income comes from its exports which form the income account.

If a country **imports more than it exports,** the deficit will reduce the **income account.** This will also feed to the financial account and balance sheet. If a nation's income falls, it has less money to invest in assets and it may have to increase its liabilities in order to support its industries.

2.2 Fiscal policy

KEY TERM

FISCAL POLICY refers to government policy on taxation and government spending.

Fiscal policy is based on the theories of British economist *John Maynard Keynes*. Keynesian economics is based around the theory that governments can influence macroeconomic productivity levels by increasing or decreasing tax levels and public spending.

The aim, generally, is to keep inflation relatively low (between 2% and 3%) while maintaining high employment levels. This is a balancing act, as stimulating a stagnant economy to increase demand and employment may result in a decrease in the value of money - inflation.

2.2.1 Taxation

Direct taxes are levied on earnings or profits, for example income tax for individuals and corporation tax for companies.

Indirect taxes are levied on spending or expenditure. For example, Value Added Tax, specific sales taxes such as those imposed on tobacco and petrol, import duties, road tax etc.

Ultimately, just as a household or a business aims to spend no more than it earns, over the long term a government aims to **run a balanced budget**.

2.3 Monetary policy

KEY TERM

MONETARY POLICY refers to government policy on the money supply, the monetary system, interest rates, exchange rates and the availability of credit.

Monetary policy can be used as a means of achieving economic objectives for inflation, the balance of trade and economic growth. Most economists believe that an increase in the money supply will increase demand leading to increases in prices (inflation) and incomes.

Monetary policy focuses on three factors, **interest rates**, **exchange rates** and **national income**.

2.3.1 Interest rates

The government may use interest rates in an attempt to influence the level of expenditure in the economy and/or the rate of inflation.

A rise in interest rates increases the price of borrowing for both companies and individuals. If companies see the rise as relatively permanent, rates of return on investments will become less attractive and **investment plans may be curtailed**. Corporate profits will fall as a result of higher interest payments. Companies will reduce inventory levels as the cost of having money tied up in stocks rises. Individuals should be expected to reduce or postpone consumption in order to reduce borrowings, and should become less willing to borrow for house purchases.

Although it is generally accepted that there is likely to be a connection between interest rates and investment (by companies) and consumer expenditure, the connection is **not a stable and predictable one**. Interest rate changes are only likely to affect the level of expenditure after a **considerable time lag**.

The table below explains some **impacts of a rise in interest rates**.

Impact	Comment
Spending falls	Higher interest rates increase the cost of credit. The higher interest rate makes it more attractive to hold money than to spend it.
Investment falls	The higher rate will increase the opportunity cost of investment (for example in new projects) and reduce the net present value of the investment. This will discourage organisations from investing.
	The increased interest rates will make borrowing more expensive.
Foreign funds are attracted into the country	Interest rates are the reward for capital, so a rise in interest rates will encourage overseas currency investors because of the increased rate of return relative to other countries.
Exchange rate rises	The inflow of foreign funds (above) increases the demand for the home currency and therefore strengthens the exchange rate making exports more expensive and imports cheaper.
Inflation rate falls	This is often the main goal of an interest rate rise. The reduction in spending and investment will reduce aggregate demand in the economy.
	The stronger exchange rate means imported goods will be cheaper.

An increase in interest rates will have a **deflationary** impact on the economy.

Note, however, the **potential conflicting objectives** which monetary policy faces. A change in interest rates will have effects on both the domestic economy and on a country's international trade position (for example through exchange rate movements). It may be the case that the interest rate movement required for the domestic economy **conflicts** with that required to achieve a balance on the external current account.

2.3.2 Exchange rates

Exchange rates are often used in monetary policy for two reasons.

(a)   If the **exchange rate falls** (or weakens), exports become cheaper to overseas buyers and so the nation becomes more competitive in export markets. Imports will become more expensive and so less competitive against goods produced by manufacturers at home. A fall in the exchange rate might therefore be good for the domestic economy, by giving a **stimulus to exports** and **reducing demand for imports**.

(b)   An increase (or strengthening) in the **exchange rate** will have the opposite effect, with dearer exports and cheaper imports. If the exchange rate rises and imports become cheaper, there should be a reduction in the rate of domestic inflation. A fall in the exchange rate, on the other hand, tends to increase the cost of imports and adds to the rate of domestic inflation.

When a country's economy is heavily dependent on **overseas trade** it might be appropriate for government policy to establish a target exchange value for the domestic currency. However, the exchange rate is dependent on both the domestic rate of inflation and the level of interest rates. Targets for the exchange rate cannot be achieved unless the rate of inflation at home is first brought under control.

2.3.3 National income

The authorities might set targets for the level of **national income**. For example, the policy might be for the growth in the national income to be X% per annum for Y years. However, it takes time to collect information about national income.

For this reason, although a **target growth rate** in national income itself is, in theory, probably the most suitable target of monetary policy, it is the least practical because the authorities would always be working with out-of-date information.

Question 2.1	Exchange and inflation rates

Learning outcome A1(vi)

Briefly explain how a nation's exchange and inflation rates may affect its national income.   **(4 marks)**

Section summary

Key elements of the **macro economy** include, **interest rates**, **exchange rates** and levels of **demand** and **supply**.

A number of **factors influence a nation's balance of trade** because they affect the price of domestic goods compared to foreign imports.

A nation's **balance of trade** forms part of its **national account balance**.

Fiscal policy refers to government policy on taxation and government spending.

Monetary policy refers to government policy on money supply, the monetary system, interest rates, exchange rates and the availability of credit. It can directly affect a nation's balance of trade.

3 Market regulation

Introduction

Regulation can be defined as any form of state interference with the operation of the free market.

3.1 Regulation and Competition Policy

Regulation could involve regulating demand, supply, price, profit, quantity, quality, entry, exit, information, technology, or any other aspect of production and consumption in the market

An example of regulation in practice can be seen in the £270 million fines imposed on British Airways in July 2007 after an investigation by the UK's Office of Fair Trading, in conjunction with the US Department of Justice, into BA's collusion in fixing the price of fuel surcharges.

3.1.1 The Competition Act 1998

In the UK, this Act sought to encourage competition by introducing the presumption that anti-competitive arrangements are against the public interest and so should be illegal.

3.1.2 Industry regulators

Most countries have **specific industry regulators** to monitor the activities of private companies in 'essential' industries. For example, the UK has OFCOM to regulate the telecommunications market, while OFGEM regulates the gas industry.

The regulators aim to promote competition, for example by **imposing price caps** and **performance standards** or **removing barriers** preventing new organisations entering the market.

3.2 The Competition Commission

In the UK, the **Competition Commission's** (CC's) role is to promote competition. For example, the CC may investigate **proposed mergers** where the assets involved exceed £70 million in value and recommend whether or not it should be allowed to proceed.

3.3 The Restrictive Practices Court

The UK **Restrictive Practices Court (RTP)** has jurisdiction to declare that certain agreements are contrary to the public interest and to restrain parties from enforcing them.

The RTP considers applications made by **the Director General of Fair Trading** in respect of agreements under which at least two parties are imposing restrictions on the price or supply of goods.

3.4 European Union competition policy

European Union competition policy is intended to ensure free and fair competition in the EU. The **Commission of the European Union** has authority under the Treaty of Rome (Articles 81 to 89) to prohibit price fixing and other uncompetitive arrangements, including limiting production or seeking to exclude competitors from a market.

The Commission also has authority to prevent national governments within the EU offering subsidies or other **state aid** to organisations in their countries which will distort competition across the wider market.

3.5 Self-regulation

In many markets, the participants may decide to maintain a system of **voluntary self-regulation**, possibly in order to try to avert the imposition of government controls. Self-regulation often exists in the professions.

3.6 Costs of regulation

The **costs of regulation** include:

(a)   **Enforcement costs**. Direct costs of enforcement include the setting up and running of the regulatory agencies. Indirect costs are those incurred by regulated organisations in conforming with the regulations relevant to them.

(b)   **Regulatory capture**. This refers to the process by which the regulator becomes dominated and controlled by the regulated companies, such that it acts increasingly in the latter's interests, rather than those of consumers. This is a phenomenon which has been observed in the USA.

(c)   **Unintended consequences of regulation.** Organisations will not react passively to regulatory constraints on their behaviour – instead they try to limit their effectiveness. In general, theory and observation suggest that if it's practical, businesses will move away from regulated activities towards those which are less constrained or completely unregulated.

3.7 Deregulation

Deregulation can be defined as the removal or weakening of any form of statutory (or voluntary) regulation of free market activity. Deregulation allows free market forces more scope to determine the outcome.

There was a shift in policy in the 1980s in the UK and in the USA towards greater deregulation of markets, in the belief that this would **improve efficiency**.

A rational assessment of deregulation should weigh the potential benefits against the costs. If there will be a net gain to society, we can say that the deregulation should proceed. It would be simplistic to contend that all regulation is detrimental to the economy.

3.7.1 Advantages and disadvantages of deregulation

Deregulation measures are also known as **liberalisation**.

Those who favour deregulation quote **possible benefits** such as:

(a) **Increased incentive to find internal cost savings and efficiency**. Increased competition should lead to the most efficient organisations being the most successful.

(b) **Improved allocative efficiency**. Competition should result in prices closer to marginal cost and therefore result in overall production that is closer to the socially optimal output level.

In some industries, liberalisation could have certain **disadvantages**.

(a) **Loss of economies of scale**. If increased competition means that each organisation produces less output on a smaller scale, unit costs will be higher.

(b) **Lower quality or quantity of service**. The need to reduce costs may lead organisations to reduce quality or eliminate unprofitable but socially valuable services.

(c) **Need to protect competition**. It may be necessary to **implement** a regulatory regime to protect competition where inherent forces have a tendency to eliminate it.

Section summary

Regulation can be defined as any form of state interference with the operation of the free market.

In the UK there have been various pieces of **legislation** enacted to maintain competition in the market place and there are a number of industry regulators.

European Union competition policy is intended to ensure free and fair competition in the EU.

Deregulation can be defined as the removal or weakening of any form of statutory (or voluntary) regulation of free market activity.

4 Corporate governance

Introduction

Although shareholders own a company, the responsibility for directing and controlling it rests largely with the board of directors. In the UK, a series of high profile corporate scandals in the 1980s and 1990s led to a range of corporate governance controls.

KEY TERM

CORPORATE GOVERNANCE is the system by which companies and other entities are directed and controlled.

(CIMA Official Terminology)

4.1 Stakeholders

Stakeholders are persons or groups that have a **legitimate interest in a business's conduct** and whose concerns should be addressed as a matter of principle. Many stakeholder groups have influence over the way in which organisations are managed and operated. They can therefore be fundamental to corporate governance.

STAKEHOLDERS are those persons and organisations that have an interest in the strategy of an organisation.

(CIMA Official Terminology)

There are three broad types, or **constituencies**, of stakeholder in an organisation.

- **Internal** stakeholders such as employees and management
- **Connected** stakeholders such as shareholders, customers, suppliers and financiers
- **External** stakeholders such as the community, government and pressure groups

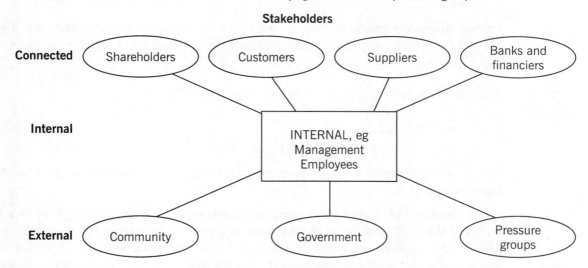

The extent to which external stakeholders are interested and recognised is linked in some ways to the size of the organisation. For example the policies and actions of **larger organisations** are more likely to be of interest to **national governments** and even **international bodies** than are those of smaller organisations.

Stakeholders may also be analysed into those who have a **formal contractual relationship** with the organisation and those who do not. These two groups are called **primary** and **secondary** stakeholders. Internal and connected stakeholders fall into the primary category, while external stakeholders are secondary stakeholders.

You will use your understanding of the types of stakeholders in paper E3 when you study how to manage them.

Mendelow classifies stakeholders on a matrix whose axes are **power** (or influence) and degree of **interest** in the organisation's activities. These factors help define the type of relationship the organisation should seek with its stakeholders.

		Level of interest	
		Low	High
Power/influence	**Low**	A	B
	High	C	D

(a) **Key players** are found in segment D. Any strategy must be *acceptable* to them, at least. An example would be a major customer. These stakeholders may **participate** in decision-making.

(b)   Stakeholders in segment C must be **treated with care**. While often passive, they may be capable of moving to segment D. They should, therefore be **kept satisfied.** Large institutional shareholders might fall into segment C.

(c)   Stakeholders in segment B do not have great ability to influence strategy, but their views can be important in **influencing more powerful stakeholders**, perhaps by lobbying. They should therefore be **kept informed.** Community representatives and charities might fall into segment B.

(d)   **Minimal effort** should be expended on segment A. An example might be a contractor's labour force.

Internal stakeholder groups are likely to have both more influence and more interest than external groups. Coalitions of stakeholder groups are likely to have more influence than single stakeholders or small uniform groups.

Stakeholder mapping is also part of the syllabus for Paper E2.

4.2 Failures of corporate governance

Though mostly discussed in relation to large quoted companies, governance is an issue **for all organisations**.

An increasing number of **high profile corporate scandals** and collapses, including Polly Peck International, BCCI and Maxwell Communications Corporation prompted the development of governance codes in the early 1990s. However, scandals since then, such as Parmalat and Enron, have raised questions about further measures that may be necessary. These scandals have highlighted the need for guidance to tackle the various **risks and problems** that can arise in organisations' systems of governance.

4.2.1 Domination by a single individual

A feature of many corporate governance scandals has been boards dominated by a single senior executive with other board members merely acting as a rubber stamp. Sometimes the single individual may bypass the board to action their own interests. The report on the UK *Guinness* case suggested that the Chief Executive, *Ernest Saunders* paid himself a substantial reward without consulting the other directors. The presence of non-executive directors on the board is felt to be an important safeguard against domination by a single individual.

4.2.2 Lack of involvement of board

Boards that meet irregularly or fail to consider systematically the organisation's activities and risks are clearly weak. Sometimes the failure to carry out proper oversight is due to a **lack of information** being provided.

4.2.3 Lack of adequate control function

An obvious weakness is an ineffective **internal audit function,** since this is one of the most important aspects of internal control.

Another important weakness is a **lack of adequate technical knowledge** in key roles, for example in the audit committee or in senior compliance positions. A rapid turnover of staff involved in accounting or control may suggest inadequate resourcing and the constant change will make control more difficult.

4.2.4 Lack of supervision

Employees who are not properly supervised can create large losses for the organisation through incompetence, negligence or fraudulent activity. The behaviour of *Nick Leeson*, the employee who caused the collapse of *Barings* bank was not challenged because he appeared to be successful, whereas he was using unauthorised accounts to cover up his large trading losses. Leeson was able to do this because he was in charge of both dealing and settlement, a systems weakness or **lack of segregation of key roles** that has also featured in other financial frauds.

4.2.5 Lack of independent scrutiny

External auditors may not carry out the necessary questioning of senior management because of fears of losing the audit and internal audit may avoid awkward questions because the chief financial officer determines their employment prospects. Often corporate collapses are followed by criticisms of external auditors; such as the *Barlow Clowes* affair where poorly planned and focused audit work failed to identify illegal use of client monies.

4.2.6 Lack of contact with shareholders

Board members may be out of touch with the **interests and views** of shareholders. One possible symptom of this is the payment of remuneration packages that do not appear to be warranted by results. Equally, the directors may choose to pursue their own interests and ignore the requirements of the shareholders.

4.2.7 Emphasis on short-term profitability

Emphasis on short-term results can lead to the **concealment** of problems or errors, or **manipulation** of accounts to achieve desired results.

4.2.8 Misleading accounts and information

Often, misleading figures are symptomatic of other problems (or are designed to conceal them). In many cases, poor quality accounting information is a major problem if markets are trying to make a fair assessment of the company's value. Giving out misleading information was a major issue in the UK's *Equitable Life* scandal where the company gave contradictory information to savers, independent advisers, media and regulators.

4.3 Benefits of improving corporate governance

4.3.1 Risk reduction

Clearly, the ultimate risk is of the organisation **making such large losses** that **bankruptcy** becomes inevitable. The organisation may also be closed down as a result of **serious regulatory breaches,** for example misapplying investors' monies. Proper corporate governance reduces such risks by aligning directors' interests with the company's strategic objectives and by providing for measures to reduce fraud.

4.3.2 Performance

Performance should improve if **accountabilities** are made clear and directors' motivation is enhanced by performance-related remuneration. Also, the extra breadth of experience brought by non-executive directors and measures to prevent domination by a single powerful figure should improve the quality of decision-making at board level.

4.3.3 External support

External perceptions of the company should be enhanced. This can have wide-ranging benefits.

- Improved ability to raise finance
- Improved corporate image with public and government
- Improved relations with stakeholders such as customers and employees

4.4 The UK Corporate Governance Code (an example)

The UK Corporate Governance Code applies to listed companies in the UK. These companies must either comply with the code or explain any departures from it in a note to their financial statements ('**comply or explain**').

The key principles of the code are explained briefly below.

4.4.1 Leadership

Every company should be headed by an **effective board**.

The roles of chairman and chief executive should not be exercised by the same individual. If the board decides that the roles of chief executive and chairman should be held by the same individual, they should consult major shareholders in advance, setting out their reasons.

The board should include sufficient **non-executive directors** who constructively challenge and help develop proposals on strategy.

4.4.2 Effectiveness

The board should have an appropriate **balance of skills, experience, independence and knowledge**.

There should be a formal and transparent procedure for the appointment of new directors. The board should undertake a formal annual evaluation of its performance.

All directors should receive induction on joining the board and should regularly update and refresh their skills and knowledge. Directors should be submitted for re-election at regular intervals.

The board should be supplied in a timely manner with information in a form and of a quality appropriate to enable it to discharge its duties.

The board should include an appropriate combination of executive and non-executive directors such that no individual or small group of individuals can dominate.

4.4.3 Accountability

The board should **present a balanced and understandable assessment of the company's position and prospects**.

The board is responsible for determining the nature and extent of risks it is willing to take to achieve strategic objectives.

The board should establish an audit committee of at least three (or in the case of smaller companies two), independent non-executive directors. At least one member of the audit committee should have recent and relevant financial experience.

The main role and responsibilities of the audit committee should include monitoring the integrity of the financial statements, reviewing the company's internal controls and risk management, reviewing the effectiveness of the internal audit function, and monitoring the external auditor's independence and objectivity.

4.4.4 Remuneration

Director remuneration should be **sufficient** to attract, retain and motivate **directors of the quality required**, but should not be more than is necessary. A significant proportion of executive directors' remuneration should be linked to corporate and individual performance.

There should be a formal and transparent procedure for developing policy on executive remuneration and for fixing the remuneration of individual directors. No director should be involved in deciding his or her own remuneration.

4.4.5 Relations with shareholders

There should be a **dialogue with shareholders** based on the mutual understanding of objectives. The board as a whole has responsibility for ensuring that a satisfactory dialogue with shareholders takes place.

Exam skills

You may be asked to read a scenario and identify any corporate governance issues. Learn the **principles of good corporate governance** rather than the specific requirements of the UK Corporate Governance Code or any other country-specific regime.

Corporate governance is a popular topic – it appears on **several syllabuses.**

Further details of the UK Corporate Governance code are available on the web. Visit **www.frc.org.uk**

Question 2.2	Corporate governance and directors

Learning outcome A2(i)

Briefly explain what is meant by corporate governance and explain three measures concerning directors recommended by the UK Corporate Governance Code. **(4 marks)**

Section summary

Corporate governance is the system by which companies and other entities are directed and controlled.

Stakeholders are persons or groups that have a **legitimate interest in a business's conduct** and whose concerns should be addressed as a matter of principle.

Since their interests may be widely different, **conflict between stakeholders** can be quite common.

An increasing number of **high profile corporate scandals** and collapses prompted the development of governance codes in the early 1990s.

The **UK Corporate Governance Code** sets out standards of best practice in relation to issues such as board composition, remuneration and accountability.

5 Corporate social responsibility   11/10

Introduction

Corporate social responsibility (CSR) refers to the expectation in society that companies are accountable for the social and ethical effects of their actions.

In most countries, some CSR issues are covered by legal regulations (eg pollution and child labour). Increasingly, consumers are demanding that producers of the products and services they use do more than simply comply with laws - they expect companies to behave ethically and with moral responsibility.

KEY POINT

The term Corporate Social Responsibility (CSR) is used to describe a wide range of obligations that an organisation may feel it has towards its secondary or external stakeholders, including the society in which it operates.

5.1 Caroll and Buchholtz's layers of corporate social responsibility

Caroll and Buchholtz argued that there are **four main 'layers' of corporate social responsibility**.

5.1.1 Economic responsibilities

Companies have **economic responsibilities** to shareholders demanding a good return, to employees wanting fair employment conditions and to customers seeking good-quality products at a fair price. Businesses are formed to be **properly functioning economic units** and so economic responsibilities form the basis of all other responsibilities.

5.1.2 Legal responsibilities

Since **laws codify society's moral views**, obeying them must be the foundation of compliance with social responsibilities. Although in all societies corporations will have some legal responsibilities, there is perhaps more emphasis on them in continental Europe than in the Anglo-American economies. In Anglo-American economies the focus of discussion has often been whether many legal responsibilities are unnecessary burdens on business.

5.1.3 Ethical responsibilities

These are responsibilities that require corporations to act in a **fair and just way** even if the law does not compel them to do so. If customers demand this, acting ethically may be as much a business decision as a moral one.

5.1.4 Philanthropic responsibilities

According to *Carroll and Buchholtz*, these are **desired** rather than being required of businesses. They include charitable donations, contributions to local communities and providing employees with the chances to improve their own lives.

5.2 Corporate citizenship

The concept of **corporate citizenship** provides a different perspective on organisations and society. It seeks to explain what determines how much and in what ways organisations engage with society. Again there are different views of how far it should extend.

5.2.1 Limited view

This is based on **voluntary philanthropy** undertaken in the organisations' interests. The main stakeholder groups that the corporate citizen engages with are local communities and employees. Citizenship in action takes the form of limited focus projects.

5.2.2 Equivalent view

This is based on a wider general definition of **citizenship** that is partly voluntary and partly imposed. The organisation focuses on a broad range of stakeholders and responds to the demands of society. Self-interest is not the primary motivation, instead the organisation is focused on **legal requirements** and **ethical fulfilment**.

5.2.3 Extended view

This view is based on a partly voluntary and partly imposed view of **active social and political citizenship**. Corporations must respect citizens' rights, particularly as governments have failed to provide some necessary safeguards. Given this, corporations can make a big impact since they are the most powerful institutions in society. Again the focus is on a wide range of stakeholders.

Under the extended view, **organisations will promote**:

- **Social rights**, by provision (for example decent working conditions)

- **Civil rights**, by intervening to promote citizens' individual rights themselves or to pressurise governments to promote citizens' rights

- **Political rights**, by channelling (allowing individuals to promote their causes by using corporate power)

5.3 Corporate social responsibility in developing nations

Developing economies face different challenges to corporate social responsibility than developed nations.

Key drivers for CSR in developing economies include:

(a) **Culture**. Many developing nations already have in their culture a tradition of ethics and community. Often this has come about through religion. As businesses are part of a nation's culture it is natural for such traditions to be followed.

(b) **Politics**. Political reform and the introduction of democracy is common in developing countries as this is often the spark which drives economic development. Countries undergoing development often follow examples of good practice, such as CSR, in developed nations.

(c) **Socio-economic priorities**. Developing countries often face a conflict of priorities. For example, reducing pollution may be desirable to preserve the environment, but cleaner production methods may be more expensive and hinder economic progress.

(d) **Governance gaps**. CSR can be used as a form of governance to 'plug the gaps' that result from poor government services. For example, organisations can be used to provide healthcare or education where the government cannot afford to.

(e) **Market access**. As developed nations have high public pressure for CSR, companies in developing nations must follow the same principles if they are to sell in the same market.

(f) **Multinational companies**. Multinational companies strive for consistency across all their international subsidiaries and production units. Where these are located in developing countries, they will adopt the same policies as those in developed countries. Countries (or companies) that do not adopt CSR are less likely to receive investment (or orders) from MNCs.

Section summary

Corporate social responsibility (CSR) is a recent development brought about by pressure on companies to show an awareness of the social and ethical effects of their actions.

Developing economies face different **corporate social responsibility** challenges. For example, **culture, politics, socio-economic priorities, governance gaps, market access** and the **influence of multinational companies** all influence government, company and consumer attitudes towards corporate social responsibility.

Chapter Roundup

✓   Government influence over business extends to the **macroeconomic environment**, **legal** and **market regulations**, **corporate governance** and **social responsibility**.

✓   Key elements of the **macroeconomy** include, **interest rates**, **exchange rates** and levels of **demand** and **supply**.

✓   A number of **factors influence a nation's balance of trade** because they affect the price of domestic goods compared to foreign imports.

✓   A nation's **balance of trade** forms part of its **national account balance**.

✓   **Fiscal policy** refers to government policy on taxation and government spending.

✓   **Monetary policy** refers to government policy on money supply, the monetary system, interest rates, exchange rates and the availability of credit. It can directly affect a nation's balance of trade.

✓   **Regulation** can be defined as any form of state interference with the operation of the free market.

✓   In the UK there have been various pieces of **legislation** enacted to maintain competition in the market place and there are a number of industry regulators.

✓   **European Union competition policy** is intended to ensure free and fair competition in the EU.

✓   **Deregulation** can be defined as the removal or weakening of any form of statutory (or voluntary) regulation of free market activity.

✓   **Corporate governance** is the system by which companies and other entities are directed and controlled.

✓   **Stakeholders** are persons or groups that have a **legitimate interest in a business's conduct** and whose concerns should be addressed as a matter of principle.

✓   Since their interests may be widely different, **conflict between stakeholders** can be quite common.

✓   An increasing number of **high profile corporate scandals** and collapses prompted the development of governance codes in the early 1990s.

✓   The **UK Corporate Governance Code** sets out standards of best practice in relation to issues such as board composition, remuneration and accountability.

✓   **Corporate social responsibility** (CSR) is a recent development brought about by pressure on companies to show an awareness of the social and ethical effects of their actions.

✓   **Developing economies** face different **corporate social responsibility** challenges. For example, **culture**, **politics**, **socio-economic priorities**, **governance gaps**, **market access** and the **influence of multinational companies** all influence government, company and consumer attitudes.

Quick Quiz

1   Briefly explain the impact a falling exchange rate will have on a nation's balance of trade.

2   The primary consequence of an increase in a nation's interest rates is:

A   To make imports more expensive
B   To make borrowing more expensive
C   To make imports cheaper
D   To make borrowing cheaper

3   Which of the following is an external stakeholder?

A   Shareholders
B   Customers
C   Suppliers
D   Pressure groups

4   Which of the following is **not** an example of a corporate governance failure?

A   Domination by a single individual
B   Lack of contact with shareholders
C   Strong corporate finance controls
D   Short-term profitability is pursued

5   Charitable donations are an example of which layer of corporate social responsibility according to *Caroll and Buchholtz*?

A   Economic
B   Legal
C   Ethical
D   Philanthropic

Answers to Quick Quiz

1   If an **exchange rate falls**, exports become cheaper to overseas buyers and so the nation becomes more competitive in export markets. Imports will become more expensive and so less competitive against goods produced by manufacturers at home. A fall in the exchange rate might therefore be good for the balance of trade, by giving a **stimulus to exports** and **reducing demand for imports**. However, if the demand for imported goods remains constant at the higher price level (for example demand for oil-related products such as petrol tends to be inelastic), the falling exchange rate may have an adverse effect on the balance of trade.

2   B   An increase in interest rates makes company and individual borrowing more expensive.

3   D   Pressure groups are external stakeholders. The others are connected stakeholders.

4   C   Strong corporate finance controls would be an example of good corporate governance.

5   D   Charitable donations are an example of the philanthropic layer of corporate social responsibility according to *Caroll and Buchholtz*.

Answers to Questions

2.1 Exchange and inflation rates

Exchange rates affect the relative cost of a nation's imports and exports. If its currency falls in value, imports become more expensive and exports cheaper. This leads to an improvement in national income as the country exports more than it imports.

Inflation rates affect the cost-base of organisations. If a nation experiences rising inflation, then the cost of producing goods will rise. As a result, organisations have to raise their prices. This makes the price of goods produced locally relatively more expensive compared to imports. Consequently, this will lead to a worsening national income as the local demand for cheaper imports increases and overseas demand for expensive exports decreases.

2.2 Corporate governance and directors

Corporate governance can be defined as the system by which an organisation is directed and controlled.

It is concerned with **systems, processes, controls, accountability** and **decision making** at the highest level of an organisation. Therefore, it affects the way in which board members and senior managers **execute their responsibilities** how they account for that authority to those who have entrusted them with assets and resources.

Three recommendations of the UK Corporate Governance Code concerning directors are:

(a)   Companies should appoint **non-executive directors** to the board. They are intended to provide a check or balance against the power of the chairman and chief executive.

(b)   **The posts of chairman and chief executive** should not be held by the same person. This is to prevent excessive executive power being held by one individual.

(c)   **Directors** should have to **apply for re-election** regularly, and **should not set their own remuneration**.

Note: These are just three possible examples, your answer may have included other examples.

Now try this question from the Exam Question Bank	Number	Level	Marks	Time
	2	Examination	20	36 mins

INFORMATION SYSTEMS

Part B

50

THE ROLE OF INFORMATION SYSTEMS

In this chapter we introduce **information systems** and explain their role within organisations.

In particular, we are interested in how developments in technology have provided organisations **new ways of** **working** and how IT enabled **'transformations'** have led to new forms of organisation both **real** and **'virtual'**.

Later, we consider two major issues concerning information systems – **privacy** and **security**.

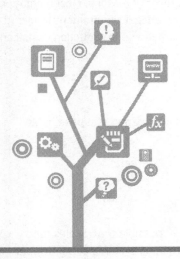

topic list	learning outcomes	syllabus references	ability required
1 The role of information systems in organisations	B1(a)	B1(i)	comprehension
2 Data and information	B1(a)	B1(i)	comprehension
3 Types of information systems	B1(a)	B1(i)	comprehension
4 Emerging trends in information systems	B1(a)	B1(ii)	comprehension
5 IT enabled transformation	B1(c)	B1(iii)	analysis
6 IT and new forms of organisation	B1(b)	B1(iii), B1(iv)	analysis
7 Privacy and security	B2(a)	B2(ii)	analysis

1 The role of information systems in organisations

Introduction

In this section we look at the role information systems play in organisations. Two main roles can be identified:

- **Support operations** through the processing and storing of transactions
- **Suppprt managerial activities** such as decision making, planning, performance measurement and control

These two purposes can be broken down into five elements.

KEY POINT

Organisations **require information** for a range of purposes.

- Recording transactions
- Decision making
- Planning
- Performance measurement
- Control

1.1 Recording transactions

Information about **each business transaction or event** is required for a number of reasons. Documentation of transactions can be used as **evidence** in a case of dispute. There may be a **legal requirement** to record transactions, for example for accounting and audit purposes. Detailed information on production costs can be built up allowing a better **assessment of profitability**.

1.2 Decision making

Information is also required to make **informed decisions**. Information and information systems enable **informed decisions** to be made.

Information used by information systems may be classified as **internal** and **external**.

1.3 Planning

Planning requires a knowledge of, among other things, available **resources**, possible **time-scales** for implementation and the likely **outcome under alternative scenarios**. Information systems can provide a number of **planning tools**.

1.4 Performance measurement

Just as individual operations need to be controlled, so overall performance must be measured in order to enable **comparisons against budget or plan** to be made. This may involve the collection of information on, for example, costs, revenues, volumes, time-scale and profitability. The **collection, analysis** and **presentation** of such data can be performed by information systems.

1.5 Control

Once a plan is implemented, its actual performance must be controlled. Information is required to assess **whether it is proceeding as expected** or whether there is some unexpected deviation from the plan. It may consequently be necessary to take some form of corrective action. Information systems can be used to **monitor** and **control the outcomes of plans**.

2 Data and information

Introduction

When discussing information systems the terms data and information often crop up. It is worth defining these terms.

- **Data** consists of raw, unprocessed facts and figures.
- **Information** is data that has been processed in a way that makes it meaningful for planning or decision making.

The process of turning data into information involves a number of stages.

 Data collection

Data gathering from internal and external sources.

 Data evaluation

The data collected is examined and filtered. Irrelevant data may be deleted or ignored.

 Data analysis

Data collected is compared against benchmarks or yardsticks, for example actual versus budget..

 Interpretation

Data is considered, interpreted and meaning added. For example an explanation as to why actual differs from budget.

 Reporting

Information is distributed to those who require it, for example as a report sent out as an email attachment.

2.1 Internal data and information

This is data and information that is held within the organisation's own files. The following are examples of internal information.

2.1.1 Accounting records

Accounts receivable ledgers, **accounts payable** ledgers, **general ledgers** and **cash books** etc hold information that may be of great value outside the accounts department, for example, sales information for the marketing function.

2.1.2 Personnel records

Information about **personnel** will be held, possibly linked to the **payroll** system. Additional information may be obtained from this source if, say, a project is being costed and it is necessary to ascertain the availability and rate of pay of different levels of staff, or the need for and cost of recruiting staff from outside the organisation.

2.1.3 Production data

Much information will be produced by a **production** department about machine capacity, fuel consumption, movement of people, materials, work in progress, set up times, maintenance requirements and so on.

2.1.4 Timesheets

Many **service** businesses, notably accountants and solicitors, need to keep detailed records of the **time spent** on various activities, both to justify fees to clients and to assess the efficiency and profitability of operations.

2.2 External data and information

Organisations often need to collect information concerning environmental factors. The following table describes some of these factors using PEST analysis.

Factor	Comment
Political/legal	National or local politics may affect how an organisation operates. Changes in legislation may put new responsibilities or liabilities on an organisation. For example, the Data Protection Act.
Economic	Economic factors affect an organisation's finances such as the availability of loans or sales levels.
Social	Society's views may put pressure on how the organisation is run, for example pressure to reduce environmental pollution.
Technological	Technological advances may affect an organisation's production and/or management processes. Technology may also allow the development of new products and services which were not previously possible.

Organisations may also require external information relating to:

(a)   **Competitors** – how successful are they, are they developing new products?

(b)   **Customers** – what are their needs, how large is the potential market, are there any new market segments? (see Chapter 8)

(c)   **Suppliers** – what are their prices, what is the quality of their products like, are there any new potential suppliers in the market?

Formal collection of data from outside sources includes the following.

(a)   A company's **tax specialists** will be expected to gather information about changes in tax law and how this will affect the company.

(b)   The company's **legal expert** or **company secretary** would collect relevant information relating to any new legislation on health and safety at work, or employment regulations.

(c)   **Research and development** (R & D) work often relies on information about other R & D work being done by another company or by government institutions.

(d)   **Marketing managers** need to know about the opinions and buying attitudes of potential customers. To obtain this information, they might carry out market research exercises.

KEY TERM

The phrase ENVIRONMENTAL SCANNING is often used to describe the process of gathering external information from a wide range of sources.

Sometimes additional external information is needed, requiring an active search outside the organisation. The following **additional external sources** may be identified.

(a)   The government.

(b)   Advice or information bureaux.

(c)   Consultancies.

(d)   Newspaper and magazine publishers.

(e)   Specific reference works which are used in a particular line of work.

(f)   Libraries and information services.

(g)   Customer or supplier systems can be a source of information, for instance via electronic data interchange (EDI).

(h)   Web-based sources of information are becoming ever more important.

2.2.1 Informal data and information gathering

Informal gathering of data and information from the environment goes on all the time, when employees learn **what is going on in the world around** them – perhaps from trade magazines, newspapers, websites, television reports or meetings with business associates.

2.3 The qualities of information

To be useful, information requires a number of specific qualities. The mnemonic ACCURATE, shown in the following table, is a useful way of remembering them. Information systems should aim to produce information that possesses these qualities.

Quality	Example
Accurate	Figures in a report should add up, the degree of rounding should be appropriate, there should be no typos, items should be allocated to the correct category, assumptions should be stated for uncertain information.
Complete	Information should include everything relevant to the decision being considered. if relevant, comparative information should be included. Information should be **consistent**, for example it should be collected on the same basis each time, to allow for meaningful **comparison**.
Cost-beneficial	It should not cost more to obtain the information than the **benefit** derived from its use. Information collection and analysis should be **efficient**. Presentation should be clear, such that users do not waste time working out what the information means.
User-targeted	The **needs of the user** are paramount. For example, senior managers may require summaries, operational managers may require more detail.
Relevant	Information that is **not needed** for a decision should be omitted. All significant information that is relevant to the decision being considered should be included.
Authoritative	The **source** of the information should be a reliable one (not, for instance, 'Joe Bloggs Predictions Page' on the Internet - unless Joe Bloggs is known to be a reliable source for that type of information.
Timely	The information should be available **when it is needed** and in time for required action to be effective.
Easy to use	Information should be **understandable**. It should be clearly presented, not excessively long, and sent using the right medium and communication channel (e-mail, telephone, hard-copy report etc).

Section summary

Information systems play a key role within organisations. In particular they are used in **planning**, **controlling**, **recording transactions**, **performance measurement** and **decision making**.

Data consists of raw, unprocessed facts and figures. **Information** is data that has been processed in a way that makes it meaningful for planning or decision making.

Information used by organisations comes from a variety of **internal** and **external sources**.

Information systems should provide information that possesses certain specific **qualities** (ACCURATE).

3 Types of information systems

Introduction

There are a large **range of information systems** available to an organisation, with different purposes. In this section we shall look at common forms of information system, and later, some **recent trends** and **developments in information systems**.

3.1 Information systems at different organisational levels

The term '**information system**' is a general concept that refers to the people, data and activities, both computer-based and manual, that effectively gather, process, store and disseminate information. Most information systems utilised in a business context today rely on information and communications technologies (**ICT**).

Organisations require different types of information system to provide information at **different levels** of the organisation, and in a range of functional areas.

System level	System purpose and features	Examples
Strategic	**Purpose**: To help senior managers with long-term planning. **Time focus**: Long term **Coverage**: Whole organisation **Uncertainty and subjectivity**: High **Accuracy**: Less critical than at other levels	Key ratios and performance indicators Ad hoc market analysis Strategic plans
Management or tactical	**Purpose**: To help middle managers monitor and control. **Time focus**: Short to medium term **Coverage**: Department(s) or function(s) **Uncertainty and subjectivity**: Moderate **Accuracy**: Moderate level, not as detailed as operational level	Variance analyses Exception reports
Operational	**Purpose**: To process transactions and help operational managers track the organisation's day-to-day operational activities. **Time focus**: Immediate **Coverage**: Specific activities **Uncertainty and subjectivity**: Low **Accuracy**: A high level of accuracy is required	Transaction listings Daily receipts and payments Real-time production data

Different types of information systems exist with different characteristics – reflecting the different roles they perform. The most common are described below.

3.2 Transaction Processing Systems (TPS)

KEY TERM

A TRANSACTION PROCESSING SYSTEM (TPS) performs and records routine transactions.

TPS are used for **routine tasks** in which data items or transactions must be processed so that operations can continue. TPS support most business functions in most types of organisation.

Transaction Processing Systems are sometimes referred to as **Data Processing Systems (DPS)**.

The following table shows a range of TPS applications.

Transaction processing systems				
	Sales/ marketing systems	**Manufacturing/ production systems**	**Finance/ accounting systems**	**Human resources systems**	**Other types (eg university)**
Major functions of system	• Sales management • Market research • Promotion pricing • New products	• Scheduling • Purchasing Shipping/ receiving • Engineering • Operations	• Budgeting • General ledger • Billing • Management accounting	• Personnel records • Benefits • Salaries • Labour relations • Training	• Admissions • Student academic records • Course records • Graduates
Major application systems	• Sales order information system • Market research system • Pricing system	• Materials resource planning • Purchase order control • Engineering • Quality control	• General ledger • Accounts receivable /payable • Budgeting • Funds management	• Payroll • Employee records • Employee benefits • Career path systems	• Registration • Student record • Curriculum/ class control systems • Benefactor information system

3.3 Management Information Systems (MIS)

KEY TERM

MANAGEMENT INFORMATION SYSTEMS (MIS) convert data from mainly internal sources into information (eg summary reports, exception reports). This information enables managers to make timely and effective decisions for planning, directing and controlling the activities for which they are responsible.

An MIS provides **regular reports** and **access** to the organisation's current and historical performance.

MIS usually **transform data** from **underlying transaction processing systems** (TPS) into summarised **files** that are used as the basis for management reports.

MIS have the following characteristics:

- Support **structured** decisions at operational and management control levels
- Designed to report on **existing** operations
- Have **little analytical capability**
- Relatively **inflexible**
- Have an **internal** focus

3.4 Executive Information Systems (EIS) 05/11

KEY TERM

An **EXECUTIVE INFORMATION SYSTEM (EIS)** pools data from internal and external sources and makes information available to senior managers in an easy-to-use form. EIS help senior managers make strategic, unstructured decisions.

An EIS should provide senior managers with easy access to key **internal** and **external** information. The system summarises and tracks strategically critical information, possibly drawn from internal MIS and DSS (see below), but also including data from **external sources** eg competitors, legislation and external databases such as Reuters.

Executive Information Systems are sometimes referred to as **Executive Support Systems** (ESS). An ESS/EIS is likely to have the following **features**.

- Flexibility
- Quick response time
- Sophisticated data analysis and modelling tools

A model of a **typical EIS** follows.

An Executive Information System (EIS)

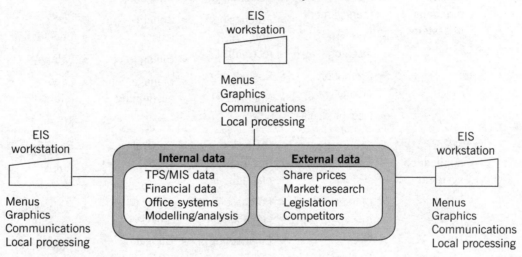

Exam alert

Exam questions may require you to explain the value of a good MIS or EIS. To gain good marks you must think about the benefits these systems bring to an organisation.

3.5 Decision Support Systems (DSS) 05/11

KEY TERM

DECISION SUPPORT SYSTEMS (DSS) combine data and analytical models or data analysis tools to support semi-structured and unstructured decision making.

DSS are used by **management to assist in making decisions** on issues which are subject to high levels of uncertainty. They are intended to provide a wide range of alternative information gathering and analytical tools with a major emphasis upon **flexibility** and **user-friendliness**.

DSS have more **analytical power** than other systems, enabling them to analyse and condense large volumes of data into a form that aids managers' decision making. The objective is to allow the manager to consider a number of **alternatives** and evaluate them under a variety of potential conditions.

3.6 Knowledge Work Systems (KWS)

KEY TERMS

KNOWLEDGE WORK SYSTEMS (KWS) are information systems that facilitate the creation and integration of new knowledge into an organisation.

KNOWLEDGE WORKERS are people whose jobs primarily involve creating new information and knowledge. They are often members of a profession such as doctors, engineers, lawyers and scientists.

KWS help **knowledge workers** create new knowledge and expertise. Examples include:

- Computer Aided Design (CAD)
- Computer Aided Manufacturing (CAM)
- Specialised financial software that analyses trading situations

3.7 Office Automation Systems (OAS)

KEY TERM

OFFICE AUTOMATION SYSTEMS (OAS) are computer systems designed to increase the productivity of data and information workers.

OAS **support the major activities** performed in a typical office such as document management, facilitating communication and managing data.

Examples include:

- Word processing, desktop publishing, presentation software
- Digital filing systems
- E-mail, voice mail, videoconferencing (or teleconferencing)
- Groupware, intranets, extranets, schedulers
- Spreadsheets, desktop databases

3.8 Expert systems

KEY TERM

EXPERT SYSTEMS are a form of DSS that allow users to benefit from expert knowledge and information. Such systems consist of a **database** holding specialised data and **rules** about what to do in, or how to interpret, a given set of circumstances.

For example, many financial institutions now use expert systems to process straightforward **loan applications**. The user enters certain key facts into the system such as the loan applicant's name, their most recent addresses, their income, monthly outgoings and details of other loans. The system will then:

(a) **Check the facts** given against its database to see whether the applicant has a good credit record.

(b) **Perform calculations** to see whether the applicant can afford to repay the loan.

(c) **Match up other criteria** such as whether the security offered for the loan or the purpose for which the loan is wanted is acceptable and the applicant's is risk profile. The system makes these judgements based on previous experience (as represented within the system).

A decision is then suggested, based on the results of this processing. This is why it is now often possible to get a loan or arrange insurance **over the telephone**, whereas in the past it would have been necessary to go and speak to a bank manager or send details to an actuary and then wait for them to come to a decision.

Exam skills

Do not just learn what these systems are – you need to understand which levels of an organisation's hierarchy would use them and how they support its operations.

There are many other **business applications** of expert systems.

(a)   **Legal** advice.

(b)   **Tax** advice.

(c)   **Forecasting** of economic or financial developments, or of market and customer behaviour.

(d)   **Surveillance**, for example of the number of customers entering a supermarket to decide when more checkouts need to be opened – or of machines in a factory, to determine when they need maintenance.

(e)   **Diagnostic systems** to identify causes of problems, for example in production control in a factory, or in healthcare.

(f)   **Project management**.

(g)   **Education** and **training**, diagnosing a student's or worker's weaknesses and providing or recommending extra instruction as appropriate.

An organisation can use an expert system when a number of **conditions** are met.

(a)   The problem is **reasonably well-defined**.

(b)   The expert can define some **rules** by which the problem can be solved.

(c)   The problem cannot be solved by **conventional** transaction processing or data handling.

(d)   The **expert could be released** to more difficult problems. Experts are often highly paid, meaning the value of even small time savings is likely to be significant.

(e)   The **investment** in an expert system is **cost-justified**.

Question 3.1	Expert systems

Learning outcome B1(ii)

Explain why organisations use expert systems for decision-making tasks which humans are naturally better able to perform than computers?   **(5 marks)**

3.9 Intranets and Extranets

Organisations are increasingly using **intranets** and **extranets** to **disseminate information**.

(a)   An **intranet** is like a mini version of the Internet. Organisation members use networked computers to access information held on a server. The user interface is a browser – similar to those used on the Internet. The intranet offers access to information on a wide variety of topics.

(b)   An **extranet** is an intranet that is accessible to **authorised outsiders**, using a valid username and password. The username will have access rights attached – determining which parts of the extranet can be viewed. Extranets are becoming a very popular means for business partners to exchange information.

KEY TERMS

An INTRANET is a private network inside a company or organisation accessed through web-browser like software. Intranets are for the use of staff only, they are not accessible by the public. Intranets are used to provide and distribute information.

An EXTRANET allows customers and suppliers to gain limited access to an intranet in order to enhance the speed and efficiency of their business relationship. Put another way, it is an intranet that allows some access by authorised outsiders.

3.10 Databases

KEY TERMS

A DATABASE is a collection of data organised to service many applications. The database provides convenient access to data for a wide variety of users.

A DATABASE MANAGEMENT SYSTEM (DBMS) is the software that centralises data and manages access to the database. It enables numerous applications to utilise the same files

The term '**database system**' is used to describe a wide range of systems that utilise a central pool of data.

Example of a database system

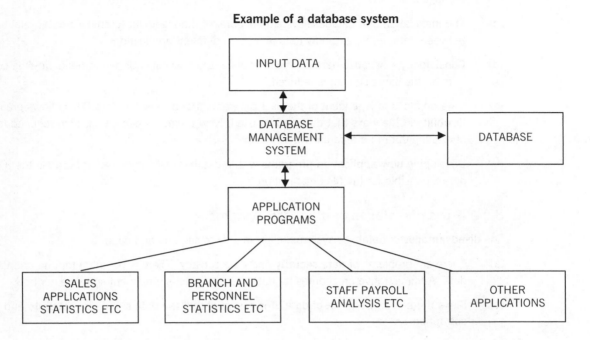

3.10.1 The characteristics of a database system

The way in which data is held on a system affects the ease with which the data is able to be accessed and manipulated. A database system has the following characteristics:

(a) **Shared**. Different users are able to access the same data for their own processing applications. This removes the need to hold the same data in different files.

(b) **Controls** to preserve the **integrity** of the database.

(c) **Flexibility**. The database system should provide for the **needs of different users**, who each have their own processing requirements and data access methods. The database should be capable of **evolving** to meet **future** needs.

3.10.2 Database queries

A database can be interrogated by a **query language**. A query language is a formalised method of constructing queries in a database system. The language provides a way of asking a database for data. Some query languages are also able to make changes within the database. SQL, short for **Structured Query Language**, is a popular language.

Databases connected to a **web server** are able to be accessed by people outside the organisation through their web browser. Microsoft ADO is an example of a **database connectivity component** that enables this functionality. Potential customers are able to view product and service information, and if the site is enabled for e-commerce, make a purchase.

3.10.3 Advantages of database systems

The **advantages** of a database system include the following:

(a) Avoidance of **unnecessary duplication** of data (data redundancy) brings time and efficiency savings and **reduced storage costs**.

(b) Data is looked upon as serving the **organisation as a whole**, not just for individual departments. The database concept encourages management to regard data as a resource that must be **properly managed**.

(c) The installation of a database system encourages management to **analyse data**, relationships between data items, and how data is used in different applications.

(d) **Consistency** – because data is only held once, the possibility of departments holding conflicting data on the same subject is reduced.

(e) Data on file is independent of the user programs that access the data. This allows **greater flexibility** in the ways that data can be used. New programs can be easily introduced to make use of existing data in a different way.

(f) Developing **new application programs** with a database system is easier because the programmer is not responsible for the file organisation.

3.10.4 Disadvantages of database systems

The **disadvantages** of database systems relate mainly to security and control:

(a) There are problems of **data security** and **data privacy**. There is potential for unauthorised access to data. Administrative procedures for data security must supplement software controls.

(b) Since there is only one set of data, it is essential that the data should be **accurate** and free from corruption.

(c) There may be disputes over who '**owns**' the data so has the right to decide how it is maintained.

(d) Since data is held once, but its use is widespread, the impact of **system failure** would be greater.

(e) If an organisation develops its own database system from scratch, **initial development costs** will be high.

Section summary

Different types of information system exist with different characteristics – reflecting the different roles they perform.

Organisations are increasingly using **intranets**, **extranets** and **database systems** to manage and provide access to data and information.

4 Emerging trends in information systems

Introduction

In recent years information systems and technology have continued to develop rapidly. Three trends in information system have emerged as being popular with many types of organisation. These are **enterprise-wide systems**, **knowledge management systems** and **customer relationship management systems**.

4.1 Enterprise-wide systems

KEY TERM

ENTERPRISE-WIDE SYSTEMS are designed to **co-ordinate** all **business functions**, **resources** and **information**,

Under an enterprise-wide system, each business area (such as accounts, HR, production and sales) is provided with a system that fulfils its needs, however each module shares a **common database** that is the basis of all the information within the organisation.

The central database allows each business area to **access** and **update information** in **real-time** and this means that information is **easy to share**, **available** to all business areas, and above all, **reliable**.

In some enterprises, even though the system spans the whole organisation individual locations have their own specific data processing capability, via a direct link to the central database. This is known as **Distributed Data Processing (DDP)**. The link is provided by either a **Local Area Network** (LAN) or a **Wide Area Network** (WAN), depending upon how far apart the different locations are.

We look at **enterprise resource planning (ERP) software** which is an example of an enterprise-wide system in Chapter 7.

A relatively recent development has been the development of **web-based enterprise-wide software**. To access these systems requires only a computer with an Internet connection and a web browser. The application is web-based, so the distance between the user and the data is irrelevant. The use of web-based software is sometimes referred to as **cloud computing**.

4.2 Knowledge management systems

KEY TERM

KNOWLEDGE MANAGEMENT SYSTEMS (KMS) record and store the knowledge held within an organisation.

Information held on a KMS is easily accessed and shared by employees. Examples of information held in a KMS include facts, solutions to problems, relevant legislation and intellectual property.

A KMS is primarily of benefit to **knowledge based organisations**, such as those involved in research and development or providing services such as legal advice. This is because their information is best suited to storing and sharing by a database.

Benefits of a KMS include:

(a)   **Valuable data is preserved** for the future and not lost, for example, where an employee leaves

(b)   The data is **easily shared**

(c)   **Data duplication** (or data redundancy) is **avoided**

(d)   It allows employees to 'get up to speed' on knowledge quickly and easily and this may **reduce the time they need to spend training**

4.3 Customer relationship management systems

KEY TERM

CUSTOMER RELATIONSHIP MANAGEMENT (CRM) systems are software applications which specialise in providing information concerning an organisation's products, services and customers.

Most CRM systems are based on a **database** which stores data about customers such as their **order history** and **personal information** such as address, age and any marketing feedback they have provided. These systems allow a personalised service to be provided to the customer as well as a swift reply to their queries.

CRM systems are often used by customer facing staff who handle **customer enquiries**, **orders** or **complaints** and who need to understand the customer's immediate needs and provide an appropriate response.

4.4 Web 2.0 and e-commerce

Two other trends are increased business use of web 2.0 applications and increased use of e-commerce.

4.4.1 Web 2.0

KEY TERM

WEB 2.0 APPLICATIONS are 'second generation' Internet-based services. These sites usually include tools that let people collaborate and share information online.

Examples of web 2.0 applications include **blogs** (short for web log), **RSS** feeds, **second life**, **wikis**, and **You Tube** (although there is some debate as to whether You Tube qualifies as web 2.0 as although users upload to it, and access content from it, they don't download from it). Social networking sites such as **Facebook** are **Twitter** are also part of the web 2.0 movement, and are increasingly being used by businesses.

4.4.2 E-commerce

E-commerce (the selling of goods or services over the Internet) has developed alongside CRM systems. The trend is towards providing the customer with a **unique shopping experience** that is tailored to their needs. The view and products presented to a customer is geared to their individual tastes, based on their profile and past behaviour on the site.

Most **organisations** have e-commerce capability on their website. Many have gone further, for example Amazon suggests potential purchases for customers when they log-on. These suggestions are driven by the customer's previous orders and their history of viewing products.

Berens (2006) identifies the following points to consider when building a website with e-commerce capability.

(a)   Ensure transactions are **secure**, and tell customers they are. Customer trust is essential.

(b)   Comply with all applicable consumer, privacy and data protection legislation.

(c)   Have clear **terms of use** for the site.

(d)   Don't require customers to provide excessive amounts of information as this may deter them.

(e)   Maintain **on-going communication** with willing customers, for example by e-mail.

The term **e-business** refers to conducting business on the Internet. It has a wider meaning than e-commerce, because it covers not only buying and selling but also servicing customers and collaborating with suppliers.

CASE STUDY

Business use of Twitter

Stuart Lynn, Head of R&D, Sage Mid Market Division, http://twitter.com/_stuartlynn

27% of UK SME's use Twitter. 27% of the 1.4 million businesses registered for VAT equals 460,000 businesses. This number rises to well over 1 million if you include businesses who are not VAT registered.

Twitter provides a ready made network to share information about your business, to set up a trading network and to build your brand. What's more, Twitter is global.

As a social networking tool Twitter has had a meteoric rise to fame with between 3 and 6 million users. When I first tried it, I was unimpressed. How can I make use of it? How do I know who to follow? How do I get followers? How could I say it in only 140 characters?

Today, I'm a convert, I use Twitter every day. It's an excellent source of news and information on just about any topic. It allows me to keep my finger on the pulse of IT and business information and to share information about Sage, as well as my other passions, with people who have chosen to follow me.

The Twitter network means if one of my follower's re-tweet's my tweet, then all of their followers see my tweet, and so on. I tweeted a link to my last blog 'The secret to successful innovation' and watched what happened.

Although I only have a few hundred followers myself, within the first hour, my original tweet had an audience of over 30,000 people. Within a couple of days my blog had turned up on other sites such as Innovation America. Others had reused parts of my blog in their own innovation blogs, a way to keep the message alive and a complement indeed. One piece of information, seen by a huge audience across the globe and recycled a second and third time.

What's more, it significantly increased traffic on sage.co.uk - all from a single tweet. The power of social networking is amazing. Remember though, Twitter is a tool to build your network, headline key information and lead people to your business. When they get there they need to find a website, or a blog, with more meaningful and relevant information, and the ability to make a purchase.

Give it a try, other than a little of your time and effort, it's free, and you might be as amazed with the results as I was.

Section summary

Enterprise-wide systems are designed to **co-ordinate** all **business functions**, **resources** and **information**.

The purpose of **knowledge management systems (KMS)** is to record and store the knowledge held within an organisation.

Customer relationship management (CRM) systems are software applications which specialise in providing information concerning an organisation's products, services and customers.

Web 2.0 applications are second generation' Internet-based services. These sites usually include tools that let people collaborate and share information online.

E-commerce (the selling of goods or services over the Internet) continues to grow rapidly.

---

5   IT enabled transformation   11/10

Introduction

Information technology and information systems allow an organisation **to transform how it does business. A dependence on IT commits an organisation to continual change**. The pace of technological change is rapid. Computer systems – both hardware and software – are likely to be superseded after a few years.

In this section we consider how IT enables an organisation to transform itself.

5.1 Information technology as an enabler of change

Information technology may be the **driving force** or **trigger of organisational change**. Even when IT is not a significant factor in the actual change, it can play an important part in the change management process.

The table below indicates the numerous ways in which **IT may enable change** within an organisation.

IT's possible role in organisational change	Comment
The type of products or services that are made and sold	For example, companies like Sony manufacture home computers, Virgin have an Internet Service Provider business. **Technological changes** affect many products, for example the introduction of tennis and squash rackets with graphite frames.

IT's possible role in organisational change	Comment
The way in which products are made	There is a continuing trend towards computer aided design and manufacture. **Computer Aided Design (CAD)** can be used to create designs which can be quickly amended. **Computer-Aided Manufacturing (CAM)** involves the use of software to control machine tools and related machinery. **Computer Integrated Manufacturing (CIM)** involves using computers to control the production process. CAM and CIM have **changed the methods and cost profiles** of many manufacturing processes. The techniques used to **measure and record costs** have also adapted to the use of IT.
The way in which employees are mobilised	The use of IT encourages de-layering of organisational hierarchies and greater **workforce empowerment** and skills. Using technology frequently requires changes in working methods.
The way in which services are provided	High-street banks encourage customers to use 'hole-in-the-wall' cash dispensers, or telephone or Internet banking. Most larger shops now use computerised **Point of Sale terminals** at cash desks. Many organisations use **e-commerce** – selling products and services over the Internet.
To enable change	IT can produce dramatic changes in individual businesses and whole industries. For example, competition in the airline industry has intensified due to information systems that allow easy fare comparison and booking. IT can be both a **cause** of major changes in doing business and a **response** to them.
To aid communication and co-ordination	Co-ordination is essential when introducing change. IT can facilitate this through the use of e-mail, project management software, an intranet, and groupware (such as Microsoft Outlook).
As a source of unity and structure	In times of restructuring, information systems can be a visible sign of the new situation. For example, an organisation-wide network, perhaps with an intranet, provides evidence of and encourages acceptance of the new situation.

 The impact of IT on an organisation is revisited in paper E3.

Question 3.2

IT transformation

Learning outcome B1(iii)

Velospeed designs, manufactures and distributes bicycles.

Designs are drawn by hand. These are passed to skilled workers who construct the bicycle frame by hand using traditional materials such as steel. Some customers have reported quality problems with frames.

The frame is the only part that Velospeed builds itself. Wheels, gears, brakes and pedals are each sourced from individual suppliers.

Orders for these parts are made over the telephone, recorded on paper and filed in a storage cabinet. The company has problems in retrieving and analysing cost data for management reports.

Required

Advise Velospeed as to how information technology could transform its business. **(9 marks)**

Section summary

IT may **enable an organisation to transform** how it does business. In particular:

- The type of products or services that are made and sold
- The way in which products are made
- The way in which employees are mobilised
- The way in which services are provided
- To enable change
- To aid communication and co-ordination
- As a source of unity and structure

6   IT and new forms of organisation

Introduction

As we have seen, information technology can affect an organisation in many ways including **changing the way it does its business**. As a consequence IT has allowed different types of organisation to emerge.

Some examples of **emerging types of organisation** are described below.

6.1 Virtual organisations

The global explosion of information technology has led to the creation of **virtual teams, virtual companies and virtual supply chains**.

6.1.1 Virtual teams

Virtual teams are groups of people who aren't based in the same office or organisation (and may even be in different areas of the world) but who:

- Share information and tasks (eg technical support provided by a supplier)
- Make joint decisions (eg on quality assurance or staff training)
- Fulfil the collaborative (working together) function of a team

Technology has facilitated this kind of collaboration, simulating team working through the use of **teleconferencing, video-conferencing**, **networked computers** and the **Internet**.

(a)   Dispersed individuals and units can use such technology to **access** and **share** product, customer, inventory and delivery information (eg using web-based databases and data tracking systems).

(b)   **Electronic meeting sites and systems** allow virtual meeting participants to talk and listen to each other while sharing data and using electronic 'white boards' on their PCs.

This has enabled organisations to:

(a)   **Outsource** areas of organisational activity to other organisations and freelance workers (even 'off-shore' in countries where skilled labour is cheaper) without losing control or co-ordination.

(b)   **Organise 'territorially'** without the overhead costs of local offices and without the difficulties of supervision, communication and control. Dispersed centres are linked to a 'virtual office' by communications technology and can share data freely.

(c)   **Centralise** shared functions and services (such as data storage and retrieval, technical support or secretarial services) without the disadvantages of 'geographical' centralisation, and with the advantages of decentralised authority. Databases and communication (eg via e-mail) create genuine interactive sharing of, and access to, common data.

(d)   **Adopt flexible cross-functional and multi-skilled working** by making expertise available across the organisation. A 'virtual team' co-opts the best people for the task – regardless of location.

6.1.2 Virtual companies and virtual supply chains

KEY TERMS

A VIRTUAL COMPANY is a collection of separate companies, each with a specific expertise, who work together, sharing their expertise to compete for bigger contracts/projects than would be possible if they worked alone.

A traditional SUPPLY CHAIN is made up of the physical entities linked together to facilitate the supply of goods and services to the final consumer.

A VIRTUAL SUPPLY CHAIN (VSC) is a supply chain that is enabled through e-business links, for example the web and extranets.

A relatively recent development is the **virtual company.** This is created out of **a network of alliances and subcontracting arrangements**. It is as if most of the activities in a particular **value chain** (see Chapter 5) are conducted by different organisations, even though the process is loosely co-ordinated.

For example, assume an organisation produces small toys. It could in theory outsource:

- The **design** to a consultancy
- **Manufacturing** to a subcontractor
- **Delivery** arrangements to a specialist logistics organisation
- **Debt collection** to a bank
- **Filing, tax returns**, **bookkeeping** to an accountancy firm

The **virtual company** relies on technology such as **remote networking**, the **Internet** and **extranets**. Many companies have become, or are becoming, more **'virtual'**. They are developing into looser affiliations of companies, organised as a supply network.

Virtual Supply Chain networks have two types of organisation: producers and integrators.

(a)   **Producers** produce goods and services. Producers must focus on delivery to schedule and within cost. The sales driver within these companies is on ensuring that their capacity is fully sold. Producers are often servicing multiple chains, so managing and avoiding capacity and commercial conflicts becomes key.

(b)   **Integrators** manage the supply network and effectively 'own' the end customer contact. The focus of the integrating organisation is on managing the end customer relationship. This includes synchronising the responses and performance of network functions and members.

Many of the most popular Internet companies are integrators in virtual companies, for example Amazon.com and Lastminute.com. These organisations 'own' **customer contact** and manage customer relationships for a range of producers.

6.2 Advantages of virtual operations

Virtual operations have various **advantages**.

- Flexibility and speed of operation
- Low investment in assets and hence less risk involved
- Injection of market forces into all the linkages in the value chain

6.3 Disadvantages of virtual operations

But there are some **disadvantages**.

- Organisations must complement each other and form close relationships if the venture is to succeed

- Quality may be a problem owing to a loss of control

- The suppliers/resources may also be available to rival operations

- Customers may recognise the virtual characteristics and this might negatively affect customer perceptions of the service or product

CASE STUDY

First Virtual Corporation, one of the few truly virtual organisations in existence, was set up in 1993 by Ralph Ungermann and it generates multi-million dollar sales of its multimedia networking equipment. Everything except the crucial design and development work is outsourced. The company has two 'core competences' according to Ungermann: technical development and forging alliances with large companies.

Section summary

The **global explosion** of information technology has led to the creation of virtual teams, companies and supply chains.

Virtual teams are interconnected groups of people who may not be present in the same office or organisation.

A **virtual company** is a collection of separate companies, each with a specific expertise, who work together, to compete for bigger contracts/projects than would be possible if they worked alone.

A **Virtual Supply Chain (VSC)** is a supply chain that is enabled through e-business links, for example the web or extranets.

7 Privacy and security   05/11

Introduction

Most of the advances in technology and information systems that we have seen in this chapter rely on the Internet as a means of communication. However, establishing Internet links makes organisations vulnerable to **privacy** and **security risks**. Therefore suitable systems, policies and procedures should be implemented to minimise them.

Computer systems with links to other systems such as the **Internet** are exposed to privacy security risks. Some of the main risks are explained below.

Privacy and security risks associated with the Internet	
Risk	**Explanation**
Hackers and eavesdroppers	Hackers attempt to gain unauthorised access to computer systems. They may attempt to damage a system or steal information. Hackers use tools like electronic password generators which enable rapid multiple password attempts.
	Data that is transmitted across telecommunications links is exposed to the risk of being intercepted or examined during transmission (eavesdropping).

Privacy and security risks associated with the Internet	
Risk	**Explanation**
Viruses	A virus is a small piece of software which performs unauthorised actions and which replicates itself. Viruses may cause damage to files or attempt to destroy files and damage hard disks. When transmitted over a network such as the Internet, into a 'clean' system, the virus reproduces and infects that system.
	Types of virus:
	E-mail viruses spread using e-mail messages and replicate by mailing themselves to addresses held in the user's contacts book.
	Worms copy themselves from machine to machine on a network.
	Trojans or Trojan horses are hidden inside a 'valid' program but perform an unexpected act. Trojans therefore act like a virus, but aren't classified as a virus as they don't replicate themselves.
	Trap doors are undocumented access points to a system allowing controls to be bypassed.
	Logic bombs are triggered by the occurrence of a certain event.
	Time bombs are triggered by a certain date.
Hoaxes	An associated problem is that of hoax virus warnings. There are a vast number of common hoaxes, most of which circulate via e-mail. Many are a variation of one of the most 'popular' early hoaxes – the Good Times hoax. This hoax takes the form of a warning about viruses contained in e-mail. People pass along the warning trying to be helpful, but they are in fact wasting the time of all concerned.
Denial of service attack	Another threat, to websites is the 'denial of service attack'. This involves an organised campaign to bombard a site with excessive volumes of traffic at a given time, with the aim of overloading the site.

A number of websites provide information on hoaxes and 'real' viruses – for example www.sophos.com. If you receive a warning of a virus or the promise of rewards for forwarding an e-mail to a number of others, this is a good place to look to establish if the warning is a hoax or not.

7.1 Minimising privacy and security risks

The risks identified above can be minimised through a variety of **controls** that provide network and communications security.

7.1.1 Anti-virus software

The main protection against viruses is **anti-virus software**. Anti-virus software, such as McAfee or Norton search systems for viruses and remove them. Anti-virus programs include an auto-update feature that downloads profiles of new viruses, enabling the software to check for all known or existing viruses. Very new viruses may go undetected by anti-virus software (until the anti-virus software vendor updates their package – and the organisation installs the update).

Additional precautions include **disabling external media** to prevent viruses entering an organisation via external storage devices. However, this can disrupt work processes. At the very least, organisations should ensure all files received via external media and e-mail are virus checked.

7.1.2 A firewall

External e-mail links can be protected by way of a **firewall** that may be configured to virus check all messages, and may also prevent files of a certain type being sent via e-mail (eg .exe files, as these are the most common means of transporting a virus). Firewalls can be implemented in both hardware and software, or a combination of both. A firewall disables part of the telecoms technology to prevent **unauthorised intrusions**. However, a determined hacker may well be able to bypass this.

7.1.3 Encryption

Data that is transmitted across telecommunications links is exposed to the risk of being **intercepted or read during transmission** (known as 'eavesdropping'). Encryption is used to reduce this risk and involves scrambling the data at one end of the line, transmitting the scrambled data, and unscrambling it at the receiver's end of the line. A person intercepting the scrambled data is unable to make sense of it.

7.1.4 Electronic signatures

One way of providing **electronic signatures** is to make use of what is known as **public key** (or asymmetric) cryptography signatures. Public key cryptography uses two keys – public and private. The private key is only known to its owner and is used to scramble the data contained in a file. The received **'scrambled' data** is checked against the original file using the public key of the person who signed it. This check confirms the file could only have been signed by someone with access to the private key. If a third party altered the message the fact that they had done so would be easily detectable.

An alternative is the use of encryption products which support key recovery, also known as **key encapsulation**. These products incorporate a **Key Recovery Agent** (KRA) which allows the authorised user to unscramble data by approaching the KRA with an encrypted portion of the message.

7.1.5 Authentication

Authentication is a technique of making sure that a message has come from an **authorised sender**. Authentication involves adding extra data in a form previously agreed between sender and recipient.

7.1.6 Dial-back security

Dial-back security operates by requiring the person wanting access to dial into the network **and identify themselves first**. The system then dials the person back on their authorised number before allowing access.

Section summary

Computer systems with links to other systems such as the **Internet** are exposed to privacy and security risks.

The **key privacy** and **security risks** come from **hackers** and **eavesdroppers**, **viruses**, **hoaxes** and **denial of service attacks**.

Organisations can take various **measures** against privacy and security risks, including **anti-virus software**, **firewalls**, **encryption**, **electronic signatures**, **authentication** and **dial-back security**.

Chapter Roundup

✓ **Information systems** support operations and management activities within organisations. In particular they are used in **recording transactions, decision making, planning, performance measurement** and **control**.

✓ **Data** consists of raw, unprocessed facts and figures. **Information** is data that has been processed in a way that makes it meaningful for planning or decision making

✓ **Information** used by organisations comes from a variety of **internal** and **external sources**.

✓ Information systems should provide information that possesses certain specific **qualities** (ACCURATE).

✓ **Different types of information system** exist with different characteristics – reflecting the different roles they perform.

✓ Organisations are increasingly using **intranets**, **extranets** and **database systems** to manage and provide access to data and information.

✓ **Enterprise-wide systems** are designed to **co-ordinate** all **business functions, resources** and **information**.

✓ The purpose of **knowledge management systems (KMS)** is to record and store the knowledge held within an organisation.

✓ **Customer relationship management (CRM)** systems are software applications which specialise in providing information concerning an organisation's products, services and customers.

✓ **Web 2.0 applications** are second generation' Internet-based services. These sites usually include tools that let people collaborate and share information online.

✓ **E-commerce** (the selling of goods or services over the Internet) continues to grow rapidly.

✓ IT may **enable an organisation to transform** how it does business. In particular:

  – The type of products or services that are made and sold
  – The way in which products are made
  – The way in which employees are mobilised
  – The way in which services are provided
  – To enable change
  – To aid communication and co-ordination
  – As a source of unity and structure

✓ The **global explosion** of information technology has led to the creation of virtual teams, companies and supply chains.

✓ **Virtual teams** are interconnected groups of people who may not be present in the same office or organisation.

✓ A **virtual company** is a collection of separate companies, each with a specific expertise, who work together, to compete for bigger contracts/projects than would be possible if they worked alone.

✓ A **Virtual Supply Chain (VSC)** is a supply chain that is enabled through e-business links, for example the web or extranets.

✓ **Computer systems** with links to other systems such as the **Internet** are exposed to privacy and security risks.

✓ The **key privacy** and **security risks** come from **hackers** and **eavesdroppers, viruses, hoaxes** and **denial of service attacks**.

✓ Organisations can take various **measures** against privacy and security risks, including **anti-virus software, firewalls, encryption, electronic signatures, authentication** and **dial-back security**.

Quick Quiz

1 Which of the following is not a type of information system?

   A   EIS
   B   MIS
   C   DSL
   D   OAS

2 A private network inside an organisation that is accessed through web-browser like software is known as:

   A   Internet
   B   Extranet
   C   Intranet
   D   Privatenet

3 Which type of system is designed to co-ordinate all an organisation's functions, resources and information?

   A   A knowledge management system
   B   A customer relationship system
   C   An expert system
   D   An enterprise-wide system

4 Web 2.0 applications have what purpose?

   A   To engage the customer in the organisation
   B   To reduce the number of customer complaints
   C   To increase an organisation's sales
   D   To collect information about the customer

5 Briefly explain what a virtual company is.

Answers to Quick Quiz

1 C DSL (Digital Subscriber Line) is a communications technology. The others are: Executive Information System, Management Information System and Office Automation System.

2 C A private network inside an organisation that is accessed through web-browser like software is known as an intranet.

3 D An enterprise-wide system is designed to co-ordinate all an organisation's functions, resources and information.

4 A Web 2.0 applications allow the customer to interact with the organisation with the purpose of engaging them in the organisation.

5 A virtual company is a collection of separate companies, each with a specific expertise, who work together to compete for bigger contracts/projects than would be possible if they worked alone.

Answers to Questions

3.1 Expert systems

The primary reason has to do with the relative costs. A 'human' expert is likely to be more expensive either to employ or to use on a consultancy basis.

Secondly, enshrining an expert's accumulated wisdom in a computer system means that this wisdom can be accessed by more people. Therefore, the delivery of complicated services to customers, decisions whether or not to extend credit and so forth, can be made by less experienced members of staff. If a manufacturing company has a complicated mixture of plant and machinery, then the repair engineer may accumulate a lot of knowledge over a period of time about the way it behaves. If a problem occurs, the engineer will be able to make a reasoned guess as to where the likely cause is to be found. If this accumulated expert information is made available to less experienced staff, it means that some of their learning curve is avoided.

An expert system is advantageous because it saves time, like all computer systems (in theory at least) but it is particularly useful as it possesses both knowledge and limited reasoning ability.

3.2 IT transformation

IT could transform Velospeed in three main areas.

The way in which bicycles are made

The current labour-intensive process of manufacture can be made more efficient. Computer Aided Design (CAD) can be used to allow efficient and accurate design, rather than relying on hand drawings which may contain inaccuracies or be unclear.

Computer Integrated Manufacturing (CIM) could be used to change the manufacturing process of the bike frames. Data from the design can be fed into an automated system that cuts and forms the metal into frames. This will ensure consistent standards of production and will reduce labour costs.

The types of bicycle which are made

The use of modern production methods will facilitate a move to new types of material in the bicycle frame. Materials not suitable for use under manual methods, such as carbon-fibre, may be used.

The combination of state-of-the-art design technology and modern materials permit new types of product to be made. For example, professional race bikes, that need to be aerodynamic and extremely light, could be produced.

To aid communication and co-ordination

Velospeed could change its paper-based ordering and filing system to one which is based on an enterprise-wide system. Orders could be made electronically over the Internet and invoices posted to an accounting system, perhaps using EDI.

Data could be stored in a database, and reports extracted. This will result in more accurate and consistent reports, as all systems will use the same source information.

Now try this question from the Exam Question Bank	**Number**	**Level**	**Marks**	**Time**
	3	Examination	30	54 mins

SYSTEMS IMPLEMENTATION AND BUSINESS STRATEGY

 In this chapter we move on from looking at the role of information systems to looking at their **implementation** and **alignment with business strategy**.

Implementing a system involves a number of stages, each of which is vital if the completed system is to be a success. We shall see that a key cause information

system failure is **user resistance** – we look at a number of ways to overcome or prevent this.

Later we consider how **aligning** a new information system with the organisation's overall business strategy can help make the system a success and even be a source of **competitive advantage**.

topic list	learning outcomes	syllabus references	ability required
1 System implementation	B2(a)	B2(iii), B2(iv)	analysis
2 Information technology and change management	B2(a)	B2(iv)	analysis
3 Introducing the change	B2(a)	B2(iv)	analysis
4 System evaluation	B2(a)	B2(i)	analysis
5 System maintenance	B2(a)	B2(iv)	analysis
6 System outsourcing	B2(b)	B2(v)	analysis
7 Aligning systems with business strategy	B2(b)	B2(vi)	analysis

1   System implementation   11/10

Introduction

Implementation is part of the systems development cycle, or systems development life cycle (SDLC).

This starts with the **identification of a problem** or a suggestion that 'things could be done better.

Next comes a **feasibility study** into relevant technical, operational, economic and social factors should be conducted.

System analysis is next. This determines the system's purpose and the features and procedures required in it. The future users of the new system should have the opportunity to provide their input, to ensure the new system satisfies their needs.

After system requirements have been documented, work can begin on **system design**. Here the component parts of the system (its hardware and software) are decided upon and purchased.

Implementation comes next. This is the process the E1 syllabus focuses on – we cover this in detail in this chapter.

Following implementation comes **system review and maintenance**.

The main steps in the **implementation** of an information system are as follows.

(a)   **Installation** of the hardware and software.
(b)   **Testing**.
(c)   **Staff training** and production of **documentation**.
(d)   **File conversion**.
(e)   **Changeover**.

The items in the list above **do not** necessarily happen in a set **chronological order** and some may be done at the same time – for example staff training and system testing can be part of the same operation. The requirements for implementation vary from system to system.

1.1 Installation

Installing a mainframe computer or a large network is a major operation that is carried out by the **manufacturer/supplier**. If just a few PCs are being installed in a small network, this may be able to be performed by non-specialists.

Most new software is provided on CD-ROM or DVD and may be able to be installed by non-specialists, depending upon the complexity of the system and the checks required to ensure it is operating correctly.

1.2 Testing

A system must be thoroughly tested before implementation, to prevent the system 'going live' with faults that might prove costly. The scope of tests and trials will vary with the size and complexity of the system. To ensure a coherent, effective approach to testing, a testing strategy should be developed.

A **testing strategy** should cover the following areas.

Testing strategy area	Comment
Strategy approach	A testing strategy should be formulated that details the approach that will be taken to testing, including the tests to be conducted and the testing tools/techniques that will be used.
Test plan	A test plan should be developed that states what will be tested, when it will be tested (sequence), and the test environment.

Testing strategy area	Comment
Test design	The logic and reasoning behind the design of the tests should be explained.
Performing tests	Detailed procedures should be provided for all tests. This explanation should ensure tests are carried out consistently, even if different people carry out the tests.
Documentation	It must be clear how the results of tests are to be documented. This provides a record of errors, and a starting point for error correction procedures.
Re-testing	The re-test procedure should be explained. In many cases, after correction, all aspects of the software should be re-tested to ensure the corrections have not affected other aspects of the software.

Four **stages of testing** can be identified as:

- System logic
- Program testing
- System testing
- User acceptance testing

1.2.1 Testing system logic

Before any programs are written, the **logic** devised by the systems analyst should be checked. This process often involves the use of flow charts or data flow diagrams. Both tools involve the manual plotting of different types of data and transactions through the system. The object is to ensure that all possibilities have been catered for and that the processing logic is correct. When all results are as expected, programs can be written.

1.2.2 Program testing

Program testing involves processing **test data** through all system programs. Test data should be of the type that the program will be required to process and should include invalid/exceptional items to test whether the program reacts as it should.

Program testing should cover the following areas.

- Input validity checks
- Program logic and functioning
- Interfaces with related modules/systems
- Output format and validity

The testing process should be **fully documented** – recording data used, expected results, actual results and action taken. This documentation may be referred to at a later date, for example if program modifications are required. Two types of program testing are **unit testing** and **unit integration testing**.

1.2.3 Unit testing and unit integration testing

KEY TERMS

Unit testing means testing one function or part of a program to ensure it operates as intended.

Unit integration testing involves testing two or more software units to ensure they work together as intended. The output from unit integration testing is a debugged module.

Unit testing involves detailed **testing of part of a program**. If it is established during unit testing that a program is not operating as intended, the cause of the error must be established and corrected. Automated diagnostic routines, that step through the program line by line may be used to help this process.

Test cases should be developed that include test data (inputs), test procedures, expected results and evaluation criteria. Sets of data should be developed for both unit testing and integration testing. Cases should be developed for all aspects of the software.

1.2.4 System testing (overall system testing)

When it has been established that individual programs and interfaces are operating as intended, **overall system testing** should begin. System testing has a wider focus than program testing. System testing should extend beyond areas already tested, to cover:

- Input documentation and the practicalities of input eg time taken
- Flexibility of the system to allow amendments to the 'normal' processing cycle
- Ability to produce information on time
- Ability to cope with peak resource requirements eg transaction volumes
- Viability of operating procedures
- Ability to produce information on time

System testing will involve testing both before installation (known as **off-line testing**) and after implementation (**on-line testing**). As many problems as possible should be identified before implementation, but it is likely that some problems will only become apparent when the system goes live.

1.2.5 User acceptance testing

KEY TERM

USER ACCEPTANCE TESTING is carried out by those who will use the system to determine whether the system meets their needs. These needs should have previously been stated as acceptance criteria.

The purpose of **user acceptance testing** is to establish whether **users are satisfied that the system meets the system specification** when used in the actual operating environment. Users process test data, system performance is closely monitored and users report whether they feel the system meets their needs. Test data may include some historical data, because it is then possible to check results against the 'actual' output from the old system.

It is **vital that users are involved** in system testing to ensure the system operates as intended when used by the people expected to utilise it. Any problems identified should be corrected – this will improve system efficiency and should also encourage users to accept the new system.

1.2.6 Types of test

To ensure as many scenarios as possible are tested, testing should include the following **four types of test**.

(a) **Realistic tests**. These involve using the system in the way it will be used in reality – ie the actual environment, users and types of data.

(b) **Contrived tests**. These are designed to present the system with unusual events to ensure these are handled correctly, for example that invalid data is rejected.

(c) **Volume tests** present the system with large numbers of transactions to see how the system copes.

(d) **Acceptance tests** are undertaken by users to ensure the system meets user needs.

1.2.7 Limitations of testing

The presence of '**bugs**' or errors in the vast majority of software/systems demonstrates that even the most rigorous testing plan is unlikely to identify all errors.

The **limitations of software testing** are outlined in the following table.

Limitation	Comment
Poor testing process	The test plan may not cover all areas of system functionality. Testers may not be adequately trained. The testing process may not be adequately documented.
Inadequate time	Software and systems are inevitably produced under significant time pressures. Testing time is often 'squeezed' to compensate for project over-runs in other areas.
Future requirements not anticipated	The test data used may have been fine at the time of testing, but future demands may be outside the range of values tested. Testing should allow for future expansion of the system.
Inadequate test data	Test data should test 'positively' – checking that the software does what it should do, and test 'negatively' – that it doesn't do what it shouldn't. It is difficult to include the complete range of possible input errors in test data.
Software changes inadequately tested	System/software changes made as a result of testing findings or for other reasons may not be adequately tested as they were not in the original test plan.

1.3 Training

Staff training in the use of a new system is essential if the system is to meet its full potential. Training should be provided to **all staff** who will use the system.

Training should **focus on the specific tasks the user is required to perform** such as entering an invoice or answering a query. There are a range of options available to deliver training, as shown below.

Training method	Comment
Individual tuition 'at desk'	A trainer could work with an employee observing how they use a system and suggesting possible alternatives.
Classroom course	The software could be used in a classroom environment, using 'dummy' data.
Computer-based training (CBT)	Training can be provided using CDs, DVDs, over an intranet or via an interactive website.
Case studies and exercises	Regardless of how training is delivered, it is likely that material will be based around a realistic case study relevant to the user.
Software reference material	Users may find on-line help, built-in tutorials and reference manuals useful.

The **training method** applicable in a given situation will **depend on the following factors**:

- Time available
- Software complexity
- User skill levels
- Facilities available
- Budget

User documentation may be used to **explain** the system to users. Much of this information **may be available online** using context-sensitive help eg 'Push F1 for help'.

1.4 File conversion

KEY TERM

FILE CONVERSION, means converting **existing files** into a format suitable for the new system.

Most computer systems are based around files containing **data**. When a new system is introduced, files must be created that conform to the requirements of that system.

The various scenarios that **file conversion** could involve are outlined in the following table.

Existing data	Comment
Held in manual (ie paper) files	Data will be keyed into the new system – probably via input forms, so that data entry operators have all the data they require in one document. This is likely to be a time-consuming process.
Held in existing computer files	How complex the process is in converting the files to a format compatible with the new system will depend on technical issues and the coding systems used. It may be possible to automate much of the conversion process.
Held in both manual and computer files	Two separate conversion procedures are required.
Existing data is incomplete	If the missing data is crucial, it must be researched and made available in a format suitable for the new system – or suitable for the file conversion process.

The **file conversion process** is shown in the following diagram, which assumes the original data is held in manual files.

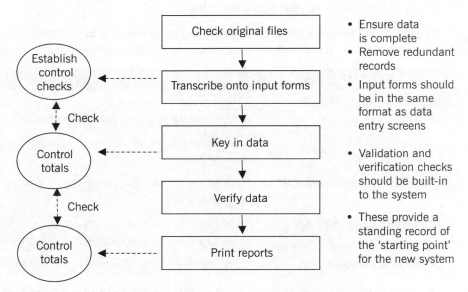

It is essential that the 'new' converted files are **accurate**. Various controls can be utilised during the conversion process.

(a) **One-to-one checking** between records on the old and new systems.

(b) **Sample checking**. Selecting and checking a sample of records. This is used if there are too many records to check individually.

(c) **Built-in data validation** routines in automated conversion processes.

(d) **Control totals** and **reconciliations**. These checks could include checking the total number of records, and the value of transactions.

LEARNING MEDIA

Exam alert

You may find it useful to remember the main system implementation stages as **FITT**. **F**ile conversion, **I**nstallation, **T**esting, **T**raining and documentation.

1.5 Changeover

Once the new system has been fully and satisfactorily tested, the final stage of implementation, **changeover**, can begin. There are **four approaches to system changeover**, each varies in terms of time required, cost and risk.

- Direct ('Big Bang') changeover
- Parallel running
- Pilot operation
- Phased or modular implementation

1.5.1 Direct ('Big Bang') changeover

The old system is **completely replaced** by the new system **in one move**. This may be unavoidable where the two systems are substantially different, or where the costs of parallel running are too great.

While this method is comparatively **cheap** and convenient, it is **risky** (system or program corrections are difficult while the system has to remain operational). The new system should be introduced during **a quiet period**, for example over a bank holiday weekend or during an office closure.

A **direct changeover** is often used where there is:

- Complete confidence in the new system
- A need to overcome a reluctance to 'let the old system go'
- A need to implement the system before staff have a chance to object
- A need on cost or convenience grounds to avoid running two systems

1.5.2 Parallel running

The **old and new** systems are **run in parallel** for a period of time. They both process current data which enables cross checking to be made. This method provides a **degree of safety** should there be problems with the new system. However, if there are differences between the two systems, cross-checking may be difficult or impossible.

Parallel running **delays** the actual implementation of the new system, which may be perceived as a **lack of confidence** in the system. Also, **more staff** are required to cope with systems running concurrently. This cautious approach, if adopted, should be properly planned, and the **plan should include**:

(a) A firm **time limit** on parallel running.
(b) Details of **cross-checking** procedures.
(c) Instructions on how **errors** in the old system are to be dealt with.
(d) Instructions on how to report and act on **any major problems** in the new system.

1.5.3 Pilot operation

Pilot operation involves selecting **part** or **parts of an organisation** (eg a department or branch) to operate the new system in parallel with the existing system. When the branch or department piloting the system is satisfied with it, they cease to use the old system. The new system is then piloted in another area of the organisation.

Pilot operation is **cheaper** and **easier to control** than running the whole system in parallel, and provides a **greater degree of safety** than a direct changeover.

1.5.4 Phased or modular changeover

Phased or **modular changeover** involves **selecting a complete section of the system** for a direct changeover, eg in an accounting system the payables ledger. When this part is running satisfactorily, another part is switched – until eventually the whole system has been changed. A phased series of direct changeovers is less risky than a single direct changeover, as any problems and disruption experienced should be isolated in an area of operations.

1.5.5 Advantages and disadvantages

The advantages and disadvantages of the various changeover methods are outlined below.

Method	Advantages	Disadvantages
Direct ('Big Bang') changeover	Quick Minimal cost Minimises workload	Risky Could disrupt operations If fails, will be costly
Parallel running	Safe, built-in safety Provides a way of verifying results of the new system	Costly, two systems need to be operated Time-consuming Additional workload
Pilot operation	Less risky than direct changeover Less costly than complete parallel running	Can take a long time to achieve total changeover Not as safe as complete parallel running
Phased or modular changeover	Less risky than a single direct changeover Any problems should be in one area – other operations unaffected	Can take a long time to achieve total changeover Interfaces between parts of the system may make this impractical

CASE STUDY

Facing frequent outages in the DSL (Digital Subscriber Line) network serving 50-plus corporate-owned gyms, Gold's Gyms management knew it was time for a significant upgrade. After looking into the various options they opted to replace DSL with a carrier-provided voice VoIP (Voice over Internet Protocol) service.

If they had to this again, however, they would take a more phased approach. 'We tried the big-bang theory, doing everything at once,' a spokesman said. That decision was driven by business needs, because the DSL network was so unreliable, and because the supplier was urging Gold's to sign a contract that included every gym. 'I think we should've done two or three gyms first, and made sure they worked OK, before we did the rest.' This would have reduced system downtime.

Adapted from Case study: VoIP implementation The problems of the 'big bang' approach
Paul Desmond, *PC Advisor*

Section summary

The main stages in the **implementation** of a computer system are:

- **Installation** of the hardware and software.
- **Testing**.
- **Staff training** and production of **documentation**.
- **File conversion**.
- **Changeover**.

2 Information technology and change management

Introduction

Any change, such as the introduction of a new information system, involves structural and behavioural factors which may result in **resistance from individuals** to that change. Many new systems fail, not because of hardware or software problems, but because the users themselves are against it.

This section considers what causes user resistance and how it can be **overcome** or **prevented** by management action.

2.1 How change affects individuals

Before looking at the causes of user resistance we must first consider how change **affects individuals**.

Change may affect individuals in several areas.

(a) There may be **physiological** changes in a person's life, both as the natural product of development, maturation and ageing, and **as the result of external factors**. For example, a change in the pattern of shift-working may temporarily throw the individual's eating, waking and sleeping routine out of synchronisation with the body's sense of time.

(b) **Circumstantial** changes – living in a new house, establishing new relationships, working to new routines – will involve letting go of things, perhaps 'unlearning' old knowledge, and learning new ways of doing things.

Above all, change affects individuals **psychologically**.

(a) It may create **feelings of disorientation** before new circumstances have been assimilated.

(b) **Uncertainty may lead to insecurity**. This is especially acute in changes involving work, where there can be very great pressures for continuity and fast acclimatisation.

(c) The secure basis of **warm, accepting relationships may be up-rooted** – the business of forging new relationships can be fraught with personal insecurity.

2.1.1 Types of change experience

Four types of **change experience** have been identified (*Torrington and Weightman* (1994)).

Type	Comment	Reaction
Imposition	Initiated and driven by someone else	Resistance
Adaptation	A change in attitude or behaviour as a result of changes by others	Uncertainty
Growth	A response to opportunities	Delight
Creativity	The individual instigates and controls the change process	Excitement

2.1.2 Reactions to proposed change

There are a range of other possible reactions to a proposed change.

(a) **Acceptance** – whether enthusiastic espousal, co-operation, grudging co-operation or resignation

(b) **Indifference** – usually where the change does not directly affect the individual: apathy, lack of interest, inaction

(c) **Passive resistance** – refusal to learn, working to rule

(d) **Active resistance** – deliberate 'spoiling', go-slows, deliberate errors, sabotage, absenteeism or strikes

John Hunt highlights a number of responses that may not **look** like resistance on the face of things, but are **behaviours aimed at reinforcing the** *status quo*. There are a number of responses that the manager should learn to recognise.

(a)   **Pleas of ignorance**: ('I need more information').

(b)   **Delayed judgement**: ('let's wait and see ...'), perhaps stalling for time with comparisons ('there are other ways ...').

(c)   **Defensive stances**: ('This isn't going to work', 'It'd be too expensive', 'It's the wrong time to ...').

(d)   The **display of various personal insecurities**: ('I won't be able to cope', 'I won't see my team anymore', 'We won't have control over our planning any more', 'Why can't we just go on as we are?'); fear, anxiety, resentment at the manner of change, frustration at perceived losses.

(e)   **Withdrawal**, or **disowning of the change**: ('Oh well. On their heads be it', 'I'm not interested in flexitime anyway').

2.2 Problems in the design stage

One common cause of dissatisfaction with new information systems is **insufficient user involvement** when establishing requirements for the new system.

Other **common causes of dissatisfaction** with information systems include:

(a)   IS project managers are often **technicians**, not managers. Technical ability for IS staff is no guarantee of management skill – an individual might be a highly proficient analyst or programmer, but **not a good manager**.

(b)   The project manager may accept **an unrealistic deadline** where the timescale is fixed early in the planning process. User demands may be accepted as deadlines before sufficient consideration is given to the realism of this.

(c)   **Poor or non-existent planning** is a recipe for disaster. Unrealistic deadlines would be identified much earlier if a proper planning process was undertaken.

(d)   A lack of **monitoring** and **control**.

(e)   Users **change their requirements**, resulting in changes to the system as it is being developed.

(f)   **Poor timetabling and resourcing**. It is no use being presented on Day 1 with a team of programmers, when there is still systems analysis and design work to do. The development and implementation of a computer project may take a considerable length of time (perhaps two years for a relatively large installation). Major projects require formal planning and scheduling.

2.3 Problems in the development process

Problems that occur when implementing a new information system can usually be traced to **deficiencies in the development process**. The table that follows outlines some common mistakes that adversely affect the implementation process – and the systems development stage or activity they relate to.

Stage/activity	Problems
Analysis	The problem the system is intended to solve is not fully understood.
	Investigation of the situation is hindered by insufficient resources.
	User input is inadequate through either lack of consultation or lack of user interest.
	The project team is unable to dedicate the time required or insufficient time spent planning the project.

Stage/activity	Problems
Design	Insufficient user input.
	Lack of flexibility. The organisation's future needs are neglected.
	The system requires unforeseen changes in working patterns.
	Failure to perform organisation impact analysis. An organisational impact analysis studies the way a proposed system will affect organisation structure, attitudes, decision making and operations. The analysis aims to ensure the system is designed to best ensure integration with the organisation.
	Organisational factors sometimes overlooked include: • Ergonomics (including equipment, work environment and user interfaces) • Health and safety • Compliance with legislation • Job design • Employee involvement
Programming	Insufficient time and money allocated to programming.
	Programmers supplied with incomplete or inaccurate specifications.
	The logic of the program is misunderstood.
	Poor programming technique results in programs that are hard to modify.
	Programs are not adequately documented.
Testing	Insufficient time and money allocated to testing.
	Failure to develop an organised testing plan.
	Insufficient user involvement.
	User management do not review and sign-off the results of testing.
Conversion	Insufficient time and money allocated to data conversion.
	Insufficient checking between old and new files.
	The process is rushed to compensate for time overruns elsewhere.
Final implementation	Insufficient time, money and/or appropriate staff mean the process has to be rushed.
	Lack of user training increases the risk of system under-utilisation and rejection.
	Poor system and user documentation.
	Lack of performance standards to assess system performance against.
	System maintenance provisions are inadequate.

2.4 Dealing with user resistance

We now look at two models relevant to dealing with user resistance.

2.4.1 Lewin/Schein: Unfreeze, Move, Refreeze

In the words of *John Hunt* (*Managing People at Work*): 'Learning also involves re-learning – not merely learning something new but trying to unlearn what is already known.' This is the thinking behind *Lewin/Schein's* **three stage approach** to changing human behaviour, which may be depicted as follows.

UNFREEZE   →   **MOVE**   →   **REFREEZE**
existing behaviour   attitudinal/behavioural change   new behaviour

Unfreeze is the most difficult (and in many cases neglected) stage of the process, concerned mainly with **selling** the change, with giving individuals or groups a **motive** for changing their attitudes, values, behaviour, systems or structures. If the need for change is immediate, clear and perceived to be associated with the survival of the individual or group (for example change in reaction to an organisation crisis), the unfreeze stage will be greatly accelerated. Routine changes may be harder to sell than transformational ones, if they are perceived to be unimportant and not survival-based.

Changing organisational **culture** is perhaps hardest of all, especially if it involves changes to long-held cultural values.

Unfreezing processes require four things.

- A trigger
- Someone to challenge and expose the existing behaviour pattern
- The involvement of outsiders
- Alterations to power structure

Move is the second stage. It is mainly concerned with identifying what the new, desirable behaviour or norm should be, communicating it and encouraging individuals and groups to 'own' the new attitude or behaviour. This might involve the adoption of a new culture. To be successful, the new ideas must be shown to work.

Refreeze is the final stage, implying consolidation or reinforcement of the new behaviour. Positive reinforcement (praise and reward) or negative reinforcement (sanctions applied to those who deviate from the new behaviour) may be used.

This model is based on the view that change is **capable of being planned**. You should note that this is not always possible.

2.4.2 Dealing with resistance

Kotter and Schlesinger (1979) identified six methods of dealing with **resistance to change**. They are:

(a) **Education** and **communication**. This method is effective where the cause of the resistance is lack of information about the change.

(b) **Participation** and **involvement**. Where those affected by the change have the power to resist it, this method reduces the resistance by taking their views into account.

(c) **Facilitation** and **support**. Where the cause of the resistance is anxiety and insecurity, support such as training is effective.

(d) **Negotiation** and **agreement**. Compensating those who lose out (for example redundancy packages) may be appropriate in some instances.

(e) **Manipulation** and **co-optation**. This method involves the presentation of partial or misleading information to those resisting change or 'buying-off' the main individuals who are at the heart of the resistance.

(f) **Explicit** and **implicit coercion**. This involves the use or threat of force to push through the change. A very last resort if parties are operating from fixed positions and are unwilling to move.

The final two options raise ethical and legal issues. They also risk alienating people, making the change even less likely to be accepted.

The six approaches are not intended to be used separately in isolation – a **combination** of them is likely to be required. Remember that people may disguise their real reason for opposing change (such as possible loss of influence or status) with technical objections.

Exam alert

Exam questions may require you to discuss potential strategies for overcoming resistance to change and identify which would be most suitable for the organisation in the scenario.

You may also be asked for an analysis of how an organisation has managed resistance to a change.

Question 4.1	Resistance to change

Learning outcome B2(iv)

Which of Kotter and Schlesinger's six methods of dealing with resistance to change is best suited to a situation where resistance is caused by a lack of information about the change?

A   Education and communication.

B   Negotiation and agreement.

C   Manipulation and co-optation.

D   Explicit and implicit coercion.

(2 marks)

Section summary

User resistance is a key cause of information systems failure.

Theories that may help when considering how to **overcome user resistance** include:
- Lewin/Schein's unfreeze, move, refreeze
- Kotter and Schlesingers' six methods of dealing with resistance

3   Introducing the change

Introduction

Rather than dealing with resistance to change after it has occurred, a better approach is to try and **prevent resistance before it occurs**.

Several theories have been developed that aim to help managers deal with change more effectively so that resistance is prevented or at least minimised.

3.1 Pace, Manner and Scope

There are **three important factors** for managers to consider when **introducing change**.

- The **pace** of change
- The **manner** of change
- The **scope** of change

3.1.1 Pace

The more **gradual** the change, the more time is available for questions to be asked, reassurances to be given and retraining (where necessary) embarked upon. People can get used to the idea of new methods and become acclimatised at each stage.

(a) Presenting the individuals concerned with change as a *fait accompli* may avoid resistance at the planning stage, but may result in resistance surfacing later – probably strengthened by resentment.

(b) **Timing** will also be crucial. Those responsible for change should be sensitive to incidents and attitudes that might indicate that 'now is not the time'.

3.1.2 Manner

The manner in which a change is put across (**communicated**) is very important. The need for change must made clear, fears soothed, and if possible the individuals concerned positively motivated to embrace the changes as their own.

(a) **Resistance should be welcomed and confronted**, not swept under the carpet. Talking thorough areas of conflict may lead to useful insights and the adaption of the programme of change to the company's advantage. Repressing resistance will only send it underground.

(b) **There should be free circulation of information** about the reasons for the change, its expected results and likely consequences. That information should appear sensible, clear, consistent and realistic. There is no point issuing information which will be seen as a blatant misrepresentation of the situation.

(c) **The change must be sold to the people concerned**. Objections must be overcome, but it is also possible to get people behind the change in a positive way. If those involved understand that there is a real problem, which poses a threat to the organisation and themselves, and that the solution is a sensible one and will solve the problem, there will be a firm rational basis, for implementing change. It may even be possible to get staff excited by the change, by emphasising the challenge and opportunity and perhaps by offering rewards and incentives.

(d) **Individuals must be helped to learn**, that is, to change their attitudes and behaviours. Few individuals will really be able to see the big picture in a proposed programmed of change. In order to put across the overall objective, the organisation should use **visual aids** to help conceptualise. Learning programmes for any new skills or systems necessary will have to be designed according to the abilities of the individuals concerned.

(e) The effects of **insecurity** and **resentment** may be lessened if people are **involved** in the planning and implementation of the change, so that it is not perceived to have been imposed from above.

3.1.3 Scope

The scope or **extent of the change** is important and should be reviewed. Total transformation will create greater insecurity – but also provides the opportunity for greater excitement – than moderate innovation.

There may be **hidden changes** to take into account. For example, a change in technology may necessitate changes in work methods, which may in turn result in the breaking up of work groups. Management should be aware of how many various aspects of their employees' lives they are proposing to alter – and therefore on how many fronts they are likely to encounter resistance.

3.2 Commitment, co-ordination and communication

Commitment, **co-ordination** and **communication** are often cited as playing an important role in the context of introducing any form of change.

(a) **Commitment.** Commitment to the change must be universal. Senior management must ensure adequate resources are provided (people, money, time etc) to achieve change.

(b) **Co-ordination.** To implement change successfully requires co-ordination. This involves ensuring those involved in the process work in an efficient and effective way towards an agreed common goal. This requires planning and control.

(c) **Communication.** Successful change requires good communication. The right people must communicate the right things at the right time and in the right way. Good communication early in the process should ensure all are aware of what the process hopes to achieve. Communication during the process should aid co-ordination and to maintain momentum. Upon completion, communication is likely to focus on ensuring there is no return to the previous behaviour – and a review of the process itself to see if any lessons may be learnt.

3.3 Successful implementation of information systems

A recurring theme when examining the reasons for **information system failure** is user resistance. Three types of theory explain the causes user resistance against new information systems together with how they are overcome.

Theory	Description	Overcoming the resistance
People-oriented	User-resistance is caused by factors internal to users as individuals or as a group. For example, users may not wish to disrupt their current work practices and social groupings.	User training. Organisation policies. Find 'change champions' who already see the benefits of the system and can persuade others who are resisting. User involvement in system development.
System-oriented	User-resistance is caused by factors inherent in the new system design, relating to ease of use and functionality. For example, a poorly designed user-interface will generate user-resistance.	User training and education. Improve the user-interface. Ensure users contribute to the system design process. Ensure the system 'fits' with the organisation.
Interaction	User-resistance is caused by the interaction of people and the system. For example, the system may be well-designed but its implementation will cause organisational changes that users resist eg reduced chance of bonuses, redundancies, monotonous work.	Re-organise the organisation before implementing the system. Redesign any affected incentive schemes to incorporate the new system. Promote user participation and encourage organisation-wide teamwork. Emphasise the benefits the system brings.

Section summary

It is better for the organisation to **prevent or minimise resistance** occurring in the first place. Theories aimed at achieving this include:

- Pace, manner and scope

- Commitment, co-ordination and communication

4 System evaluation

Introduction

A system should be **reviewed** after implementation, and periodically when in operation, so that any unforeseen problems may be resolved and to confirm that it is achieving the desired results. The system should have been designed with clear, specified **objectives**, and justification in terms of **cost-benefit analysis** or other **performance criteria**.

4.1 Cost-benefit review

A cost-benefit review is similar to a cost-benefit analysis, except that **actual** data can be used. For instance when a large project is completed, techniques such as **DCF appraisal** can be performed **again**, with actual figures being available for much of the expenditure.

Question 4.2	Cost-benefit review

Learning outcome B2(i)

A cost-benefit review might categorise items under the five headings of **direct benefits**, **indirect benefits**, **development costs**, **implementation costs** and **running costs**.

Required

Give two examples of items which could fall to be evaluated under each heading. **(5 marks)**

4.2 Measuring system performance

KEY TERM

METRICS are quantified measurements used to measure system performance.

The use of metrics enables some aspects of **system quality** to be **measured**. Metrics may also allow the early identification of problems – for example, by highlighting instances of system failure, the causes of which may then be investigated.

Metrics should be carefully thought out, objective and **stated clearly**. They must measure significant aspects of the system, be used consistently and agreed with users. **Examples** of metrics include system response time, the number of transactions that can be processed per minute, the number of bugs per hundred lines of code and the number of system crashes per week.

Many facets of system quality are not easy to measure **statistically** (eg user-friendliness). Indirect measurements such as the number of calls to the help-desk per month can be used as an indication of overall quality/performance.

4.3 Performance reviews

Performance reviews can be carried out to look at a wide range of systems functions and characteristics. They will vary in content from organisation to organisation, but may include the following.

(a)   The **growth** rates in file sizes and the number of transactions processed by the system. Trends should be analysed and projected to assess whether there are likely to be problems with lengthy processing time or an inefficient file structure due to the volume of processing.

(b)   The **staffing** requirements of the system, and whether they are more or less than anticipated.

(c)   The identification of any **delays** in processing and an assessment of their consequences.

(d) An assessment of the efficiency of **security** procedures, in terms of number of breaches, or number of viruses encountered.

(e) A check of the **error rates** for input data. High error rates may indicate inefficient preparation of input documents, an inappropriate method of data capture or poor design of input media.

(f) An examination of whether **output** from the computer is being used for a good purpose. (Is it used? Is it timely? Does it go to the right people?)

(g) Operational **running costs** can be examined to discover any inefficient programs or processes. This examination may reveal excessive costs for certain items although in total, costs may be acceptable.

4.4 Post-implementation review

A **post-implementation review** establishes whether the objectives and targeted performance criteria have been met, and if not, why not, and what should be done about it. In appraising the operation of the new system immediately after the changeover, comparison should be made between **actual and predicted performance**.

This will include:

(a) Consideration of **throughput speed** (time between input and output).
(b) Use of computer **storage** (both internal and external).
(c) The number and type of **errors/queries**.
(d) The **cost** of processing (data capture, preparation, storage and output media, etc).

A special **steering committee** may be set up to ensure that post-implementation reviews are carried out, although the **internal audit** department may be required to do the work of carrying out the reviews.

The post-implementation measurements should **not be made too soon** after the system goes live, or else results will be abnormally affected by 'teething' problems, lack of user familiarity and resistance to change. A suitable period is likely to be between one month and one year after completion (the appropriate length of time will depend upon the role of the system, and how complex it is).

Post-implementation audits are on the paper E2 syllabus in connection with project management.

4.4.1 The post-implementation review report

The findings of a post-implementation review team should be formalised in a **report**.

(a) A **summary** of their findings should be provided, emphasising any areas where the system has been found to be **unsatisfactory** so the organisation can learn from its mistakes.

(b) A review of **system performance** should be provided. This will address the matters outlined above, such as run times and error rates and whether it meets users' needs.

(c) A **cost-benefit review** should be included, comparing the forecast costs and benefits identified at the time of the feasibility study with actual costs and benefits.

(d) **Recommendations** should be made as to any **further action** or steps which should be taken to improve performance. It will also make recommendations on how the project was managed to help future initiatives.

Section summary

After implementation the system should be **evaluated** to see if it is a success and whether there are any lessons to be learned.

Evaluation often takes the form of a **cost-benefit review** or **performance measurement** using metrics or other measurable features of the system.

A **post-implementation review** compares actual and expected performance levels and is a formal report that should be compiled after a suitable period of time following implementation.

5 System maintenance

Introduction

After implementation, the system will require **regular maintenance** if it is to continue operating as expected and to develop with the organisation.

There are **three types of systems maintenance**.

KEY TERMS

CORRECTIVE MAINTENANCE is carried out when there is a systems failure of some kind, for example a defect in processing or in an implementation procedure. Its objective is to ensure that systems remain operational.

PERFECTIVE MAINTENANCE is carried out in order to perfect the software, or to improve it so that processing inefficiencies are eliminated and performance is enhanced.

ADAPTIVE MAINTENANCE is carried out to take account of anticipated changes in the processing environment. For example new taxation legislation might require changes to be made to payroll software.

Corrective maintenance usually consists of action in response to a **problem**.

Perfective maintenance consists of making enhancements requested by **users** to improve or extend the facilities available. The user interface may be amended to make software more user friendly.

There are many examples of **adaptive maintenance**, for example:

(a)   The system needs minor modifications to cope with changes in the computer user's procedures or volume of business.

(b)   The system can benefit from advances in computer hardware technology without having to switch to another system altogether.

5.1 The causes of system maintenance

Besides environmental changes, **three factors** contribute to the need for maintenance.

Factor	Comment
Errors	However diligently a system is tested, it is likely that **bugs** will exist in a newly implemented system. These require fixing.
Poor documentation	If old systems are accompanied by poor documentation, or even a complete lack of documentation, they may be difficult to understand. It is difficult to update or maintain these systems. Programmers may opt instead to patch up the system with new applications using newer technology.

Factor	Comment
Changes in requirements	Although users should be consulted at all stages of systems development, problems may arise after implementation, for example users may have found it difficult to express their requirements, or not participated fully in development.
	Cost constraints may have meant that certain requested features were not incorporated. Time constraints may have meant that requirements suggested during development were ignored in the interest of prompt completion.

5.1.1 Testing the effect of changes

A problem with systems development and maintenance is that it is **hard to predict all the effects of a change** to the system. A 'simple' software change in one area of the system may have unpredicted effects elsewhere. It is important therefore to carry out **regression testing**.

KEY TERM

REGRESSION TESTING involves the retesting of software that has been modified to fix 'bugs'. It aims to ensure that the bugs have been fixed **and** that no other previously working functions have failed as a result of the changes.

Regression testing involves **repeating system tests** that had been executed correctly before the recent changes were made. Only the changes expected as a result of the system maintenance should occur under the regression test – other changes could be due to errors caused by the recent change.

Problems with regression testing include:

- Deciding on the extent of testing required
- Envisaging all areas possibly affected
- Convincing users and programmers that the tests are necessary

5.2 Hardware maintenance

Provision must also be made to ensure computer hardware is maintained. A **hardware maintenance contract** should specify service response times in the event of a breakdown, and include provision for temporary replacement equipment if necessary. Maintenance services may be provided by the computer manufacturers or suppliers, or by a third-party maintenance company.

Section summary

Corrective Maintenance is carried out when there is a systems failure of some kind, for example a defect in processing or in an implementation procedure. Its objective is to ensure that systems remain operational.

Perfective Maintenance is carried out in order to perfect the software, or to improve it so that processing inefficiencies are eliminated and performance is enhanced.

Adaptive Maintenance is carried out to take account of anticipated changes in the processing environment. For example new taxation legislation might require changes to be made to payroll software.

6 System outsourcing   05/10

Introduction

We came across outsourcing in Chapter 1. We now consider its application to information systems.

There are four **broad classifications** of IT outsourcing.

Classification	Comment
Ad-hoc	The organisation has a short-term requirement for increased IT skills. An example would be employing programmers on a short-term contract to help with the programming of bespoke software.
Project management	The development and installation of a particular project is outsourced. For example, a new accounting system. This approach is sometimes referred to as **systems integration**.
Partial	Some services are outsourced. Examples include hardware maintenance, network management or ongoing website management.
Total	An external supplier provides the vast majority of an organisation's IS services. For example, a third party owns or is responsible for IT equipment, software and possibly staff.

6.1 Levels of service provision

The degree to which the provision and management of IS services are transferred to the third party varies according to the situation and the skills of both organisations.

(a) **Time-share**. The vendor charges for access to an external processing system on a time-used basis. Software ownership may be with either the vendor or the client organisation.

(b) **Service bureaux** usually focus on a specific function. Traditionally bureaux would provide the same type of service to many organisations, eg payroll processing. As organisations have developed their own IT infrastructure, the use of bureaux has decreased.

(c) **Facilities management (FM)** . The terms 'outsourcing' and 'facilities management' are sometimes confused. Facilities management traditionally involved contracts for premises-related services such as cleaning or site security.

In the context of IS, facilities management involves an **outside agency** managing the organisation's IS facilities. All equipment usually remains with the client, but the responsibility for providing and managing the specified services rests with the FM company. FM companies operating in the UK include Accenture, Cap Gemini, EDS and CFM.

CASE STUDY

The retailer Sears outsourced the management of its vast information technology and accounting functions to Accenture. First year *savings* were estimated to be £5 million per annum, growing to £14 million in the following year, and thereafter. This is clearly considerable, although re-organisation costs relating to redundancies, relocation and asset write-offs are thought to be in the region of £35 million. About 900 staff were involved: under the transfer of undertakings regulations (which protect employees when part or all of a company changes hands), Accenture was obliged to take on the existing Sears staff. This provided new opportunities for the staff who moved, while those who remained at Sears were free to concentrate on strategy development and management direction.

6.2 Developments in outsourcing

Outsourcing arrangements are becoming increasingly flexible to cope with the ever-changing nature of the modern business environment.

Examples of outsourcing arrangements include:

(a) **Multiple sourcing**. This involves outsourcing different areas of the IS function to a range of suppliers. Some suppliers may form alliances to present a stronger case for selection.

(b) **Incremental approach**. Organisations progressively outsource selected areas of their IS function. Possible problems with outsourced services are solved before progressing to the next stage.

(c) **Joint venture sourcing**. This term is used to describe an organisation entering into a joint venture with a supplier. The costs (risks) and possible rewards are split on an agreed basis. Such an arrangement may be suitable when developing software that could be sold to other organisations.

(d) **Application Service Providers (ASP)**. ASPs are third parties that manage and distribute software services and solutions to customers across a Wide Area Network. ASPs could be considered the modern equivalent of the traditional computer bureaux.

6.3 Managing outsourcing arrangements

Managing outsourcing arrangements involves deciding **what** will be outsourced, **choosing and negotiating** with **suppliers** and **managing the supplier relationship**.

When **considering** whether to outsource a particular service the following questions are relevant.

(a) Is the system of **strategic importance**? Strategic IS are generally not suited to outsourcing as they require a high degree of specific business knowledge that a third party IT specialist cannot be expected to possess.

(b) Can the system be **relatively isolated**? Functions that have only **limited interfaces** are most easily outsourced, eg payroll.

(c) **Do we know enough about the system to manage the outsourced service agreement**? If an organisation knows very little about a technology it may be difficult to know what constitutes good service and value for money. It may be necessary to recruit additional **expertise** to manage the relationship with the other party.

(d) Are our **requirements likely to change**? Organisations should avoid tying themselves into a long-term outsourcing agreement if requirements are likely to change.

A key factor when **choosing and negotiating** with external vendors is the contract offered and subsequently negotiated with the supplier. The contract is sometimes referred to as the **Service Level Contract** (SLC) or **Service Level Agreement** (SLA).

The **key elements of the contract** are described below.

Contract element	Comment
Service level	The contract should clearly specify minimum levels of service to be provided. Penalties should be specified for failure to meet these standards. Relevant factors will vary depending on the nature of the services outsourced but could include: • Response time to requests for assistance/information • System 'uptime' percentage • Deadlines for performing relevant tasks
Exit route	Arrangements for an exit route, addressing how the transfer to another supplier, or the move back in-house would be conducted.

Contract element	Comment
Timescale	When does the contract expire? Is the timescale suitable for the organisation's needs or should it be renegotiated?
Software ownership	Relevant factors include: • Software licensing and security • If the arrangement includes the development of new software who owns the copyright?
Dependencies	If related services are outsourced, the level of service quality agreed should group these services together.
Employment issues	If the arrangement includes provision for the organisation's IT staff to move to the third party, employer responsibilities must be specified clearly.

If full **facilities management** is involved and almost all management responsibility for IS lies with the entity providing the service, then a close relationship between the parties is necessary (a '**partnership**'). Factors such as organisation culture need to be considered when entering into such a close and critical relationship.

On the other hand, if a relatively simple function such as payroll were outsourced, such a close relationship with the supplier would not be necessary. A 'typical' supplier – customer relationship is all that is required.

Regardless of the type of relationship, a **legally binding contract** is the key element in establishing the obligations and responsibilities of all parties.

6.4 Advantages of outsourcing arrangements

The **advantages** of outsourcing are as follows.

(a)   Outsourcing can remove uncertainty about **cost**, as there is often a long-term contract where services are specified in advance for a **fixed price**. If computing services are inefficient, the costs will be borne by the outsourcing company. This is also an incentive to the third party to provide a high quality service.

(b)   Long-term contracts (maybe up to ten years) encourage **planning** for the future.

(c)   Outsourcing can bring the benefits of **economies of scale**. For example, an outsourcing company may conduct research into new technologies that benefits a number of their clients.

(d)   A specialist organisation is able to retain **skills and knowledge**. Many organisations would not have a sufficiently well-developed IS department to offer IS staff opportunities for career development. Talented staff would leave to pursue their careers elsewhere.

(e)   New skills and knowledge become available. A specialist company can **share** staff with **specific expertise** (such as programming in HTML to produce Web pages) between several clients. This allows the outsourcing company to take advantage of new developments without the need to recruit new people or re-train existing staff, and without the cost.

(f)   **Flexibility** (contract permitting). Resources may be able to be scaled up or down depending upon demand. For instance, during a major changeover from one system to another the number of IT staff needed may be twice as large as it will be once the new system is working satisfactorily.

     An outsourcing organisation is more able to arrange its work on a **project** basis, whereby some staff will expect to be moved periodically from one project to the next.

6.5 Disadvantages of outsourcing arrangements

Some possible **drawbacks** are outlined below.

(a)   It is arguable that information and its provision is **an inherent part of the business and of management**. Unlike office cleaning, or catering, an organisation's IS services may be too important to be contracted out. Information is at the heart of management.

(b)   A company may have highly **confidential information** and to let outsiders handle it could be seen as **risky** in commercial and/or legal terms.

(c)   Information strategy can be used to gain **competitive advantage**. Opportunities may be missed if a third party is handling IS services, because there is no onus upon internal management to keep up with new developments and have new ideas. Any new technology or application devised by the third party is likely to be available to competitors.

(d)   An organisation may find itself **locked in** to an unsatisfactory contract. The decision may be very difficult to reverse. If the outsourcing company supplies unsatisfactory levels of service, the effort and expense the organisation would incur to rebuild its own computing function or to move to another provider could be substantial.

(e)   The use of outsourcing does not encourage **awareness** of the potential costs and benefits of IS within the organisation. If managers cannot manage in-house IS resources effectively, then it could be argued that they will not be able to manage an arrangement to outsource effectively either.

6.6 Information systems and broader management operations

The information systems within an organisation should complement and **support other functional areas** such as finance, human resources and marketing. For example, an intranet facilitates the sharing of information.

Effective information systems and information management **contribute towards the attainment of organisational goals**. To best achieve this, **a cohesive IS strategy** should be developed that supports the organisation's overall strategy.

As with any expenditure, the **benefits** of information systems should be **greater than their costs**.

Section summary

Four broad **types of information systems outsourcing are ad-hoc**, **project management**, **partial** and **total**.

Examples of **outsourcing arrangements** include **multiple sourcing, incremental approach, joint venture sourcing, Application Service Providers (ASP)**.

7   Aligning systems with business strategy

Introduction

An organisation's **information systems (IS)** should **support** the **overall strategy of the business**.

The **identification of business needs** and the information technology framework to satisfy them is at the **heart of a strategy for information systems**. However, this is not always feasible, especially if an organisation's use of technology has grown in a haphazard fashion. The purpose of the strategy in this situation may be to impose some sort of order on a disorganised situation.

We shall begin by looking at the **effect** information systems have on an industry.

7.1 The effect of IS on an industry

Porter and Millar state that IS has the potential to **change the nature of competition** within an industry.

The ways in which IS can **impact an industry** according to *Porter and Millar* are:

- Change the industry structure
- Create new businesses and industries
- Be used to create competitive advantage

7.2 Changing the industry structure

Porter's five forces model can be used to analyse the effect of IS on an industry.

Porter identified **five competitive forces** operating in a competitive environment.

(a) The threat of **new entrants**.
(b) The bargaining power of **suppliers**.
(c) The bargaining power of **customers**.
(d) The threat of **substitute** products/services.
(e) The **existing competitive rivalry** in the industry.

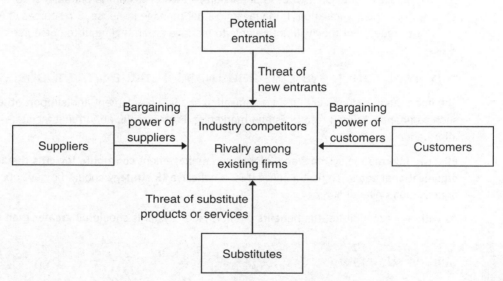

7.2.1 New entrants

IS can have two possible roles in relation to **barriers to entry**.

(a) **Defensively**. IS can increase economies of scale, raise the capital cost of entry (by requiring an investment in IS) or effectively colonising distribution channels by tying customers and suppliers into the supply chain.

(b) **Offensively**. IS can leap over entry barriers. An example is the use of telephone banking, which sometimes obviates the need to establish a branch network.

7.2.2 Suppliers

Supplier power can derive from various factors such as geographical proximity and the fact that the organisation requires goods of a certain standard in a certain time.

The bargaining power of suppliers can be **eroded** by IS in three ways.

(a) By **increasing competition** between suppliers. IS can provide a purchases database, which enables easy scanning of prices from a number of suppliers.

(b) Suppliers' power can be **shared**. An example is using CAD to **design components in tandem with suppliers**. Such relationships might be developed with a few key suppliers. The supplier and the organisation both benefit from performance improvement.

(c) Suppliers can be **integrated**, in purely administrative terms, by a system of **electronic data interchange (EDI)**.

7.2.3 Customers

The bargaining power of **customers** can be affected by using IS to **'lock them in'**.

(a) IS can **raise switching costs** (in both cash terms, and in terms of operational inconvenience). An example is where IS provides a distribution channel for certain services (eg airline tickets). Another example comes from the computer industry itself. Until the advent of the PC, most computers were run with proprietary software: in other words, you could not run ICL software, say, on IBM mainframes. This made any switch in supplier (of hardware or software) too much trouble to contemplate.

(b) Customer information systems can enable a **thorough analysis of marketing information** so that products and services can be **tailored to the needs** of certain market segments.

7.2.4 Substitutes

IS has the following relationships to existing and substitute products and services.

(a) In some cases IS itself **is the 'substitute'**. PC-based word processing packages were originally a substitute for typewriters, e-commerce is a substitute for a high street shop.

(b) Technology is the basis for **new leisure activities** (eg computer games). Alternatively, IT based systems can imitate existing goods (eg electronic keyboards imitating pianos).

(c) Technology can **add value to existing services** by allowing more detailed analysis, by generating cost advantages, or by extending the market.

7.2.5 Rivalry

IS can be used to compete – as a source of **competitive advantage** (see below).

Porter's five forces is another important strategy for analysing an organisation's environment. Be prepared to use it again as it is part of the syllabus for Paper E2.

7.3 Using IS for competitive advantage

As the importance of information has increased, organisations have realised that **information systems** can be used as a source of **competitive advantage**.

Where the majority of organisations in an industry use IS for competitive advantage, or the industry is based on IS to a large extent, there may be a **competitive necessity** to use it.

KEY TERM

COMPETITIVE ADVANTAGE is a profitable and sustainable position. It exists in the minds of customers, who believe the value they will receive from a product or service is greater than both the price they will pay and the value offered by competitors.

7.3.1 Generic strategies for competitive advantage

Porter proposes **three generic strategies** for achieving competitive advantage.

(a) **Cost leadership** means being the lowest-cost producer in the industry as a whole. A cost leadership strategy seeks to achieve the position of lowest-cost producer in the industry.

(b)   **Differentiation** is the exploitation of a product or service which the industry as a whole believes to be unique. A differentiation strategy assumes that competitive advantage can be gained through **particular characteristics** of a product or service.

(c)   **Focus** involves a restriction of activities to only part of the market (a segment or niche) through:

     (i)   Providing goods and/or services at lower cost **to that segment** (**cost-focus**).

     (ii)   Providing a differentiated product or service to that segment (**differentiation-focus**).

Cost leadership and differentiation are **industry-wide** strategies. Focus involves segmentation – pursuing **within the segment** a strategy of cost leadership or differentiation.

Examples of how IS can **support** each of these strategies are shown in the following table.

Strategy	How IS can support the strategy
Cost-leadership	By facilitating reductions in cost levels, for example by reducing the number of administration staff required.
	Allowing better resource utilisation, for example by providing accurate stock information allowing lower 'buffer' inventories to be held.
	Using IS to support just-in-time and advanced manufacturing systems.
Differentiation	Differentiation can be suggested by IS, perhaps in the product itself or in the way it is marketed. For example moving away from paper-based products to electronic.
Focus	IS may enable a more customised or specialised product/service to be produced.
	IS also facilitates the collection of sales and customer information that identifies targetable market segments.

7.4 Porter's value chain

Porter analyses the various activities of an organisation into a **value chain**. This is a model of value activities (which procure inputs, process them and add value to them in some way, to generate outputs for customers) and the relationships between them.

The value chain is covered in more detail in Chapter 5 on **operations management**. We are considering it briefly here as it can be applied to IS strategy as well.

Value chain analysis can be used to assess the impact of IS, and to identify **processes where it could be used to add value**. The activities and how IS can benefit them are described below.

7.4.1 Logistics

In both **inbound** logistics and **outbound** logistics IS can have an impact.

(a)   The use of IS in **inbound logistics** includes inventory control systems such as MRP, MRPII, ERP and JIT (we cover these systems in a later chapter).

(b)   **Warehousing**. The use of barcodes facilitates accurate inventory data.

(c)   It is possible to create computer models, or **virtual warehouses**, of inventory held at different locations.

7.4.2 Marketing

Marketing and services can be made more effective by **customer databases** enabling market segmentation.

(a)   Buying and analysing a mailing list is a more precise method of targeting particular groups of consumers than television advertising.

(b)   A variety of market research companies use IS to monitor consumers' buying habits.

(c)   Supermarkets can use automated EPOS systems to have a precise hour-by-hour idea of how products are selling to enable speedy ordering and replenishments.

Customer relationship management (CRM) systems can encourage closer relationships, as described in the previous chapter.

7.4.3 Support activities

As far as **support** activities are concerned IS has some impact.

(a)   **Procurement**. IS can automate some purchasing decisions. Paperwork can be saved if the organisation's purchase systems are linked directly to the sales order systems of some suppliers (eg by electronic data interchange).

(b)   **Technology development**. Computer Aided Design (**CAD**) is, in a number of areas, an important influence.

   (i)   **Drafting**. CAD produces engineer's drawings, component design, layout (eg of stores, wiring and piping) and electronic circuit diagrams in complex systems.

   (ii)   **Updating**. It is easy to change design in CAD systems and to assess ramifications of any changes. Some CAD systems have archive data (eg for reference).

   (iii)   CAD enables modelling to be **checked** without the necessity of producing working prototypes. Some 'stress testing' can be carried out on the model.

(c)   There is perhaps less impact on **human resources**. However, HR applications include the maintenance of a skills database, staff planning, computer based training, time attendance systems, payroll systems, pension systems.

7.5 IS and strategy - other writers

7.5.1 Ward and Griffiths

Ward and Griffiths suggested four ways that IS could be used for competitive advantage:

(a)   Linking the organisation to customers or suppliers.
(b)   Creating effective integration of the use of information in a value-adding process.
(c)   Enabling the organisation to develop, produce, market and distribute new products or services.
(d)   Giving senior management information to help develop and implement strategy.

7.5.2 Clegg

Clegg (2003) stated that an organisation's information strategy is a plan for ensuring that information is appropriate, accurate, available, timely and effective.

He emphasised that information strategy should not be left in the hands of IT experts. It's the managers within the organisation that know what information they require.

7.5.3 Boomer

Boomer (2007) identified a number of issues relevant when planning information systems.

Strategic issues relevant when planning information systems:

  • The corporate plan and the organisation's priorities expressed in it
  • How technology could be used to meet corporate objectives
  • Trends in the use of IT in the organisations industry and in other industries

Tactical issues relevant when planning information systems:

- What skills and abilities do people within the organisation possess?
- How are information systems and IT resources managed? Is outsourcing used - and should it be?
- What is the budget and timescale?

Question 4.3

Five forces

Learning outcome B2(vi)

Using each of Porter's five forces, identify and briefly explain five ways that information systems could be used to create a competitive advantage for an organisation that manufactures wooden furniture for sale through a chain of its shops. **(10 marks)**

Section summary

The ways in which **IS can impact an industry** according to *Porter and Millar* are, **change the industry structure, create new businesses and industries** and **be used to create competitive advantage**.

Porter identified **five competitive forces** operating in a competitive environment.

Porter proposes **three generic strategies** for achieving competitive advantage, **cost leadership, differentiation** and **focus**.

Value chain analysis can be used to assess the impact of IS, and to identify **processes where it could be used to add value**.

Chapter Roundup

✓ The main stages in the **implementation** of a computer system are:

- **Installation** of the hardware and software.
- **Testing**.
- **Staff training** and production of **documentation**.
- **File conversion**.
- **Changeover**.

✓ **User resistance** is a key cause of information systems failure.

✓ Theories to **overcome user resistance** include:

- Lewin/Schein's unfreeze, move, refreeze
- Kotter and Schlesingers' six methods of dealing with resistance

✓ It is better for the organisation to **prevent or minimise resistance** occurring in the first place. Theories aimed at achieving this include:

- Pace, manner and scope
- Commitment, co-ordination and communication

✓ After implementation the system should be **evaluated** to see if it is a success and whether there are any lessons to be learned.

✓ Evaluation often takes the form of a **cost-benefit review** or **performance measurement** using metrics or other measurable features of the system.

✓ A **post-implementation review** compares actual and expected performance levels and is a formal report that should be compiled after a suitable period of time following implementation.

✓ **Corrective Maintenance** is carried out when there is a systems failure of some kind, for example a defect in processing or in an implementation procedure. Its objective is to ensure that systems remain operational.

✓ **Perfective Maintenance** is carried out in order to perfect the software, or to improve it so that processing inefficiencies are eliminated and performance is enhanced.

✓ **Adaptive Maintenance** is carried out to take account of anticipated changes in the processing environment. For example new taxation legislation might require changes to be made to payroll software.

✓ Four broad **types of information systems outsourcing are ad-hoc**, **project management**, **partial** and **total**.

✓ Examples of **outsourcing arrangements** include **multiple sourcing, incremental approach, joint venture sourcing, Application Service Providers (ASP)**.

✓ The ways in which **IS can impact an industry** according to *Porter and Millar* are, **change the industry structure, create new businesses and industries** and **be used to create competitive advantage**.

✓ *Porter* identified **five competitive forces** operating in a competitive environment.

✓ *Porter* proposes **three generic strategies** for achieving competitive advantage, **cost leadership, differentiation** and **focus**.

✓ **Value chain analysis** can be used to assess the impact of IS, and to identify **processes where it could be used to add value**.

Quick Quiz

1   Which of the following is the final step in Lewin and Schien's three stage model of change?

   A   Refreeze
   B   Move
   C   Unfreeze
   D   Fix

2   Which of the following describes corrective maintenance?

   A   Maintenance carried out when there is a systems failure
   B   Maintenance carried out to perfect the system
   C   Maintenance carried out to adjust the system for changes in the processing environment
   D   Maintenance carried out to improve user-friendliness

3   How does a cost-benefit review differ from a cost-benefit analysis?

4   Which level of service provision by an IS outsourcing organisation is described below?

   'The vendor charges for access to an external processing system on a time-used basis.'

   A   Service bureaux
   B   Timeshare
   C   Facilities management
   D   Processing rental

5   Who developed value chain analysis?

   A   Lewin
   B   Schein
   C   Porter
   D   Clegg

Answers to Quick Quiz

1 A The final stage in Lewin and Schien's three stage model of change is refreeze.

2 A Option B is perfective maintenance, C is adaptive maintenance, D is also perfective maintenance

3 The review uses actual data. The analysis relies on estimates.

4 B Timeshare is where the vendor charges for access to an external processing system on a time-used basis.

5 C Porter developed value chain analysis.

Answers to Questions

4.1 Resistance to change

A Education and communication is effective where the cause of the resistance is lack of information about the change.

4.2 Cost-benefit review

Direct benefits might include reduced operating costs, for example lower overtime payments.

Indirect benefits might include better decision-making and the freeing of human 'brainpower' from routine tasks so that it can be used for more creative work.

Development costs include systems analysts' costs and the cost of time spent by users in assisting with fact-finding.

Implementation costs would include costs of site preparation and costs of training.

Running costs include maintenance costs, software leasing costs and on-going user support.

4.3 Five forces

The following are just some ideas that are possible, you may have thought of others.

Potential entrants

Technology can reduce the labour cost of manufacturing and speed up the production process so that substantial economies of scale are created. This may mean that new entrants cannot compete with the organisation on cost.

Suppliers

The organisation can store price, and other data, regarding suppliers on a database. This will allow it to quickly scan which suppliers provide the best deal, increasing the competition between them and therefore reducing their bargaining power.

Customers

The organisation can store marketing data that it collects from its customers on a database. This information can be analysed and used to improve the targeting of the marketing effort, therefore reducing customer bargaining power.

Substitutes

The organisation can develop a website and an in-store product database that allows customers to analyse and compare the products that are on offer. For example by colour, size and style. Such value-added activities can help reduce the threat of substitutes.

Industry rivalry

Porter proposed three strategies for competitive advantage. Cost leadership, differentiation and focus.

We have already seen how IS can help the organisation compete on cost. Differentiation can be achieved through the provision of the website and in-store database – not all of the organisation's competitors will provide this.

IS can also help focus the organisation's activities by allowing it to trade under two different brands on the Internet. For example one brand could compete on cost – this would sell cheaper products. Another brand could compete on product differentiation such as stylish or luxury products. Each brand could have a separate website and be marketed differently, even though the organisation that manufactures their products is the same.

	Number	Level	Marks	Time
Now try this question from the Exam Question Bank	4	Examination	25	45 mins

OPERATIONS MANAGEMENT

Part C

OPERATIONS MANAGEMENT AND THE ORGANISATION

In this chapter we begin our study of **operations management** by discussing what it is and the important role it plays in organisations.

We then continue by considering an organisation's broad **operations strategy**. This is concerned with how the

organisation **structures itself** and its **relations with suppliers**, to meet the needs of the customer.

Finally, we look at the issue of **sustainability in operations management**. This is a recent development that many organisations are under pressure from customers to address.

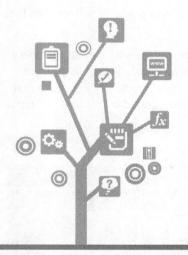

topic list	learning outcomes	syllabus references	ability required
1 Operations management	C1(a), C1(c)	C1(i), C1(iii), C1(iv)	comprehension
2 Operations strategy	C1(a), C1(b), C2(b), C2(e)	C1(i), C1(ii), C1(iii), C2(v), C2(xii)	comprehension
3 Sustainability in operations management	C1(d)	C1(v)	comprehension

1 Operations management

Introduction

The overall objective of operations is to use a **transformation process** to add value and create **competitive advantage**. It involves taking input resources and transforming them into outputs of products or services for customers. Operations management involves the design, implementation and control of these processes.

KEY TERM

OPERATIONS MANAGEMENT is concerned with the transformation of 'inputs' into 'outputs' that meet the needs of the customer.

1.1 The operations function

Organisations will invariably have an **operations function**. The operations function might be considered as one of the three traditional 'core functions'.

(a) **Operations**. This is responsible for fulfilling customer orders and requests through production of the goods or services, and for delivery of products or services to the customer.

(b) **Marketing and sales**. This is responsible for identifying customer needs and perhaps more significantly, for communicating information about the organisation's products or services to customers so as to procure sales orders.

(c) **Product and service development**. This is responsible for designing new products and services that will meet customer needs, to generate sales orders.

There are also **support functions** within an organisation that help the core functions to operate effectively. Traditionally, support functions might include accounting, HR and IT. However, what is actually a core function or a support function will depend on the particular organisation. For example, organisations that rely heavily on technology (eg the use of computer-aided manufacturing) may consider IT a core function.

The functions within an organisation **overlap**, and for any particular task or process, input is often required from more than one core function or support function.

The core functions: examples		
	Publishing company	**Hotel**
Operations	Editing Printing Distribution	Reservations Housekeeping Building maintenance Catering
Marketing and sales	Advertise through trade magazines Book fairs Negotiate sale of rights Sell into bookshops and other outlets	Advertise across media Liaise with tour operators, travel agents and booking agents
Product/ service development	Commission new titles Vet submitted scripts Develop new media forms, eg Internet delivery	Develop accommodation offerings, creative ambience, catering and ancillary facilities such as gym, business centre, conference facilities, entertainment etc Devise new packages Identify new locations

At its simplest, operations management tries to ensure that organisations are run as **efficiently** as possible.

1.2 Mintzberg's operating core

Henry Mintzberg suggested one way of looking at organisations. His theory published in 1983 suggested organisations are made up of **five parts**.

Five parts of an organisation (Mintzberg)

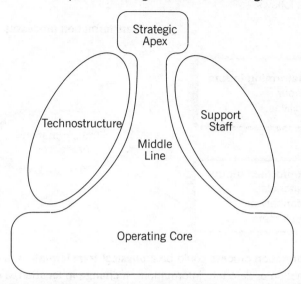

Mintzberg's five basic parts of an organisation	
Part	**Comment**
Operating core	People involved producing products and services by transforming inputs such as stock using operations such as manufacturing.
Middle line	The hierarchy linking the strategic apex to the operating core. Usually comprises first line supervisors up to senior managers.
Strategic apex	Formulates and implements strategy – and if applicable links the organisation to those who own or control it.
Technostructure	Co-ordinates work through standardising processes, outputs and skills, eg HR managers includes expert advice, research and work study.
Support staff	Provide services and assistance outside the work flow, eg catering, cleaning, PR.

1.3 The transformation process model

An operation takes **input resources** and, through one or more **processes**, **transforms** these into **outputs**. Input resources are transformed in the process into a product or service that satisfies customer needs. This generalised concept of the transformation process model applies to all processes and may be depicted as follows.

Transformation processes

Transforming inputs
- Labour
- Facilities

Transformation processes

Outputs
Products
Services

Transformed inputs
- Materials
- Information
- Customers

The **transformation process** could be a **physical transformation**, a **change in nature or form** (for example, a transformation of data into information), a **change in location**, a **change in ownership**, or, in the case of customers, a **psychological change** (eg giving enjoyment).

Inputs to the transformation process can be categorised as either transformed resources or transforming resources.

(a)   **Transformed resources** are manipulated and formed into a different condition by the process. These resources can be materials, information or customers themselves.

(b)   **Transforming resources** are the resources that are used to alter the condition of the transformed resources. These consist of the work force of the organisation and facilities such as buildings, equipment and vehicles.

Here are some **practical examples of the transformation process**.

(a)   In a manufacturing process, inputs of raw materials and components are manipulated into a finished product. The **output** is the **product**. This is then distributed to the customer.

(b)   In the legal profession, a client seeks clarification about a legal problem. A lawyer holds a meeting with the client and provides the necessary advice. The **output** is an **informed client**.

(c)   In the rail industry, rail service providers take customers, and use their work force and facilities (eg trains) to deliver the customers from one location to another. The **output** is a **re-located customer**.

(d)   In banking, instructions from a customer (information) are processed using the facilities of the bank, and the instructions are carried out, for example by the transfer of money. The **output** is the **completed transfer**.

(e)   In the entertainment industry, the customer might be provided with entertainment input such as a comedian telling a joke. The **output** is an **entertained customer**.

1.3.1 Product and service outputs

Many operations produce a **mixture** of product and service outputs. Remember also that in many countries the service economy may be more significant than the manufacturing economy. Here are some examples of the close interrelationships between service and manufacturing operations.

(a)   The **manufacture of machine tools** is primarily concerned with the output of products. However, the organisation will also provide training and technical support services to customers.

(b)   An **education and training organisation** might provide lectures, tutorials and workshops. The service may include the provision of products in the form of study notes or books. It might also provide an online helpline.

(c)   A **restaurant** provides products in the form of food and drink. However, for the customer an essential ingredient of going to a restaurant is usually the overall dining experience that includes the enjoyment obtained from the service style, entertainment and general ambience.

Section summary

Operations is a **core** part of any organisation.

The **transformational process model** describes how **inputs** are converted through **processes** into **outputs**.

2 Operations strategy

Introduction

Organisations may employ one or more of a number of **operations strategies** to improve their processes and as a source of competitive advantage over competitors. Common strategies involve what is known as the **value chain** and **supply chain management**. This is the view that an organisation is one link in a chain that aims to turn raw materials into what the customer wants. As a result all links in the chain benefit.

2.1 The value chain

We came across the value chain in Chapter 4 where we applied it to IS strategy. We now look at it again in its more traditional context - operations management.

KEY TERM

VALUE CHAIN. 'Sequence of business activities by which, in the perspective of the end-user, value is added to the products or services produced by an entity.'   (*CIMA Official Terminology*)

In *Porter's* analysis, **business activities** are *not* the same as **business functions**.

(a)   **Functions** are the familiar departments of a business (eg production function, the finance function) and reflect the formal organisation structure and the distribution of labour.

(b)   **Activities** are what actually goes on, the work that is done. Activities are the means by which an organisation creates value in its products - sometimes referred to as *value activities.* Activities incur costs and provide a product or service which earns revenue.

An example should make this clear. An organisation needs many inputs of resources to function. It needs to secure resources from the environment. This activity can be called **procurement**. However, procurement will involve more departments than purchasing, for example the accounts department will certainly be involved and possibly production and quality assurance.

Organisations **create value** for their buyers by **performing these activities**. The ultimate value a firm creates is measured by the amount customers are willing to pay for its products or services above the cost of carrying out value activities. A business is profitable if the realised value to customers exceeds the collective cost of performing the activities.

There are two points to note here.

(a) **Customers purchase value**, which they measure by comparing an organisation's products and services with similar offerings from competitors.

(b) **The business creates value** by carrying out its activities either more efficiently than other businesses, or combined in such a way as to provide a unique product or service.

Porter's value chain is a model of value activities (which procure inputs, process them and add value to them in some way, to generate outputs for customers) and the relationships between them.

Porter's Value Chain

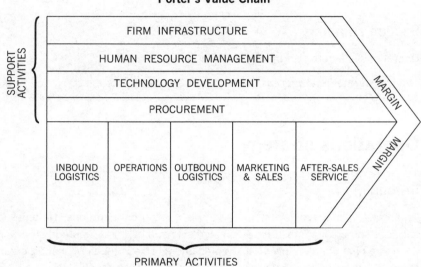

2.1.1 Primary activities

Porter distinguished between **primary activities** and **support activities**.

Primary activities are those directly related with production, sales, marketing, delivery and services.

The diagram shows **five primary activities**.

(a) **Inbound logistics** are those activities involved with receiving, handling and storing inputs to the production system.

(b) **Operations** are those activities which convert resource inputs into a final product. In a manufacturing business, this is relatively easy to identify as the factory. In a service company, operations include those activities which make up the basic service.

(c) **Outbound logistics** are those activities relating to storing the product and its distribution to customers.

(d) **Marketing and sales** are those activities that relate to informing customers about the product, persuading them to buy it, and enabling them to do so.

(e) **After-sales service** includes activities such as installing products, repairing them and providing spare parts.

2.1.2 Support activities

Support activities are those which provide purchased inputs, human resources, technology and infrastructural functions to support the primary activities.

(a) **Procurement** consists of those activities which acquire the resource inputs to the primary activities (eg purchase of materials, subcomponents, equipment).

(b) **Technology development** (in the sense of apparatus, techniques and work organisation). These activities are related to both product design and to improving processes and/or resource utilisation.

(c) **Human resource management** is the activities of recruiting, training, developing and rewarding people.

(d) **Firm infrastructure**. The systems of planning, finance, quality control and management are activities which *Porter* believes are crucially important to an organisation's strategic capability in all primary activities.

2.1.3 Other elements

Furthermore, in addition to the categories described above, *Porter* identifies three further types of activity.

(a) **Direct activities** are concerned with adding value to inputs.

(b) **Indirect activities** enable direct activities to be performed (eg maintenance, sales force administration).

(c) **Quality assurance**. This type of activity monitors the quality of other activities, and includes: inspection, review and audit (eg the quality of the financial records).

Linkages connect the interdependent elements of the value chain together. They occur when one element of the value chain affects the costs or effectiveness of another. They require co-ordination.

(a) More costly product design, or better quality production, might reduce the need for after-sales service.

(b) To deliver goods on time requires smooth functioning of operations, outbound logistics and service activities such as installation.

Porter's **Value Chain is a key theory which will crop up in other papers, for example E3 and P2.**

| Question 5.1 | Activities |

Learning outcome C1(i)

Which of the following is a support activity in the value chain?

A   Inbound logistics
B   Human resource management
C   Marketing and sales
D   Service

2.2 The value system

Activities that add value do not stop at the organisation's boundaries. For example, when a restaurant serves a meal, the quality of the ingredients – although they are chosen by the cook – is determined by the grower. The grower has also added value, and the grower's success in growing produce of good quality is as important to the customer's ultimate satisfaction as the skills of the chef. Consequently, a company's value chain is connected to what *Porter* describes as a **value system**.

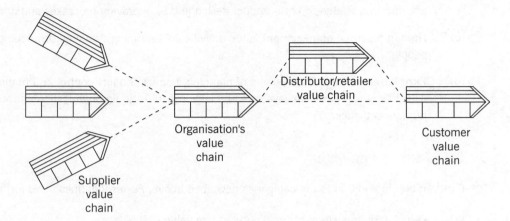

As well as managing its own value chain, a business can secure **competitive advantage** by managing the linkages with its suppliers and customers. A company can create competitive advantage by making best use of these links. An example is a **Just-in-Time system** covered in Chapter 7) where close integration of the organisation's operations with those of its suppliers is essential.

2.3 Purchasing and supply chain management   05/10

KEY TERM

SUPPLY CHAIN MANAGEMENT is concerned with the flow of goods and services through the organisation with the aim of making the firm more competitive.   (*Cousins*)

The nature of **purchasing** within organisations has changed dramatically over recent years. Historically, purchasing was viewed as a clerical function. This has changed. Purchasing today, in most organisations, is viewed as a function that impacts significantly on **organisational performance**.

2.3.1 What caused the need for closer supply chain links?

Christopher (2005) identified a number of factors.

- Shorter product life cycles requiring more efficient supply pipelines
- Increasingly global supply chains requiring greater coordination
- A move towards more flexible organisations that partner with others (organisational integration)
- More demanding customer service standards

2.3.2 Effective supply chain management

Supply chain management is concerned with the flow of goods and services through the organisation. Ultimately, the goal is to contribute to customer **satisfaction**.

Porter recognised that management of the supply chain and supply network could be a source of **competitive advantage**. He referred to the position of firms in supply chains and networks in relation to their proximity to the customer. If a firm is closer to the customer than another, it is '**downstream**' of it. If a firm is further away from the customer than another, it is '**upstream**' of it.

Supply chains today must be **responsive** and **reliable**. The relationships between members must demonstrate a high degree of **mutual understanding**. Integration between the organisation and other chain members, both upstream and downstream, should be facilitated by **integrated information systems**.

2.3.3 Reck and Long   05/11

Reck and Long (1988) devised a model that aimed to provide an insight into the evolution of the purchasing function. Their **strategic positioning tool** identified a four-phase **development of purchasing** within organisations.

The phases of Reck and Long's strategic positioning tool	
Phase	**Comment**
1 Passive	• Purchasing reacts to requests from other departments.
	• The focus is on efficient transaction processing.
2 Independent	• A more professional approach to purchasing is taken.
	• During this phase, the importance of negotiation with suppliers to securing the best prices for individual products/services purchased is recognised.
	• Often includes IT improvements and the creation of a purchasing manager position to manage supplier negotiations.
3 Supportive	• The potential for purchasing to support wider organisational goals is recognised.
	• This phase is often characterised by a centralised purchasing department with organisation-wide buying policies and systems.
	• The emphasis is co-ordination and compliance with centrally negotiated contracts.
	• The importance of careful supplier selection is recognised.
	• Policies and procedures for supplier management are developed.
4 Integrative	• Purchasing is now fully integrated in the major business activities of the organisation.
	• Pro-active purchasing strategies are developed and followed.
	• Purchasing is part of the firm's strategic planning process and purchasing strategy is aligned with corporate goals and strategy.
	• The alignment of purchasing strategy with overall organisational goals and strategy often leads to new requirements in suppliers' performance and capabilities.
	• Suppliers are viewed as partners and supplier management is viewed as relationship management.
	• Today, closely linked or joint communication and information systems would facilitate this relationship.

2.3.4 Cousins

Cousins (2000) conducted a 12-month research project to investigate the level of **strategic maturity** in the purchasing function of UK/European companies. In particular, the research aimed to establish the level of collaboration between leading UK companies (ie suppliers) and their major customers. The research looked at a range of inter-connected aspects considered important when looking at how an organisation deals with relationships relevant to overall strategy and supply strategy.

These aspects are shown in the diagram below.

Cousin's Strategic Supply Wheel

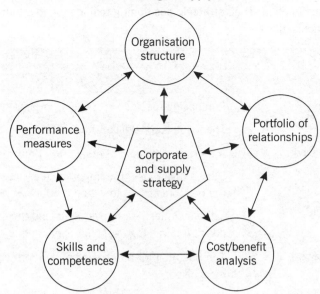

The research revealed that all of the aspects identified and shown in the **Strategic Supply Wheel** are inter-connected. *Cousins* stated that it was clear that a focus on anyone area (eg relationship development) would be to the detriment of another area (eg performance measures). Organisations need to **balance** these resources and issues.

The research also examined the **'relationship type'**, using a simple classification of **'opportunistic'** (low level of co-operation with the supplier) versus **'collaborative'** (high level of co-operation). The results showed that the more collaborative the relationship the greater the degree of strategic alignment required (between overall strategy and purchasing strategy).

2.4 Supply chain networks

KEY TERM

A SUPPLY CHAIN NETWORK is an interconnecting group of organisations which relate to each other through linkages between the different processes and activities involved in producing products/services to the ultimate consumer.

Increasingly, organisations are recognising the need for and benefits of establishing **close links** with companies in the supply chain. Historically, businesses in the supply chain have operated relatively **independently** of one another to create value for an ultimate customer. Independence was maintained through holding buffer stocks and managing lead-times. There was very little control over other channel members, and no wider perspective on the system as a whole.

Market and competitive demands are now, however, **compressing lead times** and businesses are reducing inventories and excess capacity. Linkages between businesses in the supply chain must therefore become much tighter. This new condition is shown in the **'Integrated supply chain'** model (the second model in the following diagram).

There seems to be increasing recognition that, in the future, it will be **whole supply chains** which will compete and not just individual organisations – we saw earlier how *Porter's* value chain achieves this.

Traditional and integrated supply chain models

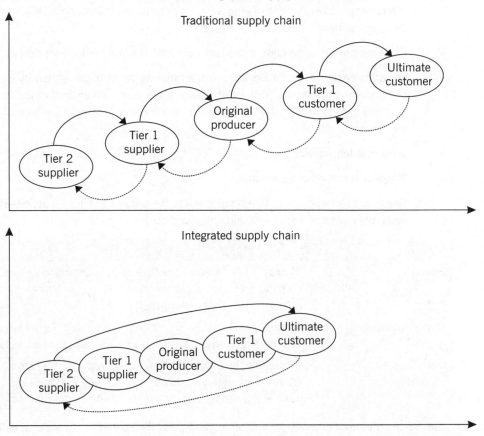

Traditional supply chain

Integrated supply chain

The aim is to co-ordinate the whole chain, from raw material suppliers to end customers. The chain should be considered as a **network** rather than a **pipeline** - a network of vendors support a network of customers, with third parties such as transport businesses helping to link the companies. In marketing channels, organisations have to manage the trade-off between the desire to remain **independent and autonomous**, and the need to be **interdependent and co-operative**.

KEY TERMS

INDEPENDENCE: each channel member operates in isolation and is not affected by others, so maintaining a greater degree of control.

INTERDEPENDENCE: each channel member can affect the performance of others in the channel.

If the supplier 'knows' what its customers want, it does not necessarily have to guess, or wait until the customer places an order. It will be able to better plan its own delivery systems. The potential for using the **Internet** to allow customers and suppliers to acquire up-to-date information about forecasted needs and delivery schedules is a recent development, but one which is being used by an increasing number of companies. Some supply chain relationships are strengthened and communication facilitated through the use of **extranets** (intranets accessible to authorised outsiders).

2.4.1 Implications for supply chain management

Supply chain management involves optimising the activities of companies working together to produce goods and services. The trend towards closer links with suppliers and the development of supply chain networks has implications for supply chain management.

- **Reduction in customers served**. For the sake of focus, companies might concentrate resources on customers of high potential value.

- **Price and inventory co-ordination**. Businesses co-ordinate their price and inventory policies to avoid problems and bottlenecks caused by short-term surges in demand, such as promotions.

- **Linked computer systems**. Closer links may be facilitated through the use of **Electronic Data Interchange** (EDI), for example to allow paperless communication, billing and payment and through the use of a computer **extranet**.

- **Early supplier involvement** in product development and component design.

- **Logistics design**. Hewlett-Packard restructured its distribution system by enabling certain product components to be added at the distribution warehouse rather than at the central factory. For example user-manuals which are specific to the French market would be added at the French distribution centre.

- **Joint problem-solving**.

- **Supplier representative on site**.

The business case for supply chain management is the **benefit** to **all** the **participants** in terms of the performance objectives of speed, dependability and cost.

Performance objective	Example
Speed	Plumbers need to manage their supply chains to ensure they are able to get hold of parts such as water tanks, boilers, valves etc so they can respond quickly to customer emergencies.
Dependability	A mail order business promises delivery within 10 days of receipt of order. It will need to ensure good supply chain management to fulfil its promise.
Cost	A company providing mortgages will need to manage its supply chain with great skill with one of its objectives being to obtain the cheapest sources of finance in keeping with the profile and risks of their mortgage lending.

Businesses that are perceived by customers and potential customers to excel at delivering the desired performance objectives are likely to derive a **competitive advantage**.

2.5 Demand networks

Demand networks are a recent evolution of supply chains. The key difference between them is how they are formed.

KEY POINT

In a traditional **supply chain**, producers form links between themselves in order to produce a product that the customer wants at an appropriate selling price and cost to the producer. The chain is formed to '**push**' the product out into the market.

By contrast, products produced by **demand networks** are '**pulled**' into existence in response to demand signals. Organisations within a demand network share information and collaborate to produce a product or service the market is demanding.

A **demand network** is the result of companies **evolving** internally (or within their departments) and externally (with their partners). This evolution is a four-stage process.

 Reacting

Departments optimise their operations to meet demand. Reacting organisations cannot sense demand or tie it into corporate strategy – they simply react to market conditions.

 Anticipating

Anticipating companies have developed internally to **respond to long and short-term demand**. They often use lean production or six sigma (see later) to bring order to their operations. They can anticipate upstream demand (the demand which is coming to them) but not downstream demand.

Collaborating

Collaborating organisations have established **external relationships** with business partners that allow **intelligence** to be gathered on downstream demand. This allows better forecasting and adjustment of plans.

 Orchestrating

Supply and demand have evolved into a **flow of information** throughout the network. Companies plan new products and product life cycles, and can begin to influence demand patterns. Production decisions are based on costs and profitability.

Demand network evolution

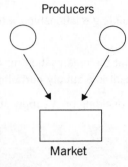

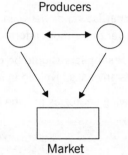

Reacting
Producers estimate demand and push products to market

Anticipating
Some communication between producers. The product continues to be pushed to market

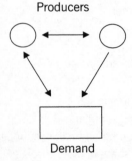

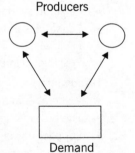

Collaborating
Use of intelligence allows the market to be manipulated – the pull process begins

Orchestrating
Producers are fully networked and can control the pull process

To create **competitive advantage**, organisations within a demand network have to manage **three factors**:

- **Alignment** – of shared incentives
- **Agility** – to respond to demand quickly
- **Adaptability** – to adjust the structure of the supply chain to meet demand

 Exam alert

Exam questions may require you to consider a range of operations strategies and decide which is the most suitable in a given scenario.

2.6 Supply portfolios and sourcing strategies

Organisations may use a number of suppliers for their raw materials, and there are a range of possible **strategies** open to an organisation when deciding who they will purchase their supplies from. For example

- Certain suppliers may produce a **better quality** of product.

- Some suppliers may be **cheaper on price.**

- Suppliers may also be selected from **a number of countries** to guard against the risk of supplies from one country being affected by circumstances such as bad weather.

- Suppliers are of **different sizes** so buyers can match order sizes to appropriate suppliers (ie small suppliers may not be suitable for larger orders).

- **Expertise** varies between suppliers so building relationships with a number of them can help the buyer make more **informed choices**.

The **mix of suppliers should be optimised** so that the organisation maximises the benefits they offer and minimises any risks involved in supply – the result is a **supply portfolio**.

The following strategies may be followed when deciding on a **supply strategy**.

Supply sourcing strategies	
Option	**Comment**
Single	**Description** • The buyer chooses one source of supply. **Advantages** • Stronger relationship with the supplier. • Possible source of superior quality due to increased opportunity for a supplier quality assurance programme. • Facilitates better communication. • Economies of scale. • Facilitates confidentiality. • Possible source of competitive advantage. **Disadvantages** • Vulnerable to any disruption in supply. • The buyer is dependent on the supplier. • Supplier power may increase if no alternative supplier. • The supplier is vulnerable to shifts in order levels.
Multiple	**Description** • The buyer chooses several sources of supply. **Advantages** • Access to a wide range of knowledge and expertise. • Competition among suppliers may drive the price down. • Supply failure by one supplier will cause minimal disruption – it is easy to switch between suppliers. **Disadvantages** • Not easy to develop an effective quality assurance programme. • Suppliers may display less commitment. • Economies of scale are neglected.

Supply sourcing strategies	
Option	Comment
Delegated	**Description**
	• A supplier is given responsibility for the delivery of a complete sub-assembly. For example, rather than dealing with several suppliers a 'first-tier' supplier would be appointed to deliver a complete sub-assembly (eg a PC manufacturer may delegate the production of keyboards).
	Advantages
	• Allows the utilisation of specialist external expertise.
	• Frees-up internal staff for other tasks.
	• The purchasing entity may be able to negotiate economies of scale.
	Disadvantages
	• Quality control is difficult to maintain.
	• Loss of confidentiality if products use trade secrets.
	• Competitors may utilise the same external organisation so it is unlikely to be a source of competitive advantage.
Parallel	**Description**
	• Parallel sourcing involves mixing/combining the other three approaches to maximise the benefits of each.
	Advantages
	• If used correctly should provide an efficient/effective strategy.
	• Supplier failure will not halt production.
	• Price competition is created between suppliers.
	Disadvantages
	• Can be complicated to manage.
	• Quality control is difficult to maintain.

Strategic supply chain management is also part of the Paper E3 syllabus.

| Question 5.2 | Sourcing and supplier performance |

Learning outcome C2(xii)

(a)   List four methods organisations use to source materials. **(4 marks)**

(b)   Which method would you recommend to an organisation whose product is based upon a trade secret and relies on quality for competitive advantage? **(1 mark)**

(c)   List four criteria that could be used to assess supplier performance. (*Hint*: Come up with these yourself based on what you have read and your own experience when you order a product or service.) **(4 marks)**

2.7 Information flows across supply chains and networks

For supply chains and networks to operate successfully information must flow smoothly between all participating organisations. One way of analysing and representing information flows is with the use of

process maps. Process maps are a **diagrammatic representation** of a process. A number of techniques or notations may be used to produce a process map.

2.8 Process mapping

Process mapping aims to **identify** and **represent** the **steps** and **decisions** involved in a process, in diagrammatic form.

Process maps:

- Describe the flow of materials, information and documents
- Display the tasks contained within the process
- Show that the tasks transform inputs into outputs
- Indicate the decisions that need to be made
- Demonstrate the relationships and dependencies between the process steps

There are many types of **process maps** (sometimes referred to as process charts) and many charting conventions.

Two **common types** of process map are:

- A **'basic' flowchart** – which provides a basic 'birds eye' view

- A **deployment chart** – which provides an overview and also indicates where or by whom actions are performed

Process maps should be simple enough for the process under review to be understood by almost anyone, even someone unfamiliar with the process.

2.8.1 Why process map?

Process maps are **important** for several reasons.

(a) Changing systems and working methods without understanding the underlying processes can lead to costly mistakes. It can also create conditions that make it difficult for staff to work effectively.

(b) If organisations don't understand a process they will not be able to manage it effectively - and if they cannot manage a process they cannot improve it.

(c) Process mapping enables businesses to clearly define current processes, identifying problem areas such as bottlenecks, delays or waste. This knowledge provides a solid basis from which to develop solutions and plan new improved processes.

(d) Process mapping enables an organisation to:

- Establish what is currently happening and why

- Measure how efficiently the process is working

- Gather information to understand where waste and inefficiencies exist and their impact on employees, customers and/or partners

- Develop new improved processes to reduce or eliminate inefficiency.

2.8.2 Process map types and symbols

Two common types of process map are a basic flowchart and a deployment flowchart.

(a) **Basic process map flowchart**

Process map flowcharts set out the sequence of activities and decision points. They illustrate the main steps and decisions in the process. Labels showing the type and level of staff doing each step can be added if required.

(b) **Deployment process map flowchart**

Deployment process map flowcharts are similar to basic process maps, but also show who does what, including interactions between the parties involved. This type of chart is sometimes referred to as a 'swim lane' chart - as the page is divided into vertical lanes for each person or party involved.

2.8.3 Process map flowcharting symbols

Below are examples of **commonly used flowcharting symbols**. You should remember though that different people and organisations may use different symbols, or may use only some of the symbols below. Factors such as the complexity of the process being modelled and simple personal preference play a part.

Flowcharting symbols

Start/End

This symbol marks the starting or ending point of the system.

Action or process

A box can represent a single step ('add two cups of flour'), or an entire sub-process ('make bread') within a larger process.

Document

A printed document or report. This symbol is not always used – it depends upon the level of detail required in the model.

Decision

A decision or branching point. Lines representing different decisions emerge from different points of the diamond.

Input/ Output

Represents material or information entering or leaving the system, such as customer order (input) or a product (output). Again, the use of this symbol is not consistent – some people may identify a customer placing an order at a retail counter as an action – others may identify it as Input.

Flow →

This arrow indicate the sequence of steps and the direction of flow.

2.8.4 Constructing a process flowchart

Maps are most-easily produced using relatively specialised software, for example Microsoft Visio. General purpose software packages such as Word, Excel and PowerPoint can also be used.

 Organise the sequence out by working down rather than across.

 Having thought through the main 'steps' of the process, flowchart them in the sequence they are performed.

 Use rectangles for 'tasks' and diamonds for 'decisions'. Use connecting arrows between boxes to represent the direction of the sequence.

 Concisely describe each task or decision in its own box. Boxes may be numbered and a key provided where the activity is described in more detail.

 If the process includes decision points, this will normally imply some 'return-routing' causing some boxes to have more than one input. 'Return routing' or 'loops' often indicate an inefficiency or waste.

 Decisions usually (but not always) pose questions answerable by 'Yes' or 'No'. Structure questions so that the preferred answer is 'Yes'.

STAGE 7 Conventions include drawing the 'Yes' route out of the bottom of the diamond (ie normal flow downward through the chart) and the 'No' route as a line to the side of the box).

2.8.5 A simple process flowchart

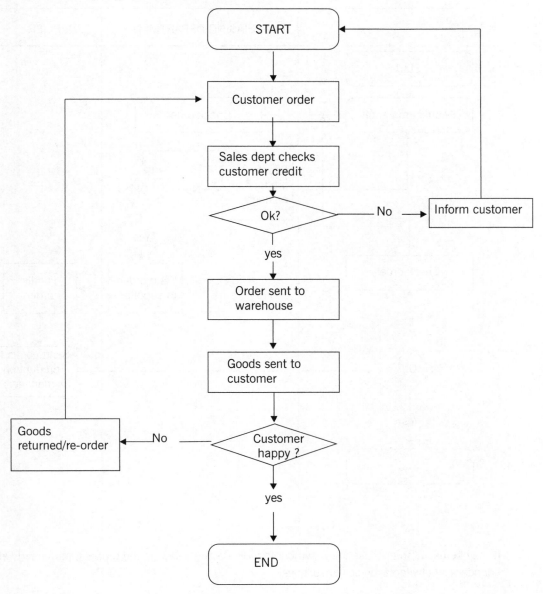

2.8.6 Constructing a deployment flowchart

Deployment flowcharts include a 'department' or 'unit' dimension along the top of the chart. They may include individuals, groups, departments, agencies, organisations, functions etc - whatever 'units' involved in the process.

The following should be considered when **constructing deployment flowcharts**:

- Draw vertical lines to separate the functional boundaries.

- When the flow moves from one function to another, this is ideally denoted by a horizontal line.

- Apart from the horizontal moves between functions, aim when possible to sequence activities from top to bottom.

- Always connect symbols with arrows indicating the direction of flow.

2.8.7 A simple deployment flowchart

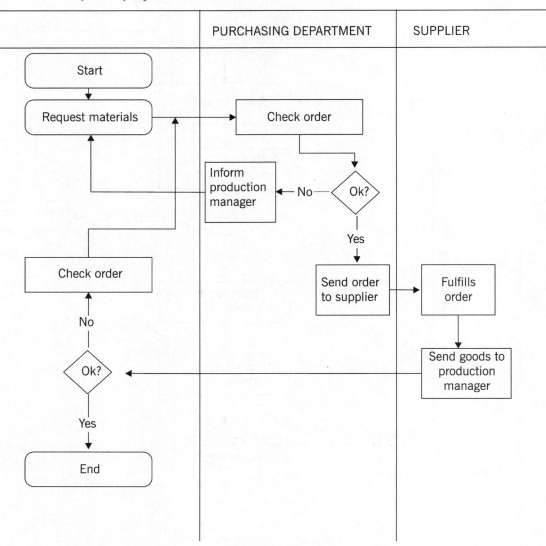

It may be useful to also use the D symbol to indicate any delays in the process, particularly at the boundaries between agencies or sections.

2.9 Process design

Process mapping is also often used when designing organisational processes.

Bowhill (2008) saw process design as a way of **highlighting inefficiencies and designing improved processes** that ultimately lead to increased customer satisfaction.

Many management techniques covered elsewhere in this book could be used to improve processes, for example supply chain management, TQM, Kaizen and Business Process Re-engineering.

2.10 Operations strategy – Brown

Brown (2001) identified six items that should be considered when devising an organisation's operations strategy.

Item	Comment
Capability required	What is it that the organisation wants to 'do' or produce?
Range and location of operations	How big and/or widespread does the organisation want to be?
Investment in technology	How will processes and production be performed?
Strategic buyer-supplier relationships	Who will be key strategic partners?
New products/services	What are the expected product life-cycles?
Structure of operations	How will staff be organised and managed?

2.11 General points

Operations strategy theories are simply illustrations of approaches to operations strategy formulation. In broad terms, **strategy formulation** in practice will include many of the **following concepts**.

(a) Setting **operational objectives** that are consistent with the organisation's overall business strategy.

(b) Translating **business strategy** or **marketing strategy** into **operations strategy**, by means of identifying key competitive factors.

(c) Assessing the relative importance of different **competitive factors**.

(d) Assessing current operational performance by **comparison** with the performance of **competitors**.

(e) Using the idea of a clean-slate or 'green-field' approach to strategy selection. Managers are asked to consider how they would ideally design operations if they could **start again from scratch**. The ideal operations design is then compared with actual operations, and important differences identified. Strategy decisions are then taken to move actual performance closer towards the ideal.

(f) Formulating strategy could be based on other types of **gap analysis**, such as comparing what the market wants with what the operation is actually achieving, and taking decisions aimed at closing the significant gaps.

(g) Emphasising the iterative process of strategy selection. Strategies should be **continually reviewed, refined and re-developed** through experience and in response to changes in the environment.

Section summary

Porter saw organisations as **value chains** that are made up of different processes. A competitive advantage can be gained by ensuring these processes are efficient.

Organisations can become part of a larger **supply chain**. They purchase from suppliers and sell to other organisations which are buyers. Eventually raw materials are converted into what the end-customer wants.

Supply chains are a source of **competitive advantage** as each organisation works towards a common goal.

Demand networks are an evolution of supply chains. They are formed by demand acting as a stimulus to produce a product.

Supply portfolios are the mix of suppliers selected by an organisation to balance the benefits and risks involved in relying on them.

Process maps can be used to present the processes involved in supply chains and networks.

3 Sustainability in operations management

KEY POINT

In relation to the world's resources, sustainability has been defined as ensuring that development meets the needs of the present without compromising the ability of future generations to meet their own needs.

For organisations, sustainability involves developing strategies with the eventual aim that the organisation only uses resources at a rate that allows them to be replenished, and that emissions of waste are at a level the environment is able to absorb.

3.1 Sustainability

KEY TERM

SUSTAINABILITY is a long-term programme involving a series of sustainable development practices, aimed at improving organisational efficiency, stakeholder support and market edge.

Goldsmith and Samson (2004)

Let's examine three aspects of *Goldsmith and Samson's* definition above.

3.1.1 Sustainability and efficiency

Sustainable efficiency practices an organisation could pursue include:

- Reducing waste
- Using less energy
- Recycling

3.1.2 Sustainability and stakeholder support

Sustainable practices that might gain stakeholder support include:

- Reducing greenhouse gas emissions would gain the support of environmentalists and some others
- Employee cycle schemes
- Encouraging employee flexible working (reduce commuting)
- Reduced business travel, utilise technology eg web conferencing
- Sourcing from green suppliers

3.1.3 Sustainability and market edge

Sustainable practices that could provide 'market edge' include:

- Innovation
- Supply chain improvements
- Research and development (eg greener motor vehicles)

CASE STUDY

In the year since Comerica Bank opened its first **L**eadership in **E**nergy and **E**nvironmental **D**esign (LEED®) certified banking centre, the bank has received recognition for its progress in implementing its commitment to sustainability.

'Integrating green practices into the way we do business is a core commitment and allows us to enhance our performance as a company and **create long-term value for our stakeholders**,' said Richard J. Plewa, Comerica Bank's Chief Sustainability Officer.

In 2009, Comerica Bank was named to the following **sustainability leadership indices** in recognition of its recent sustainability successes:

The Carbon Disclosure Project's (CDP) Carbon Disclosure Leadership Index. The CDP represents 534 global investors responsible for the management of $64 trillion of assets. For the second year in a row, Comerica was named to the CDP's Carbon Disclosure Leadership Index, which rates firms according to the level and quality of their disclosure and reporting on greenhouse gas emissions and climate change strategy. In 2009, Comerica's index score of 91 was top among S&P 500 companies.

Maplecroft Climate Innovation Leaders Index. The Maplecroft Index focuses on U.S. companies with at least $1 billion of market capitalisation and identifies top performers in climate-related innovation and carbon management. Comerica was ranked number 61 overall and number 5 in the finance sector.

FTSE4Good Index. The FTSE4Good Index is a leading global responsibility investment index designed to measure the performance of companies that meet globally recognised corporate responsibility standards. Companies named in the FTSE4Good Index have demonstrated that they have put policies and management systems in place to help address relevant corporate responsibility risks as they pertain to social and environmental change.

Comerica launched the following sustainability initiatives to **increase the efficiency of resources and decrease greenhouse gas emissions**:

Energy and Emissions. During 2009, Comerica implemented a range of initiatives to reduce energy use, corporate travel and the related greenhouse gas emissions. Total corporate emissions decreased by almost 5 percent from 2008 to 2009, partly reflecting the positive contributions of these initiatives.

Reducing Paper Use. Other initiatives implemented in 2009 were designed to reduce the use of paper throughout the company. Paper purchases were down by almost 19 percent for the year, a reduction of almost 6 million printed pages.

Greener Procurement. A Green Procurement Work Group was established in 2009 and a new Supplier Questionnaire & Scorecard was developed to help identify environmentally preferred providers of goods and services. Comerica plans to use this tool to improve the sustainability performance of its supply chain.

Eco-Friendly Buildings. All of Comerica's newly constructed banking centres in 2010 will have green features. Specifically, Comerica has five new banking centres that are LEED-certified by the U.S. Green Building Council. Comerica also is seeking LEED certification for three additional banking centres opening in 2010. In addition, four existing Comerica buildings received Energy Star certification in 2009 from the U.S. Environmental Protection Agency.

Sustainability Reporting. Comerica published its Inaugural Sustainability Report in September 2009. The report was based on the Global Reporting Initiative framework and included a wealth of information on Comerica's sustainability programs and performance, including baseline environmental performance data against which future progress can be measured.

'We've also been working hard to develop awareness of sustainability issues among our employees and to tap into the deep reservoir of creativity they possess when it comes to identifying better and more sustainable ways to operate,' noted Plewa. 'For example, on Earth Day 2010, Comerica teams will be sponsoring and participating in a range of educational and service projects at Comerica locations and beyond.'

For more information visit www.comerica.com/sustainability.

Section summary

Sustainability in operations is concerned with **efficient use of resources** and **minimising the effect** of an organisation's **activities** on **society** and the **environment**.

Chapter Roundup

✓ **Operations** is a **core** part of any organisation.

✓ The **transformational process model** describes how **inputs** are converted through **processes** into **outputs**.

✓ *Porter* saw organisations as **value chains** that are made up of different processes. A competitive advantage can be gained by ensuring these processes are efficient.

✓ Organisations can become part of a larger **supply chain**. They purchase from suppliers and sell to other organisations which are buyers. Eventually raw materials are converted into what the end-customer wants.

✓ Supply chains are a source of **competitive advantage** as each organisation works towards a common goal.

✓ **Demand networks** are an evolution of supply chains. They are formed by demand acting as a stimulus to produce a product.

✓ **Supply portfolios** are the mix of suppliers selected by an organisation to balance the benefits and risks involved on relying on them.

✓ **Process maps** can be used to present the processes involved in supply chains and networks.

✓ **Sustainability** in operations is concerned with **efficient use of resources** and **minimising the effect** of an organisation's **activities** on **society** and the **environment**.

Quick Quiz

1   Which of the following are parts of an organisation according to *Mintzberg*?

(i)   Strategic apex
(ii)   Support staff
(iii)   Middle core
(iv)   Technostructure

A   (i), (ii), and (iii) only
B   (i), (ii), and (iv) only
C   (ii) and (iv) only
D   All of the options

2   Which of the following is a primary activity according to *Porter's* value chain?

A   Firm infrastructure
B   Technology development
C   Procurement
D   Marketing and sales

3   Who developed the strategic supply wheel?

A   *Porter*
B   *Mintzberg*
C   *Cousins*
D   *Reck and Long*

4   Organisations within a demand network need to manage which three factors to create a competitive advantage?

A   Acceptability, agility and adaptability
B   Agility, adaptability and access
C   Adaptability, access and acceptability
D   Alignment, agility and adaptability

5   List the six items *Brown* identified that should be covered by an organisation's operations strategy.

Answers to Quick Quiz

1   B   The 'middle core' is fictitious, made up from the middle line and operating core.

2   D   Marketing and sales is a primary activity according to *Porter's* value chain.

3   C   *Cousins* developed the strategic supply wheel.

4   D   Organisations within a demand network need to manage alignment, agility and adaptability to create a competitive advantage.

5   Capability required, range and location of operations, investment in technology, strategic buyer-supplier relationships, new products/services and the structure of operations.

Answers to Questions

5.1 Activities

B   Human resource management is a support activity.

5.2 Sourcing and supplier performance

(a)   **Single sourcing** – the buyer chooses one source of supply.

   Multiple sourcing – the buyer chooses several sources of supply.

   Delegated sourcing – the buyer chooses a supplier to deliver a complete sub-assembly of part of the product.

   Parallel sourcing – the buyer mixes the other three approaches to maximise their benefits.

(b)   **Single sourcing**. This method allows a strong relationship to develop between buyer and supplier and helps to ensure confidential treatment of trade secrets and allows the development of a quality assurance programme.

(c)   **Quality** – whether the product or service is fit for purpose, defect rates.

   Flexibility and capability – is the supplier open to reasonable requests and able to meet them?

   Timeliness – is the product or service delivered on time?

   Price – value for money relative to competitors.

Now try this question from the Exam Question Bank	Number	Level	Marks	Time
	5	Examination	30	54 mins

QUALITY MANAGEMENT

 A significant trend in all business sectors over recent years has been an increased **emphasis on quality**. In an increasingly **competitive** environment, quality is seen as vital to success.

As with many topics in this paper, you must learn the relevant theory, but also be able to apply it to a practical situation. For example, a **theoretical** question may require you to evaluate various contemporary approaches to the management of quality – while a more **practical** question could ask you to identify and analyse problems with management of quality in an organisation described in the question.

The purposes of **external quality standards** (eg the various ISO standards appropriate to products and organisations) are also highly examinable.

We start this chapter by looking at the **concept** of quality, before moving on to the various **approaches** used to ensure quality in both the product or service produced and the systems used by the organisation.

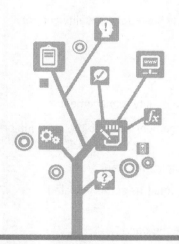

topic list	learning outcomes	syllabus references	ability required
1 The scope of quality management	C2(a), C2(d)	C2(ii)	application
2 Quality management approaches	C2(a), C2(d)	C2(i)	application
3 Total quality management (TQM)	C2(a), C2(d)	C2(ii)	application
4 Managing quality using TQM	C2(a), C2(d)	C2(ii), C2(ix)	application
5 Processes of continuous improvement	C2(a), C2(d)	C2(ix)	application
6 Lean production	C2(c), C2(d)	C2(x), C2(xi)	application
7 International Organisation for Standardisation	C2(c), C2(d)	C2(iii)	application
8 Total productive maintenance (TPM)	C2(a), C2(d)	C2(ii)	application
9 The TQMEX model	C2 (a), C2(d)	C2(ii)	application
10 Service quality	C2(c), C2(d)	C2(viii)	application

1 The scope of quality management

Introduction

In the modern commercial environment, there has been a change in emphasis **away from quantity** (produce as much as we can) **to quality** (produce the best we can). Customers have become more sophisticated and discerning. Poor quality products and services are no longer tolerated.

Quality applies to both goods and services. Whether a customer goes shopping for food or visits a dentist, they expect a quality experience. More importantly, quality is increasingly a source of **competitive advantage**.

Quality is concerned with **'fitness for purpose'**. **Quality management** is concerned with ensuring that products or services meet their planned level of quality and conform to specifications.

KEY TERMS

QUALITY is 'the totality of features and characteristics of a product or service which bears on its ability to meet stated or implied needs'. (*Holmes*, 1992)

QUALITY MANAGEMENT is concerned with controlling activities with the aim of ensuring that products or services are fit for their purpose, and meet specifications. Quality management encompasses quality assurance and quality control.

QUALITY ASSURANCE focuses on the way a product or service is produced. Procedures and standards are devised with the aim of ensuring defects are eliminated (or at least minimised) during the development/production process.

QUALITY CONTROL is concerned with checking and reviewing work that has been done. Quality control therefore has a narrower focus than quality assurance.

1.1 Quality as a concept

Throughout this chapter, the following four themes reappear in relation to quality management.

(a) **Commitment**. A commitment to quality is required from top management down to the most junior-level employees.

(b) **Competence**. Employees must 'know what they are doing'. Training is important.

(c) **Communication**. The need for quality, and the benefits of quality, must be communicated throughout the organisation.

(d) **Continuous improvement**. Quality involves always looking to 'raise the bar'.

1.2 Quality control versus quality assurance

Traditional approaches to quality were focused on **inspection**. Modern approaches to quality focus on the **prevention** of defects through quality standards and processes.

1.2.1 Quality control

In the past, 'quality' usually meant **quality control** – which meant **inspection**. Inspection was usually carried out at three main points.

- Receiving inspection
- Floor or process inspection
- Final inspection or testing

The **problem** with this 'inspection' approach is that it allows for and often entails **built-in waste**.

(a)   The inspection process itself does not add value. If it could be guaranteed that no defective items were produced there would be no need for a separate inspection function.

(b)   The inspection function itself involves requires resources, both people and facilities.

(c)   The production of substandard products is a waste of materials, machine time, human efforts, and overheads.

(d)   The production of defects is not compatible with newer production techniques such as just-in-time – there is no time for inspection.

(e)   Working capital is tied up in inventory which cannot be sold.

(f)   In a service industry, damage will have been done to customer relations before inspection takes place.

Quality control involves establishing standards of quality for a product or service, implementing procedures that are expected to produce products of the required standard in most cases and monitoring output to ensure sub-standard output is rejected or corrected.

1.2.2 Quality assurance

The demand for better quality has led to the acceptance of the view that quality management should aim to **prevent** defective production rather than simply detect it.

Most **modern approaches** to quality have therefore tried to assure quality in the **production process**, (quality assurance) rather than inspecting goods or services after they have been produced.

The term **'quality assurance'** is used where a supplier guarantees the quality of goods or services they supply. Quality assurance programmes usually involve a close relationship between supplier and customer, which may extend to allowing customer representatives to view and/or monitor production procedures.

Quality assurance emphasises the **processes** and **procedures** used to produce a product or service – the logic being that if these are tightly controlled and monitored the resulting product and service will be high quality. As quality has been 'built-in', the need for **inspection** after production should be **eliminated**.

Section summary

Most **modern approaches** to quality try to assure quality in the **production process** (quality assurance) rather than inspecting goods or services after they have been produced.

2   Quality management approaches

Introduction

For any **quality policy** to be successful a suitable system should be developed and the levels of **quality measured** to enable the system's success to be monitored. In recent years a number of approaches to quality management have been developed.

2.1 Quality management

In general terms, any quality management system should involve the activities outlined below.

 Plan. Establish:

(a) **Standards** of quality for a product (eg a software package) or service (eg an IT helpdesk).

(b) **Procedures** or production methods that ought to ensure that these required standards of quality are met.

 Devise suitable instruments and techniques to **monitor** actual quality.

 Compare actual quality with planned quality using quality measures.

 Take **control action** when actual quality falls below standard.

Quality auditing involves a systematic inspection to establish whether quality objectives are being met.

 Review the plan and standards to ensure continuous improvement.

The activities and steps above describe a **general approach** to quality management. In the following sections, we will look at some specific methodologies or approaches associated with quality.

2.2 Measuring quality

A number of methods of measuring quality have been developed, including **SERVQUAL**, **the balanced scorecard** and **value for money audits**.

2.2.1 SERVQUAL

SERVQUAL was developed in the 1980s by *Zeithaml, Parasuraman and Berry* as a method of **measuring quality in service organisations**. It was primarily concerned with measuring the gap between a customer's preconceived **expectations** and the **actual experience** they receive.

When it was first introduced, SERVQUAL **measured ten aspects of service quality** – understanding the customer, tangibles, courtesy, security, credibility, competence, communication, access, reliability and responsiveness. However in the 1990s the model was refined and is now known as **RATER**.

Aspect	Description
Reliability	Employee ability to perform the service dependably and accurately
Assurance	Employee ability to inspire confidence and trust in the customer
Tangibles	The tangible environment, for example facilities, equipment and staff appearance
Empathy	The extent to which a caring, personal service is provided
Responsiveness	Employee willingness to help and respond to customer requests

SERVQUAL and RATER are not without their critics. *Francis Buttle*, for example, noted that the five aspects are not universals and that the model is not based on established economic, statistical or psychological theory.

2.2.2 Balanced scorecard

Deciding how to measure quality is an important aspect of quality management. **Quality measures** should cover **operational**, **financial** and **customer aspects**. One approach, originally developed by *Kaplan and Norton* (1990), is the use of a 'balanced scorecard'.

The balanced scorecard focuses on **four different perspectives**.

Perspective	Question	Explanation
Customer	What do existing and new customers value from us?	Gives rise to targets that matter to customers: cost, quality, delivery, inspection, handling and so on.
Operational: internal operations	What processes must we excel at to achieve our financial and customer objectives?	Aims to improve internal processes and decision making.
Operational: innovation and learning	Can we continue to improve and create future value?	Considers the business's capacity to maintain its competitive position through the acquisition of new skills and the development of new products.
Financial	How do we create value for our shareholders?	Covers traditional measures such as growth, profitability and shareholder value but set through talking to the shareholder or shareholders direct.

The scorecard is 'balanced' in the sense that managers are required to think in terms of **all four perspectives**, to prevent improvements being made in one area at the expense of another.

The types of measure which may be monitored under each of the four perspectives include the following. The list is **not exhaustive** but it will give you an idea of the possible scope of a balanced scorecard approach. The measures selected will vary considerably with the type of organisation and its objectives.

Perspective	Measures
Customer	• New customers acquired • Customer complaints • Customer satisfaction • Telephone response times • Delivery speeds
Operational: internal operations	• Quality control rejects • Productivity levels • Speed of producing management information • Streamlining/systems simplification
Operational: innovation and learning	• Training days for employees • Skills enhancement • Percentage of revenue generated by new products and services • Average time taken to develop new products and services
Financial	• Return on capital employed • Revenue growth • Cash flow • Earnings per share

2.2.3 Value for Money (VFM) audit

Originally associated with the **public sector**, VFM techniques are now increasingly being applied to private sector businesses.

The basic approach involves identifying and **measuring key aspects of performance**, such as: money spent, inputs purchased, outputs and outcomes achieved.

The relationship between **money** spent and inputs purchased provides a measure of **economy**. The relationship between **inputs and outputs** provides a measure of **efficiency**. Comparing **outputs with outcomes** achieved provides a measure of **effectiveness**, eg ten clients serviced (output), nine 'extremely satisfied' clients (outcome).

2.3 Possible problems when attempting to measure quality

Measuring quality involves taking into account many **variables**, which can lead to problems.

Problem	Explanation
Conflicting measures	Some measures in the scorecard such as research funding and cost reduction may naturally conflict. It is often difficult to determine the balance which will achieve the best results.
Selecting measures	Not only do appropriate measures have to be devised but the number of measures used must be agreed. Care must be taken that the impact of the results is not lost in a sea of information.
Expertise	Measurement is only useful if it initiates appropriate action. Non-financial managers may have difficulty with the usual profit measures. With more measures to consider this problem will be compounded.
Interpretation	Even a financially-trained manager may have difficulty in putting the figures into an overall perspective.
Too many measures	The ultimate objective for commercial organisations is to maximise profits or shareholder wealth. Other targets should offer a guide to achieving this objective and not become an end in themselves.

Section summary

Three methods of measuring quality include:

SERVQUAL – this can be used to measure quality in a service organisation. It measures the gap between customer expectations and their actual experience.

Balanced scorecards – these rate quality across four financial and non-financial perspectives.

Value for money audits – these identify and analyse key aspects of performance which are often related to economy, efficiency and effectiveness.

3 Total quality management (TQM)   11/10

Introduction

The development of **total quality management** (TQM) heralded a new era and philosophy of dealing with quality. Rather than 'fire-fighting' quality issues, the approach aims to **continuously improve** quality in all aspects of the organisation. **Customer satisfaction** is a key objective of TQM.

KEY TERM

TOTAL QUALITY MANAGEMENT (**TQM**) is the continuous improvement in quality, productivity and effectiveness obtained by establishing management responsibility for processes as well as output.

The **principles of TQM** evolved through a number of management theorists and 'quality gurus', it is therefore an amalgamation of related but different ideas.

3.1 Deming (TQM)

Deming (1982) is credited with the development of **TQM** in Japan. He took the view that as process variability (the amount of unpredictability in a process) decreases, quality and productivity increase. Quality can therefore be improved by reducing process variability.

His **14 points for quality improvement** stressed the need for statistical control methods, participation, education, openness and improvement.

1   Create a constancy of purpose.
2   Adopt a new quality-conscious philosophy.
3   Cease dependence on inspection.
4   Stop awarding business on price.
5   Continuous improvement in the system of production and service.
6   Institute training on the job.
7   Institute leadership.
8   Drive out fear.
9   Break down barriers between departments.
10   Eliminate slogans and exhortations.
11   Eliminate quotas or work standards.
12   Give employees pride in their job.
13   Institute education and a self-improvement programme.
14   Put everyone to work to accomplish it.

3.2 Ouchi (Theory Z)

Theory Z was devised by *William Ouchi* in the early 1980s. It emphasises the following **elements**.

- Interpersonal skills
- Building relationships
- Group interaction and decision-making
- Participative management
- Free flow of information
- Trust
- Retention of hierarchical rules and control
- Formal procedures for planning and setting objectives

Theory Z combined aspects of **US management practice** (which *Ouchi* referred to as Theory A) and Japanese management practices (Theory J).

3.3 Juran (Fitness for use)

Juran (1988) argued that quality should focus on the role of the customer, both internal and external. This user-based approach to quality emphasises **fitness for use**.

Juran emphasised that quality management should aim to ensure that the way in which work is performed (ie systems and processes) facilitated high quality output. He believed 85% of quality problems were the result of ineffective systems.

3.4 Ishikawa (Quality circles)

Ishikawa (1985) stressed the importance of people and participation to improve quality. He is often credited with the idea of **quality circles**, and their use to achieve participation and overcome resistance to quality initiatives. We cover quality circles later in this chapter.

3.5 Crosby (Quality costs)

Crosby (1979) wrote about quality costs. Like other quality gurus, he argued for **worker participation** and the need to **motivate** individuals to do something about quality.

His **'absolutes of quality management'** were:

1   Quality is conformance to requirements.
2   Prevention is required, not an appraisal of the costs of poor quality.
3   **Zero defects** in production.
4   Organisations should measure the cost or price of 'non-conformance'.
5   There is no such thing as a 'quality problem'.

We look at quality costs in more detail later in this chapter.

3.6 The elements of TQM

TQM has been described as a natural extension of previous approaches to quality management, such as:

(a)   **Inspection**, ie inspecting output in order to detect and rectify errors.

(b)   **Quality control**, ie using statistical techniques to establish quality standards and monitor process performance.

(c)   **Quality assurance**. This extended quality management to areas other than direct operations, and uses concepts such as quality costing, quality planning and problem solving.

The following **table of principles** should help you remember the key elements of TQM.

Principle	Description
Prevention	Organisations should take measures that prevent poor quality occurring.
Right first time	A culture should be developed that encourages workers to get their work right first time.
Eliminate waste	The organisation should seek the most efficient and effective use of all its resources.
Continuous improvement	The Kaizen philosophy should be adopted. Organisations should seek to improve their processes continually.
Everyone's concern	Everyone in the organisation is responsible for improving processes and systems under their control.
Participation	All workers should be encouraged to share their views and the organisation should value them.
Teamwork and empowerment	Workers across departments should form team bonds so that eventually the organisation becomes one.

The mnemonic **PRECEPT** should help you remember them.

Section summary

Total quality management (TQM) is the continuous improvement in quality, productivity and effectiveness obtained by establishing management responsibility for processes as well as output.

The key **principles of TQM** are, prevention, right first time, eliminate waste, continuous improvement, everyone's concern, participation and teamwork/empowerment.

4 Managing quality using TQM

Introduction

The introduction of TQM requires **new ideas** and methods of **managing quality** within an organisation. In particular, relationships between an organisation's departments and its culture are affected.

4.1 Internal customers and internal suppliers

In a TQM approach, **all parts** of the organisation are involved in quality issues, and need to work together. Every person and every activity in the organisation affects the work done by others.

TQM promotes the concept of the **internal customer** and **internal supplier**. The work done by an internal supplier for an internal customer will eventually affect the quality of the product or service to the external customer.

Internal customers are therefore linked in **quality chains**. Internal customer A can satisfy internal customer B who can satisfy internal customer C who in turn can satisfy the external customer.

4.2 Service level agreements

Some organisations formalise the internal supplier-internal customer concept by requiring each internal supplier to make a **service level agreement** with its internal customer. A service level agreement is a statement of the standard of service and supply that will be provided to the internal customer and will cover issues such as the range of services supplied, response times, dependability and so on.

Service level agreements have been criticised, however, for over-formalising the relationship between the internal supplier and internal customer, therefore **creating barriers** to the development of a constructive relationship and **genuine co-operation** between them.

4.3 Quality culture

A purely **procedures-driven** approach is unlikely to secure a culture of quality. Interpersonal factors such as employee empowerment, teamwork and commitment are likely to be important considerations.

Every person within an organisation has an impact on quality and it is the **responsibility of everyone** to **get quality right**.

Individuals should be encouraged not just to comply with performance standards and procedures, but to also be proactive improving their performance and the performance of others. This requires the **empowerment** of employees (covered in the next section). Customers are better served by employees who are in a position to make decisions in meeting their needs without having to obtain authorisation from others.

Teamworking skills are a key competence required of modern management. This recognises that employees are individuals with individual strengths and weaknesses. They need to work together to optimise their personal attributes for the collective benefit of the company.

Commitment is also important in achieving quality. This will require management to apply their skill in persuading and motivating staff into a true commitment to quality. Ultimately it is the employees that will have to deliver the quality.

4.4 Empowerment

KEY POINT

Empowerment recognises that employees are likely to know how best to perform their role and to improve quality. It contrasts with traditional '**top down management**' which assumes that management is best qualified to make decisions.

Empowerment includes two key aspects.

(a)   Allowing workers to have the **freedom to decide how to do** the necessary work, using the skills they possess and acquiring new skills as necessary to be an effective team member.

(b)   Making workers **responsible** for achieving production targets and for quality control.

Empowerment may be more appropriate in **service organisations** where formal procedures might hamper the flexibility of employees responding quickly to a customer's needs.

The concept of **empowerment** must be **embraced by management and staff at all levels** to be effective.

4.5 Continuous improvement or Kaizen

Quality management is not a one-off process but is the **continuous** examination and improvement of processes. This continuous improvement is sometimes referred to as '*Kaizen*'. Some authors explain Japan's competitive success in the world market place as the result of the implementation of the *Kaizen* concept.

Kaizen looks for uninterrupted **incremental change**. It can be implemented by improving every aspect of a business process in a step-by-step approach, while gradually developing employee skills through training, education and increased involvement.

The **principles** of **continuous improvement/Kaizen** are:

(a)   People are the most important organisational asset.
(b)   Processes should evolve by **gradual improvement** rather than radical change.
(c)   Improvement should be based on **statistical / quantitative evaluation** of process performance.
(d)   Resources, measurements, rewards, and incentives all need to be **aligned**.
(e)   Continuous improvement enables **changing customer needs** to be taken into account.
(f)   Continuous improvement enables **new technologies** to be introduced.

Tools used in the Kaizen process include:

(a)   **The five why process.** This encourages the employee to ask 'Why' to issues and questions until the solution or reason is discovered. This process was developed by Toyota.

(b)   **Fishbone diagrams.** These are cause and effect diagrams used to analyse all causes (or inputs) that result in a single effect (or output). A map in the form of a Fishbone is created and the route of continuous improvement is drawn. Potential problems that may be encountered will 'splinter' off from the path.

(c)   **Plan-do-check-act (PDCA).** The use of a plan-do-check-act cycle to encourage continuous improvement.

4.6 Quality costs

The **cost of quality** may be looked at in a number of different ways.

Some argue that producing higher quality output increases costs, as more expensive resources are likely to be required to achieve a higher standard.

Others argue that poor quality output will lead to customer dissatisfaction, which generates costs associated with complaint resolution and loss of revenue as customers move to competitors.

There are **four types of quality cost** – prevention, appraisal/inspection, internal and external failure.

Type of cost	Definition	Examples
Prevention cost	Costs incurred prior to making the product or delivering the service – to prevent substandard quality products or services being delivered.	The cost of building quality into the product design or service design. The cost of training staff in quality improvement and error prevention. The cost of prevention devices (eg fail-safe features).
Appraisal cost or inspection cost	This is a cost incurred after a product has been made or service delivered, to ensure that the output or service performance meets the required quality standard or service performance.	The cost of inspecting finished goods or services, and other checking devices such as supplier vetting. Customer or client feedback forms (although these may be a way of keeping service staff 'on their toes').
Internal failure cost	This is a cost arising from inadequate quality, where the problem is identified before the transfer of the item or service from the organisation to the customer or client.	Cost of materials scrapped due to inefficiencies in stockholding procedures. Cost of materials and components lost during production or service delivery. Cost of output rejected during the inspection process. Cost of re-working faulty output. Cost of reviewing product and service specifications after failures or customer dissatisfaction. Losses due to selling faulty output cheaply. Not charging for a service so as to pacify dissatisfied and angry customers or clients.
External failure cost	This is a cost arising from inadequate quality, where the problem is identified after the transfer of the item or service from the organisation to the customer.	Cost of product liability claims from customers or clients. Cost of repairing products returned by customers, including those forming part of service. Cost of replacing sub-standard products including those included with a service. Delivery costs of returned units or items. Cost of the customer services section and its operations. Loss of customer goodwill and loss of future sales.

4.6.1 Traditional v TQM approaches to quality costs

The **traditional approach to quality management** is that there is an optimal level of quality effort, that minimises total quality costs, and that spending more in an attempt to improve quality beyond this point is not cost-effective. Diminishing returns set in beyond the optimal quality level.

The **TQM philosophy** is different.

(a) **Failure and poor quality are unacceptable**. The inevitability of errors is not something that an organisation should accept. The target should be zero defects.

(b) Quality costs are difficult to measure, and **failure costs** in particular are often **seriously under-estimated**. The real costs of failure include not just the cost of scrapped items and re-working faulty items or placating an unhappy customer or client. There is also all the management time spent sorting out problems and the loss of confidence between different parts of the organisation whenever faults occur.

(c) A TQM approach does not accept that the prevention costs of achieving **zero defects** becomes unacceptably high. If everyone in the organisation is involved in improving quality, the cost of continuous improvement need not be high.

(d) If an organisation accepts an **optimal quality level** that it believes will minimise total quality costs, there will be no further challenge to management to improve quality further.

The **TQM quality cost model** is based on the view:

(a) **Prevention costs and appraisal costs** are subject to management influence or control. It is better to spend money on prevention, before failures occur, than on inspection.

(b) **Internal failure costs and external failure costs** can be reduced through additional effort on prevention.

In other words, higher spending on prevention will eventually lead to lower total quality costs. The emphasis should be on **getting things right first time** and **designing quality** into the product or service.

4.7 Common reasons for failure of TQM initiatives

Participation is important in TQM, especially in the process of continuous improvement, where workforce views are valued. Management should encourage everybody to contribute.

Common reasons for failure in TQM programmes include:

(a) **Lack of management buy-in**. Managers continue to monitor, control and punish rather than being facilitators of open communication and worker involvement.

(b) **Tail-off**. After the initial enthusiasm, interest and support fades.

(c) **Deflection**. Other initiatives or problems take over from TQM.

(d) **Rejection**. TQM is not compatible with managers who feel their authority is threatened and make decisions with the aim of maintaining their position.

(e) General **cynicism** about quality and its role in fulfilling customer needs.

Question 6.1	TQM and consistency

Learning outcome C2(ii)

A key word in the TQM philosophy is **consistency**.

Briefly explain what in TQM needs to be consistent, and why consistency is important. **(4 marks)**

Section summary

In a TQM approach, **all parts** of the organisation are involved in quality issues, and need to work together. Every person and every activity in the organisation affects the work done by others.

Some organisations formalise the internal supplier-internal customer concept by requiring each internal supplier to make a **service level agreement** with its internal customer.

Kaizen is the **continuous** examination and improvement of existing processes.

There are four types of **quality costs – prevention**, **appraisal/inspection**, **internal failure** and **external failure**.

5 Processes of continuous improvement

Introduction

The concept of **Kaizen** and **continuous improvement** has led to the development of new management strategies and processes to handle it. **Multinational organisations**, often those which are American or Japanese, have been at the forefront of this development.

5.1 Quality circles

KEY TERM

A QUALITY CIRCLE is a team of workers from within the organisation which meets at intervals to discuss issues relating to the quality of the product or service produced.

A typical quality circle comprises employees from **many levels** of the organisation who meet regularly. The frequency of meetings varies across organisations – every three months would normally be sufficient.

Suggestions are encouraged regarding how the **product** or **service** produced could be made better, and how **processes** and **working practices** could be improved. Members are encouraged to analyse issues in a logical way.

Wider issues may also be discussed, as it is recognised that the complete working environment will affect quality levels. In some organisations this has led to quality circles having input on issues such as health and safety, employee benefits and bonuses, and training and education programmes.

5.1.1 Developing quality circles

An organisation can encourage the use of quality circles by:

- **Rewarding the circle** for suggestions that are implemented (eg a share of any savings made).

- **Providing a budget and support** to run the quality circle in terms of room provision, refreshments, staff to take minutes etc.

- **Ensuring management are supportive** and prepared to act on useful suggestions from the circle.

- **Providing an explanation** as to why **suggestions not implemented** were rejected.

- **Management asking the circle** for **suggestions** and **comments** on specific issues and problems facing the company, without anticipating the outcomes.

5.1.2 Benefits of quality circles

The **benefits of quality circles** include:

(a)   Employee involvement improves morale.
(b)   Practical improvements/solutions are likely as workers know the processes involved.
(c)   Organisation unity is fostered as the circle includes all levels.
(d)   Suggestions can result in valuable savings.
(e)   A 'culture' of quality is fostered.

5.1.3 Drawbacks of quality circles

Possible **drawbacks** of quality circles include:

(a)   Employee 'power' is hard to control.
(b)   The scope of influence can become very wide.
(c)   Rejected suggestions may cause resentment.
(d)   Business practicalities (eg cost) may not be fully understood.

The concept of quality circles has expanded to now include groups drawn from **separate organisations** but with a common interest.

5.2 The 5Ss

Often associated with **lean production** (covered later in this chapter), the overriding idea behind the 5Ss is that there is 'a place for everything and everything goes in its place'. Discipline, simplicity, pride, standardisation and repeatability are emphasised in the 5Ss as being critical to efficiency.

The 5Ss			Comment/meaning
Seiri	or	Structurise	Segregate or discard. Introduce order where possible.
Selton	or	Systemise	Arrange and identify for ease of use. Approach tasks systematically.
Seiso	or	Sanitise	Clean daily. Be tidy, avoid clutter.
Seiketsu	or	Standardise	Revisit each 'S' frequently. Be consistent in your approach.
Shitsuke	or	Self-discipline	Sustain via motivation. Do the above daily.

5.3 Six Sigma

KEY TERM

SIX SIGMA is a process that is designed to assist organisations to focus on developing and delivering near-perfect products and services.

The expression is derived from the discipline of statistics. Sigma is a statistical measure of variation in output. A score of six times the Sigma within a specification means 99.999% of the manufactured items are within the specification (3.4 defects per million opportunities). A Three Sigma level of quality implies a 93.32% specification compliance (67,000 defects per million).

5.3.1 Elimination of defects

Six Sigma ensures the progressive **elimination of defects** by:

•   Identifying the root causes of error
•   Confirming the critical root causes
•   Implementing corrective action

By minimising defects, **customer satisfaction** should improve and this should improve **profitability**. The thinking might be summarised as follows.

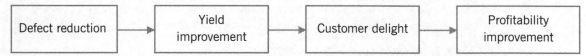

A key advantage of Six Sigma is that it can be implemented alongside other initiatives such as TQM and ISO 9000. However, where Six Sigma is different is that it is **customer focused**, rather than operations orientated. It looks at strategically critical outcomes that affect customer satisfaction.

The method was first devised by **Motorola** in the USA in 1985 to help manufacture a virtually defect free pager. It has been successfully implemented by recognised corporations such as Polaroid, Kodak, and IBM. However, it was General Electric that propelled it to current prominence and popularity.

5.3.2 Example of Six Sigma in practice

General Electric (GE) introduced Six Sigma and there are **three elements** to its approach.

(a)   **Delighting customers**

   (i)   The customer sets the quality standard, rather than some manager within the company.

   (ii)   A focus on performance, reliability, price, delivery, service and transaction processing.

(b)   **Outside-in thinking**

   (i)   The company must be seen form the customer's perspective.

   (ii)   There is a need to understand what the customer is seeing and feeling as regard the company's processes.

   (iii)   Customer knowledge is used to improve company processes and add value.

(c)   **Leadership commitment**

   (i)   GE recognises that people are key to creating quality and generating results.

   (ii)   There is a commitment to providing opportunities for employees to develop themselves in the services may provide to customers.

   (iii)   There is a focus on ensuring employee training needs are satisfied.

CASE STUDY

Tiffinwallah system of Mumbai

The Tiffinwalla system in Mumbai, India, was recently singled out by Forbes Magazine as an outstanding example and awarded a Six Sigma grading.

Each day, 175,000 tiffins (lunchboxes) are delivered to offices and schools throughout Mumbai and later returned home, by approximately 5,000 people called tiffinwallahs. Each tiffin holds a variety of dishes of food. Each tiffin is collected by a tiffinwallah and taken to one of Mumbai's suburban railway stations, where they are sorted. They are collected at the destination station and taken to the building.

There is a fairly simple method of coding which manages a very low failure rate. Each tiffinwallah does not have to deal with too many tiffin boxes. The tiffinwallas make only one error in 16 million transactions. Statistically this represents 99.999% of correctness, thereby achieving Six Sigma.

Section summary

A **quality circle** is a team of workers from within the organisation which meets at intervals to discuss issues relating to the quality of the product or service produced.

The **5Ss** is a Japanese approach to quality that focuses on the five aspects of structurise, systemise, sanitise, standardise and self-discipline.

Six Sigma is a process that is designed to assist organisations to focus on developing and delivering **near-perfect** products and services.

6   Lean production   11/10

Introduction

Lean production is a manufacturing methodology developed originally for Toyota. It is also known as the Toyota Production System. Its goal is 'to get the right things to the right place at the right time, the first time, while **minimising waste** and being open to change'.

KEY TERM

LEAN PRODUCTION (sometimes referred to as lean manufacturing or lean process improvement) is a philosophy of production that aims to minimise the amount of resources (including time) used in all activities. It involves identifying and eliminating all non-value-adding activities.

Lean production or lean process improvement involves the **systematic elimination of waste**, such as:

- **Overproduction** and early production
- **Waiting** – time delays, idle time, any time during which value is not added to the product
- **Transportation** – multiple handling, delay in materials handling, unnecessary handling
- **Inventory** – holding or purchasing unnecessary raw materials, work in process and finished goods
- **Motion** – actions of people or equipment that do not add value to the product
- **Over-processing** – unnecessary steps or work elements/procedures (non added value work)
- **Defective units** – production of a part that is scrapped or requires rework

Ohno (an engineer) is generally credited with developing the principles of lean production. He argued that it **eliminated waste** and led to **improved product flow** and **improved quality**.

Lean production focuses on reducing system response time so that the **production system is capable of rapid change to meet market demands**.

6.1 Characteristics of lean production

The **characteristics of lean production** are:

- Integrated, single piece continuous workflow.
- Integration of the whole value chain through partnerships with suppliers and distributors.
- Just-in-Time processing.
- Short order-to-ship cycle times synchronised with small batch production.
- Production based on orders rather than forecasts.
- Minimal inventories at each stage of the production process.
- Quick changeovers of machines and equipment.
- Production layout based on work flow.
- Active involvement by workers in problem solving to improve quality and eliminate waste.
- Defect prevention (rather than inspection and rework) by building quality into the process.
- Team-based work with multi-skilled staff empowered to make decisions.

6.2 Applications of lean techniques

During the 1980s **lean production methods** were adopted by many manufacturing plants in the US and Europe, with varying degrees of success.

Recent years have seen a renewed interest in lean techniques, particularly since the reduction of inventory. Dell Computers and Boeing Aircraft have embraced the philosophy of lean production with great success.

Lean techniques are applicable not only in manufacturing, but **also in a service environment**. Every system contains waste (ie something that does not provide value to the customer).

Lean supply chains occur when lean techniques are applied in firms across the chain. This requires a high degree of trust and coordination. Integrated information systems would be required to ensure each organisation in the chain is aware of the activities of other chain members.

6.3 Benefits of lean production

Supporters of lean production believe it enables a company to **deliver** on demand, **minimise** inventory, **maximise** the use of multi-skilled employees, **flatten** the management structure and **focus** resources where they are most effective.

Other benefits include:

- Waste reduction (up to 80%)
- Production cost reduction (50%)
- Manufacturing cycle times decreased (50%)
- Labour reduction (50%) while maintaining or increasing throughput
- Inventory reduction (80%) while increasing customer service levels
- Capacity increase in current facilities (50%)
- Higher quality
- Higher profits
- Higher system flexibility in reacting to changes in requirements improved
- More strategic focus
- Improved cash flow through increasing shipping and billing frequencies

6.4 Criticisms of lean principles

In many situations, organisations supposedly using lean principles have not experienced the improvements in productivity and profitability expected. It is difficult to know whether this is due to shortcomings in the lean philosophy or whether the techniques involved are being interpreted and applied correctly.

For example, the **5Ss** concept should be used with the aim of creating a workplace with **real organisation** and **order** which creates pride by employees in their work, improves safety and results in better quality. However, in some organisations 5S has become a cleaning and housekeeping exercise only.

Lean techniques should be seen and treated as outward signs of a more **fundamental approach** to **operations** and **quality**. Real improvements require a change in thinking and in culture – which are difficult to achieve.

Many companies use lean manufacturing and Six Sigma techniques to reduce costs, rather than a fundamental commitment to eliminating waste and adding value.

6.5 World class manufacturing

In a **manufacturing environment** a commitment to quality (and to the customer) may be referred to as 'world class manufacturing'. This approach involves a **focus on customer requirements** and then ensuring products meet these requirements.

As customer requirements often change, **flexibility** in manufacturing operations is a key feature of world-class manufacturing.

Three factors Japanese manufacturing organisations focussed on that contributed to world class manufacturing are:

- Integrated operations processes enabling smooth production flow

- Team leaders that involved employees' (team members) in quality issues and developed both their own and employees problem-solving skills

- Tightly integrated value chains with close, productive relationships between supply chain partners

6.6 Flexible manufacturing

Manufacturing operations designed to emphasise flexibility are sometimes referred to as '**flexible manufacturing**'.

Flexible manufacturing describes the situation where '**economies of scope**' make it economical to produce **small batches of a relatively wide range of products** using the same machines or production facilities.

This is the opposite of traditional large-scale assembly lines with their emphasis on **economies of scale**.

Exam alert

Exam questions may require you to associate flexible operations with demand management, in particular chase demand strategies, covered in the next chapter.

TQM, Kaizen, lean production and the balanced scorecard all feature in papers P2 and E3.

Section summary

The goal of **lean production** is 'to get the right things to the right place at the right time, the first time, while **minimising waste** and being open to change'.

In a **manufacturing environment** a commitment to quality (and to the customer) may be referred to as 'world class manufacturing'.

---

7 International Organisation for Standardisation 05/11

Introduction

A number of organisations produce quality standards. The most widely used are those published by the **International Organisation for Standardisation (ISO)**.

The ISO 9000 quality standards have been adopted by many organisations world-wide.

ISO issue standards are applicable to **many types of organisation** and they are updated periodically. The ISO 9000:2000 series of standards consists of four primary standards: ISO 9000, ISO 9001, ISO 9004, and ISO 19011.

(a)   **ISO 9001:2000** contains ISO's current quality management system requirements. This is the standard you need to use if you wish to become certified (registered).

(b)   **ISO 9000:2000 and ISO 9004:2000** contain ISO's quality management system guidelines. These standards explain ISO's approach to quality management presenting definitions and a set of guidelines for improving performance, but they are not intended to be used for certification purposes.

(c)   **ISO 19011** covers quality auditing standards.

(d)   **ISO 14001** relates to environmental management systems. It specifies a process for controlling and improving an organisation's environmental performance. Issues covered include:

   (i)   Use and source of raw materials
   (ii)   Waste
   (iii)   Noise
   (iv)   Energy use
   (v)   Emissions

7.1 ISO certified/registered or ISO compliant?

KEY POINTS

When a company claims that they are **ISO 9000 certified** or **registered**, they mean that **an independent registrar** has audited their processes and certified that they meet the ISO requirements.

When an organisation says that they are **ISO 9000 compliant**, they mean that they have **met ISO's quality system requirements**, but have **not been formally certified** by an independent registrar. In effect, they are **self-certified**.

Of course, official certification carries more weight in the market place.

The ISO 9000 standards are **process standards**, not product standards. Organisations are granted certified or compliant status on the basis that their **processes** rather than their products and services meet ISO 9000 requirements. The logic is that high quality processes ensure high quality output.

7.2 Criticisms of quality accreditation

Many writers and managers have criticised **formal quality schemes**. These criticisms tend to emphasise the following points.

(a)   Documentation is **expensive** (in terms of time) to produce.

(b)   Rigid policies and procedures encourage **management by manual**, **discourage innovation** and initiative.

(c)   The schemes **encourage bureaucracy**.

(d)   The formal methods may not be consistent with ways of working in small and medium-sized organisations.

7.3 The European Quality Foundation model

There are now many smaller self-assessment models for business/organisation improvement. In Europe, one of the most popular is the **European Quality Foundation** model.

This provides a **structured methodology for organisations** to measure their own performance in areas that are critical to businesses.

The model provides a basis for measurement of '**enablers**' (leadership, policies, strategies, processes and resources) and '**results**' in relation to customers, employees, society and performance indicators.

Criticisms of this and similar schemes include their **expense** (in terms of time) and the fact that scoring is largely **subjective**.

Section summary

ISO certified organisations have had their **processes and procedures checked and verified** by an independent auditor.

ISO compliant organisations **self-certify that they meet the ISO requirements**, however such claims have not been verified.

8 Total productive maintenance (TPM)

Introduction

Quality issues do not just affect production processes. They filter into every part of the organisation including the maintenance of production equipment. **Total productive maintenance** or **TPM** originated in Japan. It is defined as 'the productive maintenance carried out by all employees through small group activities'.

8.1 Five goals of TPM

The goals of TPM are:

(a) **Improve equipment effectiveness**. The goal should be to examine how the facilities of an operation are contributing to its effectiveness. Loss of effectiveness could be caused by defects, down-times and loss of operating speed.

(b) **Achieve autonomous maintenance**. The employees who use an item of equipment should be allowed to take on some of the responsibility for its maintenance. Specialist maintenance staff should be encouraged to take on the responsibility for improving maintenance performance.

(c) **Plan maintenance**. Maintenance should be planned, and the frequency and level of preventive maintenance and standards for condition-based maintenance should be specified.

(d) **Train all staff in maintenance skills**.

(e) **Achieve early equipment management**. This goal is linked to maintenance prevention, by which the causes of failure and the ease of maintenance of an item of equipment are considered at the design, manufacture, commissioning and installation stages, ie before the equipment is brought into operation.

8.2 Benefits of TPM

Benefits of TPM include:

- **Reduced** instances of **breakdowns**
- **Production consistency** and **uniform output**
- **Reduction** in **waste** and **cost of quality**
- **Improved accuracy** of **production schedules**
- Facilitation of an **on-time delivery**

One **possible approach** is shown in the steps below.

Step 1

Discover what the nature of the failure has been, its possible consequences, and the reasons why it has happened. Finding out the reason for a failure is not, at this stage, an in-depth investigation. Being aware of the reason for the failure can, however, help with making a decision about what the recovery procedure should be.

Step 2

Act by:

(I)   Telling people involved what you propose to do about the failure, for example by keeping customers informed

(ii) Containing the failure in order to stop the consequences from spreading

(iii) Following up to make sure that the containing action has been successful

Step 3

Learn. Use the failure as a learning opportunity, to find out in some depth why the failure occurred and 'engineering out' the cause to prevent it from happening again.

Step 4

Plan. Operations managers should incorporate the lessons learned from past failures to plan how they would deal with similar failures in the future. This involves identifying what failures might occur and their reasons and devising formal procedures to be followed if and when it **occurs.**

8.3 Business continuity

Business continuity is a term used to describe measures to help an operation to **prevent or recover from failures**, and to continue operating in the event of a **disaster**. A disaster is a critical malfunction that stops normal operations (eg a key supplier going out of business, a major computer system failure, a bomb blast at a key location and so on).

One approach to **business continuity** planning is to:

(a)   **Identify and assess the risks** of various disasters happening.

(b)   **Identify core business processes**, and rank them in order of priority. Make sure that employees understand these priorities.

(c)   **Quantify recovery times**.

(d)   **Determine what resources will be needed** to carry out the recovery, and make sure that the resources will be available if and when required.

(e)   **Communicate** with everyone in the organisation and others involved in the recovery process to ensure they know what they will be required to do in the event of a disaster.

> **Section summary**
>
> **Total productive maintenance** is a policy that ensures quality is reflected in the maintenance of production equipment.

9 The TQMEX model

> **Introduction**
>
> As we explained earlier, **TQM focuses on the needs of customers**. In order to fully understand TQM we need to understand how all elements of an organisation work towards the ultimate goal – customer satisfaction (or if possible, customer delight).

Ho (1999) devised his TQMEX model to indicate the relationship between quality management and other aspects of operations management. The model demonstrates how contemporary **approaches** to quality may be **integrated** to achieve a **philosophy of quality** throughout the organisation.

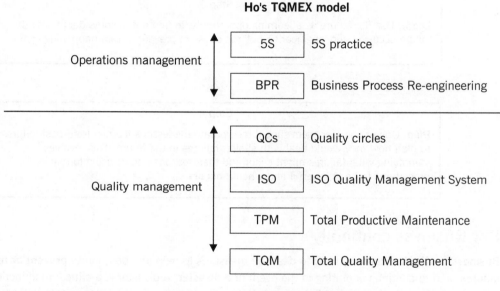

Ho's TQMEX model

The one tool mentioned in Ho's model that we haven't covered in this book is Business Process Re-engineering (BPR).

9.1 Business Process Re-engineering (BPR)   05/10

The changing of business processes is sometimes referred to as Business Process Re-engineering (BPR).

KEY TERM

BUSINESS PROCESS RE-ENGINEERING is the fundamental rethinking and radical redesign of business processes to achieve dramatic improvements in critical contemporary measures of performance, such as cost, quality, service and speed. *Hammer and Champy* (2001).

As the definition states, BPR involves **fundamental** changes in the way an organisation operates. Other key words from the definition are '**radical**', '**dramatic**' and '**process**'.

(a) **Fundamental** and **radical** indicate that BPR assumes nothing: it starts by asking basic questions such as 'why do we do what we do', without making any assumptions.

(b) **Dramatic** means that BPR should achieve 'quantum leaps in performance', not just marginal, incremental improvements.

(c)   A **process** is a collection of activities that takes one or more kinds of input and creates an output. For example, order fulfilment is a process that takes an order as its input and results in the delivery of the ordered goods.

9.1.1 Four themes of BPR

Hammer and Champy identify four themes of BPR.

(a)   **Process reorientation**. There should be a focus on resources, tasks and constraints.
(b)   **Creative use of IT** should be explored.
(c)   **Ambition**. Don't be restricted by current ways of working. Think widely and ambitiously.
(d)   Challenge and **break rules**. Think radically. Old rules may not apply to new processes.

9.1.2 Five phases of BPR

BPR involves five phases.

- Planning
- Internal learning
- External learning
- Redesign
- Implementation

CASE STUDY

Example of BPR

A company employs 25 staff to perform the standard accounting task of matching goods received notes with orders and then with invoices. A process review established that 50% of employee time was spent trying to match the 20% of document sets that do not agree.

One way of improving the situation would be to computerise the existing process to facilitate matching. This would help, but BPR would go further.

A BPR approach may question why **any** incorrect orders are accepted. To enable incorrect orders to be identified before being accepted, all orders could first be entered in to a computerised database. When goods arrive, they either agree to goods that have been ordered (as recorded in the database) or they don't.

Goods that agree to an order are accepted and paid for. Goods that are not agreed are *sent back* to the supplier. Time is not wasted trying to sort out unmatched documents.

Gains would include staff time saved, quicker payment for suppliers, lower stocks, and lower investment in working capital.

9.1.3 Limitations of BPR

Some BPR projects have **failed to bring the benefits expected**. To succeed, a BPR initiative requires sustained management **commitment** and leadership, **realistic scope** and expectations, and a **willingness to change**.

BPR has become associated with narrow targets such as **reductions in staff numbers** and other **cost-cutting** measures. Some companies, attracted by the latest high-tech gadgetry, believed they could enhance their performance solely by re-deploying office automation systems (and laying off workers) rather than through the much harder task of significant organisational process redesign, which may involve neither IT investment nor redundancies, just the better use of people.

Exam alert

BPR could be examined together with process mapping – redesigning a process requires an understanding of the process that may best be obtained from a process map.

Section summary

Ho's **TQMEX model** indicates the relationship between quality management and other aspects of operations management.

10 Service quality

Introduction

Many of the models and techniques that we have already studied can be applied to the **service industry**. We have already seen how **SERVQUAL** can be used to measure quality in service organisations by reference to customer expectations. Therefore managing these expectations and the actual service provided are key to service quality.

KEY TERM

SERVICE QUALITY is the totality of features and characteristics of that service which bears on its ability to meet stated or implied needs.

10.1 Dimensions of service quality

Service quality has a number of dimensions.

(a)   **Technical quality** of the service encounter (ie what is received by the customer). Was the meal edible? Was the train on time? Were the shelves fully stocked? Problems of this sort must be addressed by improving the processes of production and delivery.

(b)   **Functional quality** of the service encounter (ie how the service is provided). This relates to the psychological interaction between the buyer and seller and is typically perceived in a very subjective way.

     (i)   **Relationships between employees**. For example, do these relationships appear to be professional? Do they chat to each other whilst serving the customer? Does each appear to know their role in the team and the function of their colleagues?

     (ii)   **Appearance and personality of service personnel**. For instance, do they seem interested in the customer and the customer's needs? Are they smartly presented? Do they convey a positive image?

     (iii)   **Service-mindedness of the personnel**. For example, do they appear to understand and identify with the needs of the customer? Do they convey competence? Do they show willingness to help?

     (iv)   **Accessibility of the service to the customer**. Do the service personnel explain the service in language which the customer can understand?

     (v)   **Approachability of service personnel**. For instance, do the service personnel appear alert, interested or welcoming? Or are they day-dreaming, yawning or looking at their watches?

10.2 Role of customer

For many service operations, the **customer** represents both the input and the output of a transformation process eg a patient visiting a dentist.

10.3 Satisfaction as a measure

Service quality therefore focuses on the extent of success achieved in creating a **transformed customer**. This can be answered in terms of customer satisfaction. *Johnston and Clark* (2001) state that customer satisfaction levels may be 'represented on a continuum from (extreme) delight to (extreme) dissatisfaction'.

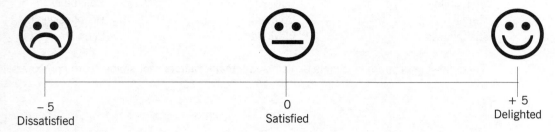

10.4 Customer expectations

Going back to the beginning of the transformation process the **input is a customer with certain expectations**. The organisation delivers a service that is intended to meet those customer expectations. This overall process is depicted as follows.

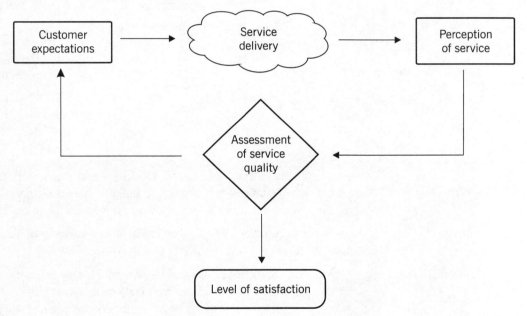

10.4.1 Influencing customer expectations

A prerequisite to being able to manage customers' expectations or designing services to meet expectations is to accurately identify and understand them.

A customer's preconceived expectations is likely to influence a **customer's assessment of service quality** eg a guest at an expensive hotel is likely to expect a high level of attentiveness from the hotel staff.

Various authors have tried to identify **generic factors** that determine a customer's assessment of service quality. The following is a useful list of 18 **service quality factors**. (*Johnston and Clark*, 2001)

Access	Comfort	Friendliness
Aesthetics	Commitment	Functionality
Attentiveness	Communication	Integrity
Availability	Competence	Reliability
Care	Courtesy	Responsiveness
Cleanliness	Flexibility	Security

The following diagram and table explain some **major factors** that shape customer expectations.

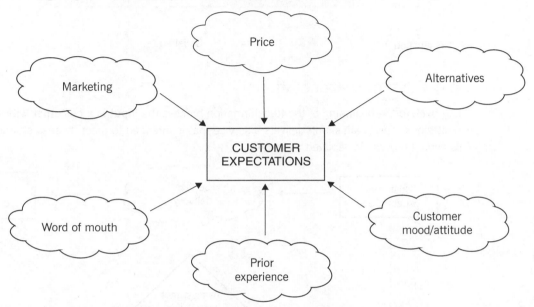

Factor	Example
Marketing	Claims may be difficult to deliver eg an optician advertises that no appointments are required, but a client has to actually wait 50 minutes for an eye test.
Price	Customer expectations usually increase as price increases eg if a hair salon charges high prices, clients expect a good cut and styling.
Alternatives	A good past experience at one service provider is likely to set the standard next time for an alternative service provider eg a tasty meal at one burger chain is likely to engender expectations of a similar dining experience when visiting another outlet.
Word of mouth	Often this is the most influential source for setting up customer expectations.
Previous experience	This helps the customer develop a clearer view of what to expect. This adds to the challenge faced by the service provider but on the other hand also helps to moderate the consumers' expectations eg experience of travelling with a certain rail service may inject a certain sense of reality into what a passenger can expect.
Customer's mood and attitude	It is inevitable that a customer's mood and attitude is likely to influence their expectations eg a guest at a restaurant who has received some good news (got a promotion or passed an exam etc) is more likely to be tolerant of slow service.

There are various ways in which service quality factors may be **classified**.

Classifications	Comment
Hygiene factors	These are very much base line factors. If not present will tend to dissatisfy a customer, eg a hotel guest will expect proper security but it is unlikely to delight.
Enhancing factors	These may partially delight but will not be a source of dissatisfaction if absent eg a hotel guest is likely to really appreciate friendly staff but might not be dissatisfied if they are not all that cheerful.
Critical factors	These have the potential to delight as well as dissatisfy eg a hotel guest will expect staff responsiveness.
Neutral factors	These usually have little impact on satisfaction eg a hotel guest may be delighted if a hotel is aesthetically pleasing with nice wallpaper, smart fittings etc, but may well not miss them if not present.

Question 6.2	Service quality factors

Learning outcome C2(viii)

You have recently been appointed to manage an underground rail system for a major international city.

Required

Classify the 18 service quality factors (from the previous section) in terms of the four key categories; **Hygiene factors**; **Critical factors**; **Neutral factors** and **Enhancing factors**.   **(8 marks)**

10.5 Perception of service

In product operations there is a physical output which is relatively easy to measure in terms of quality. With service operations, the expression 'perception is reality' applies. Differences arise between the **service delivered** and the **customers' perception of quality** because people filter what they see and experience.

Exam alert

The concepts of quality, quality assurance and quality management are now well-established in the business world. Quality proved highly popular as a topic for examination questions in the past, and can be expected to feature prominently in the future.

Section summary

Service quality is the totality of features and characteristics of that service which bears on its ability to meet stated or implied needs.

Chapter Roundup

✓   Most **modern approaches** to quality try to assure quality in the **production process** (quality assurance) rather than inspecting goods or services after they have been produced.

✓   **Three methods of measuring quality** include:

  •   **SERVQUAL** – this can be used to measure quality in a service organisation. It measures the gap between customer expectations and their actual experience.

  •   **Balanced scorecards** – these rate quality across four financial and non-financial perspectives.

  •   **Value for money audits** – these identify and analyse key aspects of performance which are often related to economy, efficiency and effectiveness.

✓   **Total quality management** (TQM) is the continuous improvement in quality, productivity and effectiveness obtained by establishing management responsibility for processes as well as output.

✓   The key **principles of TQM** are, prevention, right first time, eliminate waste, continuous improvement, everyone's concern, participation and teamwork/empowerment.

✓   In a TQM approach, **all parts** of the organisation are involved in quality issues, and need to work together. Every person and every activity in the organisation affects the work done by others.

✓   Some organisations formalise the internal supplier-internal customer concept by requiring each internal supplier to make a **service level agreement** with its internal customer.

✓   Kaizen is the **continuous** examination and improvement of existing processes.

✓   There are four types of **quality costs – prevention**, **appraisal/inspection**, **internal failure** and **external failure**.

✓   A **quality circle** is a team of workers from within the organisation which meets at intervals to discuss issues relating to the quality of the product or service produced.

✓   The **5Ss** is a Japanese approach to quality that focuses on the five aspects of structurise, systemise, sanitise, standardise and self-discipline.

✓   **Six Sigma** is a process that is designed to assist organisations to focus on developing and delivering **near-perfect** products and services.

✓   The goal of **lean production** is 'to get the right things to the right place at the right time, the first time, while **minimising waste** and being open to change'.

✓   In a **manufacturing environment** a commitment to quality (and to the customer) may be referred to as '**world class manufacturing**'.

✓   **ISO certified** organisations have had their **procedures and procedures checked and verified** by an independent auditor.

✓   **ISO compliant** organisations **self-certify that they meet the ISO requirements**, however such claims have not been verified.

✓   **Total productive maintenance** is a policy that ensures quality is reflected in the maintenance of production equipment.

✓   *Ho's* **TQMEX model** indicates the relationship between quality management and other aspects of operations management.

✓   **Service quality** is the totality of features and characteristics of that service which bears on its ability to meet stated or implied needs.

Quick Quiz

1 List five principles of TQM.

1 ....

2 ....

3 ....

4 ....

5 ....

2 Which of the following is not one of the 5Ss?

A Structurise
B Systemise
C Simplify
D Self-discipline

3 An ISO 9000 compliant organisation:

A Has its processes independently checked and verified as meeting the ISO requirements
B Has self-certified the fact that its processes meet the ISO requirements
C Aims to meet the ISO requirements
D Meets ISO 9000 requirements at least 90% of the time.

4 Which of the following is not a critical service quality factor?

A Responsiveness
B Integrity
C Communication
D Competence

5 Who devised the TQMEX model?

A Kaplan and Norton
B Deming
C Ouchi
D Ho

Answers to Quick Quiz

1   Any five from the following: prevention, right first time, eliminate waste, continuous improvement, everybody's concern, participation and teamwork.

2   C   The other elements are sanitise and standardise.

3   B   An ISO compliant organisation self-certifies the fact that its processes meet the ISO requirements. ISO certified or registered organisations have their claims independently verified.

4   B   Integrity is a hygiene factor.

5   D   *Ho* devised the TQMEX model.

Answers to Questions

6.1 TQM and consistency

When producing a product or service, consistency means using the same standard of resources and employing the same methods and procedures (processes). Consistency in processes should result in consistently high quality output, and a consistently satisfied customer.

6.2 Service quality factors

Hygiene factors	Critical factors	Neutral factors	Enhancing factors
Access	Responsiveness	Comfort	Attentiveness
Availability	Communication	Aesthetics	Care
Functionality	Competence		Cleanliness
Integrity			Commitment
Reliability			Friendliness
Security			Courtesy
			Flexibility

Now try this question from the Exam Question Bank	Number	Level	Marks	Time
	6	Examination	25	45 mins

MANAGING CAPACITY AND INVENTORY

In this final chapter on operations management, we turn our attention to strategies for **balancing capacity with demand** and the **management of inventory**.

Capacity management is concerned with the organisation's ability to meet the demand for its products or services. Capacity is a limiting factor on how much an organisation can produce, and how much it can earn.

Today's business environment demands **speed** and **efficiency** in the delivery of products and services. This changing nature of business has implications for **inventory management**.

The **just-in-time** philosophy, covered in the final section of this chapter, is one approach that minimises holding costs while allowing timely production and delivery of products and services.

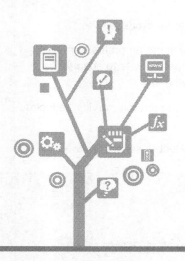

topic list	learning outcomes	syllabus references	ability required
1 Capacity management	C2(b)	C2(vii)	comprehension
2 Balancing capacity and demand	C2(b)	C2(vii)	comprehension
3 Capacity planning	C2(b)	C2(vii)	comprehension
4 Capacity control	C2(b)	C2(iv)	comprehension
5 Inventory management	C2(b)	C2(vi)	comprehension
6 Just-in-time (JIT)	C2(b)	C2(vi)	comprehension

1   Capacity management

Introduction

Capacity is a measure of what an operation is able to produce within a specified period of time. Capacity management aims to maximise the returns an organisation achieves on the assets and systems it utilises.

KEY TERM

CAPACITY has been defined as the maximum level of value added activity over a period of time that can be achieved by a process or production unit under normal working conditions.

Overcapacity or undercapacity can be detrimental to the business activities of an organisation.

1.1 Overcapacity

Overcapacity means **resources** available for production are **not fully utilised**.

(a)   Resources are underutilised and return on assets is lower than it could be. If an attempt is made to increase selling prices to improve the return, products and services may become expensive relative to competitors.

(b)   In the service industry it could send out the wrong messages to customers eg a restaurant that is not full may give that impression that the food is not good.

1.2 Undercapacity

Undercapacity means **more production is being demanded than is able to be produced**.

(a)   If the organisation is unable to satisfy customer demand it is missing out on profits from the products or services the market was ready to buy. Also, the customer is likely to acquire the product or service from a rival organisation and the customer may be lost.

(b)   In the service industry, undercapacity may result in slower or less comfortable service, reducing customer satisfaction and customer retention.

Capacity planning aims to **balance capacity** with the **demand** for the product or service.

Section summary

Overcapacity means resources available for production are not fully utilised.

Undercapacity means more production is being demanded than is able to be produced.

2   Balancing capacity and demand

Introduction

One important operations management task within an organisation is **balancing** the amount it is able to produce (**capacity**) with the amount it is able to sell (**demand**).

2.1 Dealing with uncertainty

KEY POINTS

Uncertainties in capacity could be caused by a number of factors, for example the shortage or a delay in the supply of a resource.

Uncertainties in demand are often due to the unpredictable nature of customers and potential customers.

Dealing with uncertainty requires a flexibility in **planning and control**.

Dependent demand is demand that **is predictable** because it is based on a factor that is known. For example, an organisation providing school meals can predict the demand for its meals because the size of each school population is known.

Dependent demand occurs often in manufacturing, where the demand for raw materials and components can be predicted from the demand for the main product. **Materials requirement planning (MRP)** (covered later in this chapter) is a form of **dependent demand planning and control**.

However, many organisations and / or operations within organisations aren't able to predict demand as easily. They have to make capacity decisions based on **experience** and **judgement** about the **likely** level of **demand**.

CASE STUDY

Fast turnaround time is important for airlines because, by minimising time on the ground, an airline can maximise the productivity of its planes in the air (ie maximise capacity).

To help airlines achieve the benefits of a fast turnaround time, the Airbus A320 family aircraft has the following features.

- Larger passenger doors
- Wider aisles
- Larger overhead storage compartments
- Convenient access to underfloor baggage holds
- Wider outward-opening cargo doors

2.2 Planning and control activities

There are **four planning and control activities** associated with balancing capacity and demand.

(a) Loading
(b) Sequencing
(c) Scheduling
(d) Monitoring and controlling

2.2.1 Loading

Loading is the **amount of work that is allocated to an operating unit**. The term was traditionally applied to the allocation of work to a machine or group of machines, but is applicable to any operating unit (eg a hair salon).

2.2.2 Sequencing

Decisions have to be taken when work comes in about **the order in which different jobs will be done** or different orders fulfilled. **The sequencing of operations** could be on the basis of any of the following.

(a) Customer priority
(b) Due date
(c) Last in first out
(d) First in first out

(e)   Longest operation time first

(f)   Shortest operation time first

The preferred sequencing criteria should be the one that **optimises operational performance** in terms of:

(a)   Dependability of delivery (ie meeting the due dates promised to customers)

(b)   Speed of delivery (ie minimising the amount of time that jobs spend in the process)

(c)   Cost

(d)   Minimising idle time in work centres (which is an aspect of cost)

(e)   Minimising inventory levels (which is another aspect of cost)

2.2.3 Scheduling

Once work has been sequenced, it might be necessary to prepare **a detailed timetable,** specifying the time that jobs should be started and when they should end.

Formal schedules are only needed when detailed planning is necessary to make sure that **customer demand can be met**. In operations where demand is unpredictable, scheduling is impracticable, and the operation must simply **react to orders as they arrive**, for example petrol stations.

For an operation that processes a large number of jobs, there is a risk that with poor scheduling, **bottlenecks** will occur in different parts of the operation at different times.

2.2.4 Monitoring and controlling

Having loaded, sequenced and scheduled the work, management must monitor the operation to make sure that the **work is proceeding as planned**. If a deviation from the plan is shown, corrective measures may be required so that the work can be re-scheduled.

The terms 'push control' and 'pull control' refer to when control action is taken to manage the flow of work. With **push control**, the focus is on pushing work through each stage of the process, regardless of whether the next stage is ready to receive it.

With **pull control**, the focus is on each stage of the process calling for work to be delivered from the previous process when it is needed. The work is not delivered from the previous process until it is needed. With pull control, there should be less inventory in the system.

Section summary

There are **four planning and control activities** associated with balancing capacity and demand, **loading**, **sequencing**, **scheduling** and **monitoring and controlling**.

3 Capacity planning

Introduction

Capacity planning aims to balance the **capacity** of an operation with the **demand** from customers. The objective is to maximise both **profits** and **customer satisfaction**.

3.1 Purpose of capacity planning and control

Planning and controlling capacity involves:

(a)   Planning the **normal capacity** of the operation, and

(b)   Reacting to **changes** in demand.

Long-term **strategic decisions** have to be made about what the capacity of an operation should be, and investment decisions taken to achieve the planned capacity.

Capacity planning in the short- and medium-term has several implications for operational performance.

Implication	Comment
Cost	Costs are affected by planned capacity. When the capacity of an operation exceeds demand, there will be under-utilised resources and costs will be higher than if capacity were more closely matched to demand.
Revenue	On the other hand, revenues could also be affected by the capacity of an operation. If demand exceeds the capacity of an operation to meet it, revenues will be forgone that could otherwise have been earned.
Quality	The quality of an operation could be affected by capacity planning. For example, if an operation varies its capacity by using part-time or temporary staff, the quality of the product or service might be impaired.
Speed of response to demand	The speed of response to demand can be improved either by building up finished goods inventories (which has a cost) or by providing sufficient capacity to avoid customers having to queue or to wait (which also has a cost).
Dependability of supply	The closer an operation works to its capacity limit, the less easily will it be able to cope with unexpected disruptions to the work flow. Supply will therefore be less dependable.
Flexibility	The flexibility of an operation, and in particular its ability to vary the volume of output it can produce, will be improved by having surplus capacity. An operation working at or close to its capacity limit is much less flexible.

3.2 Measuring demand and capacity

3.2.1 Forecasting demand

In most organisations, the **sales and marketing department** is responsible for forecasting demand. However, demand forecasts are relevant to operations management and capacity planning.

(a) For operations management purposes, demand forecasts should be expressed in terms of units rather than in terms of sales revenue. For example, for a manufacturing operation it is more relevant to express demand in terms of labour hours or machine hours.

(b) Forecasts should be as **accurate** as possible, because capacity will be planned on the basis of the forecasts.

(c) Forecasts of demand should give some indication of the degree of uncertainty. Where possible, the **variation** in demand should be **assessed statistically**, perhaps on the basis of demand patterns from the past.

3.2.2 Measuring capacity

Measuring capacity is not a straightforward task, except for standardised and repetitive operations. When an operation produces a range of different products or services, measuring capacity in terms of output produced is difficult, because there isn't a standard measure of output.

Capacity might therefore be measured either in terms of **input resources available** or in terms of **output produced**.

Operation	Capacity measure in terms of input resources	Capacity measure in terms of output produced
Football club	Ground capacity Squad size Number of matches	Number of paying spectators
Doctors' surgery	Number of doctors Number of surgery hours	Number of patients treated
Department store	Shelf space or volume, or floor area	Number of customers through the check-outs
Air travel	Number of seats available on a route	Number of passengers carried on the route each week

Where output is non-standard, any capacity measurement based on output will have to use an **average** measure. For example, a doctors' surgery might measure its capacity in terms of being able to treat 400 patients each week, this might be based on the assumption that an average time for treating each patient is ten minutes. In practice, some patients will need more than ten minutes and some less.

Often, one or more parts of an operation will work at their capacity limit. The parts of an operation that work at their capacity limit are the **capacity constraints for the entire operation**. Capacity constraints limit the total output achievable. They can cause bottlenecks in the work flow and result in unsatisfied demand. For example, if visitors to an out-of-town shopping centre all use the centre's car park and the car park is limited to 1,000 spaces, the number of car parking spaces is a capacity constraint for the centre.

3.3 Planning for capacity

There are different ways of **planning for capacity**.

* A level capacity plan
* A chase demand plan
* A demand management plan
* A mix of the above three types of plan

3.3.1 Level capacity plan

A **level capacity plan** is a plan to maintain **activity at a constant level** over the planning period and to ignore fluctuations in forecast demand. Staffing and other resource levels are kept constant.

In a manufacturing operation, when demand is lower than capacity, the operation will produce goods for inventory.

In a service operation, there will be idle resources when demand is low and delays and probably lower service quality when demand is high.

3.3.2 Chase demand plan

This plan is the opposite of a level capacity plan - it aims to **match capacity to** forecast **fluctuations in demand**.

To achieve this, **resources must be flexible**. For example, staff numbers might have to be variable and staff might be required to work overtime or shifts. Variations in equipment levels might also be necessary, perhaps by means of short-term rental arrangements.

Project-based teams and **virtual organisations** may help provide the flexibility needed to implement a chase demand plan.

3.3.3 Demand management planning

Some organisations attempt to **stabilise demand** and then plan capacity accordingly.

The aim of **demand management planning** is to reduce peak demand by switching it to the off-peak periods.

The most obvious way of managing demand is through **price discrimination**. Examples include:

(a)   Offering low off-peak fares on trains to encourage some customers to switch their travelling time.

(b)   Off-peak telephone charges.

(c)   Off-peak holiday prices to build up demand out of the holiday season.

Producers can also use **advertising** and other **marketing** tools to attempt to **stabilise demand**.

3.3.4 Mixed plans

In practice, capacity planning is often a **mixture** of level capacity planning, chase demand planning and demand management planning.

3.3.5 Yield management

In operations with a fairly fixed short-term and medium-term capacity, such as hotels, restaurants, theatres and airlines, an objective could be to achieve as much revenue as possible from the available fixed resources.

A **yield management approach** is particularly well-suited to an operation where:

(a)   Capacity is fairly fixed in the short- to medium-term.
(b)   The market can be segmented, to allow some price discrimination.
(c)   The service cannot be sold in advance.
(d)   The marginal cost of making an additional sale is low.

Yield management techniques have been evident in airline operations, where the techniques used include:

(a)   **Price discounting**. When demand is expected to be low, an airline might sell a block of tickets at a very cheap price.

(b)   **Varying the capacity of different types of service**. In an airline operation, this could mean switching the space in an aircraft from first class or business seats to economy class, or *vice versa*.

(c)   **Over-booking**. An airline will expect a percentage of its customers who have booked in advance to fail to arrive for their flight. Airlines therefore tend to book more passengers on to a flight than they have seats. If more passengers arrive than there are seats, some passengers will be offered inducements to take a later flight, or will be upgraded to first-class or business class travel.

Section summary

There are four different ways of **planning for capacity**, **level capacity** plans, **chase demand** plans, **demand management** plans and a **mix of the other three** types of plan.

CASE STUDY

Balancing capacity and demand

One of the biggest challenges electronics companies are facing in 2010 is lengthening component lead-times. After a year of slow sales, just as demand is picking up, lead-times are stretching out.

The problem is that component suppliers are unwilling to increase capacity or inventory until recovery is clearly underway. Given the economic uncertainties that still exist, it is hard to blame component manufacturers for being reluctant to take a leap of faith and increase inventories and/or capacity.

At the same time, electronics manufacturers are seeing revenues drop, not because of order cancellations, but because of an inability to get materials. What can these companies do?

At this point, the best business strategy is to address the current situation both reactively and proactively.

The reactive strategy should focus on bringing quality components in as quickly as possible in the given current market conditions. While creative sourcing may be required, reactive measures should continue to support customer approved vendor list integrity and avoid questionable sources of supply.

The proactive strategy focuses on longer term solutions that help address a market that could have extended lead-times for several more quarters and prevent excess inventory liability. Proactive strategy steps should include:

- Working with customers to develop extended forecasts so that orders can be placed with sufficient lead-time.

- Working with the customer to expand the approved vendor list, where possible to increase sourcing options on critical components

- Careful monitoring of total company inventories of critical components. Companies should have ERP systems and component numbering practices which allow real-time visibility into inventory by customer and inventory across the company.

- Careful monitoring of lead-time trends and pricing.

Strong supply chain relationships will help.

The good news is that lengthening lead-times are often indicative of a recovering market.

Adapted from an article by Susan Mucha, www.emtworldwide.com, March 2010

4 Capacity control

Introduction

Capacity control involves **reacting** to actual demand and influences on actual capacity as they arise.

4.1 Materials requirements planning (MRP I)

MRP I is a technique for deciding the volume and timing of materials, in manufacturing conditions where there is dependent demand.

The purpose of an MRP I system is to:

(a)   Calculate the **quantity** of materials required, for each type of material, and
(b)   Determine **when** they will be required.

The **materials requirements** are calculated from:

(a)   Known future orders, ie firm orders already received from customers, plus
(b)   A forecast of other future orders that, with a reasonable degree of confidence, will be received.

The quantities of each type of materials required for the product or service will be defined in its **bill of materials**. Estimates of firm and likely demand can therefore be converted into a **materials requirements schedule**.

MRP I enables manufacturing organisations to determine **when to order material**, by working back from when they will be required for production, and allowing the necessary lead time for production or for purchasing from the external supplier.

4.2 Manufacturing resource planning (MRP II)

Manufacturing resource planning, or MRP II, evolved out of **materials requirements planning** (MRP I). It is a plan for **planning and monitoring** all the **resources** of a **manufacturing company**: manufacturing, marketing, finance and engineering.

MRP II is a computerised system that incorporates a **single database** used by many different areas of the organisation. The engineering department, manufacturing function and finance function will all be using the same version of the bill of materials. All functions work from a **common set of data**.

MRP II is a sophisticated system that enables **optimal inventory control** based on the matching of supply and demand.

Features include:

- Production planning
- Capacity planning
- Forecasting
- Purchasing
- Order-entry
- Operations control
- Financial analysis

Brown (2001) believes **possible benefits** include:

- Reduced stock-outs – better customer service
- Reduced inventory holding costs
- Improved plant/facilities utilisation
- Reliable order fulfilment times
- Reduced 'crisis management' time

However, MRP II implementations are not always successful. Some potential **drawbacks** are illustrated in the following case study.

CASE STUDY

A family-owned building construction company builds residential and commercial buildings. At any time, the company is working on about 12 projects.

The operations department is organised around project managers, each responsible for between two and four projects at any time, and a foreman for each site. Full-time employees are organised into work groups of two, three or four individuals, and each work group has a specialist skill. The company also uses sub-contractors for many aspects of building work.

The company has recently installed a MRP II system.

One of the projects it is working on is the construction of a new residential estate of 50 houses. The houses on the estate will be of three different designs. Each design differs in terms of size, layout, window sizes, roof tile design, electricity supply features, water supply and central heating, furnishings and kitchen fittings. House buyers also have the option to pay for extra items, such as additional or more expensive bathroom fittings.

Project managers and site foremen have complained about the MRP II system. They identified the following issues.

1   The system generates a lot of figures, often using complex formulae (algorithms) to estimate the required quantities and timing of materials. The figures are produced by production planning staff, but a large number of people need to be kept informed – the foremen, project managers, possible sub-contractors and possibly also specialist work teams. This is bureaucratic.

2   The material requirements are estimated by a computer system of the production planning section. The final users of the information – and of the materials – have no sense of ownership of the figures. The figures, having been computer-produced, will be difficult to check. Project managers

and foremen etc will probably have no incentive to check the figures to see whether they appear to make sense.

3   Small hold-ups or difficulties in the building work can have a significant effect on materials requirements. For example, bad weather could hold up production. Whenever scheduling has to be changed, there will be a new materials requirements schedule, and this new information will have to be distributed to all the people affected. This will add to the problems of information over-load.

4   MRP II methods work reasonably well for standardised building, but are not easily applied to one-off construction work, where materials requirements and scheduling have to be done on a one-off basis.

4.3 Optimised production technology (OPT)

OPT is a computer-based method for scheduling production that focuses on the known capacity constraints (**bottlenecks**) of the operation.

It is used to:

(a)   Identify the capacity constraints in the system.
(b)   Schedule production to these capacity constraints.
(c)   Try to identify ways of overcoming the capacity constraint, so as to increase capacity.
(d)   Having done that, identify the next capacity constraint and schedule production to this constraint.

4.4 Enterprise resource planning (ERP)

Enterprise resource planning developed out of MRP II. ERP performs a similar function but on a wider basis, integrating and using databases from all parts of the organisation.

Enterprise Resource Planning (ERP) software attempts to integrate all departments and functions of an organisation in a computer system able to meet the needs of users from across the whole organisation.

An ERP system includes a number of integrated modules designed to support all of the key activities of an enterprise. This includes managing the key elements of the supply chain such as production planning, purchasing, inventory control and customer service including order tracking.

ERP has been extended to the growing number of e-business applications, connecting to customers and supply chain members.

One of the most popular ERP systems has been the R/3 system supplied by **SAP**. The R/3 system integrates most of an organisation's business applications and contains sections for manufacturing and logistics, sales and distribution, financial accounting and human resource management.

ERP has been effective in some situations, for example where it has been implemented as a means of **rationalising and integrating systems** where mergers and acquisitions have led to an uncoordinated mix of systems. ERP also provides efficiencies in supply chain management through facilitating reduced lead times.

However many ERP implementations **have failed to live up to expectations**, failing to deliver significant efficiency gains.

As they cover many areas of an organisation, ERP implementations are relatively expensive. They also carry significant 'hidden' costs through requiring organisations to change the way they operate. Some businesses have been restructured simply to fit the restrictions of the ERP software.

Question 7.1   Capacity management

Learning outcome C2(vii)

Identify the ways that service organisations differ from manufacturing organisations when considering capacity management.   **(5 marks)**

MRP and ERP are included on the paper P1 syllabus in connection with integrating accounting functions with other systems.

Section summary

MRP I, MRP II, OPT and **ERP** systems all include elements of capacity control.

5 Inventory management

Introduction

Inventories held in any organisation can generally be classified under four main headings.

- Raw materials
- Spare parts/consumables
- Work in progress
- Finished goods

For example, the raw materials of a furniture company would be wood and upholstery. Consumables would be items such as nails, screws and castors. Work in progress would be partly completed furniture. Finished goods would be tables, chairs, desks etc ready for sale. Not all organisations will have inventories of all four general categories.

Inventory control includes the functions of inventory ordering and purchasing, receiving goods into store, storing and issuing inventory and controlling the level of inventory.

5.1 Why hold inventories?

Brown (2001) identified the following reasons for holding inventory.

- **Protection** against supply problems
- To **meet unexpected increases** in demand
- To **improve delivery times** to customers
- To **allow bulk purchases** and associated **discounts**
- To **provide** a **buffer protecting against quality problems** in raw materials of newly finished goods
- To **improve reliability**
- To **smooth** out production when **demand fluctuates**.

5.2 Controls

There should be controls over the following functions.

- The **ordering** of inventories
- The **purchase** of inventories

- The **receipt** of goods into store
- **Storage**
- The **issue** of inventory and maintenance of inventories at the most appropriate level

Inventory controls are **required** for a number of reasons.

(a)   Holding costs of inventory may be expensive.
(b)   Production will be disrupted if the company runs out of raw materials.
(c)   If inventory with a short shelf life is not used or sold, their value may decline.
(d)   If customer orders cannot be supplied immediately, customer satisfaction will suffer.

5.3 Importance of keeping inventory records

Proper records should be kept of the **physical procedures** for ordering and receiving a consignment of goods to ensure the following.

- That enough inventory is held
- That there is no duplication of ordering
- That quality is maintained

5.4 Storage of inventories

Storekeeping involves storing materials to achieve the following objectives.

- Speedy **issue** and **receipt** of goods
- Full **identification** of all goods at all times
- Correct **location** of all goods at all times
- **Protection** of goods from damage and deterioration
- Provision of **secure stores** to avoid pilferage, theft and fire
- **Efficient** use of storage space
- **Maintenance** of correct inventory levels
- Keeping correct and up-to-date **records** of receipts, issues and inventory levels

One of the objectives of storekeeping is to maintain **accurate records** of current inventory levels. This involves the accurate recording of inventory movements (issues from and receipts into stores).

5.5 Perpetual or continuous inventory

Continuous or **perpetual inventory** is the name for a system that involves recording every **receipt and issue** of inventory **as it occurs**. This means that there is a continuous record of the balance of each item of inventory.

When the inventory levels drops below a predetermined level, an order for a fixed amount is issued to replenish inventory.

5.6 Periodic inventory systems

These systems involve a check of inventory levels at **specific time intervals**. The checks may trigger an order for new inventory. The quantity ordered depends on the current inventory level.

5.7 ABC system

Under this system, items may be **classified as expensive, inexpensive or in a middle-cost range**. Because of the practical advantages of simplifying stores control procedures without incurring unnecessary high costs, it may be possible to segregate materials for selective stores control.

(a)   Expensive and medium-cost materials are subject to careful stores control procedures to minimise cost.

(b)   Inexpensive materials can be stored in large quantities because the cost savings from careful stores control do not justify the administrative effort required to implement the control.

This selective approach to stores control is sometimes called the **ABC method** whereby materials are classified A, B or C according to their **value**. A refers to **high** value inventory, B to **medium** and C to **low** value inventory. It is based upon the Pareto 80/20 rule which suggests that 20% of the items are likely to account for 80% of the overall value.

5.8 Obsolescence and wastage

Obsolete inventories are those items which have become **out-of-date** and are **no longer required**. Obsolete items are disposed of and treated as an expense in the company's financial statements.

From the perspective of operations management, proper controls should be instituted to minimise the incidence of losses arising from obsolescence or wastage.

Slow-moving inventories are items which are likely to take a long time to be used up.

5.9 Holding costs

If stocks are too high, **holding costs** will be incurred unnecessarily. Such costs occur for a number of reasons.

(a)   **Costs of storage and stores operations.** Larger stocks require more storage space and possibly extra staff and equipment to control and handle them.

(b)   **Interest charges**. Holding inventory involves the tying up of capital (cash) on which interest must be paid.

(c)   **Insurance costs**. The larger the value of inventory held, the greater insurance premiums are likely to be.

(d)   **Risk of obsolescence**. The longer an inventory item is held, the greater is the risk of obsolescence.

(e)   **Deterioration**. When materials in store deteriorate to the extent that they are unusable, they must be thrown away with the likelihood that disposal costs would be incurred.

5.10 Costs of obtaining inventories

If inventories are kept low, small quantities will have to be ordered more frequently, thereby increasing the following **ordering or procurement costs**.

(a)   **Clerical and administrative costs** associated with purchasing, accounting for and receiving goods

(b)   **Transport costs**

(c)   **Production run costs**, for stock which is manufactured internally rather than purchased from external sources

5.11 Running out of inventory (stock-outs)

An additional type of cost which may arise if inventories are kept too low is the type associated with **running out of inventories**.

- Lost contribution from lost sales
- Loss of future sales due to disgruntled customers
- Loss of customer goodwill

- Cost of production stoppages
- Labour frustration over stoppages
- Extra costs of urgent, small quantity, replenishment orders

5.12 Objective of inventory control

The overall objective of inventory control is, therefore, to **maintain inventory levels** so that the total of the following costs is minimised.

- Holding costs
- Ordering costs
- Stockout costs

5.13 Inventory control levels

KEY POINT

Inventory control levels can be calculated in order to maintain inventory at the optimum level. The three critical control levels are **reorder level**, **minimum level** and **maximum level**. The **Economic Order Quantity (EOQ)** is the order quantity which minimises inventory costs.

Based on an analysis of past inventory usage and delivery times, a series of control levels can be calculated and used to maintain inventories at their **optimum level** (in other words, a level which minimises costs). These levels will determine 'when to order' and 'how many to order'.

(a) **Reorder level**. When inventories reach this level, an order should be placed to replenish stocks. The reorder level is determined by considering the rate of consumption and the lead time (lead time is the time between placing an order with a supplier and the stock becoming available for use).

(b) **Minimum level**. This is a warning level to draw management attention to the fact that inventories are approaching a dangerously low level and that outages are possible.

(c) **Maximum level**. This acts as a warning level to signal to management that stocks are reaching a potentially wasteful level.

(d) **Reorder quantity**. This is the quantity of inventory which is to be ordered when stock reaches the reorder level. If it is set so as to minimise the total costs associated with holding and ordering inventory, then it is known as the **economic order quantity**.

(e) **Average inventory**. The formula for the average inventory level assumes that inventory levels fluctuate evenly between the minimum (or safety) inventory level and the highest possible inventory level (the amount of inventory immediately after an order is received, ie safety inventory + reorder quantity).

Exam skills

You need to understand that holding inventories and ordering inventories involve costs and that these should be minimised and balanced against the risk of stock-outs.

Section summary

Continuous or **perpetual inventory** is the name for a system that involves recording every receipt and issue of inventory as it occurs.

These systems involve a check of inventory levels at **specific time intervals**.

Under the **ABC method of inventory control** materials are classified A, B or C according to their **value. A** refers to **high** value inventory, **B to medium** and **C to low** value inventory. It is based upon the Pareto 80/20 rule which suggests that 20% of the items are likely to account for 80% of the overall value.

If inventory levels are too high, **holding costs** will be incurred unnecessarily.

If inventories are kept low, small quantities will have to be ordered more frequently, thereby increasing **ordering or procurement costs**.

There are also **costs** involved in **running out of inventory** (stockouts).

The overall **objective** of inventory control is to **maintain inventory levels** so that the total of holding, ordering and stockout costs is **minimised**.

Inventory control levels can be calculated in order to maintain inventory at the optimum level. The three critical control levels are **reorder level**, **minimum level** and **maximum level**. The **Economic Order Quantity (EOQ)** is the order quantity which minimises inventory costs.

6 Just-in-time (JIT)

Introduction

Just-in-time (JIT) is an approach to operations based on the idea that goods and services should be produced **only when they are needed** – neither too early (so that inventories build up) nor too late (so that the customer has to wait). JIT is also known as 'stockless production' and may be used as part of a lean production process. In its extreme form, a JIT system seeks to hold **zero inventories**.

6.1 Operational requirements of JIT

Just-in-Time (JIT) requires the following **characteristics** in operations.

(a)   **High quality**. Any errors in quality will reduce throughput and reduce the dependability of supply.

(b)   **Speed**. Throughput in the operation must be fast, so that customer orders can be met through production rather than out of inventory.

(c)   **Reliability**. Production must be reliable and not subject to hold-ups.

(d)   **Flexibility**. To respond immediately to customer orders, production must be flexible, and in small batch sizes (often a 'batch' of one).

(e)   **Lower costs**. As a consequence of high quality production, and with a faster throughput and the elimination of errors, costs will be reduced.

Under JIT, if there is no immediate demand for output the operation should not produce goods.

6.2 The JIT philosophy

The **JIT philosophy** originated in Japan in the 1970s, with companies such as the car manufacturer Toyota.

6.2.1 Three key elements in the JIT philosophy

Element	Comment
Elimination of waste	Waste is defined as any activity that does not add value. Examples of waste identified by Toyota are: • **Overproduction**, ie producing more than is immediately needed by the next stage in the process. • **Waiting time**. Waiting time can be measured by labour efficiency and machine efficiency. • **Transport**. Moving items around a plant does not add value. Waste can be reduced by changing the layout of the factory floor so as to minimise the movement of materials. • **Waste in the process**. There could be waste in the process itself. Some activities might be carried out only because there are design defects in the product, or because of poor maintenance work. • **Inventory**. Inventory is wasteful. The target should be to eliminate all inventory by tackling the things that cause it to build up. • **Simplification of work**. An employee does not necessarily add value by working. Simplifying work is an important way of getting rid of waste in the system because it eliminates unnecessary actions. • **Defective goods** are quality waste. This is a significant cause of waste in many operations.
The involvement of all staff in the operation	JIT is a cultural issue, and its philosophy has to be embraced by everyone involved in the operation if it is to be applied successfully. Critics of JIT argue that management efforts to involve all staff can be patronising.
Continuous improvement	The goal is to meet demand immediately with perfect quality and no waste. In practice, this ideal is never achieved. However, the JIT philosophy is that an organisation should work towards the ideal, and continuous improvement is both possible and necessary. The Japanese term for continuous improvement is *Kaizen*.

6.2.2 Criticism of JIT

A **criticism of JIT**, in its extreme form, is that to have no inventory between any stages in the production process ignores the fact that some stages, by their very nature, could be less reliable than others. It could therefore be argued that some inventory should be held at these stages to provide a degree of protection to the rest of the operation.

6.3 JIT techniques

JIT is a **collection of management techniques**. Some of these relate to basic working practices.

(a)   **Work standards**. Work standards should be established and followed by everyone at all times.

(b)   **Flexibility in responsibilities**. The organisation should provide for the possibility of expanding the responsibilities of any individual to the extent of their capabilities. Grading structures and restrictive working practices should be eliminated as far as possible.

(c)   **Equality of all people working in the organisation**. Equality should exist and be visible. For example, there should be a single staff canteen.

(d)   **Autonomy**. Authority should be delegated to the individuals responsible directly in the activities of the operation. Management should support people involved in production, not direct them.

(e)   **Development of personnel**. Individual workers should be developed and trained.

(f)   **Quality of working life**. The quality of working life should be improved, through better work area facilities, job security and involvement of everyone in job-related decision-making.

(g)   **Creativity**. Employees should be encouraged to be creative in devising improvements to the way their work is done.

(h)   **Use several small, simple production units**. Small machines can be moved around more easily, and so offer greater flexibility in a shop floor layout. The risk of making a bad and costly investment decision is reduced, because relatively simple small machines usually cost much less than sophisticated large machines.

(i)   **Work floor layout and work flow**. Work can be laid out to promote the smooth flow of operations. Work flow is an important element in JIT, because the work needs to flow without interruption in order to avoid a build-up of inventory or unnecessary down-times.

(j)   **Total productive maintenance (TPM)**. Total productive maintenance seeks to eliminate unplanned breakdowns and the damage they cause to production and work flow. Staff operating on the production line are brought into the search for improvements in maintenance.

(k)   **JIT purchasing**. With JIT purchasing, an organisation establishes a close relationship with trusted suppliers, and develops an arrangement with the supplier for being able to purchase materials only when they are needed for production. The supplier is required to have a flexible production system capable of responding immediately to purchase orders.

6.4 JIT planning and control

Holding inventories is one source of waste. Not having materials when they are needed is another. In other words, both having inventories in hand and having stock-outs is wasteful practice.

6.4.1 Kanban

Kanban is the Japanese word for **card** or **signal.** A kanban system controls the flow of materials between one stage in a process and the next. In its simple form, a card is used by an 'internal customer' as a signal to an 'internal supplier' that the customer now requires more parts or materials. The card will contain details of the parts or materials required.

The receipt of a card from an **internal customer** sets in motion the movement or production or supply of one unit of an item, or one standard container of the item.

6.5 JIT in service operations

The JIT philosophy can be applied to **service operations**. Whereas JIT in manufacturing seeks to eliminate inventories, JIT in service operations seeks to eliminate queues of customers.

Queues of customers are **wasteful** because:

(a) They waste customers' time.
(b) Queues require space and this space does not add value.
(c) Queuing lowers the customers' perception of the quality of the service.

The application of JIT to a service operation calls for **multiskilling**, so that employees can be used more flexibly and moved from one type of work to another, in response to work flow requirements.

CASE STUDY

A postal delivery service has delivery staff allocated to their own routes. However, there may be scenarios where, say, Route A is overloaded while Route B has a relatively small number of deliveries.

Rather than have items for Route A piling up at the sorting office, the person responsible for Route B could finish their route and then help out on Route A.

Teamwork and flexibility can be difficult to introduce because some people are more comfortable with clearly defined boundaries and responsibilities.

However, the customer is only interested in receiving a timely service.

Some service organisations use a **buffer operation** to minimise customer queuing or minimise the likelihood of customer dissatisfaction during queuing.

For example, hairdressers often give clients a shampoo to reduce the impact of waiting for the stylist. Restaurants may have an area where guests may have a drink if no vacant tables are available immediately. Such facilities may even encourage guests to plan in a few drinks before dinner thereby increasing the restaurant's revenues.

Question 7.2	Capacity management and JIT

Learning outcomes C2(vi), C2(vii)

Discuss why a level capacity strategy might be difficult for a firm wishing to adopt a just-in-time (JIT) philosophy. **(5 marks)**

You will meet JIT again in paper P2.

Section summary

Just-in-time is an approach to operations based on the idea that goods and services should be produced **only when they are needed**.

The key elements of JIT are **elimination of waste, the involvement of all staff in the operation** and **continuous improvement**.

Kanban is the Japanese word for **card** or **signal**. A kanban control system is a system for controlling the flow of materials between one stage in a process and the next.

JIT philosophy can be applied to **service operations**. Whereas JIT in manufacturing seeks to eliminate inventories, JIT in service operations seeks to **remove queues of customers**.

Chapter Roundup

- ✓ **Overcapacity** means resources available for production are not fully utilised.

- ✓ **Undercapacity** means more production is being demanded than is able to be produced.

- ✓ There are **four planning and control activities** associated with balancing capacity and demand, **loading, sequencing, scheduling** and **monitoring and controlling**.

- ✓ There are four different ways of **planning for capacity, level capacity** plans, **chase demand** plans, **demand management** plans and a **mix of the other three** types of plan.

- ✓ **MRP I, MRP II, OPT** and **ERP** all include elements of capacity control.

- ✓ **Continuous** or **perpetual inventory** is the name for a system that involves recording every receipt and issue of inventory as it occurs.

- ✓ These systems involve a check of inventory levels at **specific time intervals**.

- ✓ Under the **ABC method of inventory control** materials are classified A, B or C according to their **value. A** refers to **high** value inventory, **B** to **medium** and **C** to **low** value inventory. It is based upon the Pareto 80/20 rule which suggests that 20% of the items are likely to account for 80% of the overall value.

- ✓ If inventories are too high, **holding costs** will be incurred unnecessarily.

- ✓ If inventories are kept low, small quantities will have to be ordered more frequently, thereby increasing **ordering or procurement costs**.

- ✓ There are also **costs** involved in **running out of inventory**.

- ✓ The overall **objective** of inventory control is to **maintain inventory levels** so that the total of holding, ordering and stockout costs is **minimised**.

- ✓ **Inventory control levels** can be calculated in order to maintain inventory at the optimum level. The three critical control levels are **reorder level, minimum level** and **maximum level**. The **Economic Order Quantity (EOQ)** is the order quantity which minimises inventory costs.

- ✓ **Just-in-time** is an approach to operations planning and control based on the idea that goods and services should be produced **only when they are needed**.

- ✓ The key elements of JIT are **elimination of waste, the involvement of all staff in the operation** and **continuous improvement**.

- ✓ *Kanban* is the Japanese word for **card** or **signal**. A kanban control system is a system for controlling the flow of materials between one stage in a process and the next.

- ✓ JIT philosophy can be applied to **service operations** as well as to manufacturing. Whereas JIT in manufacturing seeks to eliminate inventories, JIT in service operations seeks to **remove queues of customers**.

Quick Quiz

1   An organisation is unable to produce enough output to fulfil demand. This is this an example of:

    A   Overcapacity
    B   Undercapacity
    C   Demand-pull production
    D   Stockouts

2   'A plan to maintain activity at a constant level over the planning period.' This statement defines:

    A   A chase demand plan
    B   A steady capacity plan
    C   A level capacity plan
    D   A demand management plan

3   Which inventory control level indicates that inventories are nearing a potentially wasteful level?

    A   Re-order level
    B   Minimum level
    C   Maximum level
    D   Economic order quantity

4   'A perpetual inventory system may be referred to as a continuous inventory system.'

    True   ☐

    False   ☐

5   The main feature of the *Kanban* system is that:

    A   Cards are used to signal that more items of inventory are required
    B   Stocks are ordered when they reach the minimum level
    C   Stockouts are commonplace
    D   Holding costs are maximised

Answers to Quick Quiz

1   B   Undercapacity occurs where an organisation is unable to produce enough output to fulfil demand.

2   C   A level capacity plan seeks to maintain constant activity over a planning period.

3   C   The maximum level indicates that inventories are nearing a potentially wasteful level.

4   True.   A perpetual inventory system can also be referred to as a continuous inventory system.

5   A   The main feature of the *Kanban* system is that cards are used to signal that more items of inventory are required.

Answers to Questions

7.1 Capacity management

Service organisations differ from manufacturing organisations when considering capacity management in the following ways.

- **Production** and **consumption** occur at the same time. Inventories of services can't be built up in quieter times, which makes the balancing of capacity and demand more difficult.

- **Greater interaction**. The customer plays an active role in the delivery process. Customer service quality is integral to the customer experience.

- **Output** is **different each time**. Each customer service interaction is different in some way eg different conversation, attitude etc. Achieving a consistently high level of output is more challenging.

- **Generally greater reliance on staff**. Service delivery depends on the people delivering the service. The 'mood' of staff on the front line shouldn't adversely impact upon the customer experience.

- **Intangible output** makes **measuring** the **quality level** of output more difficult as there is no physical product to inspect. Obtaining feedback of customer satisfaction is important.

7.2 Capacity management and JIT

A **level capacity strategy** involves building up an inventory buffer to enable orders to be met from stores when demand exceeds capacity.

A **Just in Time (JIT)** approach involves producing goods when they are needed – eliminating the need to hold inventory.

The **build up of inventory** required under a level capacity strategy contradicts the no inventory approach required under JIT. Therefore, the two approaches are **incompatible**.

Under **JIT, production** is **driven** by **immediate demand**. The capacity management approach consistent with JIT is a **chase strategy** – which involves adjusting production levels to match demand. This would allow nil (or minimal) inventory, as required under JIT.

Now try this question from the Exam Question Bank	Number	Level	Marks	Time
	7	Examination	30	54 mins

MARKETING

Part D

MARKETING AND BUSINESS STRATEGY

In Part D of this Text we cover the **marketing** area of the syllabus.

We start this chapter with an explanation of marketing, the **marketing concept** and the **marketing environment** which organisations operate in.

The bulk of this, and the next, chapter concern an organisation's **marketing activities**. We begin by looking at how marketing plans are **organised** and **managed** – and the role of marketing within an organisation.

The key activities that we are concerned with in this chapter are market research, segmentation, targeting and positioning – the **marketing strategy**.

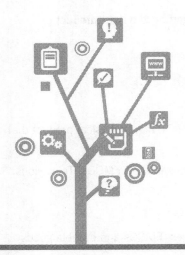

topic list	learning outcomes	syllabus references	ability required
1 The marketing concept	D1(a)	D1(i)	comprehension
2 The marketing environment	D1(b)	D1(ii)	comprehension
3 Marketing and corporate strategy	D2(d)	D2(x)	comprehension
4 Marketing strategy	D2(a)	D2(i), D2(ii)	comprehension

1 The marketing concept

> **Introduction**
>
> We begin our study of marketing by considering what marketing is and what adopting a marketing orientation means We consider the **marketing concept**, as a business philosophy.
>
> Later in the chapter we look at marketing as a core element of an organisation's **corporate strategy** and the **processes** involved in creating a **marketing plan**.

1.1 What is marketing?

KEY TERM

MARKETING is the process of planning and executing the concepts of pricing, promotion and distribution of ideas, goods and services in order to create exchanges that satisfy individual and organisational objectives.

Another definition is given by the UK's **Chartered Institute of Marketing**.

> 'Marketing is the management process which identifies, anticipates and supplies customer requirements efficiently and profitably.'

This definition emphasises the **wide scope of marketing**, ranging from initial identification of customer needs by means of **research**, right through to eventual, **profitable satisfaction of those needs**. This definition is important because it stresses the importance of the customer and, more particularly, **customer satisfaction**.

Kotler, on the other hand, emphasised the importance of marketing as getting 'the **right product** or **service** to the customer, at the **right price**, at the **right time**'.

1.2 Products, goods and services: a note on terminology

A **product** is something that is offered to a market.

(a) Soap powder is an example of a **fast moving consumer good** (FMCG). It is a physical product that is bought often.

(b) **Durable goods** are purchased less often and tend to be more expensive than FMCGs. Televisions, cars and computers are examples of durable goods.

(c) A haircut is also a type of product – it is an example of a **service** product.

Broadly speaking, the word **product** can refer to physical **goods** or **services**. FMCGs and durable goods combined are sometimes referred to as **consumer goods**.

1.3 Strategic and tactical marketing

Marketing involves several types of activity and many types of decision. For many organisations, the products they provide are **fundamental** to their existence.

(a) **Strategic marketing** is tied in with corporate strategy, by identifying which products and markets the organisation wishes to operate in.

(b) **Tactical marketing** is focused more on the short term and on particular elements of the marketing mix.

Example: retail	
Strategic marketing	A fashion retailer decides to open in the capital city of a country it had not operated in before as it believes there are new, wealthy customers.
Tactical marketing	End of season sale to make way for new stock.

Question 8.1

Strategic and tactical marketing

Learning outcome D1(i)

Distinguish between strategic and tactical marketing, and provide an example. **(4 marks)**

1.4 Exchanges

The role of marketing is to **identify**, **anticipate** and **supply satisfactions** to **customers**, to facilitate mutually beneficial exchanges.

Mutually beneficial exchanges

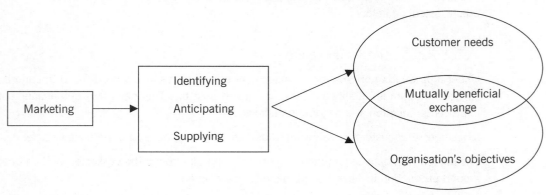

1.5 The marketing concept and a marketing orientation

The **marketing concept** and **marketing orientation** are two interrelated terms. The definitions that follow are from *Brassington and Pettit* (2000).

Marketing concept	Marketing orientation
A philosophy of business, permeating the whole organisation, that holds that the key to organisational success is meeting customers' needs more effectively and more closely than competitors.	An approach to business that centres its activities on satisfying the needs and wants of its customers.
= A BELIEF SYSTEM	= ACTUAL PRACTICES

1.6 The marketing concept

The **marketing concept** is a belief system. A belief system can be incorporated into the culture of the organisation. Culture involves beliefs and patterns of behaviour.

The organisation as a whole can claim to be **'customer orientated'**. Many organisations refer to customer satisfaction in their statements of corporate purpose (mission statements). But official claims to be customer orientated are often just claims - with little basis in fact.

As part of becoming properly 'customer orientated', organisations need to **seek out gaps in the market** where the organisation or its competitors fail to meet customer demand. They should then produce appropriate products.

1.6.1 The marketing concept in practice

Even though the marketing concept, with its attempt to match goods to consumer needs, is widely accepted, most organisations will still require salespeople. The sales team's effort will be more successful if products and services meet market needs.

A **market-led approach** will make what is on sale more appealing to customers. Salespeople will be able to devote a greater proportion of their time to more productive activities such as developing leads, providing better customer service and identifying changes in customer requirements.

All good **sales presentations** focus **on the benefits that customers will receive** from the company's product or service.

1.7 Marketing orientation (or market orientation) and other orientations

The marketing concept and marketing orientation are often compared to other '**orientations**' which are briefly described below.

1.7.1 Production orientation

Under a **production orientation**, management believe that success is achieved through producing goods or services of optimum quality as cost-efficiently as possible. The major task of management is to pursue improved production and distribution efficiency.

It assumes that customers will want to buy products that have been produced efficiently.

The comparison between a **marketing orientation** built around the **customer** and an orientation built around **production** is illustrated in the following diagram.

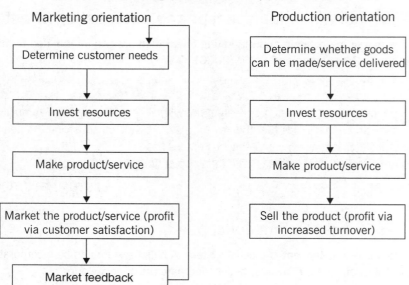

Comparison of marketing orientation with production orientation

Perhaps the most well-known example of **production orientation** was the **Model T Ford**, one of the earliest motor cars to be produced for the mass market. *Henry Ford* famously said that Ford's customers could have the (mass-produced) Model T in any colour, so long as it was black.

1.7.2 Sales orientation

Under a sales orientation the tendency is to make the product and then **actively** and perhaps aggressively **sell it**. Underlying this philosophy is a belief that a good sales force can sell just about anything to anybody.

Selling is preoccupied with the seller's need to convert their product into **cash**. **Marketing** is concerned with **satisfying the needs of the customer** by means of the product and the whole cluster of things associated with creating, delivering and finally consuming it.

1.7.3 Product orientation

Product orientated organisations focus on **product development**, for example the introduction of new product features. This approach is based upon the belief that a more advanced product or one with more features will be perceived as superior.

1.8 The potential impact of a marketing orientation

The marketing concept suggests that companies should focus on customer needs. The organisation needs to interpret customer needs and then produce products and services that meet them, at a price that customers accept. Do this and, in theory at least, minimal sales effort will be needed.

CASE STUDY

Customers of banking services generally have expectations that their accounts will be updated efficiently and effectively, over a period of time, so that they have access to funds. They may also have other needs.

(a) **Traditional 'western' banking**

Banks like to offer other products to their customers, so that a customer with a current account may also open a savings account. The bank is able to use the money to lend, at higher interest rates, to other customers, thereby earning a profit. Competition between banks is often based on interest rates.

(b) **'Islamic' banking**

The classic banking model is held by some Muslims to contradict certain tenets of Islam. The difficulty involves the payment of interest, which is frowned upon. Many banks are now able to structure lending transactions in a fashion that is acceptable to Islam.

In both cases (a) and (b) the bank is providing a service and, over the long term, engaging in a relationship with its customers.

| Question 8.2 | Product and production orientation |

Learning outcome D1(i)

Compare and contrast product orientated organisations and production orientated organisations.

(4 marks)

1.9 Push v Pull marketing

Traditionally, marketing activities focus on **pushing** goods out to resellers and consumers. Product promotion is by the final seller in the value chain.

A **'pull' approach** on the other hand, aims to produce a product that consumer demand will **pull** into retail outlets. Product promotion is shared between the manufacturer and final seller.

1.10 The marketing concept: summary

To conclude, **marketing has three dimensions**.

(a)   It is a **culture**. The marketing concept is to focus on consumer needs.

(b)   It involves **strategy**. A company must select the markets it intends to sell to and the products or services it will sell. These selections are strategic decisions.

(c)   It involves **tactics**. Marketing tactics can be considered as the 7Ps of the marketing mix (see Chapter 9).

Exam skills

The syllabus refers to the marketing concept as a business philosophy. Therefore when answering questions in this area you need to demonstrate that you understand 'marketing' means much more than the traditional view of 'advertising' and 'public relations'.

Section summary

Marketing is the process of planning and executing the concepts of pricing, promotion and distribution of ideas, goods and services in order to create exchanges that satisfy individual and organisational objectives.

The **marketing concept** is a business philosophy which attempts to **match goods to consumer needs**.

A **production orientation** may be defined as the management view that success is achieved through producing goods or services of optimum quality and cost.

Under a **sales orientation** the tendency is to make the product and then actively and aggressively sell it.

Product orientated organisations focus on product development.

---

2   The marketing environment

Introduction

All organisations **exist in, interact with** and are **influenced by factors** in their **environment.** It is important for organisations to **identify** and **monitor** these factors as they often have a direct effect on the performance of the business.

The marketing environment consists of three levels.

The **macro-environment** includes all factors that can influence the organisation, such as the PESTEL factors explained in the next section. The macro-environment is generally out of the organisation's control.

The **micro-environment** is comprised of factors specifically related to the organisation, such as the organisation's customers and suppliers. The organisation can have some influence over these factors.

The **internal environment** refers to factors within the organisation, such as its assets, employees and finance. These factors are able to be controlled by the organisation.

2.1 PESTEL factors

Factors in the environment that influence marketing can be classified using the PESTEL framework, as shown below.

PESTEL factors					
Political	Economic	Social/Cultural	Technological	Ecological	Legal

These factors influence the organisation in many ways. However in marketing, we are particularly interested in how they impact on **markets** and **customers.**

Environment and markets

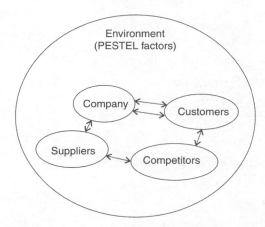

For example, **political factors** may influence the market for financial services by encouraging customers to take out certain types of investment. **Economic factors** may influence customers' buying power. The following table shows the type of impact on customers.

Factor	Impact on customers
Political factors • Changes in government and/or changes in government policy. • Political instability could lead to warfare or civil unrest.	This can affect consumers' confidence in the future, their spending power or their rights. Clearly this fundamentally affects normal business. Government policy could give consumers more rights in relation to business.
Economic factors These include overall rate of economic growth, inflation, interest rates, exchange rates, consumers propensity to save.	Ultimately, this determines consumers' effective demand for products and services. Uncertainty about the future may lead to more saving and less spending. General prosperity may lead to more spending on luxury items.
Social/cultural factors Demography relates to the composition of the population, where people live, social classification. Culture relates to people's values and beliefs. There may be many subgroups (subcultures) within a culture.	Demographic factors suggest the size and purchasing power of customer groups. Some products may indicate high status. Culture has significant consequences for the acceptability of marketing communications messages, attitudes to products (eg alcoholic drinks), attitudes towards purchasing, and so on.

Factor	Impact on customers
Technological factors • New products • New processes • New working methods • New communication methods • New ways of distribution	Companies may be able to change the products or services they offer, but they can also communicate in different ways. Customers may have different attitudes to innovation, some preferring to stay with tried and trusted products or patterns of behaviour.
Ecological factors • Long-term trends in the global physical environment, such as climate change. • Natural climatic impacts, such as flooding, earthquakes and so on. • As well as considering the physical environment, we should consider customers' attitudes to it, as a developing cultural factor with an influence on political decision-making.	The effect on customers is two-fold. Changing attitudes enable businesses to satisfy new needs with new products, for example organic vegetables. Natural disasters are a business opportunity for insurance companies, but also those supplying aid and construction companies.
Legal factors • The law affects ways of doing business. • Specific laws exist for particular areas of economic activity.	• Do legislation and judicial decisions increase the customer's rights? • Particular classes of customer may be protected in some cases (eg funeral services) • Are customers increasingly willing and able to take legal action?

Exam skills

Exam questions may require you to evaluate the environment an organisation operates in. You could use the PESTEL factors as headings and generate ideas for each of them. This way you can earn marks quickly and demonstrate good breadth of knowledge.

2.2 SWOT analysis

Another method of environmental analysis looks at an organisation's internal **strengths** and **weaknesses** as well as external **opportunities** and **threats**. This is known as **SWOT** analysis.

2.2.1 Internal appraisal: strengths and weaknesses

An internal appraisal will identify:

(a)   The areas of the organisation that have **strengths** that should be exploited by suitable strategies

(b)   The areas of the organisation that have **weaknesses** which need strategies to improve them.

The strengths and weaknesses analysis is intended to shape the organisation's approach to the external world. For instance, the identification of shortcomings in products could lead to a programme of product development.

2.2.2 External appraisal: opportunities and threats

The external appraisal identifies **opportunities** that can be exploited by the organisation's strengths and also to anticipate environmental **threats** against which the company must protect itself.

Opportunities

(a)   What opportunities exist in the business environment?

(b)   What is their inherent profit-making potential?

(c)   Can the organisation exploit the worthwhile opportunities?

(d)   What is the comparative capability profile of competitors?

(e)   What is the company's comparative performance potential in this field of opportunity?

Threats

(a)   What threats might arise to the company or its business environment?

(b)   How will competitors be affected?

(c)   How will the company be affected?

2.2.3 Using a SWOT analysis

The SWOT analysis can be used in one of two ways.

(a)   The organisation can develop **resource-based strategies** which enable the organisation to extend the use of its strengths. This is common in retailing, for example, as supermarket chains extend their own brands from food to other areas.

(b)   The business can develop **positioning-based strategies**. In other words identifying what opportunities are available and what the firm has to do exploit them.

Section summary

An organisation's **marketing environment** can be analysed into **political**, **economic**, **social**, **technological**, **ecological** and **legal factors** (PESTEL).

---

3   Marketing and corporate strategy

Introduction

In this section we look at how an organisation develops and implements a **marketing plan.** The process begins by considering what the overall **corporate strategy** is – the marketing plan is driven by the overall corporate strategy.

Later in the chapter we explain the **structure of a marketing plan.**

3.1 Corporate and marketing strategies

The process of corporate planning and the relationship with marketing strategy is shown in the following table.

	Corporate	Marketing
Set objectives	For the organisation as a whole: eg increase profits by X%.	For products and market: eg increase market share by X%; increase turnover.
Internal appraisal (*strengths and weaknesses*)	Review the effectiveness of the different aspects of the organisation.	Conduct a marketing audit: a review of marketing activities. Does the organisation have a marketing orientation?

	Corporate	Marketing
External appraisal (*opportunities and threats*)	Review political, economic, social, technological, ecological factors impacting on the whole organisation.	Review environmental factors as they affect customers, products and markets.
Gaps	There may be a gap between desired objectives and forecast objectives. How should the gap be closed?	The company may be doing less well in particular markets than it ought to. Marketing will be focused on growth.
Strategy	Develop strategies to fill the gap: eg diversifying, entering new markets.	A marketing strategy is a plan to achieve the organisation's objectives by specifying: • Resources to be allocated to marketing • How those resources should be used In the context of applying the marketing concept, a marketing strategy would: • Identify target markets and customer needs in those markets • Plan products which will satisfy the needs of those markets • Organise marketing resources, so as to match products with customers
Implementation	Implementation is delegated to departments of the business.	The plans must be put into action, eg advertising space must be bought.
Control	Results are reviewed and the planning process starts again.	Has the organisation achieved its market share objectives?

3.2 The marketing plan

The **marketing plan** must be **consistent** with the **corporate strategy**. It might take the following form (based on *Kotler*, 1994).

Section	Content
The executive summary	This is the finalised planning document with a summary of the main goals and recommendations in the plan.
Situation analysis	This consists of a SWOT analysis and forecasts.
Objectives and goals	What the organisation is hoping to achieve, or needs to achieve, perhaps in terms of market share or 'bottom line' profits and returns.
Marketing strategy	This considers the selection of target markets, the marketing mix and marketing expenditure levels, as described in the preceding table.
Strategic marketing plan	• Three to five or more years long • Defines scope of product and market activities • Aims to match the activities of the organisation to its distinctive competences
Tactical marketing plan	• One year time horizon • Generally based on existing products and markets • Concerned with marketing mix issues

Section	Content

Action plan	This sets out how the strategies are to be achieved.
	
	• Marketing mix strategy
	
	  – The product – People
	  – The price – Processes
	  – Place (distribution) – Physical evidence
	  – Promotion (advertising etc)
	
	• The mix strategy may vary for each segment.

Budgets	These are developed from the action programme.
Controls	These will be set up to monitor the progress of the plan and the budget.

To summarise, the following diagram shows how **marketing planning** fits into the corporate plan.

Marketing and corporate planning

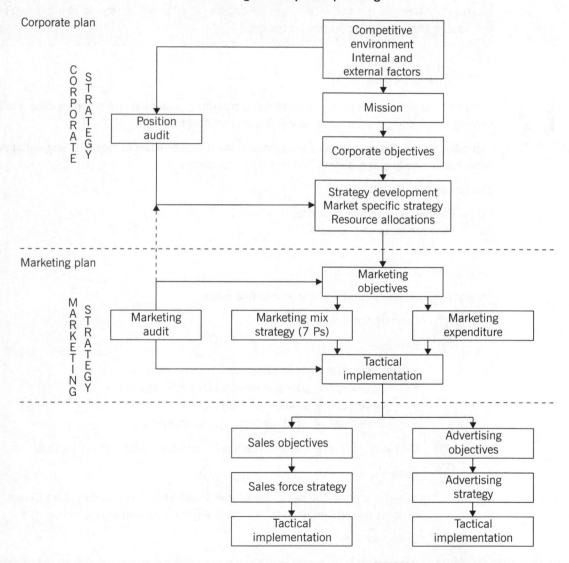

Section summary

An organisation's **marketing plan** is **driven by** and must therefore be **consistent** with its **corporate strategy**.

4 Marketing strategy

Introduction

In this section we look at **marketing strategy** – in other words how the organisation decides which markets to attack and how to position itself within each market. The **key activities** in this process are **market research**, **market segmentation**, **targeting** and **positioning**.

Market research is the initial stage in which the organisation obtains data about its customers and their needs.

A **market segment** is a group of customers with similar characteristics who can be **targeted** with the same **marketing mix**. Segmentation bases can include **objective classifications** (eg age) as well as more **subjective approaches** such as lifestyle or attitudes.

Having analysed the **attractiveness of a segment**, the organisation chooses one or more **target markets**.

Market positioning is the act of designing the company's offer and image so that it occupies a **distinct** and **valued place** in the **target** customer's mind.

4.1 Market research

KEY TERM

MARKET RESEARCH is the process of gathering, recording, analysing and reporting data and information relating to the company's market, customers and competitors.

Typically, market research is used to determine the **characteristics of markets**, suggest **opportunities for products** and **selling approaches** and to suggest **segments**.

The research can relate to:

(a) **Existing products** and services
(b) **New products** and services

4.1.1 A market research plan

Market research plans can be analysed into **five steps**.

Defining the problem

Example

- Explaining a fall in sales
- Investigating potential demand for a new product
- Investigating attitudes to the brand
- Investigating what matters most to consumers

Developing the hypotheses to be tested, and the purpose of the research

Example

In some studies, the researchers have a particular question they want to test. The purpose of some research may be to see if it is worth doing further research.

Collecting data

Example

A variety of approaches are used, such as surveys or questionnaires.

Analyse and interpret the data

Example

The type of analysis depends on the type of research. Not all research is quantitative with statistical validity. The emphasis on statistical assumptions is important – statistics can be misunderstood and misused.

Report the findings

Example

The results of the research are written up and presented in a report to the client.

4.1.2 Quantitative vs qualitative data

KEY POINTS

Quantitative data enables measurement. The purpose is to measure the response of a sample of consumers, on the assumption that measurable conclusions can be drawn from it. An example could be a survey of structured questionnaires sent out to a sample of a population.

Qualitative data is not measurable, but it is useful to get people to say what they feel and think, as opposed to giving relatively simple answers to unstructured questions.

4.1.3 Secondary vs primary data

KEY POINT

Secondary data may be generated by sources internal or external to the organisation. It is termed secondary because its intended use is not the specific research the organisation is using it for. Secondary data is usually gathered before primary data as it is often cheaper to collect and is used to guide the primary research. It is not normally sufficient for research purposes by itself.

Secondary data	
Source	**Uses**
Internal	
• From existing information systems • Accounting data • Customer databases • Data produced by other departments (eg complaints)	• Before primary research to give guidance • Instead of expensive primary research – some questions may already be answered
External	• Some information can only be acquired via secondary data
• Published statistics from government, professional/ trade bodies • Review of journals • Research already collected by market research agencies can be purchased, eg Nielsen Index on grocery chains and random surveys	• Where primary research is not possible

Primary data may be collected from sources internal or external to the organisation and may be qualitative or quantitative in nature. Primary data is collected for a specific research purpose.

Primary data	
Data collection method	**Comment**
Questionnaires, such as the following.	A number of precise questions requiring precise responses. Ensuring questions are free of ambiguity is absolutely vital.
• Post surveys	
• Telephone	Survey must be relevant to the data required.
• In street, via market researchers	Questionnaires often move from the general to the specific.
• Over the Internet	The interviewer always has to locate suitable respondents.
• At home	A danger with postal questionnaires is that the response is self-selected.
• In hotels	
• In shops	
Experiment	The researcher may set up artificial surroundings or may test a product in real surroundings (eg asking software purchasers to try out Beta versions of certain packages).
Observation	People can be observed using product.
Unstructured interviews	There is no structure to what is effectively a conversation but the interviewer may have a checklist of topics to be covered.
Depth interviews	The aim is to explore attitudes and motives for behaviour that may not be conscious. If conducted properly, respondents can be encouraged to say what they feel.
Projective techniques	People often say that they will act in a different way than they actually behave. Researchers have borrowed methods from psychologists, and seek to uncover unconscious motives. Examples include: • Inkblot tests ('What images do you see in this inkblot?') • Word association • Thematic apperception tests ('What is going on in this picture?')
Focus groups	Focus groups usually consist of 8 to 10 respondents and an interviewer taking the role of group moderator. The group moderator introduces topics for discussion and intervenes as necessary to encourage respondents or to direct discussions if they threaten to wander too far off the point. The moderator will also need to control any powerful personalities and prevent them from dominating the group.

4.2 Forecasting demand

Forecasting demand for new products can be difficult. A **forecast** could be developed based on a range of information and mathematical techniques. Possible types of data and information are explained below.

4.2.1 Current demand

An estimate of demand as it would be 'today' could involve considering a number of factors, such as:

- Total market potential
- Area market potential (geographic)
- Total industry sales
- Relative market shares

4.2.2 Forecasting future demand

Preparing a sales (income) or demand forecast usually involves five stages:

 Prepare a **macroeconomic forecast** – what will happen to overall economic activity in the relevant economies in which a product is to be sold.

 Prepare an **industry sales forecast** – what will happen to overall sales in an industry based on the issues that influence the macroeconomic forecast.

 Prepare a **company sales forecast** – based on what management expect to happen to the company's market share.

 Prepare a **demand forecast** – based on three types of information:

- What customers are currently doing in the market (industry sales data, company sales data)

- Customer intentions in relation to buying products (survey of buyers' intentions, market tests, sales force opinions, expert opinions)

- What customers have done in the past in the market (past-sales analysis)

 Prepare an **income forecast** – based on the information created in Steps 1-4. Income is dependent on forecasted demand and prices.

4.2.3 Survey of buyers' intentions

There are many market research agencies that undertake surveys of **customer intentions** – and sell this information on. The value of a customer intention survey increases when there are a relatively small number of customers, the cost of reaching them is small, and they have clear intentions.

4.2.4 Market tests

Instead of simply asking customers about their intentions, marketers may conduct **market tests**. Tests may be particularly useful when **finalising product design**. Alternative designs may be evaluated, with different features.

4.2.5 Sales force opinions

Another option is to use opinions from members of the **sales force** to forecast sales. This may be difficult if the product is new, although salespeople may be able to get a feel for the market by talking with clients and potential clients.

Unfortunately, **sales people may try to forecast low sales** if these forecasts will form the basis of their future sales targets. On the other hand, **marketing executives** may provide **over-optimistic forecasts** to help gain approval for the project or motivate the sales force.

4.2.6 Expert opinions

Expert opinion studies are widely used for forecasting marketing problems. For example, forecasts may be obtained from **industry experts, distributors** or **consultancies**. Sometimes independent forecasts from more than one expert source may be combined to produce what should be a more realistic forecast.

4.2.7 Past-sales analysis

Many businesses use past sales as a starting point for future sales forecasts. Figures may then be processed through a model (for example a spreadsheet) that aims to take into account various factors, such as:

- Trends: are sales growing, remaining steady ('flat-lining') or in decline?
- Seasonal or cyclical factors that occur in a regular pattern.
- Likely competitor activity.
- Sales and marketing campaigns.

4.2.8 Sales potential

The amount of sales that a product can achieve is known as **sales potential**. Factors that influence sales potential include:

- How '**essential**' the product is to consumers
- The **overall size** of the **market**
- The **level of competition** in the market
- Whether consumers may **delay purchasing** the product (non-essential luxury items)
- **Price** – high prices may restrict the market
- **Promotional expenditure** – investment in promotion may broaden the market.

4.3 Market segmentation

A **market** is not a single homogeneous group of customers wanting an identical product. Markets consists of **potential buyers** with **different needs**, and **different buying behaviour**.

KEY TERM

MARKET SEGMENTATION may be defined as the subdividing of a market into distinct and increasingly homogeneous subgroups of customers, where any subgroup can conceivably be selected as a target market to be met with a distinct marketing mix.

Although the total market consists of widely different groups of consumers, each group consists of people (or organisations) with **common needs and preferences**, who perhaps react to 'market stimuli' in much the same way.

Each market segment can become a **target market for an organisation**, and would require a unique marketing mix if the organisation is to exploit it successfully.

The organisation can then **position its offer** to account for the roles of each segment.

4.3.1 The bases for segmentation

There are many different **bases for segmentation**. One basis will not be appropriate in every market, and sometimes two or more bases might be valid at the same time. One **segmentation variable** might be 'superior' to another in a hierarchy of variables.

Simple segmentation could be on one of the bases below.

- Geographical area
- Age
- End use (eg work or leisure)
- Gender
- Level of income
- Occupation
- Education
- Religion
- Ethnicity
- Nationality

- Social class
- Buyer behaviour
- Lifestyle (see below)

Lifestyle segmentation deals with the **person** as opposed to the product and attempts to discover the particular lifestyle patterns of customers. Lifestyle refers to 'distinctive ways of living adopted by particular communities or subsections of society'. It involves combining a number of behavioural factors, such as motivation, personality and culture.

One simple example generalises **lifestyle** in terms of **four categories**, as follows.

Lifestyle categories	
Upwardly mobile, ambitious	These individuals seek a better and more affluent lifestyle, principally through better paid and more interesting work, and a higher material standard of living. A customer with such a lifestyle will be prepared to try new products.
Traditional and sociable	Here, compliance and conformity to group norms bring social approval and reassurance to the individual. Purchasing patterns will therefore be 'conformist'.
Security and status seeking	This group stresses 'safety' and 'ego-defensive' needs. This lifestyle links status, income and security. It encourages the purchase of strong and well known products and brands, and emphasises those products and services which confer status and make life as secure and predictable as possible. Products that are well established and familiar inspire more confidence than new products, which will be resisted.
Hedonistic preference	This lifestyle places emphasis on 'enjoying life now' and the immediate satisfaction of wants and needs. Little thought is given to the future.

4.3.2 Segment validity

A market segment will only **be valid if it is worth designing and developing a unique marketing mix** for it. A general rule is that a valid segment must be **substantial**, **measurable** and **accessible**. The following questions are commonly asked to decide whether or not the segment can be used for developing marketing plans.

Criteria	Comment
Can the segment be measured?	It might be possible to conceive a market segment, but it is not necessarily easy to measure it. For example, with a segment based on people with a conservative outlook to life, can conservatism of outlook be measured by market research?
Is the segment big enough?	There has to be a large enough potential market to be profitable.
Can the segment be reached?	There has to be a way of getting to the potential customers via the organisation's promotion and distribution channels.
Do segments respond differently?	If two or more segments are identified by planners, but each segment responds in the same way to a marketing mix, the segments are effectively one and the same. Consequently there is no point in distinguishing them from each other.
Can the segment be reached profitably?	Do the identified customer needs, cost less to satisfy than the revenue they earn?
Is the segment suitably stable?	The stability of the segment is important, if the organisation is to commit huge production and marketing resources to serve it. The organisation does not want the segment to 'disappear' next year. Of course, this may not matter in some industries.

4.3.3 Segment attractiveness

A segment might be valid and potentially profitable, but is it potentially **attractive?** Segments which are most attractive will be those whose needs can be met by building on the company's strengths and where forecasts for demand, sales profitability and **growth** are favourable.

4.3.4 Benefits of market segmentation

The organisation may be able to identify **new marketing opportunities**, because it will have a better understanding of customer needs in each segment, with the possibility of spotting further sub groups.

Specialists can be used for each of the organisation's major segments. For example, small business counsellors can be employed by banks to deal effectively with small organisations. A computer consultancy can have specialist sales staff for, say, shops, manufacturers, service industries and local government authorities. This builds competences and establishes effective marketing systems.

The **total marketing budget** can be allocated proportionately to each segment and the likely return from each segment. This optimises return on investment.

The organisation can **make small adjustments** to the product and service offerings and to the promotional aspects for each segment. This again promotes efficient use of resources.

The organisation can try to **dominate particular segments**, therefore gaining competitive advantage. Advantages created may function synergistically, promoting improved competitive ability – in other words, the outcome is more than the sum of its parts.

The **product range** can more closely reflect differences in customer needs. Marketing relies on responsiveness to the consumer. When this is improved, benefits can flow.

Question 8.3	Market segmentation

Learning outcome D2(ii)

Identify and briefly explain five benefits that a company may obtain through market segmentation.

(10 marks)

4.4 Target markets

Limited resources, competition and large markets make it ineffective and inappropriate for companies to sell to the entire market – that is, every market segment. For the sake of efficiency they must select target markets. A **target market** is a market or segment selected for special attention by an organisation (possibly served with a distinct marketing mix). The management of a company may choose one of the following policy options.

Marketing strategy	Comment	Alignment to competitive strategy
Mass (or undifferentiated) marketing	This policy is to produce a single product and hope to get as many customers as possible to buy it – segmentation is ignored entirely.	The mass (or undifferentiated) marketing approach can be pursued by cost leaders or companies pursuing a differentiation strategy with a single market.

Marketing strategy	Comment	Alignment to competitive strategy
Concentrated marketing	The company attempts to produce the ideal product for a single segment of the market (for example, Rolls Royce cars). The disadvantage of concentrated marketing is the business risk of relying on a single segment of a single market.	Concentrated marketing is effectively a focus strategy, whether by cost or differentiation.
Differentiated marketing	The company markets several product versions, each aimed at a different market segment. The disadvantage of differentiated marketing is the additional costs of marketing and production. When the costs of further differentiation of the market exceed the benefits from further segmentation and target marketing, an organisation is said to have 'over-differentiated'.	Differentiated marketing is effectively a multi-focus strategy, with a company pursing different opportunities in different segments.

CASE STUDY

Reaching Out to an Older Crowd

For decades, marketing has been youth-focused. But the fact is, 90 million Americans are 50 and over – that's 42% of the adult population of the U.S. And during the next decade that number will grow by 22 million.

'Small-business owners who start recognising **the needs and preferences of middle-aged and older consumers** have the chance to gain an advantage over larger firms', says Dick Stroud. Stroud is the founder of 20plus30, a London-based marketing consultancy. He spoke recently with columnist Karen E. Klein, edited excerpts of their conversation follow.

'When talking about older people, the U.S. media and marketing industry uses the term 'boomers.' Europe has adopted the term '50-plus.' These groups represent **a very large number of potential customers**. During the next decade, their numbers will increase six times faster than their children and grandchildren's age group of 15- to 34-year-olds.

'The other reason why the over-50s are so important relates to their **purchasing power**. Older consumers are the primary purchasers of transportation, healthcare, housing, food, pensions, and personal insurance. More than half of all cars purchased by an average American household occur after the head of the household turns 50; and they are big spenders on vacations and travel.

To market to this group effectively, business owners should decide **what segment** of the over-50 population is appropriate to their product or service. This could be done on the basis of geography, income, lifestyle, gender, or any number of other factors. Then, **research** is needed to understand what the target customers really want.

The most dangerous stereotype is to view all over 50s as a single group. The next mistake is to believe any of the nonsense about older people being averse to trying new brands, not wanting to use technology, or not seeking new life experiences. None of these assumptions is substantiated by research.

The Internet is a really important marketing tool for this group. The physiological effects of aging need to be considered here – image size, colour, contrast and website structure are all important.

I think the bottom line is that smaller companies are already leading the way in marketing to this demographic and they're going to continue to do so. For example, there are an awful lot of small travel companies that focus almost exclusively on 50-plus customers because they do spend a lot on travel. They have found, maybe by accident, that this is a growth market for them, and they've become very successful at it.

I've also seen this in the insurance industry. Real estate, with the amount of people who sell their property and move as they reach this age group, is another huge sector. But there are lots of other ways to think about it, if business owners get creative and pay attention.

Adapted from an article by Karen E. Klein, *Business week online,* April 3, 2006

4.5 Positioning

Market position refers to how customers perceive a brand or product relative to other brands or products. When positioning their products and services, most organisations want to achieve a clear, unique, and positive position, such as the cheapest supermarket or highest quality vehicle manufacturer.

(a)   Many products are, in fact, very similar, and the key issue is to make them distinct in the customer's mind.

(b)   Few products occupy a market space on their own. Inevitably they will be positioned in relation to competing products and companies.

(c)   People remember 'number 1', so the product should be positioned as 'number 1' in relation to a positioning variable.

(i)   Attributes (eg size)
(ii)   Benefits (eg convenience)
(iii)   Use/application (ease of use; accessibility)
(iv)   User (the sort of person the product is meant to appeal to)
(v)   Product category (consciously differentiated from competition)
(vi)   Image
(vii)   Quality/price (premium price)

4.6 Developments in market segmentation and product positioning

Approaches to **market segmentation** and **product positioning** are continually changing. Here are a few developments in recent years.

Development	Comment
There is a growing awareness that consumers should be segmented according to the purpose of the segmentation.	For example, the same customers of a retail bank can be segmented by their account profile, for the purpose of product cross-selling, by their attitudes to risk-taking for the purpose of delivering advertising messages and by socio-economic type for the purpose of selecting a marketing medium.
There is growing interest in customer database analysis, and the idea of 'letting the data speak for itself'.	Customer information on a database is analysed in order to identify segments or patterns of behaviour. This technique, known as 'data mining' is likely to increase in significance as e-commerce grows in popularity.
There is growing emphasis on segmentation by 'soft' data.	Consumer attitudes and needs and lifestyles (as distinct from 'hard data' such as age, lifestyle, socio-economic grouping, and so on).
There is a growing use of sub-segmentation or 'hybrid segmentation' methods.	Consumers within a particular segment can be sub-divided into different segments, and each sub-segment is targeted in a different way.
Computer models are used.	These will discover suitable additions to a product line, that will appeal to a separately-distinguished market segment.

4.7 The Ansoff matrix

Ansoff (1987) devised a matrix showing **possible strategies for products and markets**.

Ansoff's competitive strategies (Ansoff matrix)

Products

		Existing	**New**
Markets	**Existing**	Market Penetration 1	Product Development 4
	New	Market Development 2	Diversification 16

The numbers in the quadrants are an approximate indication of the **risk** attached to each strategy. Diversification is the riskiest.

(a)   **Market penetration** involves increasing sales of the **existing products in existing markets**.

(b)   **Market development** entails **expansion into new markets using existing products**.

(c)   **Product development** involves the redesign or repositioning of existing products or the introduction of completely new ones in order to appeal to existing markets.

(d)   **Diversification** involves producing new products for new markets. It is much more risky than the other three because the organisation is moving into areas in which it has little or no experience.

Question 8.4   Marketing strategy

Learning outcome D2(ii)

Identify and explain *Ansoff's* possible strategies for products and markets as shown in his matrix.

(4 marks)

Section summary

Market research is used to determine the **characteristics of markets**, suggest **opportunities for products** and **selling approaches** and to **suggest segments**.

Market research information can help **forecast future sales levels**.

Market segmentation involves subdividing a market into distinct and increasingly homogeneous subgroups of customers which may be selected as a **target market** to be met with a distinct marketing mix.

Market position refers to how customers perceive a brand or product relative to other brands or products.

Market penetration involves increasing sales of **existing products in existing markets**.

Market development entails expansion into **new markets** with **existing products**.

Product development involves the redesign or repositioning of existing products or the introduction of completely new ones in order to appeal to existing markets.

Diversification involves producing **new products** for **new markets**.

Chapter Roundup

- ✓ **Marketing** is the management process which identifies, anticipates and supplies customer requirements efficiently and profitably.

- ✓ The **marketing concept** is a business philosophy which attempts to **meet consumer needs**.

- ✓ A **production orientation** may be defined as the management view that success is achieved through producing goods or services of optimum quality and cost.

- ✓ Under a **sales orientation** the tendency is to make the product and then actively and aggressively sell it.

- ✓ **Product orientated** organisations focus on product development.

- ✓ An organisation's **marketing environment** can be analysed into **political**, **economic**, **social**, **technological**, **ecological** and **legal factors** (PESTEL).

- ✓ An organisation's **marketing plan** is **driven by** and must therefore be **consistent** with its **corporate strategy**.

- ✓ **Market research** is used to determine the **characteristics of markets**, suggest **opportunities for products** and **selling approaches** and to **suggest segments**.

- ✓ **Market research information** can help **forecast future sales levels**.

- ✓ **Market segmentation** involves subdividing of a market into distinct and increasingly homogeneous subgroups of customers which may be selected as a **target market** to be met with a distinct marketing mix.

- ✓ **Market position** refers to how customers perceive a brand or product relative to other brands or products

- ✓ **Market penetration** involves increasing sales of **existing products in existing markets**.

- ✓ **Market development** entails expansion into **new markets** with **existing products**.

- ✓ **Product development** involves the redesign or repositioning of existing products or the introduction of completely new ones in order to appeal to existing markets.

- ✓ **Diversification** involves selling **new products** in **new markets**.

Quick Quiz

1   Which type of marketing involves identifying the products and markets the organisation wishes to operate in?

    A   Mass marketing
    B   Target marketing
    C   Strategic marketing
    D   Tactical marketing

2   Which of the following factors may be useful when forecasting demand'?

    A   Area Market Potential
    B   Total Industry Sales
    C   Relative Market Share
    D   All of the above

3   According to *Ansoff*, which approach should be taken when introducing a new product to an existing market?

    A   Market development
    B   Product development
    C   Market penetration
    D   Diversification

4   List five possible bases for market segmentation.

    1   ....

    2   ....

    3   ....

    4   ....

    5   ....

5   Which of the following is an example of data mining?

    A   Analysing customer information held in a database to identify behavioural patterns.
    B   Setting up a database to store customer sales records
    C   Storing and recording customer surveys in a database
    D   Statistical analysis of macroeconomic data

Answers to Quick Quiz

1   C   Strategic marketing involves identifying the products and markets the organisation wishes to operate in.

2   D   All may help forecast demand.

3   B   According to *Ansoff*, product development should be undertaken when introducing new products into an existing market. This means making sure the product will be acceptable to the market.

4   Geographical area, age, gender, income level, occupation – others may be equally valid.

5   A   Data mining involves analysing a database to identify new information such as behavioural patterns of customers.

Answer to Question

8.1 Strategic and tactical marketing

Strategic marketing covers long-term decisions such as which market to operate in.
Example: a retailer decides to set up an outlet in a new country.

Tactical marketing covers short-term decisions relating to the marketing mix.
Example: a retailer decides to cut prices to clear space for new stock.

8.2 Product and production orientation

Product orientated organisations focus on product development particularly product features.

Production orientated organisations focus on production efficiency and minimising costs.

Both production and product orientated organisations place little emphasis on market research or customer needs – and producing products takes precedence over identifying customers.

8.3 Market segmentation

Benefit	Brief explanation
Better satisfaction of customer needs	One approach will not satisfy *all* customers.
Revenue growth	Segmentation means that more customers may be attracted by, and pay more for, what is on offer, in preference to competing products.
Customer retention	By targeting customers, their needs are more likely to be met leading to repeat purchase.
Targeted communications	Segmentation enables clear communications as people in the target audience share common needs.
Innovation	By identifying un-met needs, companies can innovate to satisfy them.

8.4 Marketing strategy

Ansoff's matrix shows possible strategies for products and markets.

Market penetration – increasing sales of existing products in existing markets.

Market development – expansion into new markets using existing products.

Product development – changing existing products or introducing new ones into existing markets.

Diversification – both new products and new markets.

Now try this question from the Exam Question Bank	Number	Level	Marks	Time
	8	Examination	20	45 mins

MARKETING PLANS, BRANDING AND COMMUNICATIONS

Once an organisation has formed its overall marketing strategy work can begin on an **action plan** which consists of the **marketing activities** required for the strategy to be successful.

The **key activities** are centred around the traditional **4Ps** of the marketing mix (for **products**) and the **7Ps** of the extended marketing mix (for **services**). The

different mixes are required due to the differing nature of products and services.

Once the action plan has been developed, the organisation's **message needs to be communicated**. This can be achieved in a myriad of ways, the choice of which depends on whether a consumer or another business is the subject of the marketing campaign.

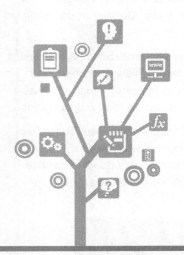

9

topic list	learning outcomes	syllabus references	ability required
1 Marketing action plans	D2(b)	D2(iv), D2(v), D2(vi), D2(xii), D2(xiv), D2(xv)	application
2 Branding	D2(e)	D2(xi)	comprehension
3 Marketing communications	D2(c)	D2(iii), D2(viii), D2(ix)	comprehension

1 Marketing action plans   11/10

Introduction

Once an organisation has determined which market segments to attack and which strategies it should use, the next stage in the marketing plan is to develop and **action plan**.

Action plans are usually based around what is known as the **marketing mix**. *Kotler and Keller* (2006) define the marking mix as 'the set of controllable variables and their levels that the firm uses to influence the target market'.

These variables should be **carefully considered** as each will directly affect the success of failure of the marketing effort.

1.1 The marketing mix   05/10, 05/11

Most of us have experience of being marketed 'to' in a variety of different ways. In developed countries and, increasingly, in developing ones, people are subjected to a variety of different marketing activities.

Media and public spaces are full of advertisements such as posters, TV ads, pop-up ads on websites, even text messages on mobile phones. In marketing terminology these are known as **promotion** (or marketing communications).

Many of these messages aim, to persuade people to want to purchase certain **products** or services. **People** are trained to produce and deliver these products or services to **places** where we can buy them. Sophisticated **processes** might be involved in production and managing the sale. Delivery is also designed and managed.

For a service (which by its nature is intangible), sometimes we require **physical evidence** that the service is to be provided. For example, a letter or guarantee for building work or testimonials or references to reassure potential customers. The **price** we pay is not arbitrary – it has been thought through. Phrases such as 'that was good value for money' suggest that price and value are important in buying decisions.

In the paragraphs above, seven words or phrases beginning with 'p' have been emboldened. These form what is known as the **extended marketing mix**. Traditionally, the marketing mix was the **'four Ps'** (**product**, **price**, **place**, **promotion**). **Three extra 'P's** have been added to describe the issues in **service industries** (eg for a restaurant: *people* waiters, *processes* the cooking process, *place* the physical environment of the restaurant).

The extended marketing mix the 7 Ps	
The traditional marketing mix (4 Ps)	You can add . . . (3 Ps)
Product	People (the '5th P')
Price	Processes
Place (distribution)	Physical evidence
Promotion	

1.2 Product

KEY TERM

A **PRODUCT** (goods or services) is anything that satisfies a need or want. It is not a 'thing' with 'features' but a package of benefits.

From the organisation's point of view the **product element** of the marketing mix is what is being sold, whether it be widgets, power stations, haircuts, holidays or financial advice. From the customer's point of view, a **product is a solution to a problem or a package of benefits.** Many products might satisfy the same customer need.

On what **basis** might a **customer choose a product**?

(a)   **Customer value** is the customer's estimate of how far a product or service goes towards satisfying their need(s).

(b)   Every product has a price, and so the customer makes a **trade-off** between the **expenditure** and **the value offered**.

(c)   According to *Kotler* a customer must feel that they get a **better deal** from buying an item than by any of the alternatives.

1.2.1 Product classification

KEY POINTS

Products can be classified as **consumer goods or industrial goods**. Consumer goods are sold directly to the person who will ultimately use them. Industrial goods are used in the production of other products.

Consumer goods can be classified as follows.

Convenience goods	Weekly groceries are a typical example. There is a further distinction between **staple goods** (eg bread and potatoes) and **impulse buys**, like the bar of chocolate found at the supermarket checkout. **Brand awareness** is extremely important in this sector.
Shopping goods	These are the more durable items that you buy, like furniture or washing machines. This sort of purchase is usually only made after a good deal of advance planning and shopping around.
Speciality goods	These are items like jewellery or the more expensive items of clothing.
Unsought goods	These are goods that the customer did not realise they needed! Typical examples are new and sometimes 'gimmicky' products, such as 'wardrobe organisers', or fire resistant car polish!

Industrial goods can be classified as follows.

- **Installations**, eg major items of plant and machinery like a factory assembly line
- **Accessories**, such as PCs
- **Raw materials**, for example plastic, metal, wood, foodstuffs and chemicals
- **Components**, eg the Lucas headlights on Ford cars, the Intel microchip in most PCs
- **Supplies**, such as office stationery and cleaning materials

1.2.2 Product levels

It is useful for marketers to think of a product, and its attributes, at different levels.

Product attributes

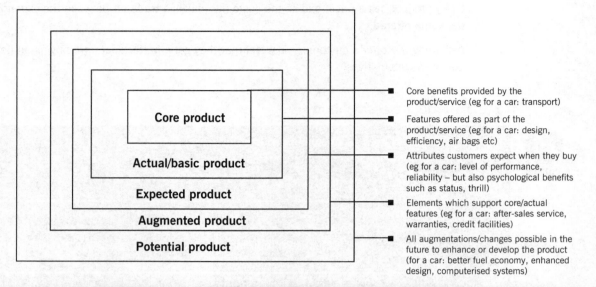

- Core benefits provided by the product/service (eg for a car: transport)
- Features offered as part of the product/service (eg for a car: design, efficiency, air bags etc)
- Attributes customers expect when they buy (eg for a car: level of performance, reliability – but also psychological benefits such as status, thrill)
- Elements which support core/actual features (eg for a car: after-sales service, warranties, credit facilities)
- All augmentations/changes possible in the future to enhance or develop the product (for a car: better fuel economy, enhanced design, computerised systems)

KEY POINTS

The **core/generic product** is those benefits that all the products in the category would have – all cars, for example, provide transport.

The **augmented product** is the core product plus extra benefits that differentiate it from other products in the category. These might include warranty, delivery, installation, after-sales support.

Many products are marketed at the **augmented product** level – the total package of the customer's experience of purchasing and consuming the product/service is relevant.

The **expected product** level is also important, because of the potential for customers to be dissatisfied (by disappointed expectations) or delighted (by exceeding expectations).

The **potential product** is important in providing the marketing organisation with future avenues to develop the product (and marketing message) in order to stay competitive and 'fresh' in the market.

Product issues in the marketing mix will include such factors as:

- Design (size, shape)
- Features
- Quality and reliability

- After-sales service (if necessary)
- Packaging

1.2.3 Product range

KEY POINT

A company's **product range** (or product portfolio, assortment or mix) is all the product lines and items that the company offers for sale.

A company's **product range** can be described in the following terms.

Characteristic	Defined by:
Width/Breadth	Number of product lines: eg cosmetics, haircare, toiletries and health products.
Depth	Average number of items per product line: eg cosmetics including moisturiser, cleanser, toner, lipstick, eyeshadow etc.
Consistency	Closeness of relationships in product range for the benefit of users and production/distribution processes.

1.2.4 Managing the product range

There are benefits to be gained from using a systematic approach to the management of the product range. It can be **reduced** (eg by discontinuing a product) or **extended** by:

- Introducing variations in models or style (eg a paint manufacturer introducing different colours, types and pot sizes)

- Differentiating the quality of products offered at different price levels (eg 'premium' paints and 'value' paints)

- Developing associated items (eg a paint roller and brushes, paint trays, colour charts)

- Developing new products with little technical or marketing relationship to the existing range (eg wallpaper and DIY accessories – or something completely different)

Managing the product range also raises **broad issues** such as:

- What role a product should play in the range. ('Flagship' brand? Profit provider? Niche filler? New market tester/developer? Old faithful, retaining customer loyalty?) The roles of products in the mix should create a balanced range, with sufficient **cash-generating** products to support **cash-using** (declining or new/market-developing) products

- How resources should be allocated between products

- What should be expected from each product

- How far products should be integrated within the brand image and be recognisable as part of the brand family

Marketing is not an exact science and there is no definitive approach or technique which can determine how resources should be shared across the product range. There are, however, techniques which can aid decision making. Ultimately the burden of the decision is a management responsibility and requires judgement, but tools such as the **BCG matrix** and the **product life cycle** can help the decision-making process.

1.2.5 The BCG matrix

KEY POINT

The **BCG matrix** classifies products or brands on the basis of their market share and according to the rate of growth in the market as a whole, as a way of assessing their role in the product range.

Relative market share

		High	Low
Market growth rate	**High**	Star	Question mark (or Problem child)
	Low	Cash cow	Dog

On the basis of this classification, each product may fall into one of four broad categories.

(a) **Question mark** (or problem child): A small market share in a high growth industry.

The generic product is clearly popular, but customer support for the particular brand is limited. A small market share implies that competitors are in a strong position and that if the product is to be successful it will require substantial funds, and a new marketing mix. If the market looks good and the product is viable, then the company should consider a 'build' strategy to increase market share by increasing the resources available for that product to permit more active marketing. If the future looks less promising, then the company should consider withdrawing the product. Which strategy is chosen will depend on the strength of competitors, availability of funding and other relevant factors.

(b) **Star**: A high market share in a high growth industry.

The star has potential for generating significant earnings, currently and in the future. At this stage it may still require substantial marketing expenditure as part of a 'maintain' strategy, but this is probably regarded as a good investment for the future.

(c) **Cash Cow**: A high market share in a mature slow-growth market.

Typically, a well established product with a high degree of consumer loyalty. Product development costs are typically low and the marketing campaign is well established. The cash cow will normally make a substantial contribution to overall profitability. The appropriate strategy will vary according to the precise position of the cash cow. If market growth is reasonably strong then a 'holding' strategy will be appropriate. However, if growth and/or share are weakening, then a 'harvesting' strategy may be more sensible by cutting back on marketing expenditure to maximise short-term profit.

(d) **Dog**: A low market share in a low-growth market.

Like the cash cow, this is a well established product, but one which is apparently losing consumer support and may have cost disadvantages. The usual strategy would be to consider divestment, unless the cash flow position is strong, in which case the product would be harvested in the short term, prior to deletion from the product range.

 The BCG matrix will be a useful tool to use in paper P2 to carry out a product mix analysis.

1.2.6 The product life cycle

KEY POINT

The classic pattern of a **product life cycle (PLC)** is in **four-stages**, an **introduction** to the market, a **growth**, **market maturity** and then **decline**. However, products can be rejuvenated so that their life cycle continues.

The priorities for performance objectives will change as a product goes through the phases of its life cycle.

(a) **Introduction stage**. The product or service offers something new to customers. There are unlikely to be any competing products, but heavy advertising costs may be incurred to raise customer awareness. Design changes may be required, as customer needs become better understood. A business needs to establish an operational capability that allows it to be flexible and capable of adapting and changing.

(b) **Growth stage**. The volume of demand for the product increases, and there are likely to be more competitors in the market. Product features may become important between different suppliers. The main objective for the operations function could be to keep up with the growing demand. Speed of response to customer orders and reliability of supply could also be significant. Quality standards will have to be maintained or improved in response to the growing competition, and cost and price are likely to be much more significant.

(c)   **Market maturity**. Demand levels off. Some early competitors are likely to have left the market, which might now be shared by a small number of organisations. Product design will be largely standardised, although organisations might try to develop new varieties of the product to extend its life cycle. Organisations in the market are likely to compete on price and/or on value for money (product differentiation). To remain competitive, it will be important to achieve low costs through productivity improvements, whilst still providing reliability of supply.

(d)   **Decline stage**. Total demand declines and competitors will start to withdraw from the market. There will nevertheless be excess capacity in the industry, and the remaining organisations will compete on price. Cost targets will remain the key operational objective. The company may also decide to stop making and selling the product, and to focus its energies instead on another developing/growing product.

Some writers refer to an additional phase between market growth and market maturity. Often at this time, some of the weaker players in the market (initially attracted by market growth) are 'shaken out' of the market by the stronger organisations. This is referred to as a '**shakeout**'.

The Product Life Cycle

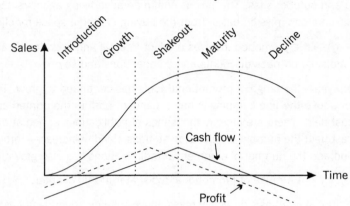

1.3 Place

Place deals with how the **product is distributed**, and how it reaches its customers.

(a)   **Channel**. Where are products sold? In supermarkets, corner shops? Which sales outlets will be chosen?

(b)   **Logistics**. The location of warehouses and efficiency of the distribution system is also important. A customer might have to wait a long time if the warehouse is far away. Arguably, the **speed of delivery** is an important issue in **place**.

An organisation can distribute the product itself (**direct distribution**) or distribute it through intermediary organisations such as **retailers**.

1.4 Promotion   05/10

Many of the practical activities of the marketing department are related to **promotion**. Promotion is the element of the mix over which the marketing department generally has most control. A useful mnemonic is AIDA which summarises the aims of promotion.

- Arouse **Attention**
- Generate **Interest**
- Inspire **Desire**
- Initiate **Action** (ie buy the product)

Promotion in the marketing mix includes all **marketing communications** which let the public know of the product or service.

- Advertising (newspapers, billboards, TV, radio, direct mail, Internet)
- Sales promotion (discounts, coupons, special displays in particular stores)
- Direct selling by sales personnel.
- Public relations

Lancaster and Withey (2005) identified the following elements of successful advertising. It must be

- **Well planned** and **executed**
- **Effective** as a method of communication
- Part of an **overall effective promotional mix**
- **Aligned** with the overall **values** and **mission** of the **company**

1.4.1 The range of promotional tools

KEY TERMS

ABOVE-THE-LINE campaigning is advertising placed in paid for media, such as the press, radio, TV, cinema and outdoor sites. The 'line' is one in an advertising agency's accounts, above which are shown its earnings on a commission basis, from the buying of media space for clients.

BELOW-THE-LINE promotion involves product-integral and negotiated sales incentives, such as packaging, merchandising, on-pack discounts and competitions and so on.

In recent years the range of **promotional tools** has continued to grow. The variety of media that can be used for **above-the-line** campaigns has expanded, both in the printed advertising field and in the broadcast field. There are literally thousands of publications aimed at different target groups. In the broadcast field the number of television stations steadily increases through satellite, cable and digital television and the number of commercial radio stations has also grown considerably.

We shall look at a range of promotional tools later in this chapter.

The traditional emphasis on heavy mass above-the-line advertising has given way to more highly targeted campaigns. Below-the-line, and even what *Fill* (2002*)* terms '**through-the-line**' promotion is now far more common. To quote Fill:

> "The shift is from an **intervention-based approach** to marketing communications (one based on seeking the attention of a customer who might not necessarily be interested), towards **permission-based communications** (where the focus is upon communications with members of an audience who have already expressed an interest in a particular offering)."

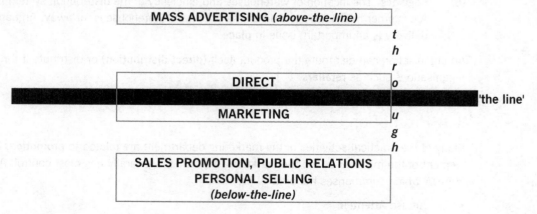

1.4.2 The product life cycle and promotional strategy

Each of the stages of the **product life cycle (PLC)**, from introduction to decline have different strategic requirements from their promotional activities.

Promotional Activities	Introduction	Growth	Maturity	Decline
Strategic focus	Strong push then pull for awareness	Pull to differentiate	Pull and push to sustain loyalty and exposure through reassurance	Some pull to remind core users
Public relations	✕		✕	
Advertising	✕	✕	✕	
Direct marketing		✕	✕	✕
Personal selling	✕	✕	✕	✕
Sales promotion	✕		✕	

The table above sets out the **strategic focus for each phase,** and the main promotional activities to be considered. What the table does not show is the way the promotional tools are used to support a push as opposed to pull approach. One particular benefit of the PLC is that it is possible to overlay the various stages of the process of **diffusion**. Through this it is possible to identify the **different types of buyer** involved with the product at each stage and through this fine tune the appropriate message and media.

1.4.3 Introduction

For consumer brands this phase is critical as the primary need is to **secure trade acceptance** (and hence shelf space) and then build **public (target audience) awareness**. Sunny Delight was developed by Proctor & Gamble in consultation with major multiple grocers. When the product was launched the multiples accepted the brand as it had been developed partly to their specification on price, ingredient and packaging/size.

1.4.4 Growth

During growth, promotional activity is used competitively to **build market share**. Customers are normally willing to buy, having been made aware, but their problem becomes one of **brand choice**. Marketing communications should therefore be used to **differentiate and clearly position** the product such that it represents significant value for the customer.

1.4.5 Maturity

Once the rapid growth in a market starts to ease, the period of maturity commences. The primary characteristic of this stage is that there is little or no growth. The battle therefore is to **retain customer loyalty**. To do this, sales promotions are often used, to encourage trial by non-users and to reward current users.

1.4.6 Decline

As sales start to decline it is normal practice to withdraw a great deal of promotion support. **Direct marketing** and a little well targeted advertising to **remind** and **reassure** brand loyalists is the most commonly used.

1.4.7 Co-ordinating promotional tools

Promotion aims to **influence customers** favourably towards an organisation's products or services. It is necessary to co-ordinate all the promotional elements to achieve the maximum influence on the customer.

This can involve trial and error, and market research to establish the effectiveness of various combinations of promotional tools (the promotion mix). The aim is optimal **effectiveness**, **economy** and **efficiency** of the promotional tools. We cover the promotion mix later in this chapter.

1.5 Price

There are three main types of influence on **price setting** in practice: **costs**, **competition** and **demand**.

1.5.1 Costs

In practice, cost is the most important influence on price. Many organisations base price on simple **cost-plus** rules. In other words, costs are estimated and then a profit margin is added in order to set the price. This method is fairly easy to apply and ensures that costs are covered.

A common example occurs with the use of **mark-up** pricing. This is used by retailers and involves a fixed margin being added to the buying-in price of goods for resale.

Because the cost-plus approach leads to price stability, with price changing only being used to reflect cost changes, it can lead to a marketing strategy which is **reactive** rather then **proactive**. In addition, there is very limited consideration of **demand** in cost-based pricing strategies. From a marketing perspective, cost-based pricing may lead to **missed opportunities** as little or no account is taken, particularly in the short run, of the price consumers are **willing** to pay for the brand, which may actually be higher than the cost-based price.

1.5.2 Competition

In some markets, **going rate pricing** in which some form of average level of price becomes the norm, perhaps, in the case of a high level of branding in the market, including standard price differentials between brands.

In some market structures **price competition may be avoided by informal agreement** leading to concentration on non-price competition – the markets for cigarettes and petrol are examples of this.

1.5.3 Demand

Rather than cost or competition as the prime determinants of price, a organisation may base pricing strategy on the **intensity** and **elasticity** of demand. **Strong demand may lead to a high price, and a weak demand to a low price** – much depends on the ability of the organisation to segment the market price in terms of elasticity.

For products or services with a typical downward sloping demand curve, fewer purchasers will buy at a **higher price**. If a supplier can identify those purchasers still willing to pay the higher price the supplier could benefit through charging them a higher price. This is called **price discrimination** or **differential pricing**.

In practice, **measurement of price elasticity** and, **implementing differential pricing** can be **very difficult**. There are a number of bases on which discriminating prices can be set.

(a)   **By market segment.** A cross-channel ferry company would market its services at different prices in England, Belgium and France, for example. Services such as cinemas and hairdressers are often available at lower prices to old age pensioners and juveniles.

(b)   **By product version.** Many car models have 'add on' extras which enable one brand to appeal to a wider cross-section of customers. Final price need not reflect the cost price of the add on extras directly. Usually the top of the range model would carry a price much in excess of the cost of provision of the extras, as a prestige appeal.

(c)   **By place.** Theatre seats are usually sold according to their location so that patrons pay different prices for the same performance according to the seat type they occupy.

(d)   **By time.** This is perhaps the most popular type of price discrimination.

Price sensitivity will vary amongst purchasers. **Those who can pass on the cost of purchases will be least sensitive** and will respond more to other elements of the marketing mix.

Pricing research is notoriously difficult, especially if respondents try to give rational rather than their 'real' response. As the respondent is not actually faced with the situation they may give a hypothetical answer that is not going to be translated into actual purchasing behaviour. Nevertheless, pricing research is increasingly common as organisations struggle to assess the perceived value customers attribute to a brand to provide an input to their pricing decisions.

1.5.4 Competitors' actions and reactions

An organisation, in setting prices, **sends out signals to rivals**. **These rivals are likely to react** in some way. In some industries (such as petrol retailing) pricing moves in unison, in others, price changes by one supplier may initiate a price war, with each supplier undercutting the others.

In established industries dominated by a few major organisations, it is generally accepted that a **price initiative by one organisation** will be countered by a **price reaction** by competitors. Here, prices tend to be fairly stable, unless pushed upwards by inflation or strong growth in demand.

In the event that a **rival cuts prices** expecting to increase market share, an organisation has several options.

(a)   It will **maintain its existing prices** if the expectation is that only a small market share would be lost, so that it is more profitable to keep prices at their existing level. Eventually, the rival organisation may drop out of the market or be forced to raise its prices.

(b)   It may **maintain its prices** but respond with a **non-price counter-attack**. This is a more positive response, because the organisation will be securing or justifying its current prices.

(c)   It may **reduce its prices**. This should protect the organisation's market share at the expense of profitability. The main beneficiary from the price reduction will be the consumer.

(d)   It may **raise its prices** and respond with a **non-price counter-attack**. The extra revenue from the higher prices might be used to finance promotion on product changes. A price increase would be based on a campaign to emphasise the quality difference between the organisation's own product and the rival's product.

1.5.5 Quality connotations

In the absence of other information, some customers tend to **judge quality by price**. Therefore a price change may send signals to customers concerning the quality of the product. A rise may be taken to indicate improvements, a reduction may signal reduced quality

1.5.6 New product pricing

Most pricing decisions for existing products relate to price changes. Such changes have a **reference point** from which to move (the existing price). But **when a new product is introduced for the first time there may be no such reference point** and therefore pricing decisions will be difficult to make.

1.5.7 Multiple products

Most organisations market not just one product but a **range of products**. These products are commonly interrelated, perhaps being complements or substitutes. The pricing strategy is likely to focus on the **profit** from the **whole range** rather than that on each single product. For example, the use of **loss leaders**. A very low price for one product is intended to make consumers buy other products in the range which carry higher profit margins.

1.6 Price setting strategies

After considering the issues above the following **price setting strategies** can be developed.

1.6.1 Market penetration

The organisation **sets a relatively low price** for the product or service in order to **stimulate growth of the market and/or to obtain a large share** of it.

This strategy is appropriate under three conditions.

- Unit costs will fall with increased output (economies of scale)
- The market is price sensitive and relatively low prices will attract additional sales
- Low prices will discourage new competitors

1.6.2 Market skimming

The organisation **sets a high initial price for a new product in order to take advantage of those buyers who are ready to pay a much higher price for it.** A typical strategy would be initially to set a premium price and then gradually to reduce the price to attract more price sensitive segments of the market.

This strategy is appropriate under three conditions.

- There is insufficient production capacity and competitors cannot increase their capacity
- Some buyers are relatively insensitive to high prices
- High price is perceived as high quality

1.6.3 Early cash recovery

The organisation **aims to recover the investment in a new product or service as quickly as possible**, to achieve a minimum payback period. The price is set to facilitate this objective.

This objective tends to be used in three circumstances.

- The business is high risk
- Rapid changes in fashion or technology are expected
- The innovator is short of cash

1.6.4 Product line promotion

The organisation **focuses on profit from the range of products** which the organisation produces **rather than to treat each product as a separate entity**.

This strategy looks at the whole range from two points of view.

- The interaction of the marketing mix
- Monitoring returns to ensure that net contribution is worthwhile

1.6.5 Cost-plus pricing

The organisation sets its price by **marking up its unit costs** by a certain percentage or fixed amount.

1.6.6 Target pricing

The organisation selects the price that gives a **specified rate of return** for a given output.

1.6.7 Price discrimination/selective pricing

The organisation **sets different prices** for **the same product** when it is **sold in different markets**.

Three sub-categories have evolved.

(a) **Category**

The product is cosmetically modified to justify a price differential. For example a 'budget' version of a product is modified into a 'premium' version.

(b) **Consumer group**

The price differential is justified by **targeting different consumer groups** for example, OAP or student prices. They are often used by leisure facilities such as leisure centres or galleries.

(c) **Peak**

The **price** is **set in accordance** with **demand**. For example, the price of train ticket is often more expensive in the morning when most people travel to work.

The danger is that price cuts to one buyer may be used as a **negotiating lever** by another buyer. This can be countered in three ways.

(a) Buyers can be split into clearly defined segments, such as overseas and home, or students' concessionary fares.

(b) Own branding, where packaging is changed for that of a supermarket, is a variation on this.

(c) Bulk buying discounts and aggregated rebate schemes can favour large buyers.

1.6.8 Going rate/competitive prices

The organisation tries to **keep in line with industry norm for prices**. This is also known as **competitive pricing** where prices are set with reference to competitors' pricing.

1.6.9 Price leadership/predatory pricing

In some markets a **price leader** (often a large corporation) emerges. A price leader dominates price levels for a class of products; increases or decreases by the price leader are followed by the market. The price dominant organisation may lead without moving at all. The price leader generally has a large market share and will usually be an efficient producer with a reputation for technical competence.

The **role of price leader** is based on a track record of having initiated price moves that have been accepted by both competitors and customers. Any dramatic changes in industry competition, (a new entrant, or changes in the board room) may endanger the price leadership role.

Predatory pricing is a similar strategy but the reason for setting a low price is to damage the competition.

1.7 Services and service marketing

Services have a different nature to goods and therefore the **marketing of services** presents a number of different challenges. As a consequence, particular marketing practices have been developed.

KEY TERM

SERVICES include:

'... those separately identifiable but intangible activities that provide want-satisfaction, and that are not, of necessity, tied to, or inextricable from, the sale of a product or another service. To produce a service may or may not require the use of tangible goods or assets. However, where such use is required, there is no transfer of title (permanent ownership) to these tangible goods.'*(Cowell, 1995)*

'... any activity of benefit that one party can offer to another that is essentially intangible and does not result in the ownership of anything. Its production may or may not be tied to a physical product.' (Kotler *et al.* 2002*)*

The following **characteristics of services distinguish them from goods,** and have marketing implications.

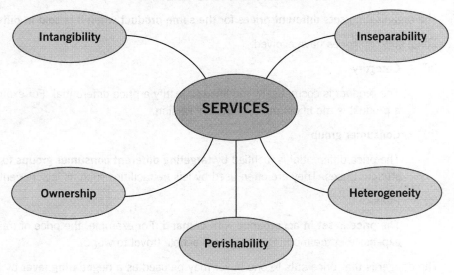

1.7.1 Intangibility

'Intangibility' refers to the **lack of substance** which is involved with service delivery. Unlike goods, there are no substantial material or physical aspects to a service – no taste, feel, visible presence and so on. This creates difficulties and can inhibit the desire to consume a service, since customers are not sure what they will receive.

Marketers and consumers need to try to overcome this problem. The marketer wishes to make the choice of the product 'safer' and make the consumer feel more comfortable about paying for something they do not then own and which has no physical form.

Dealing with intangibility may involve the following.

(a)   **Increasing the level of tangibility**. Use physical or conceptual representations/illustrations to make the customer feel more confident as to what it is that the service is delivering.

(b)   **Focusing the attention of the customer on the principal benefits of consumption**. Communicating the benefits of purchasing the service so that the customer visualises its use. Promotion and sales material could provide images or records of previous customers' experience.

(c)   **Differentiating the service and reputation-building**. Enhancing perceptions of customer service and customer value by offering excellence in the delivery of the service. This reputation can be attached to brands, which must then be managed to secure and enhance their market position, (for example, the Virgin brand).

1.7.2 Inseparability

Services often cannot be separated off from the provider, for example having dental treatment or taking a journey. Neither exists until they are actually being experienced/consumed by the person who has bought them. The 'creation' of many services is simultaneous with consumption, where the service is

- Made available
- Produced
- Sold
- Consumed

} all at the same time

Provision of the service may not be separable from the person or personality of the seller. Consequently, increasing importance is attached to the need to **instil values of quality**, **reliability** and to generate a **service ethic** in customer-facing staff. This points up the need for excellence and customer orientation and the need to invest in high quality people and high quality training.

1.7.3 Heterogeneity (lack of 'sameness' or consistency)

Many services face the problem of **maintaining consistency** in the standard of output. Variability of quality occurs because of the large number of variables involved. The quality of the service may depend heavily on who it is that delivers the service. For example, booking a holiday using standard procedures may well be quite different on a quiet winter afternoon and on a hectic spring weekend, and may well vary according to the person dealing with your case.

In terms of **marketing policy**, heterogeneity highlights the need to develop and maintain processes for:

- Consistency of quality control, with clear and objective quality measures
- Consistency of customer service and customer care, standardising as far as possible
- Effective staff selection, training and motivation in customer care
- Monitoring service levels and customer perceptions of service delivery

1.7.4 Perishability

Services cannot be stored – they are innately perishable. Seats on a bus or the services of a doctor exist only for periods of time. If they are not consumed, they 'perish'. They cannot be used later. They cannot be 'produced' in advance, to allow for peaks in demand.

This presents specific marketing problems. Meeting customer needs depends on staff being available as and when they are needed. This must be balanced against the need for an organisation to minimise unnecessary expenditure on staff wages. **Anticipating and responding to levels of demand** is, therefore, a key planning priority.

Policies must seek to **smooth out fluctuations** in supply/demand relationship, or allow for contingencies. Examples include:

- Using price variations to encourage off-peak demand (eg on travel services)

- Using promotions to stimulate off-peak demand (eg free mobile calls between certain hours)

- Using flexible staffing methods to cover fluctuations in demand (eg part-time and temporary working, outsourcing to call centres)

1.7.5 Ownership

Services do not result in the transfer of property. The purchase of a service only gives the customer access to or the right to use a facility, not ownership. This may lessen the perceived customer value of a service – particularly if the benefit does not accrue until some time in the future (like a pension, or a voucher for future use).

There are **two basic approaches** to addressing this problem.

(a)   **Promote the advantages of non-ownership**. This can be done by emphasising the benefits of paid-for maintenance, or a periodic upgrading of the product.

(b)   **Make available a tangible symbol or representation of ownership** such as a certificate, voucher, merchandise item or simple receipt. This can come to embody the benefits enjoyed.

CASE STUDY

Railways and airlines

In the UK, in the nineteenth century, railway passengers could buy tickets for first, second and third classes. Now they buy first and 'standard' classes. The UK was a society heavily stratified by wealth, and so offering three classes of tickets would seem a natural way of targeting a market segmented by wealth.

In India today, again there are first, second and third classes (with permutations based on air conditioned compartments, sleepers etc). In China there exist 'hard' and 'soft' classes.

Airlines offer a useful contrast. Segmentation is partly based on purpose of visit and time of booking. Business class was directed to people travelling on business expense accounts (who would travel economy on their own account). Some airlines offer 'premium' economy seats to those who want more legroom. The 'low-cost' airlines flying in the US and Europe designed for the 'no-frills' consumer, are increasingly frequented by business travellers, for short haul trips.

1.8 The extended marketing mix

As a consequence of the **differences** between **goods** and **services**, the **service marketing mix** developed. The intangible nature of services makes these extra three Ps particularly important (people, processes and physical evidence).

1.8.1 People

The role of employees in the marketing mix is particularly important in **service marketing**, because of the **inseparability** of the service from the service provider. Front-line staff must be selected, trained and motivated with particular attention to customer care and public relations.

In the case of some services, the **physical presence** of people performing the service is a vital aspect of customer satisfaction. The staff involved are performing or producing a service, selling the service and also liaising with the customer to promote the service, gather information and respond to customer needs.

1.8.2 Processes

Efficient **processes** can become a marketing advantage in their own right. If an airline, for example, develops a sophisticated ticketing system, it can offer shorter waits at check-in or wider choice of flights through allied airlines. Efficient order processing not only increases customer satisfaction, but cuts down on the time it takes the organisation to complete a sale.

Issues to be considered include the following.

- Policies, particularly with regard to ethical dealings (a key issue for many consumers)
- Procedures, for efficiency and standardisation
- Automation and computerisation of processes
- Queuing and waiting times
- Information gathering, processing and communication times
- Capacity management, matching supply to demand in a timely and cost effective way
- Accessibility of facilities, premises, personnel and services

Such issues are particularly important in service marketing. This is because the range of factors and people involved make it **difficult to standardise** the service offered. Quality in particular specifications will vary with the circumstances and individuals. This creates a need for **process planning** to ensure efficient work.

1.8.3 Physical evidence

As we saw earlier, services are **intangible** – there is no physical substance to them. This often means that the customer has no **evidence of ownership**. This may make it difficult for consumers to compare the qualities of service provision and reduce the incentive to consume.

Issues of **intangibility** and **ownership** can be tackled by making available **a physical symbol** or representation of the service and the benefits it confers. For example, tickets and programs relating to entertainment and certificates of attainment in training are symbolic of the service received and a provide a history of past positive experiences.

Physical evidence of service may also be incorporated into the **design** and **specification of the service environment** by designing premises to reflect the quality and type of service. Such environmental factors include finishing, decor, colour scheme, noise levels, background music, fragrance and general ambience.

Exam skills

If a question refers to **four** elements of the marketing mix the examiner is referring to the traditional elements of product, price, place and promotion – the 4Ps. If **five** elements are referred to, add 'people' to the traditional four. The other additional Ps referred to above could be referred to in longer written questions.

Question 9.1	The extended marketing mix

Learning outcome D2(v)

Briefly explain the nature of services and the three additional Ps relevant to services marketing. **(5 marks)**

Section summary

Traditionally, the **marketing mix** was the **'four Ps'** (**product, price, place, promotion**). The **three extra 'Ps'** have been added to describe additional issues relevant to **service industries** (**people, process, physical evidence**), giving an extended marketing mix of seven Ps.

2 Branding   **11/10, 05/11**

Introduction

A **brand** is a name, term, sign, symbol or design intended to identify the product of a seller and to differentiate it from those of competitors. It is a key element of marketing and corporate strategy as it generates revenue and therefore has a value.

KEY POINT

Branding is a very general term covering brand names, designs, trademarks, symbols, jingles and the like. A **brand name** refers strictly to letters, words or groups of words which can be spoken. A **brand image** distinguishes a company's product from competing products in the eyes of the user.

Branding might be discussed under any of the **four Ps**. For instance, part of the branding of a Rolls Royce is the unmistakeable design of the product, or you might buy a 'cheaper brand' of washing-up liquid if you are concerned about price.

CASE STUDY

Tesco has been named the most valuable brand on the high street, worth £8.6bn (2008), almost £4bn more than rival Sainsbury's. A report has said that Tesco's top ranking was "almost inevitable" following sales of £32bn and its market leading share in the supermarket and convenience store markets. Brands in the study were valued after looking at public sales figures for the last five years and attributing a score to measures such as future growth, price positioning, customer service and brand heritage.

Tesco's strong brand is likely to give it a better chance to weather tougher times on the UK high street, because consumers need more reasons to buy.

A **brand identity** may begin with a name, such as 'Kleenex' or 'Ariel', but extends to a range of visual features which should assist in stimulating demand for the particular product. The additional features include **typography**, **colour**, **package design** and **slogans**.

In addition a brand shares the **attributes** of a product – it is a bundle of tangible and intangible benefits which deliver customer value.

2.1 Objectives of branding

The **key benefit of branding** is product differentiation and recognition. Products may be branded for a number of reasons.

- It aids **product differentiation**, conveying a lot of information very quickly and concisely. This helps customers readily to identify the goods or services and thereby helps to create customer loyalty to the brand. It is therefore a means of increasing or maintaining sales.

- It maximises the impact of **advertising** for product identification and recognition. The more similar a product (whether an industrial good or consumer good) is to competing goods, the more branding is necessary to create a separate product identity.

- Branding leads to a **readier acceptance** of a manufacturer's goods by wholesalers and retailers.

- It reduces the importance of **price differentials** between goods.

- It supports **market segmentation**, since different brands of similar products may be developed to meet specific needs of categories of uses

- It supports **brand extension** or **stretching**. Other products can be introduced into the brand range to 'piggy back' on the articles already known to the customer (but ill-will as well as goodwill for one product in a branded range will be transferred to all other products in the range).

- It **eases the task of personal selling**, by enhancing product recognition.

The **relevance of branding** does not apply equally to all products. The cost of intensive brand advertising to project a brand image nationally may not be justified.

The decision as to whether a brand name should be given to a **range of products** or whether products should be branded **individually** depends on quality factors.

- If the brand name is associated with quality, all goods in the range must be of that standard.

- If a company produces different quality (and price) goods for different market segments, it would be unwise and confusing to give the same brand name to the higher and the lower quality goods.

2.2 Branding strategies

There are three broad **branding strategies** – **brand extension**, **multi-branding** and **family branding**.

2.2.1 Brand extension

This is the introduction of new flavours, sizes etc to a brand, to capitalise on existing brand loyalty. Examples include the introduction of Persil washing up liquid (Persil used to be a washing powder for clothes) and Mars ice cream (Mars made its name as a chocolate bar).

New additions to the **product range** are beneficial for two main reasons.

- They require a lower level of marketing investment (part of the 'image' already being known).

- The extension of the brand presents less risk to consumers who might be worried about trying something new.

2.2.2 Multi-branding

This is the introduction of a **number of brands** that all satisfy **very similar product characteristics**. This can be used where there is little or no brand loyalty, in order to pick up buyers who are constantly changing brands.

The best example is washing detergents. The two major producers, Lever Brothers and Procter & Gamble, have created a barrier to fresh competition as a new company would have to launch several brands at once in order to compete.

2.2.3 Family branding

This uses the power of the **brand name** to assist all products in a range. This strategy is being used more and more by **large companies**, such as Heinz. In part it is a response to retailers' own-label (family branded) goods. It is also an attempt to consolidate expensive television advertising behind one message rather than fragmenting it across the promotion of individual items.

2.3 Brand value

Brands are often a source of **competitive advantage**. Products with strong brands often sell themselves and can command **high prices** when compared to competitor products. Therefore a value can be attributed to them.

The following are **three approaches to valuing a brand**:

- Market approach
- Cost approach
- Income approach

2.3.1 The market approach

This approach generates a value on the basis of **market transactions**. A common method used in this form of valuation is known as **relief-from-royalty**. This reflects the fact that owners of brands have use of the brand for free, whereas they could generate an income by licensing it. This income stream, or royalty rate, is derived by reference to royalty or license agreements for similar assets and can be used to generate a value.

2.3.2 The cost approach

This approach is based on the **costs incurred to build the brand**. For example, costs involved in registering trademarks and promotional activities. However, it is not the most accurate method of valuation because the cost of building the brand is usually unrelated to its ability to generate revenue.

2.3.3 The income approach

This approach is based on **net present values**. The brand's expected future earnings, or cash flows, can be used to calculate the overall **economic benefit** that it will generate over its life. This benefit is **reduced** by all **expenditure** relating to **brand awareness** (such as advertising) that will be incurred over its life to calculate a net income figure. This income figure is then **discounted** at an interest rate that an investor would expect as a return based on the brand's **risk profile** and **characteristics**. This final value is the value of the brand.

| Question 9.2 | Branding |

Learning outcome D2(xi)

Define what a 'brand' is and briefly explain three methods by which an organisation may value its brand.

(7 marks)

Section summary

Branding is a very general term covering brand names, designs, trademarks, symbols, jingles and the like. A **brand name** refers strictly to letters, words or groups of words which can be spoken. A **brand image** distinguishes a company's product from competing products in the eyes of the user.

The key **benefit of branding** is **product differentiation** and **recognition**.

There are **three approaches to valuing a brand** – **market**, **cost** and **income**.

3 Marketing communications

Introduction

Once an organisation has decided upon its marketing plan it needs to put it into practice. This means **communicating its message** to the market and customers. There is a growing range of methods that it can employ for this purpose which we will now look at.

When conducting a **marketing campaign**, there is a range of possible communication methods and channels the campaign could utilise. The most popular methods are shown below.

Promotional tools

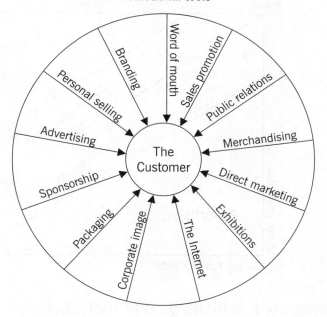

3.1 The promotion mix

The **promotion mix** consists of the blend of promotional tools that are considered appropriate for a specific marketing campaign.

These tools represent the deployment of deliberate and intentional methods calculated to bring about a **favourable response in the customer's behaviour**.

The diagram represents the most obvious **promotion methods**, though other parts of the marketing mix, including the product itself, pricing, policy and distribution channels are also important.

Choosing the **correct tools** for a particular promotions task is not easy. The process is still very much an art, though it is becoming more scientific because of the access to consumer and media databases. Computer systems may be utilised to match consumer characteristics with promotional tools.

In reality, an experienced marketing manager may be able to reach **sensible conclusions** almost intuitively, based on what has been successful in the past and on knowledge of both customers and competitors.

3.2 Consumer and business-to-business markets

The comment above about experience of a particular market can be generalised in the case of the two broad categories of consumer and business-to-business markets.

KEY POINTS

Consumer markets (or business-to-consumer markets **B2C**) are categorised as consisting of mass audiences which are cost-effectively accessible by television or national newspaper advertising. Supermarkets allow customers to serve themselves and there is little or no personal selling.

Business-to-business markets (B2B), by contrast, involve a great deal of personal selling at different levels in the organisation. The needs of individual companies are different and therefore mass advertising would be most wasteful. Building on these generalised comments it is possible to present the mix of appropriate tools in the following diagram.

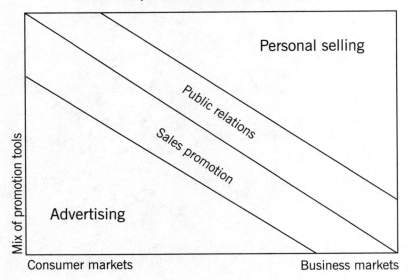

Variation of promotion tools with type of market

3.3 Integrated marketing communications

It is necessary to integrate all the promotional elements to achieve the maximum influence on the customer. **Integrated marketing communications** represent all the elements of an organisation's marketing mix that favourably influence its customers or clients. It goes beyond the right choice of promotion tools to the correct choice of the marketing mix. This is illustrated in the diagram below.

The integrated marketing communication process

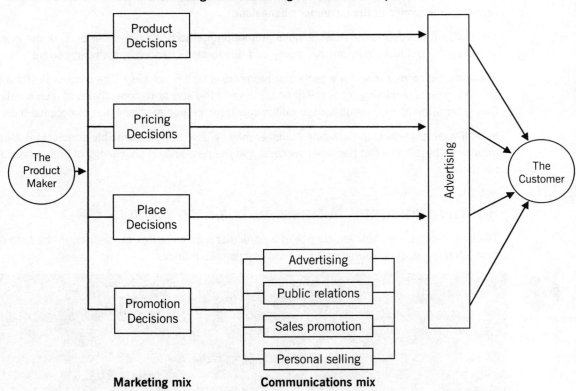

3.4 Types of marketing

The following **types of marketing** can be applied by an organisation.

- Consumer marketing (the 4Ps)
- Services marketing (the 3Ps of the extended marketing mix)
- Direct marketing
- Indirect marketing
- Guerrilla marketing
- Viral marketing
- Interactive marketing
- Experiential marketing
- E-marketing
- Internal marketing (see Chapter 9)

3.5 Direct marketing

KEY TERM

The Institute of Direct Marketing in the UK defines DIRECT MARKETING as 'The planned recording, analysis and tracking of customer behaviour to develop relational marketing strategies'.

It is worth noting some further key words and phrases associated with direct marketing.

(a)   **Response**. Direct marketing is about getting people to respond to invitations and offers.

(b)   **Interactive**. The process is two-way involving the supplier and the customer.

(c)   **Relationship**. Direct marketing is in many instances an on-going process of communicating and selling again and again to the same customer.

(d)   **Recording and analysis**. Response data is collected and analysed so that the most cost-effective procedures may be arrived at.

(e)   **Strategy**. Direct marketing should be seen as a part of a comprehensive plan stemming from clearly formulated objectives.

Because direct marketing **removes all channel intermediaries** apart from the advertising and delivery mediums, it is known as a **'zero level channel'**. There are no other parties between the seller and the customer.

Direct marketing encompasses a wide range of media and distribution opportunities, such as:

- Television
- Radio
- Direct mail

- Inserts (eg in newspapers)
- Telemarketing
- The Internet

CASE STUDY

Direct Line, the insurance company, turned the motor insurance industry on its head through its ability to by-pass the traditional brokers and offer the average consumer not only a cheaper form of insurance, but a high degree of service.

The power of the computer and the Internet has transformed the processes by which marketers relate to their customers. Improvements in database software mean the smallest of operations are able to benefit from the information era.

3.5.1 Telemarketing

One form of direct marketing is telemarketing. Telemarketing is a quick, accurate and flexible tool for gathering, maintaining and helping to exploit relevant up-to-date information about customers and prospects.

KEY TERM

TELEMARKETING is the planned and controlled use of the telephone for sales and marketing opportunities.

Characteristics of telemarketing

(a)   **Targeted**. The message is appropriately tailored to the recipient.

(b)   **Personal**. Telemarketers can determine and respond immediately to the specific needs of individuals, building long-term personal and profitable relationships.

(c)   **Interactive**. Since the dialogue is live, the conversation can be guided to achieve the desired results; the representative is in control.

(d)   **Immediate**. Every outbound call achieves an immediate result, even if it is a wrong number or 'not interested'. Customers can be given 24 hour constant access to the company (for inbound calls).

(e)   **Flexible**. Conversations can be tailored spontaneously as the representative responds to the contact's needs. Campaign variables can be tested quickly, and changes made whilst the campaign is in progress.

Possible disadvantages of telemarketing

Telemarketing can be **costly**. There are few economies of scale, and in some situations techniques such as direct mail may be more cost effective.

If poorly handled, telemarketing may be interpreted as **intrusive**. This may alienate potential customers.

3.6 Indirect marketing

KEY TERM

INDIRECT MARKETING is the marketing of products as a consequence of another activity or action.

With indirect marketing the organisation does not push products or services onto customers. Instead it performs a number of related activities that arouse interest in the product or service.

Examples include posting blogs on the internet and publishing articles. A common example is food magazines including 'advertising features' in the form of recipes which use a particular producer's products

Another form of indirect marketing is **'word of mouth'** advertising. This involves customers who have had positive experiences with the organisation recommending the organisation to their family and friends.

Recent developments in indirect marketing have been **guerrilla** and **viral marketing**.

3.7 Guerrilla marketing

Guerrilla marketing involves taking people by **surprise** and **'creating a buzz'** in **unexpected places**. It relies more use of **imagination** than large sums of money.

The term guerrilla marketing was created by Jay Conrad Levinson in the 1980s. Levinson encouraged marketers to devise their own ideas, utilising their contacts and the organisations' products and services as sources of inspiration.

3.7.1 Principles of guerrilla marketing

Levinson identified the following **principles of guerrilla marketing**:

- It is specifically geared for small organisations and entrepreneurs

- It should be based on psychology rather than experience, judgment, and guesswork

- It should be based on time, energy, and imagination rather than money

- Organisations should be judged on profit not sales

- Marketers should focus on the number of new relationships created in each time period

- Organisations should focus on creating a standard of excellence in their products and services rather than diversifying.

- Organisations should focus on increasing the numbers of customer referrals as well as the number and size of transactions, rather than just aiming to attract new customers

- Organisations should co-operate with competitors.

- A combination of marketing methods should be used in a guerrilla marketing campaign.

- The campaign should make use of technology.

CASE STUDY

Guerrilla marketing

More extreme attempts at guerrilla marketing can be risky.

In an effort to promote an online gaming site, a Canadian man leapt into an Olympic pool at the 2004 games in Athens. He was convicted of trespassing and creating a disturbance and sentenced to months in a Greek prison, but eventually released with a fine of just a few hundred dollars.

In the U.S, (Boston) in 2007, a number of flashing electronic signs designed to promote the television program Aqua Teen Hunger Force were planted around the city. Unfortunately these were mistakenly identified as explosive devices, causing huge disruption.

However, even examples of guerrilla marketing 'gone wrong' may actually be considered a success by some, as they can generate more publicity than campaigns that 'go well'.

3.8 Viral marketing   11/10

KEY POINT

Viral marketing involves the use of **pre-existing social networks** to spread brand awareness or other marketing objectives. This form of marketing is termed 'viral' because the life of the marketing message is comparable to the self replication and spread of biological and computer viruses. The **viral campaign** is successful when a customer receives the marketing message, copies it, and sends it to their friends or posts it on **social networking sites** such as Myspace or Facebook.

3.8.1 Forms of viral marketing

Examples of viral marketing include:

- Video clips (including those taken on mobile phones)
- Novelty, quirky computer games (usually created using 'Flash')
- E-books
- Text messages
- Music
- Mobile phone ringtones

Viral marketing messages will eventually run out of steam as people who receive the message fail to pass it on. They can be effective though, even with a relatively short life span.

Individuals who pass on viral marketing are said to have a **high 'Social Networking Potential'** (SNP). These people tend to use social networks for much of their time and like to become involved in spreading messages. It is the goal of viral marketers to identify these individuals and design messages that have a high probability of being passed on by them.

3.8.2 The six principles of viral marketing

Dr Ralph F Wilson describes **six principles of an effective viral marketing strategy**.

(a) Provide free products or services – free items attract attention

(b) The form of the message must be easy to pass on

(c) The transmission method must be scalable from small to large very quickly to aid the spread of the message

(d) The message must exploit common motivations and behaviours. Greed, love, success and the need to look 'cool' can provide motivation to spread the message

(e) Use existing communication networks. People have lists of contacts on their email and social networking sites – getting the message in the right place means it will multiply very quickly

(f) Take advantage of other people's resources – for example getting banner ads and links onto other websites.

3.8.3 Examples of viral marketing

Four recent examples of viral marketing are:

(a) 'Will it blend?' – a series of video clips where various items were blended in a Blendtec blender.

(b) The Cadbury Dairy Milk Gorilla advert which was made popular on YouTube and Facebook.

(c) The movie 'Cloverfield' where Myspace pages were created for the characters and websites created for fictional companies mentioned in the film.

(d) 'Compare the meerkat.com' a website created as part of a viral marketing campaign for 'Compare the Market.com'. It was featured in a national TV advertising campaign.

3.9 Interactive marketing

KEY POINT

According to *Deighton* (1996) 'interactive marketing is the ability to address the customer, remember what the customer says and address the customer again in a way that illustrates that we remember what the customer has told us'.

E-commerce has made interactive marketing easier as customer information can be 'remembered' in databases and electronic communications with the customer occur very quickly through the Internet.

An organisation which makes good use of interactive marketing is **Amazon.com**. Customers can set preferences and the site records their past transactions. In future visits they are presented with possible purchases based on this information.

3.10 Experiential marketing

KEY POINT

Experiential marketing involves providing an experience that creates an emotional connection between a person and a brand, product or idea.

Experiential marketing encourages potential customers to engage with the personality of the brand, **through experiencing it**. It is a combination of in-store promotion techniques and field marketing. It aims not only to sell more products in the short-term, but also to encourage customers and potential customers to engage with the personality of the brand.

Experiential marketing is seen as an effective way of connecting with customers, as the emotional connection encourages brand loyalty.

CASE STUDY

In Australia, Absolut Vodka launched a brand called 'Cut' using experiential marketing - combining public relations, point-of-sale, online and event marketing. Absolut leased two bars in Sydney and Melbourne, put on DJ sets, band concerts and photo exhibitions in these spaces.

Visitors to the Absolut Cut bars got a free bottle of Cut, and consumers were given a chance to contribute their photos to the exhibits, generating what Absolut hoped would be a viral element to the campaign. The campaign flew in the face of traditional ways to launch a brand. Instead of using mass marketing to blanket the millions in order to reach the few, Absolut chose to target the few to eventually reach the masses.

Question 9.3	Guerrilla and viral marketing

Learning outcome D2(viii)

Briefly explain the concepts of guerrilla and viral marketing, providing an example of each.   **(4 marks)**

3.11 E-marketing   11/10

Most companies of any size now have a **website**. A website is a **collection of screens** providing information in text and graphic form, any of which can be viewed simply by clicking the appropriate button, word or image on the screen.

E-marketing now includes the use of Short Message Service (SMS) or text messages, e-mail, online surveys and the use of social network sites such as Facebook and Twitter.

3.11.1 Successful websites

To be successful the **website** should do the following.

(a)   **Attract visitors** – with online and offline methods

(b)   **Enable participation** – interactive content, and suitable facilities to allow for transactions

(c)   **Encourage return visits** – design the site to target the needs of particular segments. Offer free services and added value facilities

(d)   **Allow for two-way information sharing** – personalisation reflecting visitor preferences, direct marketing and information retrieval provide visitors with the information they are seeking

(e)   **Integrate with back office systems** – systems must be in place to process orders and dispatch products that have been generated by the website.

3.11.2 Benefits of an effective website

Seven benefits of an effective a website and how the benefits are generated, are shown in the table below.

Benefit	How generated
Loyalty	Website offers and features
Productivity	Better management of the supply chain
Reputation	Depends on competition, and ability of web-based strategies to offer real customer benefit
Costs	Generally lower than for retail outlets
Communication	Allows quick responses to queries
Convenient	Easy customer access from home or work
Opportunity	Smaller organisations can compete globally with large, established ones
Information	Customer information can be stored and used in marketing

3.11.3 Website promotion

To encourage people to **visit** a website and then to **return** at a later date, two promotional tools have become popular. These tools are **banner advertising** and email **promotion**.

3.11.4 Banner advertising

Companies such as Yahoo! make money by **selling advertising space**. For instance, if you type in 'beer' an advertisement for **Miller Genuine Draft will appear, as well as your list of beer-related sites.** If you click on the advertisement you are taken to the advertiser's website, perhaps just to be told more about the product, perhaps to be favourably influenced by the entertainment provided by the site, or perhaps even to buy some of the product.

Banner adverts are a source of revenue for the websites they appear on. **Affiliate schemes** and **Pay-per-click advertising** pay the host site a small fee for every visitor they attract or if they make a subsequent purchase.

Search engines such as **Yahoo!** and **Google** make money in a similar way, but organisations can also pay them a fee to display an advert whenever **key words** are entered into the search box.

Advertisers may get visitors to **register their interest** in the product when they are on the site so that they can be **directly targeted** in future. At the very least advertisers know exactly how many people have viewed their message and how many were interested enough in it to click on it to find out more.

3.11.5 E-mail marketing

E-mail is cheap, relatively easily targeted and can be sent to large numbers of people quickly. It is therefore of great interest to marketers, but there is increasing concern at the prevalence of 'junk' e-mail.

There are various **uses of e-mail for marketing purposes**.

- To advertise a product/service, usually with a link to a website.
- To update a subscriber to a product/service with useful information
- To confirm an order
- To invite users to write in or to respond to a helpline

Unsolicited e-mail is probably more intrusive than traditional 'junk mail', though less so than the telephone. However, poor use of e-mail can upset large numbers of people.

Section summary

Once the organisation has decided on its **marketing plan** it needs to get its message out to the market and its customers.

Common forms of **marketing communication** include:

- Consumer marketing (the 4Ps)
- Services marketing (the 7Ps of the extended marketing mix)
- Direct marketing
- Indirect marketing
- Guerrilla marketing
- Viral marketing
- Interactive marketing
- E-marketing
- Internal marketing

Exam alert

'New' forms of marketing such as e-markeing and viral marketing are topical. CIMA are keen for their exams to be topical and up-to-date, so these topics could be examined regularly.

Chapter Roundup

✓   Traditionally, the **marketing mix** was the '**four Ps**' (**product, price, place, promotion**). The **three extra 'Ps'** have been added to describe additional issues relevant to **service industries** (**people, process, physical evidence**), giving an extended marketing mix of seven Ps.

✓   **Branding** is a very general term covering brand names, designs, trademarks, symbols, jingles and the like. A **brand name** refers strictly to letters, words or groups of words which can be spoken. A **brand image** distinguishes a company's product from competing products in the eyes of the user.

✓   The **key benefit of branding** is **product differentiation** and **recognition**.

✓   There are **three approaches to valuing a brand** – **market**, **cost** and **income**.

✓   Once the organisation has decided on its **marketing plan** it needs to get its message out to the market and its customers.

✓   Common forms of **marketing communication** include:

- Consumer marketing (the 4Ps)
- Services marketing (the 7Ps of the extended marketing mix)
- Direct marketing
- Indirect marketing
- Guerrilla marketing
- Viral marketing
- Interactive marketing
- E-marketing
- Internal marketing

Quick Quiz

1   Which of the following is included in the additional 3Ps of the extended marketing mix?

  A   Processes
  B   Product
  C   Promotion
  D   Price

2   Which of the following stages comes after 'introduction' in the product life cycle?

  A   Growth
  B   Market maturity
  C   Market penetration
  D   Decline

3   Which branding strategy uses the power of the brand name to assist all products in a range?

  A   Brand expansion
  B   Multi-branding
  C   Family branding
  D   Corporate branding

4   In the context of marketing, which type of marketing is referred to as B2B marketing?

  A   Business to brand
  B   Brand to brand
  C   Business to business
  D   Buyer to business

5   State four attributes of a successful website

  1   ....
  2   ....
  3   ....
  4   ....

Answers to Quick Quiz

1   A   Processes is one of the 3Ps of the marketing mix extended to services.

2   A   Growth follows the introduction stage as demand for the product increases.

3   C   Family branding uses the power of the brand name to assist all products in a range.

4   C   In the context of marketing, B2B means business to business marketing.

5   Four possible attributes include:

    1   Attract visitors
    2   Enable participation
    3   Encourage return visits
    4   Allow for two-way information sharing

Answer to Question

9.1 The extended marketing mix

Services have a **different nature** to traditional products. In particular they have the following characteristics that products do not. They are have no physical form, are inseparable from the provider and may lack consistency as a different member of staff may provide them each time they are provided. Additionally, they cannot be stored and usually do not result in the transfer of property.

The **three additional elements of the extended marketing mix** are:

People – services are provided by members of staff who are inseparable from the service

Process – services involve a process, for example a hair cut may involve waiting to be served, a hair wash, styling, colouring and hair drying

Physical evidence – as services are intangible, some physical item should be provided to give the customer evidence of ownership.

9.2 Branding

A **brand** is a name, term, sign, symbol or design intended to identify the product of a seller and to differentiate it from those of competitors.

There are three main methods of valuing a brand:

The market approach

This approach generates a value on the basis of **market transactions**. A common method used is known as **relief-from-royalty**. A potential income stream is calculated on the basis of what the owner of the brand could generate by licensing it to third parties and it is the value of this income stream which is used to calculate the brand's value.

The cost approach

Under this approach, the value of the brand is based on the **amount of costs incurred in building it**. However, it is not the most accurate method of valuation because the cost of building the brand is usually unrelated to its ability to generate revenue.

The income approach

This approach is based on the brand's **expected future earnings**, or cash flows – ie the amount of cash it is expected to generate less the costs of building it. The net income figure is then **discounted** at an interest rate that an investor would expect as a return based on the brand's **risk profile** and **characteristics**. This final value is the value of the brand.

9.3 Guerrilla and viral marketing

Guerrilla marketing

Guerrilla marketing is an unconventional method of marketing and involves taking people by **surprise** and 'creating a buzz' in **unexpected places**.

Example: Surprising store customers with 'for today only sales' to which they are given very little notice.

Viral marketing

Viral marketing involves the use of **pre-existing social networks** to spread brand awareness or other marketing objectives.

Example: Video clips posted on websites such as YouTube.

	Number	Level	Marks	Time
Now try this question from the Exam Question Bank	9	Examination	20	36 mins

DEVELOPMENTS IN MARKETING

In this chapter we conclude our study of marketing by considering several 'stand-alone' areas.

Consumer behaviour and the purchasing process is an important consideration for marketers since understanding how consumers think and act will help them to fine tune their marketing activities.

Not-for-profit organisations have different requirements of marketing than those for whom profit maximisation is key. There is a distinct **charity marketing mix** which is important for you to understand.

Internal marketing is about training and motivating employees to support the organisation's external marketing activities. **Employee 'buy-in'** is often critical to the success of the marketing effort – especially in service organisations.

Finally, we turn our attention to the increasingly important issue of **social marketing** and **corporate social responsibility**. Society now expects organisations to have a wider responsibility than earning profit for shareholders.

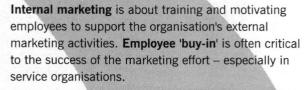

topic list	learning outcomes	syllabus references	ability required
1 Consumer behaviour	D1(e), D2(c)	D1(iv), D2(iii)	comprehension
2 Marketing not-for-profit organisations	D1(c)	D1(iii)	comprehension
3 Internal marketing	D2(c)	D2(xiii)	comprehension
4 Corporate social responsibility and social marketing	D1(d)	D1(v)	comprehension

1   Consumer behaviour

Introduction

We saw in Chapter 7 that marketing aims to produce mutually beneficial **exchanges** between **customer** and **supplier**. However, 'the customer' in a transaction can involve a number of different roles.

1.1 The customer

The table below sets out the **different roles** 'the customer' may have in a transaction.

'Customer'		Household example: a family pet animal needing vaccination	Business example: ordering of office stationery
Buyer	The person who selects a product or service	A veterinary surgeon, on the pet owner's behalf, recommends and orders a vaccine.	The office manager may order stationery for other departments.
Payer	The person who finances the purchase	The pet-owner pays for the vaccination – or perhaps an insurance company pays in the end.	The payer is the company, via the accounts department.
User	Receives the benefit of the product or service	The pet receives the benefit of the vaccination (but the owner receives emotional benefits, too, perhaps).	Users are those with access to the stationery.

The value of this distinction is that it enables **marketing efforts** and **activities** to be correctly **focused** on the people involved in the transaction. For example, an office supplies company would direct most of its marketing efforts to the office manager buying the stationery. The approach to the accounts department would be slightly different – a relationship might have to be built up to ensure speedy payment.

1.2 Buyer behaviour

Buyer behaviour describes the **activities** and **decision processes** relating to buying. Treating buying behaviour as a process enables us to distinguish between the **different buying roles** that customers sometimes assume. Typically, marketers make a distinction between:

- Consumers as buyers
- Organisations as buyers

1.3 Consumer buying behaviour

There are three main theories of consumer behaviour.

- The **cognitive paradigm** sees a purchase as the outcome of a rational decision-making process.
- The **learned behaviour** theory emphasises the importance of past purchases.
- The **habitual decision-making** theory emphasises habit and brand loyalty.

1.3.1 A consumer decision-making model

Lancaster and Withey 2003) identifies five steps in consumer decision making.

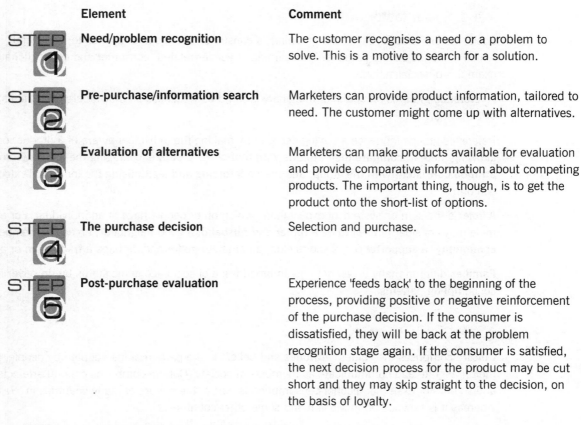

	Element	Comment
STEP ①	**Need/problem recognition**	The customer recognises a need or a problem to solve. This is a motive to search for a solution.
STEP ②	**Pre-purchase/information search**	Marketers can provide product information, tailored to need. The customer might come up with alternatives.
STEP ③	**Evaluation of alternatives**	Marketers can make products available for evaluation and provide comparative information about competing products. The important thing, though, is to get the product onto the short-list of options.
STEP ④	**The purchase decision**	Selection and purchase.
STEP ⑤	**Post-purchase evaluation**	Experience 'feeds back' to the beginning of the process, providing positive or negative reinforcement of the purchase decision. If the consumer is dissatisfied, they will be back at the problem recognition stage again. If the consumer is satisfied, the next decision process for the product may be cut short and they may skip straight to the decision, on the basis of loyalty.

Such a model provides a useful descriptive **framework** for marketers.

Question 10.1	Consumer buying

Learning outcome D1(iv)

Briefly explain the five stages of the consumer buying process.   **(5 marks)**

1.4 Influences on consumer buying

Some of the main influences on consumer buying are shown in the following diagram (based upon *Lancaster and Withey*).

Influences on buyers

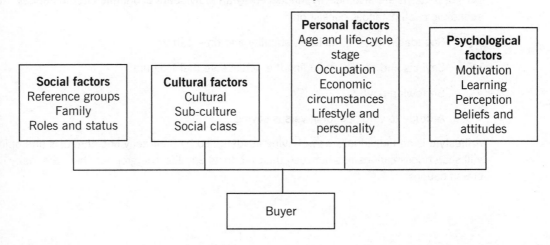

1.4.1 Social factors

Social factors relate to the social groupings a consumer belongs to or aspires to, and trends in society which influence buying patterns. The learning of gender-related, consumer and occupational roles are examples of socialisation.

A **reference group** is an actual or imaginary group that influences an individual's evaluations, aspirations or behaviour.

Reference groups influence a buying decision by making the individual **aware** of a product or brand, allowing them to **compare** their attitude with that of the group, encouraging the individual to **adopt an attitude consistent** with the group, and then **reinforcing and legitimising** the individual's decision to conform.

A 'role' is the sum or 'system' of expectations which other people have of an individual. For example, a male may consider himself to be a **father** and **husband**, a good **neighbour**, an active member of the **local community**, a **supporter** of his sports club, an amateur **golfer** and perhaps a **tradesman** or a **professional**.

Families differ in many ways, not only in broad issue of socio-economic status but in buyer behaviour and consumption patterns.

1.4.2 Cultural factors

Culture comprises the **values**, **attitudes** and **beliefs** in the pattern of life adopted by people, that help them integrate and communicate as members of society. Culture comprises cultural artefacts, lifestyles, and so on. For example, alcohol consumption is part of the culture of many countries in Western Europe, whereas it is frowned on in Muslim and some other countries.

1.4.3 Personal factors

'**Personal**' **factors** include such things as **age**, **stage of family** and **life cycle**, **occupation**, **economic circumstances** and **lifestyle**.

Individuals will buy different types of product depending on their **age**. This is particularly relevant to such products as clothes, furniture and recreation.

The **family life cycle** is used in the West to model purchase behaviour patterns. For example, couples at the early stages of their marriage before having children will have different needs and consumption patterns from those, say, after their children have left home. In the UK, where house purchase is the norm, this has particular implications for sellers of financial services.

A person's **occupation** will influence consumption and the task for marketers is to identify the occupational groups that have an above average interest in their products and services.

Buying patterns are also heavily influenced by an individual's **economic circumstances**. An individual's economic circumstances consist of:

- Spendable income: its level, stability and time pattern
- Savings and assets, including the percentage that is liquid
- Borrowing power
- Attitude toward spending versus saving

A **lifestyle** is an individual's way of living as identified by their activities, interests and opinions. Marketers will search for relationships between their products and lifestyle groups. There are many different lifestyle classifications.

1.4.4 Psychological factors

The process of buyer behaviour is also influenced by **four psychological factors**:

- Motivation
- Perception
- Learning
- Beliefs and attitudes

Motivation is an inner state that energises, activates, or moves, that directs or channels.

(a) *Maslow's* (1954) theory of motivation seeks to explain why people are driven by particular needs at particular times. Maslow argues that human needs are arranged in a **hierarchy** comprising, in their order of importance: physiological needs, safety needs, social needs, esteem needs and self-actualisation needs.

(b) *Herzberg* (1968) developed a 'two-factor theory' of motivation that distinguishes between **factors that cause dissatisfaction and factors that cause satisfaction**. The task for the marketer is, therefore, to avoid 'dissatisfiers' such as, for example, poor after-sales service, as these things will not sell the product but may well unsell it. In addition the marketer should identify the major satisfiers or motivators of purchase and make sure that they are supplied to the customer.

Perception is the process whereby people select, organise and interpret sensory stimuli into a meaningful and coherent picture. The way consumers view an object (for example, their mental picture of a brand or the traits they attribute to a brand) may vary according to their past experience, expectation, needs, interests, attitudes and beliefs.

Learning concerns the process whereby an individual's behaviour changes as a result of their experience.

A **belief** is a descriptive thought that a person holds about something. Beliefs are important to marketers as the **brand beliefs** that people have about products make up the brand images of those products.

An **attitude** describes a person's enduring favourable or unfavourable cognitive evaluations, emotional feelings, and action tendencies toward some object or idea. **Attitudes** lead people to behave in a fairly **consistent** way towards similar objects. Attitudes tend to settle into a consistent pattern – to change one attitude may entail major changes to other attitudes.

CASE STUDY

Children as consumers

What do you call a consumer who wants to buy everything you have, doesn't care what it costs and is less than five feet tall? A marketer's dream? Nope. You call them kids. -- *AdRelevance Intelligence Report, 2000*

Children are bombarded by brand messages almost from birth, including counting books for preschoolers that use M&Ms or Cheerios, exposure to brightly coloured and appealing branded packaging in the supermarket, movie and toy tie-ins in fast-food restaurants, product placement in movies, advertisements on television and the Internet, and pitches from entertainment and sports stars in a range of media. In fact, it's almost impossible to escape marketing messages. No wonder, then, that children as young as two are starting to recognize logos and request specific brands as soon as they begin to speak.

Children are a prime target for marketers. Not only do children today have more disposable income at younger ages, but they have significant influence over family purchases. YTV's 2002 Tween Report estimated that Canadian children aged 9 to 14 spend $1.9 billion and influence $20 billion in family purchases per year. Marketing experts call it "pester power," or the "nag factor" -- the ability to get kids to nag their parents to buy a specific product or take them to a specific restaurant. After all, if your child asks you for the latest toy 37 times a day for a week, the odds are that you'll eventually give in and buy it.

As a result, there is now a whole segment of the marketing industry devoted to figuring out how to sell things to kids.

Professionals who work with children are becoming increasingly concerned about this onslaught. In 2003, the Canadian Paediatric Society issued a position statement on the impact of media on children and youth that raised several concerns about advertising. In 2004, a coalition of Canadian health groups led by the Centre for Science in the Public Interest called for a ban on advertising aimed at children 13 or younger. Quebec has already banned print and broadcast advertising aimed at children under 13, although children certainly see advertising from other sources as well.

Many activists consider food advertising to be a leading cause of the increase in overweight in children. A report released in December 2005 by the Institute of Medicine, Food Marketing to Children and Youth: Threat or Opportunity?, observed that in the United States alone, over $11 billion dollars a year is spent on marketing food and beverages to children. And the food advertised to children is generally less than nutritious: most of it is highly processed, rich in saturated fat, salt, and sugar, and poor in nutrients like fibre, vitamins, calcium, and iron.

http://television-vs-children.blogspot.com/2008/11/target-market-children-as-consumers.html, November 19, 2008.

1.5 Organisations as buyers

KEY POINT

Organisations are viewed as more **rational** than individuals. The buying decision making process is likely to be formal. **Organisational (or industrial) buying** is the process organisations use to establish the need to purchase products and services and how these products and services are selected and purchased.

As we saw earlier, **transactions between organisations** are referred to as **Business-to-Business** or **B2B**, whereas transactions involving an **organisation and a consumer** are sometimes referred to as **Business-to-Consumer** or **B2C**.

When considering **organisational markets** the following factors should be taken into account:

(a) Organisational markets normally comprise **fewer buyers**, with a few buyers responsible for the majority of sales.

(b) Because of this smaller customer base and the importance and power of larger customers there is generally a **close relationship between buyer and seller**.

(c) **Demand** for industrial goods is ultimately derived from the demand for consumer goods. In addition, the total demand for many industrial products is **inelastic**, in other words, it is not affected much by price changes.

(d) The purchase decision is usually made by **consensus** in an organisational setting, rather than being the responsibility of one person.

1.5.1 Process of organisational buying behaviour

A typical **organisational buying process** is summarised in the following table.

Stage in behaviour	Comment
Stage 1. **Recognise the problem**	The stimulus may come from within or outside the organisation.
Stage 2. **Develop product specifications or service requirements to solve the problem.**	People participating in the buying decision assess the problem or need and determine what will be required to resolve or satisfy it. This may take the form of detailed specifications.
Stage 3. **Search for products and suppliers.**	The third stage of the process is similar to that of information search, utilising trade shows, trade publications, supplier catalogues, and soliciting proposals from known suppliers. This should result in a list of several alternative products.

Stage in behaviour	Comment
Stage 4. **Evaluate products relative to specifications.**	These are evaluated in order to ascertain whether they meet the product specifications developed in the second stage. Suppliers may also be evaluated according to criteria such as price, service and ability to deliver.
Stage 5. **Select and order the most appropriate product.**	The most appropriate product and supplier is then selected. In some cases an organisational buyer may select a number of suppliers in order to reduce the possibility of disruption caused by strikes, shortages or bankruptcy of suppliers. The order will then be made, often with specific details regarding terms, credit arrangements, delivery dates and technical assistance or after-sales service.
Stage 6. **Evaluate the product and supplier performance.**	The product and supplier will then be evaluated by comparing with specifications regarding product quality and so on, and the performance of the supplier over the terms of the contract for the sale.

1.5.2 The Decision Making Unit (DMU) in the organisation

A major difference between consumer and organisational buying behaviour is the fact that **organisational purchase decisions are rarely made by a single individual**. Normally, purchasing decisions are made by a number of people from different functional areas, possibly at different levels within the organisation.

Webster and Wind (1972) suggested **six groups within the Decision Making Unit** (DMU).

Groups within the DMU	
Users	Initiate the buying process and help define purchase specifications.
Influencers	Help define the specification and also provide an input into the process of evaluating the available alternatives.
Deciders	Have the responsibility for deciding on product requirements and suppliers.
Approvers	Authorise the proposals of deciders and buyers.
Buyers	Have the formal authority for the selection of suppliers and negotiating purchase terms.
Gatekeepers	By controlling the flow of information, may be able to stop sellers from reaching individuals within the buying centre.

The **size**, **structure** and **formality of the DMU** will vary depending on the specific situation. Key considerations include:

- **Who** are the principal participants in the buying process?

- In what areas do they exert the **greatest influence**?

- What is their **level of influence**?

- What **evaluative criteria** do each of the participants make use of and how **professional** is the buying process?

- To what extent is **buying centralised** in large organisations?

The **people** involved in the buying process must be convinced that the purchase will be safe for them, for example, there was an advertising slogan to the effect that 'nobody gets sacked for buying IBM'.

1.5.3 Selection criteria

The issue of precisely how **organisational buyers** make the **purchase decision**, in terms of the selection criteria determining the choice of supplier, has been the subject of various pieces of research.

Important **selection criteria** could be as follows.

- Delivery capability
- Quality
- Price
- Repair and after-sales service
- Technical capability
- Performance history
- Production facilities
- Help and advice
- Control systems
- Reputation

- Financial position
- Attitude toward the buyer
- Compliance with bidding procedures
- Training support
- Communications on the progress of the order
- Management and organisation
- Packaging
- Moral/legal issues
- Location
- Labour relations

Section summary

In consumer marketing, the customer may combine a number of roles, for example **buyer**, **payer** and **user**.

The **influences on a consumer's purchasing decision** may be classified as social, cultural, personal and psychological.

Business to business marketing reflects the more complex and **formal organisational buying process**.

2 Marketing in not-for-profit organisations

Introduction

Increasingly, public sector and charitable organisations are adopting a more commercial approach to their operations, including the use of marketing techniques.

2.1 Charity and not-for-profit marketing

Marketing has a lot to offer charities and not-for-profit organisations, for example in terms of **marketing research** and a clear understanding of **segmentation**, **targeting** and **positioning**.

Marketing techniques are now recognised as just as appropriate in NFP organisations as in a commercial environment. The tasks of setting objectives, developing strategies, devising appropriate marketing mixes and implementing controls are just as relevant for charities and NFP organisations.

Public sector organisations may use marketing tools to encourage competitive tendering to provide government services. Almost all organisations need to compete with other employers to recruit employees.

Many NFP organisations have introduced initiatives to raise money, such as hospitals selling paramedical services to local industry, and universities developing commercial centres to sell research and consultancy skills.

2.1.1 What are pubic sector organisations 'exchanging'?

Lancaster and Withey (2006) identified typical exchanges between public sector organisations and their 'customers'. For example, a university provides education, qualifications and the prospect of career advancement in return for time and fees. A local government council provides local services and contributes to the lifestyle of residents in return for taxation payments and perhaps votes.

There are many other possible examples, the key point is that even though we are talking about public sector bodies an exchange is taking place, and therefore there is likely to be a role for marketing.

2.2 Characteristics of charity and not-for profit marketing

Dibb et al suggests not-for-profit organisations need to consider their **marketing objectives**, **target markets**, **marketing mixes** and how they will **control** marketing activities.

(a)   **Objectives** will not be based on profit achievement but rather on achieving a particular response from target markets. The organisation will need to be open and honest in showing how it has managed its budget and allocated funds raised. Efficiency and effectiveness are particularly important in the use of taxpayer funds or donations.

(b)   **Target marketing** will involve identifying a number of different audiences. *Bruce* (2005) identifies three **types of customers for charities**.

   (i)   **Beneficiaries** include not only those who receive tangible support, but also those who benefit from lobbying and publicity.

   (ii)   **Supporters** provide money, time and skill. Voluntary workers form an important group of supporters. Those who choose to buy from charities are supporters, as are those who advocate their causes.

   (iii)   **Regulators** include both formal bodies, such as the Charities Commission and local authorities, and less formal groups such as residents' associations.

   The groups NFPs marketing activities try to reach can be classified as contributors (for example of time), customers (for example clients, patients, students) and volunteers.

(c)   Charities and NFP organisations often deal more with services than products. In this sense the **extended marketing mix** that includes people, processes and physical evidence is important.

   (i)   **Appearance** should be business-like rather than appearing extravagant.

   (ii)   **Process** is increasingly important; for example, the use of direct debit to pay council tax or donations reduces administration costs.

   (iii)   **People**, whether employed or volunteers, must offer good service and be caring in their dealings with clients.

   (iv)   **Distribution channels** are often shorter with fewer intermediaries than in the profit making sector. Wholesalers and distributors available to business organisations do not exist in most non-business contexts.

   (v)   **Promotion** for charities often includes personal selling with street corner and door-to-door collections. Advertising is becoming increasingly important for large charities. Direct marketing is growing due to the ease of developing databases. Sponsorship (online), competitions and special events are also widely used.

   (vi)   **Pricing**. Value for money is important. Opportunity cost, where an individual is persuaded of the value of donating time or funds, is often relevant.

(d)   **Control** aims to ensure progress is proceeding as planned. For example a charity would compare donations and expenditure to budget. To control NFP marketing activities, managers must specify what factors need to be monitored and permissible variance levels. Relevant measures could include number of employees, number of volunteers (charities), number of 'customers' served and satisfaction levels.

2.2.1 Non-governmental organisations (NGOs)

Non-governmental organisations (NGOs) are private sector, voluntary organisations that contribute to, or participate in education, training or other humanitarian, progressive, or watchdog activities. Some NGOs are accredited by the UN.

Important NGOs include the International Committee Of The Red Cross, International Organisation For Standardisation (ISO), Amnesty International and the World Wildlife Fund (WWF).

NGOs use marketing to find a position for themselves in the market, gain supporters, establish client and donor needs and to communicate with stakeholders.

2.3 The charity marketing mix

The following four elements of the **marketing mix** are particularly relevant to **charities** (product, price, processes and place). The mix adopted must suit the charity's overall philosophy.

2.3.1 Product

A charity's **product** is essentially the **cause** it supports and the **help** it provides, for example cancer research aims to reduce the suffering and improve the prospects of future cancer patients. It is important to communicate what work the charity does and what donations are used for.

When a supporter provides money to a charity, the idea of what the money will be used for is their source of satisfaction, knowing they have helped others or furthered a particular cause.

2.3.2 Price

Price is very important to larger charities since sales of goods and services provide their largest single source of income. Proper cost accounting techniques must be applied where appropriate.

2.3.3 Processes

Since supporters are crucial to a charity's income and beneficiaries are the reason why it exists, **processes** must be as customer-friendly as possible. This is certainly an area where philosophy is important.

2.3.4 Place

If charities distribute physical goods this can present challenges, for example providing disaster relief overseas.

On the other hand, charities that distribute funds, to the poor, for instance, or to pay for medical research, may have very short and easily managed distribution chains. Donations for many charities are increasingly being made online.

Section summary

Charities and **not-for-profit organisations** are increasingly utilising marketing tools and techniques, particularly in relation to **segmentation**, **targeting** and **positioning**.

Charities are **similar** in some respects to **service organisations** and the extended marketing mix is particularly relevant to them.

The **charity marketing mix** adopted must suit the charity's overall philosophy.

3   Internal marketing

Introduction

In this section we shall study what internal marketing is and its importance in motivating employees to support the marketing effort of the organisation.

KEY POINT

Internal marketing has been well summarised by *Peck et al*:

*'Internal marketing is concerned with creating, developing and maintaining an **internal service culture and orientation**, which in turn assists and supports the organisation in the achievement of its goals. ...*

*'The basic premise behind the development of internal marketing is the acknowledgement of the **impact of employee behaviour and attitudes** on the relationship between staff and external customers. The skills and customer orientation of these employees are, therefore, critical to the customers' perception of the organisation and their future loyalty to the organisation.'*

In other words, it is through internal marketing that all **employees** can develop an **understanding of how their tasks**, and the way they perform them, **create** and **deliver customer value** and **build relationships**.

CASE STUDY

LL Bean (US catalogue retailer)

To inspire its employees to practise the marketing concept, LL Bean has for decades displayed posters around its office that proclaim the following:

'What is a customer? A customer is the most important person ever in this company, in person or by mail. A customer is not dependent on us, we are dependent on him. A customer is not an interruption of our work, he is the purpose of it. We are not doing a favour by serving him, he is doing us a favour by giving us the opportunity to do so. A customer is not someone to argue or match wits with, nobody ever won an argument with a customer. A customer is a person who brings us his wants; it is our job to handle them profitably to him and to ourselves.'

3.1 Implementing internal marketing

Peck et al identify the following range of **inter-related activities** thought to be critical **in implementing internal marketing**.

- **Organisational design**: eg drawing key employees together in cross-functional customer service or quality teams

- **Regular staff surveys**: assessing the internal service culture and attitudes

- **Internal customer segmentation**: adapting the internal marketing mix to different employee groups

- **Personal development and training**: focused on core competencies for internal marketing

- **Empowerment and involvement**: enabling staff, within defined parameters, to use their discretion to deliver better service to customers

- **Recognition and rewards**: based on employees' contribution to service excellence

- **Internal communications**: ensuring information flows to support cross-functional co-ordination, and all-employee awareness of their role and contribution to service

- **Performance measures**: evaluating each individual's contribution to marketing objectives

- **Building supportive working relationships**: creating a climate of consideration, trust and support, within which internal communications and service delivery can be encouraged and improved

3.2 The internal marketing mix

Jobber directly relates the elements of the **marketing mix** to internal customers as follows.

Product	The **marketing plan** and strategies that are being proposed to employees or other functions, together with the values, attitudes and actions needed to make the plan successful (eg marketing budgets, extra staff).
Price	What internal customers are being asked to **pay or sacrifice** as a result of accepting the marketing plan (eg lost resources, lower status, new ways of working or harder work).
Promotion (or communications)	The communications **media and messages** used to inform, persuade and gain the support of internal customers for the marketing plan. The message and language will have to be adapted to the needs, concerns and understanding of the target audience (eg eliminating marketing jargon).
Place	How the product (plan) and communications are **delivered** to internal customers: eg via meetings, committees, seminars, informal conversations and so on. This may be direct or via intermediaries (eg consultants).

3.3 Segmenting the internal market

The **internal marketing mix** (like the external marketing mix) will need to be adapted to the needs and drivers of the target audience. The internal market can (like the external market) be **segmented** to allow targeting to the distinctive needs of each group. **Two methods of segmentation** have been suggested.

3.3.1 Jobber's method of segmentation

Jobber (2007) suggests segmentation of internal customers into:

- **Supporters**: those who are likely to gain from the change or plan, or are already committed to it.
- **Neutrals**: those who are likely to experience both gains and losses from the change or plan.
- **Opposers**: those who are likely to lose from the change or plan, or are traditional opponents.

The **product** (plan) and **price** may have to be **modified** to **gain acceptance** from opponents. Place decisions will be used to reach each group most effectively (eg high-involvement approaches such as consultation meetings for supporters and neutrals). Promotional objectives will also differ according to the target group, because of their different positions on issues.

3.3.2 Christopher et al's method of segmentation

Christopher et al (2002) suggest an alternative way of segmenting internal customers, according to **how close they are to external customers**:

- **Contactors** have frequent or regular customer contact and are typically heavily involved with conventional marketing activities (eg sales or customer service roles). They need to be well versed in the organisation's marketing strategies and trained, prepared and motivated to service customers on a day-to-day basis in a responsive manner.

- **Modifiers** are not directly involved with conventional marketing activities, but still have frequent contact with customers (eg receptionists, switchboard, the credit department). These people need a clear view of the organisation's marketing strategy and the importance of being responsive to customers' needs.

- **Influencers** are involved with the traditional elements of marketing, but have little or no direct customer contact (eg in product development or market research). Companies must ensure that these people develop a sense of customer responsiveness, as they influence the total value offering to the customer.

- **Isolateds** are support functions that have neither direct customer contact nor marketing input – but whose activities nevertheless affect the organisation's performance (eg purchasing, HR and data processing). Such staff need to be sensitive to the needs of *internal* customers as well as their role in the chain that delivers value to customers. *Gummesson* uses the term 'part-time marketers' to describe such employees.

3.4 The importance of internal customer communications

Information and **communication** are the foundation of all organisational activity. From a marketing point of view, internal communications may be particularly important in the following areas.

Employer branding	The **organisation's image**, mediated by communication, creates an employer brand: the organisation's image or identity as an employer in the market in which it competes for quality labour.
	Recruitment communications (job ads, application handling, interviews and so on) are public relations and marketing exercises. They must reflect the organisation's values and make an attractive offering to potential employees.
Employee communication and involvement	In many countries, there are **legal requirements** for communication and consultation with employees on matters that affect them.
	The sharing of marketing information encourages employees to **identify with the organisation**, its products/ services and its customers and other stakeholders: the marketing function effectively 'sells' quality – and customer-focused values.
	Information sharing also supports **task performance** (keeping employees informed about new products and marketing plans, and equipping them to make a competent contribution) and **decision-making** (eg by supplying market information or customer feedback to managers in other departments).
	Internal communications (eg through meetings, presentations, newsletters, intranet sites or suggestion schemes) can be used to improve **information flow** in all directions through the organisation. This may be particularly helpful where it encourages information – and ideas-sharing between management and front-line customer-facing staff, and between different organisational functions.
Employee relations	*Armstrong* (2000) describes the aims of employee relations as:
	- Building **stable and co-operative relationships** with employees.
	- Achieving **commitment** through employee involvement and communications.
	- Developing **mutuality**: a common interest in achieving the organisation's goals, through the development of a culture of shared values
	Co-operative employee relations depend on direct and open communication with employees, and giving employees a voice on matters that concern them (including customer care and corporate social responsibility).

3.5 Challenges for internal communication

Jones & Cheeseman (2005) argue that it is growing more **difficult** for organisations to maintain communication with staff, while other pressures contribute to increasing staff diversity and isolation – making such communications even more **necessary** for integration and involvement. Some of the challenges they identify include:

- **Flatter management structures**, meaning that managers have more people reporting to them (a wider 'span of control')

- **Downsizing**, creating workload pressures that may hinder communication and networking

- A trend towards **tele-working** and **'virtual' organisation**, so that staff may be geographically remote from the office, manager and each other

- **Globalisation**, creating increasingly diverse workforces and culturally distinctive units within the organisation, which pose barriers to 'mass' communication.

CASE STUDY

Jobber (2007) cites the example of software giant **Microsoft.**

'It is very easy for senior management to decide upon a set of values that represent a company's ethos, but much harder to engage employees' attention. This was the problem Microsoft faced when trying to communicate its identity as a company internally. It expressed its company values in terms of six attributes: passion, respect, accountability, integrity, self-criticism and eagerness.

Its internal marketing strategy was to ensure this ethos was communicated to employees in three stages. First, there was a campaign across the UK to generate positive feelings about the project. Second, a series of road-shows was held around the firm's UK offices to discuss the core values in depth. Third, a compulsory education programme was launched to ensure all staff understood the proposition.

The creative element of the programme was centred on the well-known David Brent character from the BBC series The Office. Actor Ricky Gervais, who played this character, became involved and a special 15-minute video in the style of the programme was filmed, adding humour to the project and raising its appeal to staff.

The result was that the project achieved high recognition levels for the main message of the campaign among employees, national press coverage and an award for the best internal marketing campaign from the magazine Marketing.'

3.6 Tools of internal communication

A variety of communication tools are used in **formal internal communications**, including: company brochures and newsletters, intranets, video presentations (often web-based), team meetings, personal presentations, conferences, one-to-one interviews, negotiating and consultative meetings (eg with employee representatives), letters, e-mail and web-based 'meetings'.

Let's consider some of these in more detail.

3.6.1 E-mail for internal communication

We looked at the use of e-mail for marketing purposes in the previous chapter. We now consider the use of e-mail for internal communication.

The **advantages of e-mail** for internal communication include:

- Messages can be sent and received very **quickly**

- E-mail is cheap

- A **'hard copy'** may be printed if required

- Messages can be sent worldwide at any time: e-mail is **24-7**, regardless of time zones and office hours

- The user can **attach complex documents** (spreadsheets, graphics, photos) where added data or impact are required

- E-mail message **management software** (such as Microsoft Outlook) enables the sending of messages to multiple recipients, integration with an 'address book' (database of contacts), corporate stationery options and facilities for mail organisation and filing.

3.6.2 Intranet

An **intranet** is an **internal, mini version of the Internet**, using a combination of networked computers and web technology.

'Inter' means 'between' and 'intra' means 'within'. This may be a useful reminder. The **Internet** is used to disseminate and exchange information among the public at large, and between organisations. An **Intranet** is used to disseminate and exchange information within an organisation: only employees are able to access this information.

The **corporate intranet** may be used for:

- **Performance data**: linked to sales, inventory, job progress and other database and reporting systems, enabling employees to process and analyse data to fulfil their work objectives

- **Employment information**: online policy and procedures manuals (health and safety, equal opportunity, disciplinary rules, customer service values and so on), training and induction material, internal contacts for help and information

- **Employee support/information**: advice on first aid, healthy working at computer terminals, training courses offered and so on

- **Notice boards** for the posting of messages to and from employees: notice of meetings, events, trade union activities and so on

- **Departmental home pages**: information and news about each department's personnel and activities, to aid cross-functional understanding

- **Bulletins or newsletters**: details of product launches and marketing campaigns, staff moves, changes in company policy – or whatever might be communicated through the print equivalent, plus links to relevant pages for details

- **E-mail facilities** for the exchange of messages and reports between employees in different locations

- **Upward communication**: suggestion schemes, feedback questionnaires, employee attitude surveys

- **Individual personnel files**, to which employees can download their training materials, references, certificates, appraisals, goal plans and so on.

Benefits of intranets include the following.

- **Cost savings** from the elimination of storage, printing and distribution of documents that can instead be exchanged electronically or be made available online

- **More frequent use** made of online documents than printed reference resources (eg procedures manuals) and more flexible and efficient searching and updating of data

- **Wider access to corporate information**. This facilitates multi-directional communication and co-ordination (particularly for multi-site working). It is also a mechanism of internal marketing and corporate culture

- **Virtual team working**. The term 'virtual team' has been coined to describe how technology can link people in structures which simulate the dynamics of team working (sense of belonging, joint goals, information sharing and collaboration) despite the geographical dispersion of team members in different locations or constantly on the move

3.6.3 Team meetings

Meetings play an important part in the life of any organisation.

- **Formal discussions** are used for information exchange, problem-solving and decision-making. For example, negotiations with suppliers, meetings to give or receive product/idea presentations or 'pitches', and employee interviews.

- **Informal discussions** may be called regularly, or on an ad hoc basis, for communication and consultation on matters of interest or concern: for example, informal briefings and marketing or project team meetings.

Despite the relative inconvenience (compared to group emails, say) of gathering people together in a physical location, team meetings are an **excellent tool of internal communication** and marketing.

Face-to-face discussion is particularly **effective in exchanging information** and **developing relationships**.

Information exchange	Developing relationships
Encourages **ideas generation:** participants encouraging and prompting each other	Brainstorming meeting for promotion planning or **customer care** improvement
Encourages **problem solving** and **conflict resolution:** allows exchange, supportive communication and sensitivity to personal factors	**Customer complaint handling**, or team conflict resolution
Improves **decision-making:** adds different viewpoints and information in real time	Team meetings to **decide plans** or **allocate roles** and tasks
Facilitates **persuasion:** use of personal charisma, logic, sensitivity to feedback	**Sales negotiations**, pitching ideas to internal customers, promoting service values
Encourages **co-operation:** information sharing and all-member participation	**Cross-functional team meetings**, briefings, project meetings
Shows the **human face** of an organisation and encourages identification with it	**Personal internal/external customer service**, internal marketing

3.6.4 The grapevine

In addition to formal attempts by the organisation to communicate with its employees, there **are informal communication channels** such as the '**grapevine**'. For example friends, colleagues and contacts developing internal networks, sharing news, information and gossip. This is a fast and effective way of transmitting information: unfortunately, it is often **inaccurate**, **subjective** – and **difficult for management to control**.

Question 10.2	Internal marketing

Learning outcome D2(xiii)

Briefly explain four benefits that an intranet will bring an organisation in terms of its internal marketing.

(4 marks)

Section summary

Internal marketing enables employees to develop an understanding of how their role delivers customer value and build relationships.

The internal market can be segmented according to the roles employees play in relation to the customer.

Internal marketing has **implications** for **employer branding**, **employee communication** and **employee relations**.

Key communication tools used in internal marketing include email, intranets, team meetings and personal/informal communication.

4 Corporate social responsibility and social marketing   11/10

Introduction

Marketing techniques may be applied to encourage consumption of products which are **potentially damaging** to the health and well-being of the individual and society. Examples include tobacco, alcohol, cars, detergents and even electronic goods such as computers.

There may be conflict between what is profitable for a business organisation and the interests of the customer, or of society.

Many organisations and businesses now accept **responsibility** for **their actions**, rather than simply setting out to provide consumer satisfaction and maximise profits.

We looked at corporate social responsibility (CSR) in Chapter 2. We now revisit this area with a focus on CSR in marketing.

KEY TERM

CORPORATE SOCIAL RESPONSIBILITY involves an organisation accepting that it is part of society and, as such, is accountable to society for the consequences of its actions.

4.1 Social responsibility, ethics and the law

Social responsibility is closely related to ethics. Ethics deal with **personal moral principles** and **values**, whereas laws are the rules that can actually be enforced in court. Behaviour which is not subject to legal penalties may still be unethical and socially irresponsible.

We can **classify marketing decisions** according to ethics and legality in four different ways.

- **Ethical and legal** (eg printing on recycled paper)

- **Unethical and legal** (eg targeting young adults in an 'alcopops' advertising campaign)

- **Ethical but illegal** (eg publishing stolen but revealing documents about mis-selling)

- **Unethical and illegal** (eg passing off cheap imitation goods as designer brands)

4.1.1 Corporate citizenship in practice

Companies have devised a number of different **definitions or approaches to corporate citizenship**.

Abbott Laboratories

CASE STUDY

Global citizenship reflects how a company advances its business objectives, engages its stakeholders, implements its policies, applies its social investment and philanthropy, and exercises its influence to make productive contributions to society.

At Abbott, global citizenship also means thoughtfully balancing financial, environmental and social responsibilities with providing quality health care worldwide. Our programs include public education; environment, health and safety; and access to health care. These efforts reflect an engagement and partnership with stakeholders in the pursuit of sustainable solutions to challenges facing the global community.

AT&T

For AT&T, corporate citizenship means caring about the communities it is involved with, keeping the environment healthy, making AT&T a safe and rewarding place to work and behaving ethically in all its business dealings.

Coca-Cola

Responsible corporate citizenship is at the heart of The Coca-Cola Promise, which is based on four core values

- **Marketplace**. We will adhere to the highest ethical standards, knowing that the quality of our products, the integrity of our brands and the dedication of our people build trust and strengthen relationships. We will serve the people who enjoy our brands through innovation, superb customer service, and respect for the unique customs and cultures in the communities where we do business.

- **Workplace**. We will treat each other with dignity, fairness and respect. We will foster an inclusive environment that encourages all employees to develop and perform to their fullest potential, consistent with a commitment to human rights in our workplace. The Coca-Cola workplace will be a place where everyone's ideas and contributions are valued, and where responsibility and accountability are encouraged and rewarded.

- **Environment**. We will conduct our business in ways that protect and preserve the environment. We will integrate principles of environmental stewardship and sustainable development into our business decisions and processes.

- **Community**. We will contribute our time, expertise and resources to help develop sustainable communities in partnership with local leaders. We will seek to improve the quality of life through locally-relevant initiatives wherever we do business.

Texas Instruments

Beyond the bottom line, the worth of a corporation is reflected in its impact in the community. At TI, our philosophy is simple and dates back to our founding fathers. Giving back to the communities where we operate makes them better places to live and work, in turn making them better places to do business. TI takes its commitment seriously and actively participates in community involvement through three ways – philanthropy, civic leadership and public policy and grass roots efforts.

4.2 Ethical marketing   11/10

Ethical issues usually revolve around **safety**, **quality**, and **value** and frequently arise from failure to provide adequate information to the customer.

Ethical issues relating to the product or service may range from **omission of uncomfortable facts** in product literature to **deliberate deception**.

A particularly serious problem is when **an unsafe product is supplied**, requiring **product recall**.

Ethical considerations are also relevant to **promotional practices**. Advertising and personal selling are areas in which there may be temptation to exaggerate, slant, conceal, distort and falsify information.

Many people think that persuading people to buy something they don't really want is intrinsically unethical, especially if 'hard sell' tactics are used.

The **targeting of children** in marketing campaigns has also attracted criticism - potentially damaging an organisation's reputation and brand.

Also relevant to this area is the issue of **inducements**. It is widely accepted that a small gift such as a mouse mat or a diary is a useful way of keeping a supplier's name in front of an industrial purchaser. Most people would however condemn the payment of substantial gifts as a way of encouraging use of a particular supplier. But where does the dividing line lie between these two extremes?

CASE STUDY

Banks accused of mis-selling risky investments to the elderly

Banks and wealth advisers are preying on vulnerable elderly people, with commission-driven staff encouraging customers in their seventies or eighties to move large sums of money from savings accounts into equities.

Many elderly people do not understand the implications of their new investments and end up losing tens of thousands of pounds when they thought their capital was secure.

Emma Parker, of the Financial Ombudsman Service (FOS), says: 'We receive thousands of complaints from elderly people who believe that they have been mis-sold a long-term investment product. Increasingly, the complaints are about bank or building society branch staff.'

With today's complex financial products, some pensioners believe they are receiving advice when they are merely hearing a sales pitch. Since April the FOS has received 1,809 investment complaints from consumers aged 65 or older. The elderly now account for 22 per cent of all investment complaints, compared with 19 per cent last year.

The Times, August 15, 2009

CASE STUDY

Toyota car recall hits US, Europe and China

Toyota has announced the recall of vehicles in the US, Europe and China over concerns about accelerator pedals getting stuck on floor mats.

The firm has announced plans to recall 1.1 million more cars in the US a day after saying it was suspending sales of eight popular US models.

According to an application to China's quality control office, it wants to recall 75,552 RAV4 vehicles there. The cars in question were manufactured between 19 March 2009 and 25 January 2010 in Tianjin, according to a notice on the website of the General Administration of Quality Supervision, Inspection and Quarantine of the People's Republic of China.

The specifics of the recall in Europe have yet to be decided - the carmaker was trying to establish how many European models shared the parts used in the cars recalled in the US.

Last week, Toyota recalled 2.3 million cars in the US with faulty pedals. It has now recalled almost 8 million cars in the US in the past four months. Last November, it recalled 4.2 million cars because of worries over pedals getting lodged under floor mats.

'Toyota's remedy plan is to modify or replace the accelerator pedals on the subject vehicles to address the risk of floor mat entrapment,' the company said.

The latest recall affects five models in the US: the 2008-2010 Highlander and the 2009-2010 Corolla, Venza, Matrix and Pontiac Vibe.

Toyota shares fell a further 3.9% in Japan, after dropping 4.3% on Wednesday, as concerns about the impact of the recalls on the carmaker's financial health and reputation gripped investors.

Separately, Ford said it would be suspending production of a van made and sold in China that has an accelerator pedal made by the same firm at the centre of Toyota's investigations.

However, Ford said it had only been using the pedal in the Transit Classic model since December, with only 1,663 vehicles produced.

www.bbc.co.uk January 28, 2010

4.3 Social marketing

KEY TERM

SOCIAL MARKETING is the application of marketing techniques to achieve non-commercial goals, for example to encourage behaviour that benefits the environment or to encourage good health.

Governments may attempt to use social marketing to encourage consumption of **merit goods** and discourage consumption of **demerit goods**.

Merit goods are goods or services provided free for the **benefit of society** by the government, for example education or healthcare.

Demerit goods are those considered by the government to be **unhealthy or damaging to society**. Examples include alcohol, cigarettes and gambling.

For example, a social marketing campaign could encourage people to stop smoking, drive safely, eat healthily or practise safe sex.

Exam skills

Corporate social responsibility and social marketing are not areas of the syllabus which you can learn and repeat textbook knowledge. Exam questions are likely to be scenario based and you may be expected to comment on issues raised in them.

Section summary

Corporate social responsibility involves an organisation accepting that it is part of society and, as such, is **accountable to society** for the consequences of its actions.

Unethical marketing practices are ultimately likely to **damage** an organisation's reputation and brand - and ultimately sales.

Social marketing is the application of marketing techniques to achieve **non-commercial goals**, for example to encourage behaviour that benefits the environment or encourages good health.

Chapter Roundup

✓   In **consumer marketing**, the **customer** may combine a **number of roles**, for example buyer, payer and user.

✓   The influences on a consumer's purchasing decision may be classified as **social**, **cultural**, **personal** and **psychological**.

✓   **Business to business** marketing reflects the more complex and **formal organisational buying process**.

✓   **Charities** and **not-for-profit organisations** are increasingly utilising marketing tools and techniques, particularly in relation to **segmentation**, **targeting** and **positioning**.

✓   **Charities** are **similar** in some respects to **service organisations** and the extended marketing mix is particularly relevant to them.

✓   The **charity marketing mix** adopted must suit the charity's overall philosophy.

✓   **Internal marketing** enables employees to develop an understanding of how their role delivers customer value and build relationships.

✓   The internal market can be segmented according to the roles employees play in relation to the customer.

✓   Internal marketing has **implications** for **employer branding**, **employee communication** and **employee relations**.

✓   **Key communication tools** used in internal marketing include email, intranets, team meetings and personal/informal communication.

✓   **Corporate social responsibility** involves an organisation accepting that it is part of society and, as such, is accountable to that society for the consequences of its actions.

✓   **Unethical marketing** practices are ultimately likely to **damage** an organisation's reputation and brand - and ultimately sales.

✓   **Social marketing** is the application of marketing techniques to achieve **non-commercial goals**, for example to encourage behaviour that benefits the environment or encourages good health.

Quick Quiz

1   Which type of customer is described as 'the person who selects a product or service'?

   A   The payer
   B   The user
   C   The consumer
   D   The buyer

2   According to *Webster and Wind* (1972), which group within an organisation's decision making unit initiates the buying process and helps define purchase specifications?

   A   Users
   B   Influencers
   C   Deciders
   D   Gatekeepers

3   Which of the following is not a type of customer of a charity?

   A   Beneficiaries
   B   Supporters
   C   Regulators
   D   Lobbyists

4   Briefly describe the purpose of internal marketing.

5   According to *Caroll & Buchholtz* (2000), what are four main layers of corporate social responsibility?

   A   Charitable, ethical, economic and philanthropic
   B   Economic, legal, ethical and philanthropic
   C   Legal, charitable, ethical and economic
   D   Social, economic, ethical and legal

Answers to Quick Quiz

1   D   The buyer selects the product or service.

2   A   According to *Webster and Wind* (1972), users are the group within an organisation's decision making unit that initiates the buying process and helps define purchase specifications.

3   D   Lobbyists are not a type of charity customer.

Beneficiaries are those who receive tangible support from the charity and who benefit from lobbying and publicity.

Supporters are those who provide the charity with money, time and skill.

Regulators include formal bodies, such as the Charities Commission, and less formal groups such as residents' associations.

4   According to *Jobber* (2007), 'Internal marketing is concerned with creating, developing and maintaining an internal service culture and orientation, which in turn assists and supports the organisation in the achievement of its goals.'

5   B   According to *Caroll & Buchholtz* (2000), the four main layers of corporate social responsibility are economic, legal, ethical and philanthropic. You should have revised this from Chapter 2.

Answer to Questions

10.1 Consumer buying

The **five stages in the consumer buying process** are:

Stage 1: Need/problem recognition

The customer recognises a need or a problem to solve. There is a motive to search for a solution.

Stage 2: Pre-purchase/information search

The customer searches for information they can use to base their decision on.

Stage 3: Evaluation of alternatives

The customer evaluates the various options they have generated.

Stage 4: The purchase decision

The purchase decision is made and the product or service selected based on how it meets their needs and other factors such as cost.

Stage 5: Post-purchase evaluation

The customer evaluates their purchase. If they are dissatisfied, they will be back at the problem recognition stage again. If they are satisfied, the next decision process for the product may be cut short and they may skip straight to the decision, on the basis of loyalty.

10.2 Internal marketing

Four benefits that an intranet will bring an organisation in relation to its internal marketing are:

Cost savings

Intranets eliminate the need to store, print and distribute documents of internal marketing. Instead they can be exchanged electronically or be made available online.

Efficiency

It is often quicker, easier and generally more efficient to search for and update material which is stored electronically.

Distribution

Intranets facilitate multi-directional communication and co-ordination. This means information can be distributed quickly to a number of sites in many countries.

Virtual team working

Employees may work in isolated locations but still be part of a team. Intranets promote virtual teams by providing a central source of information and corporate culture that enables such individuals to feel part of the organisation.

Now try this question from the Exam Question Bank	Number	Level	Marks	Time
	10	Examination	25	45 mins

MANAGING HUMAN CAPITAL

Part E

HUMAN RESOURCE MANAGEMENT

In this chapter we examine the subject of **human resource management (HRM)** and by way of introduction, we note that HRM is different from traditional personnel management.

Human resource management takes a **strategic** approach to an organisation's recruitment, training and appraisal systems. **Personnel management** is concerned with the **low-level detail** of day-to-day management.

However, we will focus most of our attention on a number of human resource theories which aim to get the maximum output from employees. In particular we will focus our attention on the factors which contribute to employee motivation.

Later in the chapter we shall consider recent developments in terms of how organisations are structured and the effect this has had on working arrangements for employees.

Before concluding with a look at **ethical issues**, we revisit HRM from a strategic perspective by looking at how organisations develop an HR plan.

topic list	learning outcomes	syllabus references	ability required
1 Human resource management	E1(a)	E1(i)	comprehension
2 Human resource management theories	E1(a)	E1(i), E1(ii), E1(iii)	comprehension
3 Employee motivation: Remuneration	E2(b)	E2(v)	analysis
4 Employee motivation: Other factors	E2(c)	E2(vii)	comprehension
5 HR management in different types of organisation	E2(c)	E2(ix)	comprehension
6 Working arrangements	E2(c)	E2(ix)	comprehension
7 The HR plan	E2(e)	E2(viii), E2(x)	analysis
8 Ethical behaviour	E1(b)	E1(iv)	comprehension

1 Human resource management

Introduction

In this chapter we look at what **human resource management** is, the **theories** behind it and how it contributes to the **success of an organisation**. We also consider the importance of **ethics** to organisations and its relevance to the line manager.

1.1 What is human resource management?

KEY TERMS

HUMAN RESOURCE MANAGEMENT (HRM) is the process of evaluating an organisation's human resource needs, finding people to fill those needs, and getting the best work from each employee by providing the right incentives and job environment. It has the overall aim of helping an organisation achieve its goals.

PERSONNEL MANAGEMENT deals with day-to-day issues such as hiring and firing and industrial relations in general. Unlike HRM it does not play a strategic role in an organisation.

1.2 The objectives of HRM

It is possible to identify **four main objectives of HRM**.

(a) To **develop an effective human component** for the organisation which will respond effectively to change.

(b) To **obtain and develop the human resources** required by the organisation and to **use** and **motivate** them **effectively**.

(c) To **create and maintain a co-operative climate** of relationships within the organisation and to this end to perform a 'firefighting' role dealing with disputes as they arise.

(d) To meet the organisation's **social and legal responsibilities** relating to the human resource.

1.3 Why is HRM important?

Effective human resource management and employee development are strategically necessary as they contribute to the success of the organisation. Particular benefits of HRM are:

(a) **Increased productivity.** Developing employee skills might make employees more productive.

(b) **Enhanced group learning.** Employees work more and more in multi-skilled teams. Each employee has to be competent at several tasks. Some employees have to be trained to work together (ie in teamworking skills).

(c) **Reduced staff turnover.** Training and developing staff often reduces turnover rates. This increases the effectiveness of operations and profitability as staff become more experienced.

(d) **Encouragement of initiative.** Organisations can gain significant advantage from encouraging and exploiting the present and potential abilities of the people within them.

1.4 Human resource management

KEY POINT

Human resource management (HRM) is based on the assumption that the management and deployment of staff is a key **strategic factor** in an organisation's competitive performance. HRM requires top management involvement and the **promotion** of **culture** and **values**, so that employees' commitment, as opposed merely to their consent, is obtained.

HRM reflects a **wider view** than **traditional personnel management** which is primarily concerned with managing day-to-day operations.

1.4.1 Armstrong

Armstrong (2003) defined HRM as 'a strategic approach to the acquisition, motivation, development and management of the organisation's human resources.'

1.4.2 Bratton and Gold

Bratton and Gold (1999) gave a more detailed definition. 'HRM emphasises that employees are crucial to achieving sustainable competitive advantage, that human resources practices need to be integrated with the corporate strategy, and that human resource specialists help organisational controllers to meet both efficiency and equity objectives.'

A precise interpretation of HRM centres on the following notions.

(a)   The **personnel function** has become centrally concerned with issues of broader relevance to the business and its objectives, such as change management, the introduction of technology, and the implications of falling birth rates and skill shortages for the resourcing of the business.

(b)   HRM should be **integrated with strategic planning**, that is, with management at the broadest and highest level. The objectives of the HR function should be directly related to achieving the organisation's goals for growth, competitive gain and improvement of 'bottom line' performance.

(c)   HRM managers should be **professionals**.

1.4.3 Tyson and Fell

S Tyson and *A Fell* (*Evaluating the Personnel Function*) suggest **four major roles** for human resource management which illustrate the shift in emphasis to the strategic viewpoint.

(a)   To represent the organisation's **central value system** (or culture).
(b)   To **maintain the boundaries of the organisation** (its identity and the flow of people in and out of it).
(c)   To provide **stability and continuity** (through planned succession, flexibility and so on).
(d)   To adapt the organisation to **change**.

Some companies will have a **separate human resource function** with staff authority over other departments. Smaller companies may not be able to afford the luxury of such a function.

HRM is therefore a **set of activities** that may or may not have a separate department to manage it.

Exam alert

You may be asked to explain the role of an 'HR' division.

Question 11.1	Human resource management

Learning outcome E1(i)

Briefly explain how human resource management contributes to the success of an organisation.

(2 marks)

1.5 The human resource cycle

A relatively simple model that provides a framework for explaining the nature and significance of HRM is the human resource cycle (*Devanna* 1984).

The model is shown below.

Human resource cycle

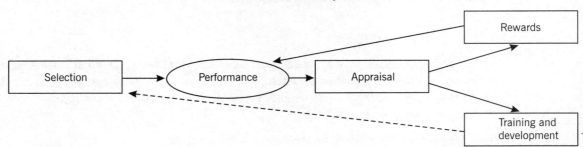

Selection is important to ensure the organisation obtains people with the qualities and skills required.

Appraisal enables targets to be set that contribute to the achievement of the overall strategic objectives of the organisation. It also identifies skills and performance gaps, and provides information relevant to reward levels.

Training and development ensure skills remain up-to-date, relevant, and comparable with (or better than) the best in the industry.

The **reward system** should motivate and ensure valued staff are retained.

Performance depends upon each of the four components and how they are co-ordinated.

1.6 The Guest model of HRM

David Guest (1997) developed a model to show the relationship between an organisation's HRM strategy and HRM activities.

Guest's six components					
① HRM strategy	② HRM practices	③ HRM outcomes	④ Behavioural outcomes	⑤ Performance outcomes	⑥ Financial outcomes
Differentiation (innovation)	Selection	Commitment	Effort	*High:*	Profits
	Training	Quality	Motivation	Productivity	Return on investment
Focus (quality)	Appraisal	Flexibility	Co-operation	Quality	
	Rewards		Involvement	Innovation	
Cost (cost reduction)	Job redesign		Organisational citizenship	*Low:*	
	Involvement			Absenteeism	
	Status and security			Employee turnover	
				Conflict	
				Customer complaints	

The model proposes that HRM practices should aim to result in **high staff commitment** and **high quality, flexible employees**. Achieving these three HRM outcomes will facilitate the achievement of the behavioural, performance and financial outcomes shown in the table.

1.7 Limitations of HRM models

Models of HRM practices (such as *Devanna's* and *Guest's*) tend to **underestimate** the influence of external **opportunities** or **threats** and internal **strengths** and **weaknesses**.

KEY POINTS

> **External factors** such as **competition**, **technology**, **political/legal factors**, **economic factors** and **social/cultural factors** will all impact upon HRM.
>
> **Internal factors** such as the **organisational structure** and **culture** will also impact upon HRM.

In addition, the way people are managed often depends upon the approach favoured by their **line manager**. Some managers favour the 'hard' or rational approach – others believe in a 'softer' approach that emphasises individual and organisational development.

Cultural, **economic** and **legal traditions** within a country will also shape HR policies. For example, in **Japan** and the **USA** there is little state intervention in business and therefore organisations are free to form their own practices. However, in former communist states such as **China** and some **Eastern European** countries there remains a relatively high degree of state intervention.

CASE STUDY

London bus drivers

The pressures faced by recruiters and, indeed, human resources managers in general is exemplified by recruiting for the bus industry. Here, problems of staff turnover, reward, recruitment catchment areas and pools, labour market trends and key stakeholder pressures are thrown into sharp focus.

London bus drivers tend to stay in a job for less than a year. The capital's bus companies are facing the highest levels of staff turnover since the 1950s. A combination of the reviving economy and the expanding London bus network means that some bus companies are having to replace up to 40 per cent of drivers a year.

Pay is one issue, shift work is another. But the bus companies, competing in a deregulated market, are under pressure to match their services to commuter needs, rather than the body clocks of their drivers.

The squeeze on numbers is now so acute that some bus companies are looking outside London for staff. Other bus companies in London believe that recruiting drivers from outside their local area spells trouble. Instead, it has broadened its recruitment policy to include significantly older and younger drivers, as well as more women.

Section summary

Human resource management (HRM) involves evaluating an organisation's human resource needs, finding people to fill those needs, and getting the best work from each employee by providing the right incentives and job environment.

HRM contributes to the success of an organisation through increased productivity, enhanced group learning, reduced staff turnover and encouragement of initiative.

HRM is important at each stage in the **human resource cycle**.

There are a number of **factors** both **internal** and **external** to the organisation which **limit the success** of any HRM policy.

2 Human resource management theories

Introduction

In this section we look at some of the most **significant theories** related to the management of people. Exam questions may require you to spot them in a scenario or you may be asked to explain them directly.

Human resource management theories often relate to three interlinked aspects, **ability**, **opportunity** and **motivation**. Many theorists believe that individual employee performance is a multiplicative function of ability and motivation and that the environment also determines the level of performance.

2.1 Ability

Ability refers the **skill**, **knowledge** and **capability** required of employees in order to fulfil the objectives of the organisation.

2.1.1 Taylor: scientific management

One of the first theorists to discover the link between employee ability and the objectives of the organisation was *Frederick W Taylor* who pioneered the **scientific management** movement. He argued that management should be based on 'well-recognised, clearly defined and fixed principles, instead of depending on more or less hazy ideas.'

Taylor was an engineer and mostly concerned with **engineering** management. His aim was increased **efficiency** in production, that is, increased productivity. His methods were later applied to many other types of work.

2.1.2 Principles of scientific management

The **principles of scientific management** are outlined below.

(a) **The development of a true science of work**. 'All knowledge which had hitherto been kept in the heads of workmen should be gathered and recorded by **management**. Every single subject, large and small, becomes the question for scientific investigation, for reduction to law.'

(b) **The scientific selection and progressive development of workers**. Workers should be carefully trained and given jobs to which they are best suited.

(c) **The bringing together of the science and the scientifically selected and trained men**. The application of techniques to decide what should be done and how, using workers who are both properly trained and willing to maximise output, should result in maximum productivity.

(d) **The constant and intimate co-operation between management and workers**. 'The relations between employers and men form without question the most important part of this art.' There is much that is relevant today in this approach and the pursuit of productivity is still a major preoccupation for management at all levels.

2.1.3 Examples of Scientific Management

The following are **examples of Scientific Management** in practice.

(a) **Work study techniques** established the 'one best way' to do any job. No discretion was allowed to the worker. Subsequently, *Henry Ford*'s approach to mass production broke each job down into its smallest and simplest component parts: these single elements became the newly-designed job.

(b) **Planning the work and doing the work were separated**. Workers did what they were told – they did not have any control over how they completed a task.

(c)   **Workers were paid incentives** on the basis of acceptance of the new methods and output norms as the new methods greatly increased productivity and profits.

(d)   All aspects of the work environment were **tightly controlled** in order to attain maximum productivity.

CASE STUDY

It is useful to consider an application of Taylor's principles. In testimony to the House of Representatives Committee in 1912, Taylor used as an example the application of scientific management methods to shovelling work at the Bethlehem Steel Works.

(a)   Facts were first gathered by management as to the number of shovel loads handled by each man each day, with particular attention paid to the relationship between weight of the average shovel load and the total load shifted per day. From these facts, management was able to decide on the ideal shovel size for each type of material handled in order to optimise the speed of shovelling work done.

(b)   By organising work a day in advance, it was possible to minimise the idle time and the moving of men from one place in the shovelling yard to another.

(c)   Workers were paid for accepting the new methods and 'norms' and received 60% higher wages than those given to similar workers in other companies in the area.

(d)   Workers were carefully selected and trained in the art of shovelling properly; anyone consistently falling below the required norms was given special teaching to improve performance.

(e)   'The new way is to teach and help your men as you would a brother; to try to teach him the best way and to show him the easiest way to do his work.'

(f)   At the Bethlehem Steel Works, Taylor said, the costs of implementing this method were more than repaid by the benefits. The labour force required fell from 500 men to 140 men for the same work.

2.2 Opportunity

Employees work within an **environment** that is provided by their employer. This environment must be **appropriate** if employees are to be given the opportunity to **perform** their role at their **maximum**.

2.2.1 Weber: Bureaucracy, rational form

In the 1940's, *Max Weber* a German sociologist developed a theory of **bureaucracy**. Under bureaucracy, authority is bestowed by dividing an organisation into jurisdictional areas (production, marketing, sales and so on) each with specified duties. Authority to carry them out is given to the officials in charge, and rules and regulations are established in order to ensure their achievement. Managers get things done because their orders are accepted as legitimate and justified. *Weber* suggested that organisations naturally evolved toward this **rational** form.

2.2.2 Lawrence and Lorsch: Contingency theory

KEY POINT

Contingency theory is a concept based upon the idea that the organisation's structure and management approach must be tailored to the situation. There is no one best way to manage.

One form of contingency theory was developed by *Lawrence and Lorsch* (1967). They concluded that organisations in a **stable environment** are more effective if they have more detailed procedures and a more centralised decision-making process while organisations in an **unstable environment** should have decentralisation, employee participation, and less emphasis on rules and procedures to be effective.

2.3 Motivation

KEY POINT

Motivation is an **employee's desire to perform their role**. It is often linked to the outcome and any reward.

It is in an organisation's interests to know the reasons or **motives** behind **people's behaviour**. Motivation influences employee productivity and their quality of work. By understanding what motivates their staff, an organisation is better equipped to provide an environment that maximises employee performance.

We now outline some of the main theories of motivation.

2.3.1 Taylor, maximising prosperity

In the late nineteenth and early twentieth centuries, *Taylor* established four principles to achieve the **maximum prosperity** for employers and employees.

(a)   **Science** should be used to **determine fair pay** for a **day's work**.

(b)   **Scientific methods** should be used in the **recruitment** and **selection** of staff who should be developed to ensure they are capable of **meeting output** and **quality targets**.

(c)   **'Mental revolution'**. Staff should be encouraged to fulfil their potential.

(d)   There should be **constant** and **intimate co-operation** between **management** and **staff**.

Taylor appreciated how productivity would improve if staff were specialised and equipped with the **knowledge** and **skills** required to perform their role. Jobs should be broken down into functions that would each be performed by an individual. However, this view resulted in over-staffing in some organisations as a relatively large number of middle managers controlled the other workers.

Taylor also held the view that as **workers were rational** and would be **motivated** by the **highest remuneration** that was possible.

2.3.2 Mayo, Schein: Human relations

In the 1930s, a critical perception of scientific management emerged. *Elton Mayo* pioneered a new (then) approach called **human relations**. This concentrated mainly on the concept of *Schein's* 'Social Man' where **people are motivated by 'social' or 'belonging' needs**, which are satisfied by the social relationships they form at work.

Attention shifted towards people's **higher psychological needs** for **growth**, **challenge**, **responsibility** and **self-fulfilment**. *Herzberg* suggested that only these things could positively motivate employees to improved performance.

The human relations approaches contributed an important awareness of the influence of the **human factor** at work on organisational performance.

(a)   Most theorists offer **guidelines** to enable practising managers to satisfy and motivate employees and so (theoretically) to obtain improved productivity.

(b)   However, as far as the practising manager is concerned there is still **no simple link between job satisfaction** and **productivity** or the achievement of **organisational goals**.

2.3.3 Maslow's hierarchy of needs

KEY TERM

HIERARCHY OF NEEDS: a ranked structure of behavioural stimuli within the individual, which explain motivation. It is an example of a **content theory** of motivation.

Apart from 'biogenic needs' or 'drives', that is, biological determinants of behaviour, activated by deprivation, there are **psychogenic needs** – emotional or psychological needs. The American psychologist *Abraham Maslow* argued that man has seven innate needs, and put forward certain propositions about the motivating power of these needs.

He described two **higher order** needs.

(a)   The need for **freedom of inquiry and expression**: for social conditions permitting free speech and encouraging justice, fairness and honesty.

(b)   The need for **knowledge and understanding**: to gain and order knowledge of the environment, to explore, learn, experiment. These are essential pre-requisites for the satisfaction of the remainder.

The other five needs can be arranged in a 'hierarchy of relative pre-potency'. Each level of need is **dominant until satisfied** – only then does the next level of need become a motivating factor. A need which has been satisfied no longer motivates an individual's behaviour. The need for self-actualisation can never be satisfied.

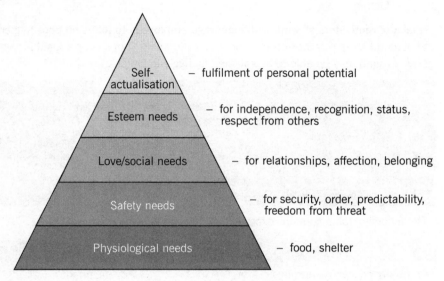

There are **various problems** associated with **Maslow's theory**.

(a)   **Empirical verification** for the hierarchy is hard to come by. Physiological and safety needs are not always uppermost in the determination of human behaviour.

(b)   **Research** does not bear out the proposition that needs become less powerful as they are satisfied, except at the very primitive level of primary needs like hunger and thirst.

(c)   It is **difficult to predict** behaviour using the hierarchy: the theory is too vague.

(d)   **Application** of the theory in work contexts presents various difficulties. For example, the role of money or pay is problematic, since it arguably represents other rewards like status, recognition or independence.

(e)   The **ethnocentricity** of Maslow's hierarchy has also been noted – it does seem broadly applicable to Western English-speaking cultures, but it is less relevant elsewhere.

2.3.4 Herzberg's two-factor content theory

The American psychologist *Frederick Herzberg* interviewed 203 Pittsburgh engineers and accountants. The subjects were asked to recall **events which had made them feel good about their work, and others which made them feel bad about it**. Analysis revealed that the factors which created satisfaction were different from those which created dissatisfaction.

Herzberg identified two groups of work related factors which caused satisfaction and dissatisfaction respectively. He called these factors **motivators** and **hygiene factors**.

KEY TERMS

MOTIVATORS produced satisfaction when present and were capable of motivating the individual.

HYGIENE FACTORS (or MAINTENANCE FACTORS) could not give satisfaction or provide motivation when present. Their absence, however, caused dissatisfaction.

In his book *Work and the Nature of Man*, *Herzberg* distinguished between **hygiene factors** and **motivator factors**, based on what he saw as two separate 'need systems' of individuals.

(a)   There is a **need to avoid unpleasantness**. This need is satisfied at work by hygiene factors. Hygiene satisfactions are short-lived: individuals come back for more, in the nature of drug addicts.

(b)   There is a **need for personal growth**, which is satisfied by motivator factors, and not by hygiene factors.

A lack of motivators at work will encourage employees to focus on poor hygiene (real or imagined) and to demand more pay for example. Some individuals do not seek personal growth: these are 'hygiene seekers' who may be able to be satisfied by hygiene factors.

KEY POINTS

Hygiene factors are essentially **preventative**. They prevent or **minimise dissatisfaction** but do not give satisfaction, in the same way that sanitation minimises threats to health, but does not give 'good' health. They are called 'maintenance' factors because they have to be continually renewed to avoid dissatisfaction.

Motivator factors create job satisfaction and are effective in motivating an individual to superior performance and effort. These factors give the individual a sense of self-fulfilment or personal growth.

The following table contains examples of **hygiene** and **motivation factors**.

Hygiene factors	Motivation factors
Company policy and administration	Advancement
Salary	Gaining recognition
Quality of supervision	Responsibility
Interpersonal relationships	Challenge
Working conditions	Achievement
Job security	Growth in role
Status (may also be a motivation factor)	Autonomy

Herzberg suggested that if there is sufficient **challenge**, **scope** and **interest** in the job, there will be a lasting **increase in satisfaction**, the employee will work well and productivity will be above normal levels.

The extent to which a job must be challenging or creative to a motivator-seeker will depend on each individual's ability and their tolerance for **delayed success**.

2.3.5 Adams: Equity theory

Equity theory deals with **issues of fairness**, in other words that people seek a fair return for their efforts, not necessarily the maximum reward.

Adams makes these suggestions.

(a)   People compare what they receive with what others receive, for a perceived level of effort.

(b)   Inequity exists if another person gets more for a given level of input.

(c)   People get more upset the more inequity there is.

(d)   The more upset someone is, the harder they will work to restore 'equity'.

Equity theory was backed up in the laboratory but is **hard to apply** in the real world.

2.3.6 McGregor's Theory X and Theory Y

Douglas McGregor categorises **managers' assumptions** into two types.

KEY TERM

THEORY X AND THEORY Y: Two contrasting managerial approaches to motivation described by *McGregor*.

(a) **Theory X. Most people dislike work and responsibility and will avoid both if possible.** Therefore, most people must be coerced, controlled, and threatened with punishment to get them to make an adequate effort towards the achievement of the organisation's objectives.

(b) **Theory Y. Individuals wants to satisfy their individual needs through work and wish to make a contribution towards goals that they have helped to establish.** Therefore managers who take a Theory Y approach seek to allow their staff to follow their own path and satisfy their own needs.

When deciding which approach to take, the following issues are important.

(i) **Strict controls** and **close supervision** may be a source of **conflict**.

(ii) **Self motivation** and **commitment** may be more **effective** and **less confrontational**.

(iii) **Treating individuals** in a **Theory X manner** may **prevent** the use of **initiative** and **encourage** doing the **minimum required**.

(iv) **Theory X is ineffective** when managing individuals who are **not financially motivated** or who are **not afraid of punishment**.

2.3.7 Vroom: Expectancy theory

The **expectancy theory** of motivation is a **process theory**, based on the assumptions of cognitive psychology that human beings are rational and are aware of their goals and behaviour.

In 1964 *Victor Vroom*, an American psychologist, worked out a formula by which human motivation could actually be assessed and measured, based on an **expectancy theory** of work motivation. *Vroom* suggested that the strength of an individual's motivation is the product of two factors.

(a) The **strength of their preference for a certain outcome**. *Vroom* called this **valence**. It may be represented as a positive or negative number, or zero – since outcomes may be desired, avoided or considered with indifference.

(b) The individual's **expectation that the outcome will result from a certain behaviour**. *Vroom* called this **subjective probability** – it is the individual's 'expectation' and depends on their perception of the probable relationship between behaviour and outcome. As a probability, it may be represented by any number between 0 (no chance) and 1 (certainty). It is also called **expectancy**.

In its simplest form, the **expectancy equation** therefore looks like this.

Force or strength of motivation to do something	=	Valence ie strength of their preference for a certain outcome	×	Expectation that behaviour will result in desired outcome

Expectancy theories suggest the following **steps** to improve **employee motivation**.

 Determine what an **individual values**.

 Identify the desired **managerial behaviour**.

 Set performance levels which are **perceived** to be **achievable**.

 Determine methods to **link managerial behaviour** to **individual performance**.

 Ensure adequate rewards are in place to **encourage performance**.

Ensure the reward system is **fair** and **equitable**.

2.3.8 Schein, common behavioural traits

Schein identified **four groups of 'man'** with common behavioural traits.

(a)   **Rational economic man**

This group is motivated by the maximisation of economic gain and by following their own self-interest.

(b)   **Social man**

Performance of this group is improved by raising morale, through socialisation at work. Rather than acting as a controller, managers should be seen as facilitators.

(c)   **Self-actualising man**

This group is motivated through self-fulfilment. In terms of work they are motivated by challenge and responsibility.

(d)   **Complex man**

Motivation is based on a 'psychological contract' between employers and employees. Each has their own expectations of the 'contract' and motivation depends on their fulfilment.

2.3.9 Goal-setting theory

Goal-setting theory suggests that **goals** can motivate.

(a)   Challenging goals, providing they have been accepted, lead to better performance than easy goals.
(b)   The best goals are specific as they focus people's attention.
(c)   Knowledge of results is essential.

Goal theory has the most **empirical support** of any motivation theory, but there are some limits to how it applies.

(a)   Research has concentrated on quantity not quality of output.

(b)   At work, people pursue several goals consecutively; achieving one may mean neglecting another. This is particularly a problem for organisations where trade offs have to be made.

2.3.10 Mullins' classifications of motivation

According to *Mullins* (2005) **motivation** is 'the driving force within individuals by which they attempt to achieve to achieve some goal in order to fulfil some need or expectation.'

Mullins also identified **three classifications** for understanding motivation.

Classification	Examples
Economic reward	Pay and benefits
Intrinsic satisfaction	Enjoyment of the job and personal development
Social relationships	Team working and forming friendships with colleagues

Question 11.2	Theory X and Theory Y

Learning outcome E1(i)

Douglas McGregor suggested that managers have one of two views or theories about subordinates.

View 1. Individuals want to satisfy their needs through work and wish to make a contribution to the goals they have helped to establish.

View 2. Most people dislike work and responsibility, and so have to be coerced, controlled, and threatened with punishment, to get them to do their job adequately.

Which of the following statements is correct?

A   View 1 is called Theory X and view 2 is called Theory Y, and McGregor suggested that the most effective managers hold view 1

B   View 1 is called Theory Y and view 2 is called Theory X, and McGregor suggested that the most effective managers hold view 2

C   View 1 is called Theory X and view 2 is called Theory Y, and McGregor suggested that the most effective managers hold view 2

D   View 1 is called Theory Y and view 2 is called Theory X, and McGregor suggested that the view held by the most effective managers depends on the circumstances

2.4 Psychological contracts

A **psychological contract** exists between individuals in an organisation and the organisation itself.

(a)   The individual expects to derive certain benefits from membership of the organisation and is prepared to expend a certain amount of effort in return.

(b)   The organisation expects the individual to fulfil certain requirements and is prepared to offer certain rewards in return.

Three types of **psychological contract** can be identified.

(a)   **Coercive contract**. This is a contract in which the individual considers that they are being forced to contribute their efforts and energies involuntarily, and that the rewards they receive in return are inadequate compensation.

(b)   **Calculative contract**. This is a contract, accepted **voluntarily** by the individual, in which they expect to do their job in exchange for a readily identifiable set of rewards. With such psychological contracts, motivation can only be increased if the rewards to the individual are improved. If the organisation attempts to demand greater efforts without increasing the rewards, the psychological contract will revert to a coercive one, and motivation may become negative.

(c)   **Co-operative contract**. This is a contract in which the individual identifies themselves with the organisation and its goals, so that they actively seek to contribute further to the achievement of those goals. Motivation comes out of success at work, a sense of achievement, and self-fulfilment.

The individual will probably want to share in the planning and control decisions which affect their work, and **co-operative contracts are therefore likely to occur where employees participate in decision-making**.

Motivation happens when the psychological contract, within which the individual's motivation calculus operates for new decisions, is viewed in the same way by the organisation and by the individual, and when both parties are able to fulfil their side of the bargain. The individual agrees to work, or work well, in return for whatever rewards or satisfactions are understood as the terms of the 'contract'.

Psychological contracts are particularly relevant when considering **staff turnover and retention rates**. Employees are more likely to stay and be loyal to an organisation where they perceive to have a co-operative contract rather than a coercive one.

Section summary

The success of any **HRM policy** can be measured by the **contribution of the employees** to the success of the organisation.

There are a number of **HRM theories** which relate to **ability**, **opportunity** and **motivation**.

Psychological contracts are the expectations that the employee and employer have of each other.

---

3   Employee motivation: Remuneration   05/11

Introduction

Pay is part of the reward system, and can be a **motivator** in certain circumstances. However, this depends on the value individuals ascribe to pay and the way in which incentive schemes are implemented. Pay is usually considered a hygiene factor.

Employees need an income to live and most probably have two basic concerns – to earn **enough** money and that their pay should be **fair**. This can be assessed in two ways.

(a)   **Equity** – a fair rate for the job
(b)   **Relativity**, or fair differentials, that is, justified differences between the pay of different individuals

3.1 Payment systems

Armstrong and *Murlis* (1998) suggested that payments to employees have two elements.

- **Pay** with scope to reward **progression** and **promotion**
- **Benefits** such as pensions, company cars and medical insurance

3.1.1 Organisational aims for payment systems

At the **organisational (strategic) level**, payment systems have the following goals.

- Aid **recruitment**
- **Retain** employees
- **Reward** employees for performance

3.1.2 Managerial aims for payment systems

At the **managerial level**, payment systems are used to:

- Reward and motivate employees fairly and consistently
- Further the organisation's objectives by providing competitive rewards
- Encourage performance and progression through development
- Recognise non-performance factors such as skill and competence
- Ensure salary costs are controlled

3.2 Pay structures

Common types of pay structure include:

- **Graded**. A pay range is attached to particular levels of job grades.

- **Broad-banded structures** usually encompass the whole workforce from the clerk to the senior manager. The range of pay in this structure is typically higher than in graded structures.

- **Individual**. Pay is allocated to individuals rather than 'bands'. It is most commonly used for senior management positions and avoids the problem of over/under payment which can result from grading.

- **Job family structures**. Jobs in specific functions such as accounts or HR are grouped into families. The jobs differ in terms of skill levels or responsibility (such as accounts technician and management accountant) and pay is determined accordingly.

- **Pay** or **profession/maturity curves**. These recognise that in certain roles, pay must be progressive to allocate pay fairly. Especially where knowledge or experience is key to the role.

- **Spot rates**. Allocate a rate of pay for a specific job often linked to the market price.

- **Rate for age**. Allocates a rate of pay or pay bracket for employees based on age.

- **Pay spines** are often used by government organisations where it is important for pay to be relative across a range of roles. They are a series of incremental points from the lowest to the highest paid jobs. Pay scales for specific jobs are superimposed onto the spine to ensure pay is relative.

- **Manual worker pay structures** recognise the difference in status between those who work in manual roles against those in other parts of the organisation. Real differentials are incorporated that reflect differences in skill and responsibility but otherwise they are similar to other pay structures.

- **Integrated structures** incorporate one grading system for all employees except senior management. They are often used where employees were paid historically under separate agreements.

The assumption behind most payment systems is that **money is the prime motivating factor**. As *Herzberg*, among others, suggested, however, it is more likely to be a cause of dissatisfaction.

Herzberg himself admitted that pay is the most important of all the hygiene factors. *Goldthorpe, Lockwood et al*, in their *Affluent Worker* study of the Luton car industry, suggested that workers may have a purely **instrumental** orientation to work – deriving satisfaction not from the work itself but from the rewards obtainable with the money earned by working. The Luton workers experienced their work as routine and dead-end, but had made a rational decision to enter employment which offered high monetary reward rather than intrinsic interest.

As expectancy theory indicates, pay is only likely to motivate a worker to improved performance if there is a clear and consistent link between performance and monetary reward and if monetary reward is valued. **Salary structures** do not always allow enough leeway to reward individual performance in a job (since fairness usually dictates a rate for the job itself, in relation to others). **Incentive schemes**, however, are often used to re-establish the link between effort and reward.

3.3 Pay differentials

Pay differentials are often key to **determining salaries for employees**. To calculate pay differentials an organisation should refer to market rates for the roles and decide a policy of how its pay levels will reflect the market rate. The following methods may be used in determining pay rates.

3.3.1 Points-factor evaluation scheme

 Evaluate the roles and calculate evaluation job scores based on the level or category of employee.

 Plot job scores on a scatter diagram and draw a line of 'best fit'.

 Plot the upper, median and lower market pay rates from the available information.

 Plot a desired pay policy line based on the market data.

 Decide on the overall shape of the pay structure based on the pay policy.

 Define pay ranges for each level taking into account flexibility for pay-progression.

3.3.2 Ranking/market method

 Rank the existing jobs and plot actual pay rates to show current pay policy.

 Plot market data and derive a 'best fit' policy.

 Decide on a pay range policy and plot upper and lower pay rates using the 'best fit' policy as the mid-range.

 Develop a grade structure and pay rates for each grade.

3.4 Incentive schemes   05/11

The purpose of incentive schemes is to **improve performance by linking it to reward**. It is believed that performance incentives take effect in several ways.

(a)   Staff members' effort and attention are **directed to where they are most needed** – performance.

(b)   **Commitment and motivation are enhanced**. This is particularly important when there are cultural obstacles to improvement.

(c)   **Achievement** can be rewarded separately from **effort**, with advantages for the recruitment and retention of high quality employees.

A further advantage is that **labour costs are linked to organisational performance**.

Schemes may be based on **individual performance** or on **group performance**.

Individual schemes are common when the work is essentially individualistic and the output of a single person is easy to specify and measure. However, much work is performed by **teams** and it is impossible to identify each person's output. Such work calls for a **group incentive scheme**.

The **main problem with team incentive payments** is that there is unlikely to be a single consistent standard of effort or achievement within the group. Inevitably there will be those who perform better than others and they are likely to be aggrieved if all group members are rewarded equally.

The ultimate group incentive scheme is the **organisation wide scheme**, in which all employees are rewarded in accordance with overall performance, usually as measured by profit . This tends to be very popular in good times and the cause of disappointment and resentment when the business is doing badly. The value of such schemes is questionable.

There are **three main types of incentive scheme**:

- Performance related pay (PRP)
- Bonus schemes
- Profit-sharing

3.4.1 Performance related pay

KEY POINT

The most common individual PRP scheme for wage earners is straight **piecework**: payment of a fixed amount per unit produced, or operation completed.

For managerial and other salaried jobs, however, a form of **management by objectives** will probably be applied.

(a) **Key results** will be identified and specified, for which merit awards (on top of basic salary) will be paid.

(b) There will be a **clear model for evaluating performance** and knowing when, or if, targets have been reached and payments earned.

(c) The **exact conditions and amounts of awards** can be made clear to the employee, to avoid uncertainty and later resentment.

For service and other departments, a PRP scheme may involve bonuses for **achievement of key results,** or points schemes, where points are awarded for performance on various criteria (efficiency, cost savings, quality of service and so on). Certain points totals (or the highest points total in the unit, if a competitive system is used) win cash or other awards.

However, *Otley* (1987) discovered that employees become **demotivated** if they fail to meet targets, resulting in a high degree of performance reduction.

3.4.2 Bonus schemes

KEY POINT

Bonus schemes are supplementary to basic salary, and have been found to be popular with entrepreneurial types, usually in marketing and sales. Bonuses are both incentives and rewards.

Group incentive schemes typically offer a bonus for a group (equally, or proportionately to the earnings or status of individuals) which achieves or exceeds specified targets. Typically, bonuses would be calculated monthly on the basis of improvements in output per man per hour against standard, or value added (to the cost of raw materials and parts by the production process).

Value added schemes work on the basis that improvements in productivity increases value added, and the benefit can be shared between employers and employees on an agreed formula. So if sales revenue increases and labour costs stay the same, or sales revenue remains constant but labour costs decrease, the balance becomes available. There has been an increase in such schemes in recent years.

3.4.3 Profit sharing schemes and employee shareholders

KEY POINT

Profit sharing schemes offer employees (or selected groups of them) bonuses, perhaps in the form of shares in the company, related directly to profits. The formula for determining the amounts may vary, but in recent years a straightforward distribution of a percentage of profits above a given target has given way to a value added related concept.

Profit sharing is in general based on the belief that **all employees can contribute to profitability**, and that that contribution should be recognised. If it is, the argument runs, the effects may include profit-consciousness and motivation in employees, commitment to the future prosperity of the organisation and so on.

The actual **incentive value** and effect on productivity may be wasted, however, if the scheme is badly designed.

(a) A **perceivably significant sum** should be made available to employees – once shareholders have received appropriate return on their investment – say, 10% of basic pay.

(b) There should be a clear, and not overly delayed, **link between performance and reward**. Profit shares should be distributed as frequently as possible – consistent with the need for reliable information on profit forecasts and targets and the need to amass a significant pool for distribution.

(c) The scheme should only be introduced if **profit forecasts** indicate a reasonable chance of achieving the target. Profit sharing is welcome when profits are high, but the potential for disappointment is great.

(d) The greatest effect on **productivity** arising from the scheme may in fact arise from its use as a focal point for discussion with employees, about the relationship between their performance and results, and areas and targets for improvement. Management must be seen to be committed to the principle.

Exam alert

Exam questions may require you to discuss the difficulties of designing and operating a reward scheme for performance.

3.4.4 Difficulties associated with incentive schemes

Incentive schemes have the following potential difficulties.

(a) **Increased earnings simply may not be an incentive** to some individuals. An individual who already enjoys a good income may be more concerned with increasing their leisure time, for example.

(b) **Workers are unlikely to be in complete control of results**. External factors, such as the general economic climate, interest rates and exchange rates may play a part in **profitability** in particular. In these cases, the relationship between an individual's efforts and their reward may be indistinct.

(c) Greater **specialisation in production processes** means that particular employees cannot be specifically credited with the success of particular products. This may lead to frustration amongst employees who think their own profitable work is being adversely affected by inefficiencies elsewhere in the organisation.

(d) Even if employees are motivated by money, the effects may not be altogether desirable. An **instrumental orientation may encourage self-interested performance** at the expense of teamwork. It may encourage attention to output at the expense of quality, and the lowering of standards and targets (in order to make bonuses more accessible).

(e) It is often all too easy to **manipulate the rules of the incentive scheme**, especially where there are allowances for waiting time, when production is held up by factors beyond the control of the people concerned. Special allowances, guaranteed earnings and changes in methods also undermine incentive schemes.

(f) **Poorly designed schemes** can produce labour cost increases out of proportion to output improvements.

All such schemes are based on the principle that people are willing to work harder to obtain more money. However, the work of *Elton Mayo* and *Tom Lupton* has shown that there are **several constraints** which prevent most people from seeking to maximise their earnings.

(a) Workers are generally capable of influencing the timings and control systems used by management.

(b) Workers remain suspicious that if they achieve high levels of output and earnings then management will alter the basis of the incentive rates to reduce future earnings. Work groups therefore tend to restrict output to a level that they feel is fair and safe.

(c) Generally, the workers conform to a group output norm. The need to have the approval of their fellow workers by conforming to that norm is more important than the money urge.

In the *Affluent Worker* study referred to above, *Goldthorpe* and *Lockwood* recognised that people do not, by and large, seek to maximise their earnings. Instead, a person will work as hard as necessary to earn the money they want – but not past the point at which the deprivations demanded of them (in terms of long hours or danger or antisocial conditions) are greater than they feel are worthwhile.

3.4.5 Total reward schemes

KEY TERM

A TOTAL REWARD SCHEME (or package) is a bundle of cash and non-cash motivators offered to staff.

Total reward schemes recognise that individuals are all different and may not all be motivated by money. The fact that an individual can supplement their remuneration package may in itself be an attraction for prospective employees.

Carrington (2004) identified the drivers for the development of total reward package. The key driver was the skills shortage in the 1990s that caused '**talent wars**' where organisations had to **attract staff** in a more **competitive manner**. Around the same time many organisations were **developing** a **vision** and **culture** – these schemes helped further this development.

Flexible benefits are another method of rewarding staff. Certain incentives have become more or less popular over time and *Prickett* (2006) identified which are growing, static and declining in popularity.

Growing	Static	Declining
Bicycles	Personal shopping and dry cleaning (city firms mainly)	Golden parachutes
Childcare	Shopping vouchers	Bonus schemes
Computers	Health and dental insurance	Share schemes
Flexible pension schemes (tax efficient)	Gym membership	Final salary pension schemes

Examples of other **non-cash benefits** that may be offered include:

- **Training**
- **Flexible working hours**
- **Working at home**
- **Career progression**
- The **pursuit** of **green** or **ethical policies** by the company (may be an attraction to individuals with strong views on these issues)

Carrington (2004) identified a number of **advantages** of such schemes. In particular they make a **positive statement** about the culture of the organisation, the **creation** of a **more inclusive** rather than a 'them and us' attitude and **improved recruitment** and retention as a result of **employer branding**.

Other **advantages** and **disadvantages** of **total reward schemes** include:

Advantages	Disadvantages
Attracts potential employees	It might have no effect
Improves employee motivation	It might cause organisational stagnation as employees may not push themselves for further reward
	It ignores employee welfare
	Employees may prefer to have cash only

3.4.6 Motivation and incentives

Gratton (2004) concluded that although money is important as a staff motivator, its importance is often over estimated. She found that money often signified **status** between employees, and that this was sometimes more important than purchasing power.

She also emphasised the importance of people being **involved** in decisions and procedures that affected them. This was an important source of motivation.

Section summary

In many circumstances **pay can be a motivator** for employees.

There are many **methods of determining the pay** of employees.

Schemes that **link reward** to **employee performance** include, **profit related pay**, **bonus schemes** and **profit sharing**.

Total reward schemes offer employees bundles of benefits from which they can pick and choose what they want.

4   Employee motivation: Other factors   05/10

Introduction

Frustration, conflict, feelings of failure and **low prospects** tend to show themselves in such effects as **high labour turnover, absenteeism** or **preoccupation with financial rewards** (in compensation for lack of other satisfactions). These can be as self-defeating for the organisation as they are unhealthy for the individual.

However, there are a great many other **work** and **non-work variables** in the equation. A happy workforce will not necessarily make the organisation profitable (if the market is unfavourable). They will not necessarily be more productive (if the task itself is badly designed or resources scarce) nor even more highly motivated.

Therefore, to ensure employee performance benefits the organisation, organisations should take into account all factors that influence employee motivation.

4.1 Job redesign, rotation, enlargement and enrichment

Job redesign, rotation, enlargement and **enrichment** can all be used to improve the motivation of employees by introducing changes to their work.

(a)   **Job redesign** aims to improve performance through increasing the understanding and motivation of employees. Job redesign also aims to ensure that an individual's job suits them in terms of what motivates them and their need for personal growth and development.

(b)   **Job rotation** allows for a little variety by moving a person from one task to another. Employees often do this spontaneously. Job rotation permits the development of extra **skills**, but does not develop **depth of skill**.

(c)   **Job enlargement** increases the *width* of the job by adding extra, usually related, tasks. It is not particularly popular with workers, many of whom prefer undemanding jobs that allow them to chat and daydream.

(d)   **Job enrichment** increase the *depth* of responsibility by adding elements of **planning** and **control** to the job, therefore increasing its meaning and challenge. The worker achieves greater autonomy and growth in the role.

4.2 Job characteristics model

Hackman and Oldham developed the **job characteristics model** that sets out the links between employee motivation, satisfaction and performance (including personal growth) and the characteristics of their job or role.

Hackman and Oldham's **motivating potential score (MPS)** is an attempt to measure a job's potential to produce motivation and satisfaction. The MPS is computed from scores in questionnaires designed to diagnose the extent to which the job displays **five core characteristics**.

(a)   **Skill variety**: the breadth of job activities and skills required
(b)   **Task identity**: whether the job is a whole piece of work with a visible outcome
(c)   **Task significance**: the impact of the job on other people
(d)   **Autonomy**: the degree of freedom allowed in planning and executing the work
(e)   **Feedback**: the amount of information provided about the worker's job performance

Hackman and Oldham suggest that the first three characteristics above contribute to the **'experienced meaningfulness of the work'** and this is borne out by empirical research. The extent to which a job's autonomy and feedback, as measured by *Hackman and Oldham*, contribute to job satisfaction is less clear-cut.

Exam alert

Motivation is an ideal topic for a Section C question. You might be introduced to a situation and asked to explain why the people in the organisation are, say, demotivated. You could be asked to comment on the motivational impact of changes proposed by management.

Section summary

There are a number of methods of **improving an employee's experience of work** and their **motivation**. These include, **job redesign**, **rotation**, **enlargement** and **enrichment**.

5 HR management in different types of organisation

Introduction

Some organisations have found a need to **develop new ways of working**. This has been brought about partly by the changing nature of business and the evolvement of different types and forms of organisations.

5.1 Project-based teams

There is a general trend in organisation structures (particularly in service organisations) away from traditional hierarchies towards **flatter structures** with reporting lines that **cross functional boundaries**. Instead of traditional departments, some organisations operate using multi-skilled employees organised into various work teams based around factors such as customer groups or particular projects.

This has implications for the HR plan and policies. For example, if a general pool of multi-skilled employees is required, **recruitment policy** should reflect that fact – rather than recruiting large numbers of specialists. Extensive training programmes are also likely to be required.

The **advantages and disadvantages of project-based organisations** can be summarised as follows.

Advantages	Disadvantages
Greater flexibility of: • **People**. Employees develop an attitude geared to accepting change. • **Workflow and decision-making**. Direct contact between staff encourages problem solving and big picture thinking. • **Tasks and structure**. The organisational structure may be readily amended, where projects are completed.	**Dual authority** threatens a conflict between functional managers and product/project area managers.

Advantages	Disadvantages
Inter-disciplinary co-operation and a mixing of skills and expertise, along with improved communication and co-ordination.	An individual with two or more bosses may suffer stress from **conflicting demands or ambiguous roles**.
Motivation and employee development: providing employees with greater participation in planning and control decisions.	**Cost**: product management posts are added, more consultation is required eg meetings.
Market awareness: the organisation tends to become more customer/quality focused.	**Slower decision making**
Horizontal workflow: Bureaucratic obstacles are removed.	Possible lack of accountability

5.2 The 'new organisation'

Some recent trends (identified by writers such as *Blyton* and *Peters*) have emerged from the focus on **flexibility** as a key organisational value.

(a) **Flat structures**. The flattening of hierarchies does away with levels of organisation which lengthened lines of communication and decision-making and encouraged ever-increasing specialisation. Flat structures are more responsive, because there is a more direct relationship between the organisation's strategic centre and the operational units serving the customer.

(b) **'Horizontal structures'**. What *Peters (Liberation Management)* calls 'going horizontal' is a recognition that functional versatility (through multi-functional project teams and multi-skilling, for example) is the key to flexibility. In the words (quoted by *Peters*) of a Motorola executive: 'The traditional job descriptions were barriers. We needed an organisation soft enough between the organisational disciplines so that ... people would run freely across functional barriers or organisational barriers with the common goal of getting the job done, rather than just making certain that their specific part of the job was completed.'

(c) **'Chunked' and 'unglued' structures**. So far, this has meant teamworking and decentralisation, or empowerment, creating smaller and more flexible units within the overall structure. *Charles Handy's* **'shamrock organisation'** (with a three-leafed structure of core, subcontractor and flexible part-time labour) is gaining ground as a workable model for a leaner and more flexible workforce, within a controlled framework.

(d) **Output-focused structures**. The key to all the above trends is the focus on results, and on the customer, instead of internal processes and functions for their own sake. A **project management** orientation and structure, for example, is being applied to the supply of services within the organisation (to internal customers) as well as to the external market, in order to facilitate listening and responding to customer demands.

(e) **'Jobless' structures**. The employee becomes not a job-holder but the vendor of a portfolio of demonstrated outputs and competences (*Bridges*). This is a concrete expression of the concept of **employability**, which says that a person needs to have a portfolio of skills which are valuable on the open labour market. Employees need to be mobile, moving between organisations rather than settling in to a particular job.

5.3 Virtual organisations

As we have seen previously, developments in technology have enabled the creation of **virtual teams** and even **virtual organisations**.

These have enabled organisations to:

(a)   **Outsource** areas of organisational activity to other organisations and freelance workers (even 'off-shore' in countries where skilled labour is cheaper), without losing control or co-ordination.

(b)   **Organise 'territorially'** without the overhead costs of local offices, and without the difficulties of supervision, communication and control. Dispersed centres are linked to a 'virtual office' by communications technology and can share data freely.

(c)   **Centralise** shared functions and services (such as data storage and retrieval, technical support or secretarial services) without the disadvantages of 'geographical' centralisation, and with the advantages of decentralised authority. Databases and communication (eg via e-mail) create genuine interactive sharing of, and access to, common data.

(d)   **Adopt flexible cross-functional and multi-skilled working**, by making expertise available across the organisation. A 'virtual team' co-opts the best people for the task – regardless of location.

Section summary

Organisations may adopt **new structures** or develop their own. Recent trends in organisational structure include **project-based teams, flat structures, horizontal structures, chunked** and **unglued structures, output-focussed structures** and **'jobless' structures**. Some have even become **virtual organisations**.

---

6 Working arrangements

Introduction

The ways in which people are **allowed** and **encouraged to work** will **affect their motivation** and performance. For example, allowing employees flexibility in when they complete their weekly hours (flexitime) may allow them to deal with domestic issues when they arise, meaning the time they actually spend working is more productive.

6.1 Attitudes and values

Working methods and arrangements cover much more then the nuts and bolts of hours and pay. For example, modern management theorists emphasise values such as the following.

(a)   **Multi-skilling**. Multi-skilled teams involve individuals who are able to perform a variety of team tasks, as required. This enables tasks to be performed more flexibly, using labour more efficiently.

(b)   **Flexibility**. Flexibility is about being able to respond and adapt quickly to rapidly-changing customer demands, or to other changes such as technological change and different working methods. This has created the following.

   (i)   Smaller, **multi-skilled**, temporary structures, such as project or task-force teams.

   (ii)   Multi-functional units, facilitating communication and co-ordination across departmental boundaries. This is sometimes referred to as a **matrix structure**, since an employee may report both to a line manager *and* to a project or product manager.

   (iii)   **Flexible deployment** of the labour resource, for example through part-time and temporary working, outsourcing, flexitime and so on.

(c)   **Empowerment**. Empowerment involves giving employees the freedom to take responsibility for their goals and actions. This may release hidden resources (creativity, initiative, leadership, innovation), which would otherwise remain inaccessible. People are allowed to use their own judgement.

The extent to which these values are incorporated into an organisation's **HR plan and policies** will depend upon the type of organisation, the role of the employees and the philosophy of top management.

6.2 Flexible working arrangements

When establishing policies and procedures on **flexible work arrangements**, organisations seek to provide employees with a means to achieve a **balance between professional and personal responsibilities** in a manner that benefits both the employee and the employer.

A **well-structured policy** should be developed that provides a **clear understanding** of the expectations and responsibilities of all parties involved in the flexible work arrangement, and ensures that the same criteria for making decisions on flexible work arrangements are applied to all employees.

KEY POINT

The key to **successful flexible work arrangements** is to tailor the arrangement to the particular needs of the individual and the organisation. When considering which flexible work arrangements to offer employees, organisations should consider the arrangement's practicality, fairness, and flexibility within the environment of the organisation.

Typical flexible work arrangements include:

(a) **Flexitime**. Flexitime is an arrangement where employees work the standard number of hours in a workday (or in some arrangements within a work week), but are given some flexibility as to when they work these hours. Most organisations establish 'core working hours', meaning there are certain hours during the day in which it is mandatory for the employee to be at the workplace. For example, an employee on flexitime may have to work 7.5 hours per day, but be able to start their day anytime between 7 and 10 a.m. and finish between 3 and 6 p.m.

(b) **Compressed week**. A compressed week is an arrangement where an employee works the standard number of hours in a one-or two-week period, but compresses those hours into fewer work days (therefore working longer hours on the days the employee is at work). For example, in a 40-hour work week an employee on a compressed work week may work four 10-hour days in a week with one day off, or nine 9-hour days with one day off every two weeks.

(c) **Job sharing**. Job sharing is an arrangement where two employees share one position. There are many combinations of work hours that are used for job sharing. For example, one employee might work Monday to Wednesday and the other employee Thursday and Friday, or one employee might work mornings and the other afternoons.

(d) **Part-time/Reduced hours**. Part-time or reduced hours are arrangements where an employee works less than the standard work week hours (and are paid only for those hours).

(e) **Telecommuting or homeworking**. Telecommuting is an arrangement where an employee works either part or all of the week from a location other than the standard place of work (office). Typically employees in such an arrangement work from their homes. For example, an employee may work three days a week at the office and two days a week from home.

Organisations introducing flexible working should compile a formal **flexible work agreement** to be completed and signed by the employer and the employee. The agreement should include the specific details of the arrangement.

Often there is an **unreasonable requirement** that individuals who work a compressed work week should be required to be available or on-call on their day off, or, on the other hand, the probably reasonable expectation that employees with the right to work at home should come into work for a meeting held on their work-at-home day. These issues should be covered by the flexible work arrangement agreement.

6.2.1 Flexibility in organisations

Three types of flexibility organisations look to achieve in the context of HRM are numerical flexibility, financial flexibility and task flexibility.

(a) **Numerical flexibility** can be achieved through the use of temporary workers – both contractors and agency staff. *Atkinson* (1984) distinguished between 'core employees' (high status, job security) and 'periphery workers' on temporary or flexible hour contracts.

(b) **Financial flexibility** is achieved through variable systems of reward (eg bonuses, performance-related pay).

(c) **Task flexibility** (sometimes referred to as functional flexibility) involves having employees able to undertake a wider range of tasks. Introducing task flexibility could involve employees undertaking a wider range of tasks at the same 'level' (horizontally) or undertaking tasks previously carried out by employees at higher or lower levels (vertically).

Exam alert

Exam questions may ask for a discussion of how an organisation could achieve workforce flexibility.

Advantages	Disadvantages
The **potential benefits to the employer** are:	Possible **disadvantages to the employer** include:
• Increased employee motivation and productivity • Increased employee commitment to the organisation • The ability to attract high performing individuals • Reduced absenteeism and staff turnover.	• Increased difficulty co-ordinating work • Loss of direct control • Dilution of the organisation's culture as employees see less of each other.
The potential **benefits to the employee** are:	Potential **disadvantages to employee** include:
• Reduction in stress due to conflicting personal and professional priorities • Increased job satisfaction, energy and creativity • Reduced cost of commuting • Wider choice of housing as employees can live further from work • Ease of balancing work/life commitments • Privacy.	• Loss of the distinction between home and office life • Increased possibility of being distracted from work tasks • Lack of space at home for office equipment • Lack of facilities such as IT equipment • Increased utility bills as the employee is at home more often • Lack of social contact with other employees.

6.2.2 Flexible HR systems and e-HR   11/10

Organisations are increasingly moving towards electronically-based HR processes and systems, sometimes referred to as **e-HR**. Enterprise-wide systems (covered in Chapter 3), usually include tools to manage and administer employees.

Section summary

Organisations are increasingly offering **flexible working schemes** for employees.

7 The HR plan

Introduction

HR planning should be based on the **organisation's strategic planning processes**, with relation to analysis of the labour market, forecasting of the external supply and internal demand for labour, job analysis and plan implementation.

KEY TERM

PLANNING '(the) establishment of objectives, and the formulation, evaluation and selection of the policies, strategies, tactics and action required to achieve them'.

7.1 HR planning   05/11

Human resource planning concerns the acquisition, utilisation, improvement and return of an enterprise's human resources. HR planning may sometimes be referred to as 'workforce planning' or 'workforce strategy'. Human resource planning deals with:

- Budgeting and cost control
- Recruitment
- Retention (company loyalty, to retain skills and reduce staff turnover)
- Downsizing (reducing staff numbers)
- Training and retraining to enhance the skills base
- Dealing with changing circumstances

The process of human resources planning

---

1. STRATEGIC ANALYSIS

- of the environment
- of the organisation's manpower strengths and weaknesses, opportunities and threats
- of the organisation's use of employees
- of the organisation's objectives

↓

2. FORECASTING

- of internal demand and supply
- of external supply

↓

3. JOB ANALYSIS

- investigating the task performed in each job
- identifying the skills required

↓

4. RECRUITMENT AND TRAINING

- recruiting and selecting required staff
- training and developing existing staff

7.2 Strategic analysis

The current and future position should constantly be kept under review.

(a)   **The environment**: population and education trends, policies on the employment of women and on pension ages and trends generally in the employment market must be monitored.

(b)   The organisation's HR **strengths, weaknesses, opportunities and threats** need to be analysed so as to identify skills and competence gaps and the level of innovation. Threats may involve competitors 'poaching' staff.

(c)   **Human resource utilisation**. An assessment should be made of how effectively the organisation is currently utilising its staff.

(d)   **Objectives.** Core and subsidiary corporate objectives should be analysed to identify the manpower implications. New products, technology, 'culture' and structure will all make demands on staff.

Timescales are very important. An immediate gap may prompt instant recruitment while long-term corporate objectives allow planned staff development, providing them with the skills required.

Human resources are hard to predict and control.

(a)   **Demand**. Environmental factors (eg the economy) create uncertainties in the demand for labour.

(b)   **Supply**. Factors such as education or the demands of competitors for labour create uncertainties in the supply of labour.

(c)   **Goals**. Employees have their own personal goals, and make their own decisions about whether to undertake further training. When large numbers of individuals are involved, the pattern of behaviour which emerges in response to any change in strategy may be hard to predict.

(d)   **Constraints**. Legislation as well as social and ethical values constrain the ways in which human resources are used, controlled, replaced and paid.

7.3 Forecasting

Estimating demand. Planning future HR needs requires accurate forecasts of turnover and productivity (eg if fewer staff are required for the same output). The demand can be estimated from:

- New venture details
- New markets (need new staff)
- New products/services
- New technology (new skills)

- Divestments
- Organisational restructuring (eg relocation)
- Cost reduction plans

Estimating supply

(a)   **Current workers. A stocks and flows analysis** will define the **internal labour market**. It describes, not just aggregate quantities, but movements in and out of certain grades, by occupation and grade and according to length and service. This can be used in **modelling**.

(b)   The **external labour market**. Labour **market research** does four things.

(i)   It measures potential employees' awareness of the organisation.

(ii)   It discerns attitudes of potential employees towards the organisation.

(iii)   It suggests possible segments for advertising purposes.

(iv)   It provides analysis of population trends for long-term forecasting.

A **position survey** compares demand and supply. Differences in the numbers required/available, their grade, skills or location can be removed by applying an integrated manpower strategy.

7.4 Closing the gap between demand and supply: the HR plan

At the business unit level, the **human resources plan** will arise out of the strategic HR plan.

(a)   The **work required to be done** will largely result **from the business plan**. Production management might determine **how** the work will be done. If, for example, the company is introducing new machinery, then the human resource requirements (eg training, possible redundancy, safety measures) need to be considered.

(b)   **The skills base** includes technical skills, interpersonal skills, and management skills. The need for **technical** and **management** skills are obvious enough. **Interpersonal skills** are important, as they deal with the service offered to customers and affect teamwork.

The HR plan is prepared on the basis of **staffing requirements** and the implications for productivity and costs. It should include **budgets**, **targets** and **standards**, and should also allocate responsibilities for **implementation** and **control** (reporting, monitoring achievement against plan).

The HR plan can be broken down into **subsidiary plans** as shown in the following table.

Plan	Comment
Recruitment plan	Numbers; types of people; when required; recruitment programme.
Training plan	Numbers of trainees required and/or existing staff needing training; training programme.
Redevelopment plan	Programmes for transferring, retraining employees.
Productivity plan	Programmes for improving productivity, or reducing manpower costs; setting productivity targets.
Redundancy plan	Where and when redundancies are to occur; policies for selection and declaration of redundancies; re-development, re-training or re-location of redundant employees; policy on redundancy payments, union consultation etc.
Retention plan	Actions to reduce avoidable labour wastage.

7.5 Tactical plans

Tactical plans can then be made, within this integrated framework, to cover all aspects of the HRM task.

*   Pay and productivity bargaining
*   Physical conditions of employment
*   Management and technical development and career development
*   Organisation and job specifications
*   Recruitment and redundancies
*   Training and retraining
*   Staffing costs

7.6 Staffing shortages or surpluses

Shortages or surpluses of labour which emerge in the process of formulating the position survey must be dealt with.

(a)   Dealing with a **shortage**

    (i)   Internal transfers and promotions, training etc
    (ii)   External recruitment
    (iii)   Reducing labour turnover, by reviewing possible causes
    (iv)   Overtime
    (v)   New equipment and training to improve productivity so reducing the need for more people

(b)   Dealing with a **surplus**

    (i)   Allowing employee numbers to reduce through natural wastage
    (ii)   Restricting recruitment
    (iii)   Introduce part-time working for previously full-time employees
    (iv)   Redundancies – as a last resort, and with careful planning

Exam alert

You may be required to describe the main issues and stages in devising a human resource plan.

7.7 Stages in human resources planning

Laurie Mullins (2002) devised a model of the different elements involved in HRM planning.

Stages in human resources planning

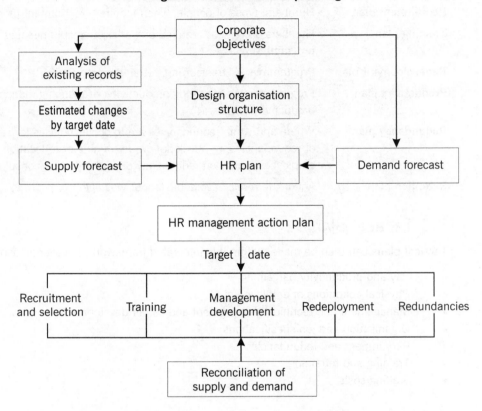

7.8 Control over the HR plan

Once the HR plan has been established, regular **control reports** should be produced.

(a) Actual numbers recruited, leaving and promoted should be compared with planned numbers. Action may be required to correct any imbalance – depending upon the cause.

(b) Actual pay, conditions of employment and training should be compared with assumptions in the HR plan. Do divergences explain any excessive staff turnover?

(c) Periodically, the HR plan itself should be reviewed and brought up to date.

Question 11.3	Employee enthusiasm/commitment

Learning outcome E2(vii)

Enthusiastic and committed employees ensure business success. Do you agree?   **(4 marks)**

Section summary

HR plans identify the needs of the organisation in terms of **numbers of staff** and their **skills** and **compare** this with the **resources that the organisation currently** has. A **plan** is formed to **close the gap** between the two.

8 Ethical behaviour

Introduction

Ethics refer to a code of **moral principles** that people follow with respect to what is right or wrong. Ethical principles are not necessarily enforced by law, although the law incorporates moral judgements (eg theft is wrong ethically, and is also punishable legally).

Companies have to follow **legal standards,** or else they will be subject to fines and their officers might face similar charges. Ethics in organisations relates to **business practice** and **social responsibility.** Increasingly, consumers and businesses prefer to purchase from and do business with organisations with high ethical standards.

8.1 Ethics in business practice   05/10

KEY TERM

ETHICS IN BUSINESS: 'The application of ethical values to business behaviour'. *CIMA*

Businesses have ethical values, based on the **norms** and **standards** of **behaviour** that their leaders believe will best help them express their identity and achieve their objectives. Some of these ethical values may be **explicit**, for example, expressed in a mission statement or in employee training programmes. Others may be **unwritten rules and customs** that form part of the organisations' culture: 'the way we do things around here'.

Business life is a fruitful source of **ethical dilemmas** because its whole purpose is material gain, the making of profit. Success in business requires a constant, avid search for potential advantage over others and business people are under pressure to do whatever yields such advantage.

The table below summarises **three elements** to ethics.

Element	Explanation
I	Ethics concern an individual's professional responsibility to act.
DO	Ethics concern the 'real world' practical actions an individual can take. It is important to consider how an individual acts and not always what they do.
BEST	Ethics concern choices between different courses of action. These may involve taking a course of action which is less unpalatable than another.

8.1.1 An issue of trust

Whatever the situation, there is a public expectation that organisations will act ethically. This is known as the **'trust me'** model and was the case for many years when most businesses were owned by families. Times have now changed and most companies are now run by directors and mangers rather than fathers and sons. The model changed to **'involve me'** as more evidence is needed of an organisation's ethical credentials.

In recent times, trust in businesses has fallen and increasingly more evidence is required to demonstrate it. The **'Show me'** stage required some demonstration of trust, **'Prove to me'** required independent verification and assurance and the final stage of **'Obey me'** would exist when the law creates legislation to cure instances of unethical behaviour. We are some way off this point currently.

What caused this trust to disintegrate? Since the 1980s, the UK has seen a procession of corporate disasters including the names of **Barings Bank**, **Polly Peck** and **Maxwell**. In an attempt to counter this lack of trust, many corporations developed **ethical strategies** and **policies** to provide **guidance** and **training** for their employees. The strategy is set by the leadership and feeds into all areas of the business, becoming part of the cultural DNA of the organisation.

8.2 Social Responsibility Policies and Reports

Many companies now produce **Corporate Responsibility Policies (CRPs)** and **Corporate Responsibility Reports (CRRs)** to demonstrate their commitment to being a 'good corporate citizen'.

8.2.1 Corporate (Social) Responsibility policies

KEY POINT

Corporate (Social) Responsibility policies explain the organisation's approach to helping the community and reducing the environmental impact of the organisation.

These policies must be consistent with the overall aims of the organisation, and should not be overstated in an attempt to paint a 'better' image. Exaggerated claims are likely to harm an organisation in the eyes of the public.

8.2.2 Corporate Responsibility Reports

KEY POINT

These reports focus included figures or statistics covering areas such as the orgnisation's carbon footprint and impact on the environment. These can be added to more conventional assessments such as staff turnover to provide a wide ranging picture of the organisation.

Corporate values also guide staff as to the expectations that employers have regarding their behaviour. The aim is to end up with consistent behaviour across the workforce in terms of personal conduct and professionalism. These policies are enforced on a voluntary basis and results are monitored through audits, surveys and interviews.

It is important that all employees, especially **line managers**, follow the policies laid down by the organisation's leadership. The media is quick to pick up on any ethical failings by employees, often resulting in adverse publicity for the organisation.

8.3 CIMA's Ethical Guidelines

All CIMA members and registered students are subject to **CIMA's Ethical Guidelines**. These guidelines make it clear that individuals must:

- Observe the highest standards of conduct and integrity
- Uphold the good standing and reputation of the profession
- Refrain from any conduct which might discredit the profession

In particular, members should pay attention to the **fundamental principles** given in the Introduction and the discussion of objectivity and the resolution of ethical conflicts that appear in Part A.

Despite being aimed at accountants, these guidelines are also **equally relevant** to **any employee** or **manager** within an organisation and are discussed briefly below.

Ethical behaviour and CIMA's ethical guidelines are core to the CIMA qualification and feature in many of the syllabuses.

CIMA's ethical guidelines are examinable. You should download a copy from the CIMA website (www.cimaglobal.com).

8.3.1 Fundamental principles

The **fundamental principles of CIMA's Ethical Guidelines** are:

(a)   **Integrity**. This is more than not telling lies – professional accountants must not be party to anything which is deceptive or misleading. You should be straightforward, honest and truthful in all professional and business relationships.

(b)   **Objectivity**. This is founded on fairness and avoiding all forms of bias, prejudice and partiality.

(c)   **Professional competence and due care**. Individuals must ensure they remain up-to-date with current developments and are technically competent. Those working under your authority must also have the appropriate training and supervision.

(d)   **Confidentiality**. Employers and clients are entitled to expect that confidential information will not be revealed without specific permission or unless there is a legal or professional right or duty to do so.

(e)   **Professional behaviour**. Accountants should behave in such a way as to protect the reputation of the professional and the professional body, and comply with relevant laws and regulations.

8.3.2 Ethical conflicts

Resolution of **ethical conflicts** is also covered by CIMA's guidance. The possibility of such conflicts arising is discussed. Potentially difficult situations include:

*   Pressure from an overbearing supervisor
*   Pressure from a friend or relation
*   Divided loyalties

A CIMA member or student should act responsibly, honour any legal contract of employment and conform to employment legislation.

In cases where the CIMA member/student is encouraged or required to act illegally, resignation may be the only option (if discussion fails to resolve the situation).

Exam alert

An exam question could require a discussion around the necessary changes to HR practices and employee attitudes when bringing in a corporate social responsibility policy.

Question 11.4	Principles

Learning outcome E1(iv)

For each of CIMA's fundamental principles, give an example of a situation where someone would be acting unethically.

(5 marks)

Section summary

Ethics are **moral principles** that people follow with respect to what is right or wrong.

Businesses have ethical values, based on the **norms** and **standards** of **behaviour** that their leaders believe will best help them express their identity and achieve their objectives.

Ethical strategies are not always visible to outsiders so many companies produce **Corporate Responsibility Policies (CRPs)** and **Corporate Responsibility Reports (CRRs)**.

It is important that all employees, especially **line managers**, follow the policies laid down by the organisation's leadership.

All CIMA members and registered students are subject to **CIMA's Ethical Guidelines**. These guidelines are also relevant to other employees.

Chapter Roundup

✓   **Human resource management** (HRM) involves evaluating an organisation's human resource needs, finding people to fill those needs, and getting the best work from each employee by providing the right incentives and job environment.

✓   **HRM contributes to the success of an organisation** through increased productivity, enhanced group learning, reduced staff turnover and encouragement of initiative.

✓   HRM is important at each stage in the **human resource cycle**.

✓   There are a number of **factors** both **internal** and **external** to the organisation which **limit the success** of any HRM policy.

✓   The success of any **HRM policy** can be measured by the **contribution of the employees** to the success of the organisation.

✓   There are a number of **HRM theories** which relate to **ability**, **opportunity** and **motivation**.

✓   **Psychological contracts** are the expectations that the employee and employer have of each other.

✓   In many circumstances **pay can be a motivator** for employees.

✓   There are many **methods of determining the pay** of employees.

✓   Schemes that **link reward** to **employee performance** include, **profit related pay**, **bonus schemes** and **profit sharing**.

✓   **Total reward schemes** offer employees bundles of benefits from which they can pick and choose what they want.

✓   There are a number of methods of **improving an employee's experience of work** and their **motivation**. These include, **job redesign**, **rotation**, **enlargement** and **enrichment**.

✓   Organisations may adopt **new structures** or develop their own. Recent trends in organisational structure include **project-based teams**, **flat structures**, **horizontal structures**, **chunked** and **unglued structures**, **output-focussed structures** and 'jobless' structures. Some have even become **virtual organisations**.

✓   Organisations are increasingly offering **flexible working schemes** for employees.

✓   **HR plans identify the needs of the organisation** in terms of **numbers of staff** and their **skills** and **compare** this with the **resources that the organisation currently** has. A **plan** is formed to **close the gap** between the two.

✓   Ethics are **moral principles** that people follow with respect to what is right or wrong.

✓   **Businesses have ethical values**, based on the **norms** and **standards** of **behaviour** that their leaders believe will best help them express their identity and achieve their objectives.

✓   **Ethical strategies** are not always visible to outsiders so many companies produce **Corporate Responsibility Policies (CRPs)** and **Corporate Responsibility Reports (CRRs)**.

✓   It is important that all employees, especially **line managers**, follow the policies laid down by the organisation's leadership.

✓   All CIMA members and registered students are subject to **CIMA's Ethical Guidelines**. These guidelines are also relevant to other employees.

Quick Quiz

1   What are the objectives of human resource management?

2   Who developed a version of contingency theory?

     A   Mayo and Schein
     B   Weber
     C   Lawrence and Lorsch
     D   Taylor

3   In terms of HRM, what is a coercive psychological contract?

     A   A contract in which the individual considers that they are being forced to contribute their efforts and energies involuntarily.

     B   A contract, accepted voluntarily by the individual, in which they expect to do their job in exchange for a readily identifiable set of rewards.

     C   A contract in which the individual identifies themselves with the organisation and its goals, so that they actively seek to contribute further to the achievement of those goals.

     D   A contract in which the individual is made to believe their working conditions will be better than they actually are.

4   Which of the following is the correct formula as stated in *Victor Vroom's* expectancy theory?

     A $F = V \times E$
     B $V = E + F$
     C $E = V \times F$
     D $F = V / E$

5   Which one of CIMA's fundamental principles is based on fairness and avoiding all forms of bias, prejudice and partiality?

     A   Integrity
     B   Objectivity
     C   Confidentiality
     D   Professional behaviour

Answers to Quick Quiz

1   The objectives of HR management include:

 •   To develop an effective human component for the organisation which will respond effectively to change

 •   To obtain and develop the human resources required by the organisation and to use and motivate them effectively

 •   To create and maintain a co-operative climate of relationships within the organisation

 •   To deal with employment disputes as they arise

 •   To meet the organisation's social and legal responsibilities relating to the human resource.

2   C   Lawrence and Lorsch developed a form of contingency theory.

3   A   A coercive psychological contract is one in which the individual considers that they are being forced to contribute their efforts and energies involuntarily.

4   A   Force = Valance x Expectation is the formula in *Victor Vroom's* expectancy theory.

5   B   Objectivity is based on fairness and avoiding all forms of bias, prejudice and partiality.

 ## Answers to Questions

11.1 Human resource management

Human resource management concerns the strategic decisions organisations take in order to get the maximum contribution from their workforce. The main benefit is increased productivity, but others include reduced staff turnover, enhanced learning and the encouragement of employees to use their initiative.

11.2 Theory X and Theory Y

D   The more effective view of managers depends on the circumstances of the work. If a manager is in charge of a large number of people doing repetitive, routine work, a Theory X approach is likely to be more effective. At other times, a Theory Y approach will be more effective, for example in dealing with subordinates who are managers or professionals.

11.3 Employee enthusiasm/commitment

Although enthusiastic and committed employees are often the driving force behind business success, they do not guarantee or ensure success.

(a)   No matter how good, loyal, committed and enthusiastic the people are, if the basic commercial strategy is wrong, the company will fail.

(b)   A strong culture of enthusiasm for all initiatives can inhibit people who have genuine valid concerns from voicing these – which may led to expensive mistakes.

11.4 Principles

There are a huge range of possible answers. Here are some examples, you probably thought of others.

- Integrity – handing over work to a colleague that you know contains errors
- Objectivity – allowing personal feelings to cloud your judgement
- Professional competence and due care – taking on work you are not qualified to do
- Confidentiality – leaving sensitive or confidential information where anyone can look at it
- Professional behaviour – cheating in professional exams

Now try this question from the Exam Question Bank	Number	Level	Marks	Time
	11	Examination	30	54 mins

HUMAN RESOURCE PRACTICES

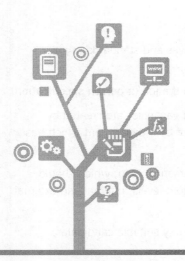

In this final chapter we shall concentrate on **good HR practice** at each stage of the employment process – from recruitment to dismissal. We shall also consider **legal and ethical issues** at each stage where relevant.

Employee development is key to maintaining the workforce's skills and providing a source of future managers for the organisation. **Appraisal** plays a major role in employee development as this is very often where training needs and future potential are discovered.

topic list	learning outcomes	syllabus references	ability required
1 Good HR practice	E1(a), E1(b), E2(c), E2(d)	E1(i), E1(iv), E2(i), E2(ii), E2(iv), E2(vii)	analysis
2 Human resource development	E2(a), E2(d)	E2(iii)	analysis
3 Appraisal	E2(a), E2(b), E2(c), E2(d)	E2(vi)	analysis

1 Good HR practice

Introduction

It is important that **effective human resource management** policies and procedures are followed if maximum employee performance is to be achieved.

Good practice at the **recruitment** and **selection stages** help ensure the most suitable candidates become employees. **Training and development policies** provide employees with skills and experience that enable them to progress through the organisation, providing them with the motivation to stay and the organisation with a **flexible workforce** that can meet its future needs.

1.1 Recruitment and selection

KEY TERMS

RECRUITMENT is concerned with finding applicants: going out into the labour market, communicating opportunities and information and generating interest.

SELECTION consists of procedures to choose the successful candidate from among those made available by the recruitment effort.

A systematic approach to recruitment and selection should be followed.

 Detailed personnel **planning**.

 Job analysis, so that for any given job there are two things.

    (a)   A statement of the component tasks, duties, objectives and standards (**a job description**).

    (b)   A definition of the kind of person needed to perform the job (**a person specification**).

 Identification of vacancies, by way of the personnel plan (if vacancies are created by demand for new labour) or requisitions for replacement staff by a department which has 'lost' a current job-holder.

 Evaluation of the sources of labour, again by way of the personnel plan, which should outline personnel supply and availability, at macro- and micro-levels. Internal and external sources, and media for reaching both, will be considered.

 Review of applications, assessing the relative merits of broadly suitable candidates.

 Notifying applicants of the results of the selection process.

 Preparing employment contracts, induction, training programmes and so on.

1.2 The recruitment process

The recruitment process begins by determining the nature of the vacancies and ends with the short-listing of candidates for selection.

1.2.1 Step 1: Job analysis

KEY TERM

JOB ANALYSIS is: 'the process of collecting, analysing and setting out information about the content of jobs in order to provide the basis for a job description and data for recruitment, training, job evaluation and performance management. Job analysis concentrates on what job holders are expected to do.'

(Armstrong)

The management of the organisation needs to analyse the sort of work needed to be done in order to **recruit effectively**. The **type of information** needed is outlined below.

Type of information	Comments
Purpose of the job	This might seem obvious. As an accountant, you will be expected to analyse, prepare or provide financial information; but this has to be set in the context of the organisation as a whole.
Content of the job	The tasks you are expected to do. If the purpose of the job is to ensure, for example, that people get paid on time, the tasks involved include many activities related to payroll.
Accountabilities	These are the results for which you are responsible. In practice they might be phrased in the same way as a description of a task.
Performance criteria	These are the criteria which measure how good you are at the job. These are largely task related.
Responsibility	This denotes the importance of the job. For example, a person running a department and taking decisions involving large amounts of money is more responsible that someone who only does what they are told.
Organisational factors	Who does the jobholder report to directly (line manager)?
Developmental factors	Likely promotion paths, if any, career prospects and so forth. Some jobs are 'dead-end' if they lead nowhere.
Environmental factors	Working conditions, security and safety issues, equipment and so on.

1.2.2 Step 2: Job design

A current approach to job design is the development and outlining of **competences**.

KEY TERM

A person's COMPETENCE is 'a capacity that leads to behaviour that meets the job demands within the parameters of the organisational environment and that, in turn, brings about desired results'. (*Boyzatis*)

Some take this further and suggest that a competence embodies the ability to **transfer** skills and knowledge to new situations within the occupational area.

Different types of competences

(a) **Behavioural/personal** competences are underlying personal characteristics and behaviour required for successful performance, for example, 'ability to relate well to others'. Most jobs require people to be good communicators.

(b) **Work-based/occupational competences** are 'expectations of workplace performance and the outputs and standards people in specific roles are expected to obtain'. This approach is used in NVQ systems. They cover what people have to do to achieve the results of the job. For example, a competence for a Chartered Management Accountant might be to 'produce financial and other statements and report to management'.

(c) **Generic competences** can apply to all people in an occupation.

Some competences for managers are shown in the following table.

Competence area	Competence	
Intellectual	• Strategic perspective • Analytical judgement • Planning and organising	
Interpersonal	• Managing staff • Persuasiveness • Assertiveness and decisiveness	• Interpersonal sensitivity • Oral communication
Adaptability	• Flexibility • Coping with change	
Results	• Initiative • Motivation to achievement • Business sense	

These competences can be elaborated by identifying **positive** and **negative** indicators.

According to *Mintzberg*, the parameters of job design include:

(a) **Job specialisation**

    (i) **How many different tasks** are contained in the jobs and how broad and narrow are these tasks? **The task may be determined by operations management**. Until recently, there has been a trend towards narrow specialisation, reinforced, perhaps by demarcations laid down by trade unions. On the production line, a worker did the same task all the time. Modern techniques, however, require workers to be **multi-skilled**.

    (ii) **To what extent does the worker have control over the work?** At one extreme ('Scientific Management') the worker has little control over the work. At the other extreme (eg an electrician) the worker controls the task.

(b) **Regulation of behaviour**. Co-ordination requires that organisations formalise behaviour so as to predict and control it.

(c) **Training** in **skills** and indoctrination in **organisational values**.

Belbin (1997) described a way of **tailoring job design** to delayered, team based structures and flexible working systems.

(a) Flattened delayered hierarchies lead to greater flexibility but also to uncertainty and sometimes to a **loss of control**.

(b) Old hierarchies tended to be **clearer** in establishing responsibilities.

1.2.3 Step 3: Job description and person specification

KEY TERM

A JOB DESCRIPTION sets out the purpose of the job, where it fits in the organisation structure, the context of the job, the accountabilities of the job and the main tasks the holder carries out.

There are **four main purposes of a job description**.

Purpose	Comment
Organisational	Defines the job's place in the organisational structure
Recruitment	Provides information for identifying the sort of person needed (person specification)
Legal	Provides the basis for a contract of employment
Performance	Performance objectives can be set around the job description

The main **contents of a job description** include:

(a)   **Job title** (eg Assistant Financial Controller). This indicates the function/department in which the job is performed, and the level of job within that function.

(b)   The **location** of the job within the organisation structure (division, department and section).

(c)   The job title of the person to whom **the jobholder is responsible to** (eg the Assistant Financial controller reports to the Financial Controller), in other words the person's immediate boss.

(d)   The job title(s) of the person(s) **responsible to the jobholder** and the number of staff directly supervised.

(e)   Responsibility and authority level for **budgets** and **expenditure**.

(f)   A brief description of the **overall purpose** of the role.

(g)   Principal accountabilities or **main tasks,** ideally listed in order of importance.

(h)   **Skills** required to perform the job including technical skills and physical skills and capabilities.

(i)   Typical working patterns or **hours of work** (eg 9 to 5), including any part-time or job-share options.

Exam alert

Exam questions may require you to produce a job description for a particular position.

Very detailed job descriptions are perhaps most suited for roles where the work is largely repetitive and predictable. In other situations, a prescriptive job description could cause problems, with employees perhaps wanting to adhere strictly to it, rather than responding **flexibly** to task or organisational requirements.

Increasingly, job descriptions are being written in terms of the **outputs and performance levels** expected. Some organisations are moving towards **accountability profiles** in which outputs and performance are identified explicitly.

An alternative to job descriptions are **role definitions**. A **role** is a part played by people in meeting their objectives by working competently and flexibly within the context of the organisation's objectives, structures and processes.

Another trend is increased use of **person specifications**. These focus on the skills and qualities required by the person who will fill the role.

Possible areas the specification may cover include:

- Personal skills
- Qualifications
- Motivation
- Personality and disposition
- Innate ability (aptitude)
- Intelligence

Alec Rodgers devised a framework for the recruitment process that identifies seven points which can be used to identify the type of person required by a particular position. It can be remembered using the mnemonic **BADPIGS**.

Point	Examples
Background/Circumstances	Location, car owner
Attainments	Qualifications, career achievements
Disposition	Calm, independent
Physical make-up	Strength, appearance, health
Interests	Mechanical, people-related
General Intelligence	Average, above average
Special aptitudes	Manual dexterity, mental sharpness

1.2.4 Step 4: Advertising job vacancies

After a job description and a personnel specification have been prepared, the organisation should **advertise** the job vacancy (**internally** or **externally**, or both).

The job description and personnel specification can be used as **guidelines** for the wording of any advertisement.

The **choice of advertising medium** will depend on **cost, frequency,** the frequency with which the organisation wants to advertise the job vacancy and its **suitability** to the target audience.

A range of **options** are available when advertising a position.

- In-house magazines
- Professional journals
- National newspapers
- Local newspapers
- Local radio
- Job centres

- Recruitment agencies
- Schools careers officers
- University careers officers
- Careers/job fairs
- Open days
- The Internet

Employment agencies may be used to ease the effort involved in both recruitment and selection. More junior posts can often be filled from among an agency's pool of registered candidates. Recruitment and selection of more senior staff may be outsourced to **executive search agencies**, who will manage the whole process. This may include preparing the job definition and person specification, advertising and word-of-mouth communication, and the initial interview process. One or two candidates will then be presented for assessment.

1.2.5 Step 5: Initial screening

The final process in the recruitment phase (before moving on to 'Selection') is the initial screening of candidates usually by reviewing curriculum vitaes (CVs) and selecting some candidates for interview.

1.3 Selection

Selection involves a filtering process, by reviewing application forms, interviewing and testing. A **variety of techniques** may be used in selection, those chosen in a particular circumstance must be:

- **Reliable** – generate consistent results
- **Valid** – accurately predict performance of employees
- **Fair** – non-discriminating
- **Cost-effective** – the benefits of obtaining good quality staff must justify the costs of selecting them

An **ineffective selection process** may result in the

- Employment of unsuitable applicants
- Rejection of suitable applicants

Both errors may be costly to put right.

1.3.1 Application forms

Job advertisements usually ask for a CV (résumé) or require an application form to be completed. The CV is more usual in applications for executive posts, except in the public sector. Application forms are usual for jobs below executive level, and at all levels in the public sector.

The application form should therefore help those making the selection to **sift through the applicants**, and to reject some at once so as to avoid the time and costs of unnecessary interviews. It should therefore:

(a)   **Obtain relevant information** about the applicant which can be compared with the requirements of the job.

(b)   **Give applicants the opportunity to write about themselves**, such as their career ambitions or why they want the job.

1.3.2 The interview: Preparation

Aims of the interview

- Finding the best person for the job, through direct assessment
- Giving the applicant the chance to learn about the business

In **preparation for the interview**, the interviewer should study three things.

(a)   The **job description** (and specification if separate), to review the major demands of the job.

(b)   The **personnel specification**, to make an assessment of the applicant's character and qualifications.

(c)   The **application form**, to decide on questions or question areas for each applicant.

1.3.3 The Interview: Conduct

The following factors should be taken into account.

(a)   The **layout** of the room and the number of interviewers should be planned carefully.

(b)   The **manner** of the interviewers, their tone of voice, and the way their early questions are phrased can all be significant in establishing the tone of the interview.

(c)   **Questions** should be put **carefully**. The interviewers should not be trying to confuse the candidate, but should be trying to obtain the information they need.

(d)   The **candidate should be encouraged** to **talk**.

(e)   The **candidate** should be **given** the **opportunity** to **ask questions**.

1.3.4 Types of job interview

There are four main types of interview.

(a)   **Individual**. A one-to-one discussion between the candidate and the interviewer.

(b)   **Tandem**. Two interviewers per candidate.

(c)   **Panel**. A group of interviewers interview the candidate together.

(d)   **Sequential**. The candidate has several one-to-one interviews with different interviewers.

1.3.5 Limitations of interviews

All of the different types of interview have advantages and disadvantages. For example, an individual interview is more likely to allow a rapport to build, but is also more subject to bias and therefore possibly less reliable.

Involving more than one interviewer could result in differing opinions, making it difficult to reach a decision.

Some general limitations of interviews are:

(a)   **Unreliable assessments**. Interviewers may disagree. A suitable candidate might be rejected or an unsuitable candidate offered a job.

(b)   **They fail to provide accurate predictions** of how a person will perform in the job. Research has shown this time and again.

(c)   The **interviewers are likely to make errors** of judgement even when they agree about a candidate.

   (i)   A **halo effect**: a **general** judgement based on a **single** attribute.

   (ii)   **Contagious bias**. Interviewers might change the behaviour of the applicant through the wording of questions or non-verbal clues.

   (iii)   Interviewers sometimes **stereotype** candidates on the basis of insufficient evidence, eg on the basis of dress, hair style, accent of voice etc.

   (iv)   **Incorrect assessment** of qualitative factors such as motivation, honesty or integrity. Abstract qualities are very difficult to assess.

   (v)   **Logical error**. An interviewer might draw conclusions about a candidate without logical justification.

Interviewers should be **trained** to conduct and assess interviews.

Question 12.1	Interviews

Learning outcome E2(a)

Some courses offer tuition in interview technique to candidates looking for jobs. Do you think this means interviews are likely to be less reliable as a means of candidate selection?   **(2 marks)**

1.3.6 Testing of candidates

Tests are used to **supplement interviews** or select applicants for interview. The following types of test may be used.

(a)   **Psychological tests and personality tests**. An individual may be required to answer a long series of questions or score a variety of statements which indicate basic attitude profiles. The best known personality test is the Cattell P16 PF (Personality Factors), covering sixteen aspects of personality.

(b)   **Cognitive tests** relate to thinking processes. These include **intelligence tests** which measure the applicant's general intellectual ability (eg IQ tests), and **aptitude tests**. Aptitude tests aim to provide information about the candidate's abilities in different areas, (eg tests in mathematics, general knowledge, reasoning, persuasion etc).

(c)   **Proficiency tests** are perhaps the most closely related to an assessor's objectives, because they measure ability to do the **work involved.**

(d) **Psychometric tests** contain features of all of the above. They are selection tests that seek to **quantify** psychological dimensions of job applicants, for example intelligence, personality and motivation. Candidates might be required to answer a list of questions. Those answers are then marked and the candidate is given a score.

CASE STUDY

The *Myers-Briggs Type Indicator* is used to categorise people as to whether they are introvert/extrovert, objective/intuitive, logical/emotional, decisive/ hesitant, and so forth. These tests may be used:

(a) In the initial selection of new recruits.
(b) In the allocation of new entrants to different branches of work.
(c) As part of the process of transfer or promotion.

1.3.7 Advantages and disadvantages of tests

Tests have the following advantages and disadvantages.

Advantages	Disadvantages
A test can be a sensitive measuring instrument.	They may over-simplify complex issues.
Tests are standardised, so that all candidates are assessed by the same yardstick.	They are culturally-specific. Many tests for managers were developed in the US. The cultures in other countries may differ.
Tests always measure the same thing (eg IQ).	Results should only be used to support other selection methods.

1.3.8 Group selection methods

Group selection methods might be used by an organisation as the final stage of a selection process for management jobs. They are not generally used for lower level staff due to their cost. They consist of a series of tests, interviews and group situations over a period of two days or so, involving a small number (eg six to eight) of candidates for a job. After an introductory chat to make the candidates feel at home, they will be given one or two tests, one or two individual interviews, and several group situations in which the candidates are invited to discuss problems together and arrive at solutions as a management team.

Advantages and **disadvantages** of group selection methods include:

Advantages	Disadvantages
Selectors have more time to study the candidates.	Time and cost.
They test interpersonal skills.	The lack of experience of interviewers/selectors.
They reveal more about the candidates' personalities.	Candidates might behave atypically in a contrived situation.
They are suitable for selection of potential managers.	

1.3.9 Assessment centres

A relatively recent development in the attempt to ensure good recruitment and selection decisions are made is the **assessment centre approach**.

An assessment centre may or may not be a particular permanent location – the term refers more the process of selection rather than to any specific building. The approach involves the candidate's **behaviour being observed and judged** by more than one assessor, using specifically developed **simulations**. This approach is generally used for senior positions, as it is time consuming (in terms of combined people hours) and therefore relatively expensive.

Trained assessors observe and **evaluate candidates** on their managerial qualities while candidates are performing a variety of situational exercises. Video is frequently used to help the assessors gather information.

Assessment centre exercises are intended to measure dimensions such as:

- Planning and organising skills
- Leadership
- Analytical skills
- Problem solving

- Decision-making
- Creativity
- Sociability and sensitivity
- Delegation

Assessor opinions are pooled and ratings discussed with fellow assessors. The exercises should allow **key job success behaviours** to be directly observed and measured. Examples could include an in-tray exercise or a report writing task.

1.3.10 Are assessment centres effective?

Assessment centres are most often used as part of a **selection process**, but may also be used to identify training and development needs or to enhance skills (through simulations).

Studies reveal that if assessment techniques are robust, targeted, well-designed and properly implemented, the assessment centre approach produces **reliable outcomes** when compared to single-method approaches such as interviews and questionnaires.

However, the approach can be costly and will only produce good results if the assessors have the required skills to make **meaningful judgements** based on the behaviour of candidates. For example, assessors should be able to organise their behavioural observations by job-related dimensions.

1.3.11 References

It is common to obtain references from the successful candidate's previous employers and other people the candidate is acquainted with. A reference enables an employer to check the **basic accuracy** of the candidate's CV – but little more than this.

1.3.12 Negotiation

A job represents an **economic exchange**. The employer obtains the **services of the employee**, who receives **benefits** such as pay and paid holiday in return. Employees may also seek **job satisfaction**, **security of employment** and **personal development**.

It is important that both employer and employee feel that the exchange they have contracted is a **fair** one. If they do not their relationship will be strained from the outset. An employee who feels undervalued will seek alternative employment. An employer who feels exploited will seek to cut pay, benefits and number employed at every opportunity.

1.3.13 Realistic job previews (RJP)

One method (suggested by *Herriot*) sometimes used to ensure both parties 'know what they are letting themselves in for' is a **realistic job preview**.

This usually involves a **prospective employee** spending some time **'shadowing' an existing employee** in a similar role.

RJPs have been found to **lower expectations** about the job and the organisation – sometimes resulting in **candidates withdrawing** from contention. Candidates that do complete a RJP and accept the role are more likely to be **committed** to the job and the organisation.

1.4 Induction

All new staff should go through a proper process of **induction**. The context of induction programmes may vary, depending on the role being undertaken, but it is unlikely that anyone can make a satisfactory start without at least some basic orientation. Induction may be carried out by the **recruit's supervisor**, by a **departmental trainer** or **mentor**, by **HR staff** or by a **combination** of all three.

1.4.1 Induction elements

An **induction programme** typically would include the following elements.

(a)   A **welcome**

(b)   **Introductions** to immediate colleagues, colleagues and supervisor

(c)   Explanation of the **nature of the job**: a written job description will make this process easier. Some detailed technical matters may be identified as suitable for deferment to a later date.

(d)   **Safety** rules and procedures

(e)   **Terms and conditions of employment**: a booklet is often provided giving full details, but essential matters such as hours of work; authorisation of absence and overtime; and any important legal obligations should be explained in full.

(f)   Orientation to the wider **mission** of the department and the organisation. This is particularly important in organisations that provide services, because of the importance of **staff attitude and motivation** in the provision of high quality service.

(g)   Explanation of any systems of continuing **training**, **coaching** or **mentoring**. Many recruits are expected (and indeed, themselves expect) to undertake significant amounts of training. Rules relating to attendance, qualification and failure to progress must be explained.

Induction should enable the **newcomer** to make a **quick start** as a productive member of staff. It also gives the recruit and the organisation a chance to become acquainted. From the point of view of the organisation this can be helpful in such matters as deciding **how best to make use** of the **recruit's particular set of abilities** and competences and how to deal with any problems. The recruit benefits by obtaining **a fuller picture of the new work environmen**t.

1.4.2 'Dialogic learning'

One element of induction emphasised by *Harrison* (1992) is integrating recruits into how the organisation operates including the **overall culture**, **beliefs** and **mission**. *Harrison* referred to this is 'dialogic learning'.

1.5 Legal and ethical issues

We now consider some of the **ethical** and **legal issues** relevant to organisations in general, with a particular emphasis on issues related to Human Resource Management (HRM). The legal issues covered are done so from a practical standpoint, rather than covering the precise legal position and legal penalties.

1.5.1 Issues relevant to employee recruitment and selection

From an **ethical standpoint**, employee selection should be made on the basis of **who can best perform the role** on offer. Other issues, such as a candidate's sex, race/ethnicity, religion or sexual orientation are irrelevant so should not play a part in the decision.

Practical steps that can be taken in the **employee recruitment process** include the following.

(a)   **Advertising**

(i)   Any wording that suggests preference for a particular group should be avoided.

(ii) Employers must not indicate or imply any 'intention to discriminate'.

(iii) Recruitment literature should state that the organisation is an Equal Opportunities employer, and actions should back this up.

(iv) The placing of advertisements only where the readership is predominantly of one race or sex could be construed as indirect discrimination.

(b) **Recruitment agencies**. Instructions to an agency should not suggest any preference.

(c) **Application forms**. These should avoid questions which are not work-related (such as domestic details) or which only one or some groups are asked to complete.

(d) **Interviews.** Any non-work-related question should be asked of all subjects, if at all, and even then, some types of question may be construed as discriminatory. Interviewers should not, for example, ask only women about plans to have a family or care of dependants.

(e) **Selection tests**. These must be wholly relevant, and should not favour any particular group.

(f) **Records**. Reasons for non-selection, and interview notes, should be recorded.

1.5.2 Issues relating to disciplinary procedures and dismissal

The grounds and procedures for **dismissing an employee** should be stated clearly in the organisation's disciplinary procedures policy. Except for instances of exceptional misconduct, dismissal should be the final step in the disciplinary process.

Many minor cases of poor performance or misconduct are best dealt with by **informal advice, coaching or counselling**.

If the problem persists, it may be decided that **formal disciplinary action** is needed. Disciplinary action is usually thought of as consecutive stages, reflecting a progressive response.

(a) **First warning**. A first formal warning could be either oral or written depending on the seriousness of the case.

(i) An **oral warning** should include the reason for issuing it, notice that it constitutes the first step of the disciplinary procedure and details of the right of appeal. A note of the warning should be kept on file but disregarded after a specified period, such as six months.

(ii) A **first written warning** is appropriate in more serious cases. It should inform the worker of the improvement required and state that a final written warning may be considered if there is no satisfactory improvement. A copy of the first written warning should be kept on file but disregarded after a specified period, such as 12 months.

(b) **Final written warning**. If an earlier warning is still current and there is no satisfactory improvement, a final written warning may be appropriate.

1.5.3 Disciplinary sanctions

The final stage in the disciplinary process is the imposition of sanctions.

(a) **Suspension without pay**

This course of action would be next in order if the employee has committed repeated offences and previous steps did not result in sufficient improvement. In the UK, suspension without pay is only available if it is provided for in the contract of employment.

(b) **Dismissal**

Dismissal is **termination of employment** by the employer. **Termination** of an employee's **employment contract** must be done in a way which follows **correct procedures**, otherwise a claim for unfair dismissal may follow.

Acceptable reasons for dismissal (UK example)	
Conduct	• Unacceptable conduct continuing after warnings/counselling
Capability	• The employee is not capable of the role (after appropriate guidance, training etc)
Breach of statutory duty	• If continuing the employment relationship would mean the employer breaching a statutory duty
Other 'substantial reason'	• Dishonesty • Loss of trust
Redundancy	• Cessation of business • Relocation of business • Cessation of work employed for

Dismissal is a drastic form of disciplinary action, and should be reserved for the most **serious offences**. For the organisation, it involves waste of a labour resource, the expense of training a new employee, and disruption caused by changing the make-up of the work team.

1.5.4 Unfair dismissal

In many countries some reasons are classed **automatically** as grounds for **unfair dismissal**. The main grounds applicable in the UK are set out below.

- Dismissal on grounds of race, sex or disability discrimination
- Pregnancy or other maternity-related grounds
- Due to a request for flexible working practices
- Trade union membership or activities
- Taking steps to avert danger to health and safety at work
- Seeking to enforce rights relating to the national minimum wage
- Refusing or opting out of Sunday working (in the retail sector)

1.5.5 Redundancy   05/10

True redundancy arises when **the role an employee performs is no longer required**, perhaps due to restructuring or different working methods. Some (unethical) organisations use redundancy as an excuse to terminate the employment of employees who are no longer wanted, but who could not justifiably be dismissed on disciplinary grounds.

Organisations should have **policies governing redundancy**. These tend to cover areas such as pre-redundancy **consultation** and post redundancy **support**. Selecting which employees will be made redundant must be fair and in accordance with established policies.

In the UK, the legal position is that an employee dismissed on the grounds of **redundancy** (that is that their position is no longer required) may claim remedies for unfair dismissal if in fact the position was not actually redundant.

Alternatives to enforced redundancies could include:

- Reduced overtime
- Recruitment limits (or a 'freeze')
- Enforced retirement (of those over retirement age)
- Voluntary early retirement (of those close to retirement age)
- Shorter hours
- Job shares (eg two employees working shorter hours)
- Voluntary redundancy

Redundancy is likely to be an **unpleasant experience**. Even if a generous redundancy payment is made, this is unlikely to provide the means to support previous expenditure levels for very long.

Managers also need to ensure **remaining employees** remain **motivated**, and **morale** is as **high** as can be expected in the circumstances.

1.5.6 Relationship management in disciplinary situations

Even if the manager uses sensitivity and judgement, imposing disciplinary action tends to generate **resentment**. The challenge is to apply the necessary disciplinary action as constructively as possible.

(a) **Immediacy** means that after noticing the offence, the manager proceeds to take disciplinary action as speedily as possible. On the other hand, care must be taken to avoid hasty decisions and on-the-spot emotions which might lead to unwarranted actions.

(b) **Advance warning.** Employees should know in advance what is expected of them and what the rules and regulations are.

(c) **Consistency.** Disciplinary action must be applied consistently. Any penalties should be connected with the act and not based upon the personality involved. No grudges should be borne.

(e) **Privacy.** As a general rule disciplinary action should be taken in private, to avoid the spread of conflict and the humiliation or martyrdom of the employee concerned.

 Your knowledge of good HR practice, in particular in regard to disciplinary proceedings will be used again when studying for paper E2.

 Section summary

Good human resource practice should be followed in **all aspects** of human resource management, such as recruitment, selection and dismissal.

There are a number of **legal issues** that should also be considered when **recruiting** and **dismissing** employees.

2   Human resource development

 Introduction

Resourcing an organisation is about building and maintaining its **skills and knowledge base**.

KEY TERMS

HUMAN RESOURCE DEVELOPMENT (HRD) is the process of extending personal abilities and qualities by means of education, training and other learning experiences.

DEVELOPMENT is 'the growth or realisation of a person's ability and potential through the provision of learning and educational experiences'.

TRAINING is 'the planned and systematic modification of behaviour through learning events, programmes and instruction which enable individuals to achieve the level of knowledge, skills and competence to carry out their work effectively'.   (*Armstrong, Handbook of Personnel Management Practice*)

The **overall purpose of employee and management development** includes:

* **Ensuring** the organisation meets current and future performance objectives by...
* **Continuous improvement** of the performance of individuals and teams, and by...
* **Maximising people's** potential for growth (and promotion).

2.1 Training and development strategy

Organisations often have a **training and development strategy**, based on the overall strategy for the business.

 Identify the skills and competences are needed by the **business plan.**

 Draw up the **development strategy** to show how training and development activities will assist in meeting the targets of the corporate plan.

 Implement the training and development strategy.

This approach produces **training** with the **right qualities**.

- Relevance
- Problem-based (ie corrects a real lack of skills)
- Action-oriented
- Performance-related

2.2 Effective learning programmes

The following **principles** are key to **effective learning programmes**:

Principle	Explanation
Participants	Must have the ability, skills, knowledge and motivation to learn.
Overview	An overview of what is to be learnt should be provided before focusing of specific tasks.
Feedback	Participants should receive, accurate and timely feedback on their progress.
Rewards	Progress should be rewarded by positive re-enforcement such as praise or tangible items such as certificates.
Active involvement	Successful learning involves taking part rather than listening or reading.
Learning curve	Training must reflect the fact that some skills are picked up quickly whereas some will take time to develop. Progress is not always at the same pace.
Job specific	Training should be as realistic as possible to the job concerned to minimise problems of applying the new skill of knowledge.

2.3 Training and the organisation

The **benefits for the organisation** of training and development programmes are outlined in the following table.

Benefit	Comment
Minimise the learning costs of obtaining the skills the organisation needs	Training and development programs ensure staff, and the organisation as a whole, have the skills required to deliver the **business strategy**.
Lower costs and **increased productivity**	Some people suggest that higher levels of training explain the **higher productivity** of German as opposed to many British manufacturers.

Benefit	Comment
Fewer accidents, and better health and safety	**EU health and safety directives** require a certain level of training. Employees can take employers to court if accidents occur or if unhealthy work practices persist.
Less need for detailed supervision	If people are trained they can get on with the job, and managers can concentrate on other things. Training is an aspect of **empowerment**.
Flexibility	Training ensures that people have the **variety** of skills needed – multi-skilling is only possible if people are properly trained.
Recruitment and succession planning	Training and development **attracts new recruits** and ensures that the organisation has a **supply of suitable managerial** and technical staff to take over when people retire.
Change management	Training helps organisations **manage change** by letting people know why the change is happening and giving them the skills to cope with it.
Corporate culture	Training programmes can be used to build the corporate culture or to direct it in certain ways, by indicating that certain **values** are espoused. Training programmes can **build relationships** between staff and managers in different areas of the business.
Motivation	Training programmes can **increase commitment** to the organisation's goals.

2.4 Training and the employee

For the individual **employee**, the **benefits of training** and **development** are more clear-cut, and few refuse it if it is offered.

Benefit	Comment
Enhances portfolio of skills	Even if not specifically related to the current job, training can be useful in other contexts, and the employee becomes **more attractive** to employers and more **promotable**.
Psychological benefits	The trainee might feel reassured that **they are of continuing value** to the organisation.
Social benefit	People's **social needs** can be met by training courses – they can also develop networks of contacts.
The job	Training can help people do their job better, thereby increasing **job satisfaction**.

2.5 Possible shortcomings of training

Training is not always the answer to **performance related problems**.

(a)   It is irrelevant to problems caused by faulty organisation, layout, methods, equipment, employee selection and placement and so on.

(b)   Cost, time, inconvenience, apathy and unrealistic expectations of training in the past may restrict its effectiveness.

(c)   Limitations imposed by intelligence, poor motivation and the psychological restrictions of the learning process also restrict its effectiveness.

2.6 Training and development needs

In order to ensure that training meets the real needs of the organisation, large businesses adopt a **planned approach to training**. This has the following steps.

Identify and define the organisation's training needs. It may be the case that recruitment might be a better solution to a problem than training.

 Define the learning required – in other words, specify the knowledge, skills or competences that have to be acquired. For technical training, this may include all finance department staff having to become conversant with a new accounting system.

 Define training objectives – what must be learnt and what trainees must be able to do after the training exercise.

 Plan training programmes – training and development can be planned in a number of ways, employing a number of techniques. It covers three things.

- Who provides the training

- Where the training takes place

- Divisions of responsibilities between trainers, line managers or team leaders and the individual personally.

 Implement the training.

 Evaluate the training: has it been successful in achieving learning objectives?

 Go back to Step 2 if more training is needed.

CASE STUDY

Training for quality

The British Standards for Quality Systems (BS EN ISO 9000) identifies training needs for those organisations registering for assessment, and also shows the importance of a systematic approach to ensure adequate control.

The training, both specific training to perform assigned tasks and general training to heighten quality awareness and to mould attitudes of all personnel in an organisation, is central to the achievement of quality.

The comprehensiveness of such training varies with the complexity of the organisation.

The following steps should be taken:

1   Identifying the way tasks and operations influence quality in total.

2   Identifying individuals' training needs against those required for satisfactory performance of the task.

3   Planning and carrying out appropriate specific training.

4   Planning and organising general quality awareness programmes.

5   Recording training and achievement in an easily retrievable form so that records can be updated and gaps in training can be readily identified.

2.6.1 Training needs analysis

Training needs analysis covers three issues.

	Current state	Desired state
1	Organisation's current results	Desired results, standards
2	Existing knowledge and skill	Knowledge and skill needed
3	Individual performance	Required standards

The difference between the two columns is the **training gap**. Training programmes are designed to improve individual performance, thereby improving the performance of the organisation.

Training surveys combine information from a variety of sources to discern what the training needs of the organisation actually are.

(a)   The **business strategy** at corporate level.

(b)   **Appraisal and performance reviews**. The purpose of a performance management system is to improve performance, and training maybe recommended as a remedy.

(c)   **Attitude surveys** of employees, asking them what training they think they need.

(d)   **Evaluation** of existing training programmes.

(e)   **Job analysis,** which deals with three things:

     (i)   Reported difficulties people have in meeting the skills requirement of the job
     (ii)   Existing performance weaknesses that could be remedied by training
     (iii)   Future changes in the job

The **job analysis** can be used to generate a **training specification** covering the knowledge needed for the job, the skills required to achieve the result, attitudinal changes required.

2.7 Setting training objectives

An investigation into the gap between job or competence requirements and current performance or competence should be undertaken. If training would improve work performance, training **objectives** can then be defined. They should be clear, specific and related to observable, measurable targets.

- Behaviour – what the trainee should be able to do
- Standard – to what level of performance
- Environment – under what conditions (so that the performance level is realistic)

Example

'At the end of the course the trainee should be able to describe ... or identify ... or distinguish x from y ... or calculate ... or assemble ...' and so on. It is insufficient to define the objectives of training as 'to give trainees a grounding in ...' or 'to encourage trainees in a better appreciation of ...': this offers no target achievement which can be quantifiably measured.

Training objectives link the identification of training needs with the content and methods of training.

Training needs	Learning objectives
To assemble clocks faster	The employee will be able to assemble each clock within thirty minutes.
To know more about the Data Protection Act	The employee will be able to answer four out of every five queries about the Data Protection Act without having to search for details.

Training needs	Learning objectives
To establish a better rapport with customers	The employee will immediately attend to a customer unless already engaged with another customer.
	The employee will greet each customer using the customer's name where known.
	The employee will apologise to every customer who has had to wait to be attended to.

Having identified training needs and objectives, the manager will have to decide on the best way to **approach training**: there are a number of types and techniques of training, which we will discuss below.

2.8 Incorporating training needs into an individual development programme

KEY TERMS

A PERSONAL DEVELOPMENT PLAN is a 'clear developmental action plan for an individual which incorporates a wide set of developmental opportunities including formal training'.

The purpose of a **personal development plan** will vary.

- Improving performance in the existing job
- Developing skills for future career moves within and outside the organisation.

SKILLS: what the individual needs to be able to do if results are to be achieved. Skills are built up progressively by repeated training. They may be manual, intellectual or mental, perceptual or social.

Preparing a personal development plan involves these steps.

Analyse the current position. You could do a personal SWOT analysis. The supervisor can have an input into this by categorising the skills use of employees on a grid as follows, in a **skills analysis**. The aim is to incorporate employees' interests into their actual roles.

Performance

		High	Low
Liking of skills	High	Likes and does well	Likes but doesn't do well
	Low	Dislikes but does well	Dislikes and doesn't do well

Set goals to cover performance in the existing job, future changes in the current role, moving elsewhere in the organisations, developing specialist expertise. Naturally, such goals should have the characteristic, as far as possible of **SMART objectives** (ie **S**pecific, **M**easurable, **A**chievable, **R**ealistic and **T**ime-bound).

Draw up action plan to achieve the goals.

2.9 Formal training

2.9.1 Formal training methods

Formal training methods include the following.

(a) **Internal courses** run by the organisation's training department or other employees.

(b) **External courses** (held either on or off-site) run by an outside organisation.

(c) There are a wide range of training course types.

    (i) **Day release**: the employee works in the organisation and on one day per week attends a local college or training centre for theoretical learning.

    (ii) **Distance learning, evening classes and correspondence courses**, which make demands on the individual's time outside work. This is commonly used, for example, by typists wishing to develop or 'refresh' shorthand skills.

    (iii) **Revision courses** for examinations of professional bodies.

    (iv) **Block release** courses which may involve four weeks at a college or training centre followed by a period back at work.

    (v) **Sandwich courses**, usually involve six months at college then six months at work, in rotation, for two or three years.

    (vi) A **sponsored full-time course** at a university for one or two years.

(d) **Techniques** used in training delivery might include:

    (i) Lectures
    (ii) Seminars, in which participation is encouraged
    (iii) Simulations

(e) **Computer-based training** involves interactive training via PC. This could involve the use of CD-ROMs, DVDs or online delivery via the Internet.

2.9.2 Methods used on courses

Common course training methods include the following.

(a) **Lectures**. Lectures are suitable for large audiences and can be an efficient way of putting across information. However lack of participation may lead to lack of interest from, and failure to understand by most of the audience.

(b) **Discussions**. Discussions aim to impart information but allow much greater opportunities to audience participation. They are often suitable for groups up to 20 and can be a good means of maintaining interest.

(c) **Exercises**. An exercise involves a particular task being undertaken with pre-set results following guidance laid down. They are a very active form of learning and are a good means of checking whether trainees have assimilated information.

(d) **Role plays**. Trainees act out roles in a typical work situation. They are useful practice for face-to-face situations. However, they may embarrass and may not be taken seriously.

(e) **Case studies**. Case studies identify causes and/or suggest solutions. They are a good means of exchanging ideas and thinking out solutions. However trainees may see the case study as divorced from their real work experience.

2.9.3 Disadvantages of formal training

(a)   An individual will not benefit from formal training unless they **want to learn**. The individual's superior may need to provide encouragement in this respect.

(b)   If the **subject matter** of the training course does not **relate to an individual's job**, the learning will quickly be forgotten.

(c)   Individuals may not be able to **carry over** what they have learnt to their own particular job.

2.10 On the job training

On the job training can include a wide range of activities. One **employee shadowing** another is one common method; being assigned a **'mentor'** is another.

Pedler (1986) pointed out that at **management level, learning** and **development** are often **accidental** or **unconscious**. Any activity that results in a manager being more willing or capable to control events has a developmental aspect to it.

More **specific or structured** on the **job training** schemes typically have the following characteristics.

(a)   The assignments should have a **specific purpose** from which the trainee can learn and gain experience.

(b)   The organisation must **tolerate any mistakes** which the trainee makes. Mistakes are an inevitable part of on the job learning.

(c)   The work should **not be too complex**.

Methods of on the job training include the following.

(a)   **Demonstration/instruction**: show the trainee how to do the job and let them get on with it. It should combine **telling** a person what to do and **showing** them how, using appropriate media. The trainee imitates the instructor, and asks questions.

(b)   **Coaching**: the trainee is put under the guidance of an experienced employee who shows the trainee how to do the job. The coach should:

   (i)   Establish learning targets.
   (ii)   Plan a systematic learning and development programme.
   (iii)   Identify opportunities for broadening the trainee's knowledge and experience.
   (iv)   Take into account the strengths and limitations of the trainee.
   (v)   Exchange feedback.

(c)   **Job rotation**: the trainee is given several jobs in succession, to gain experience of a wide range of activities.

(d)   **Temporary promotion**: an individual is promoted into their superior's position whilst the superior is absent.

(e)   **'Assistant to' positions**: a junior manager with good potential may be appointed as assistant to the managing director or another executive director.

(f)   **Action learning**: a group of managers are brought together to solve a real problem with the help of an advisor who explains the management process that actually happens.

(g)   **Committees**: trainees might be included in the membership of committees, in order to obtain an understanding of inter-departmental relationships.

(h)   **Project work**: Work on a project with other people can expose the trainee to other parts of the organisation.

2.10.1 Advantages and disadvantages of on-the-job training

Some advantages and disadvantages of on-the-job training are summarised below:

Advantages	Disadvantages
Training is provided that is **relevant** to the job being undertaken.	Training is **difficult** when **real customers** are being talked to – they may not take kindly to a person being trained when they are attempting to arrange insurance for example.
Training is '**just-in-time**' – that is specific queries are identified.	Where training is being carried out by a manager, they **may not have** the **appropriate training skills**.

2.11 The learning cycle (*Kolb*)

Kolb suggested that **formal classroom-type learning** is 'a specialist activity **cut off** from the real world and unrelated to one's life': a teacher or trainer directs the learning process on behalf of a **passive** learner.

Experiential learning, on the other hand, involves **doing** and puts the learners in an **active** problem-solving role.

Self-learning encourages learners to formulate and commit themselves to their own learning objectives.

The implication of *Kolb*'s theory is that to be effective, learning must be **reinforced by experience**.

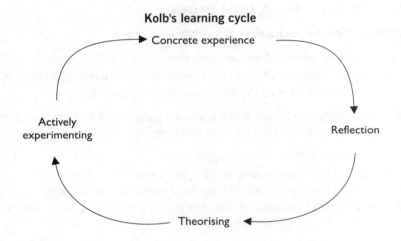

Kolb's learning cycle

2.12 Training in different industries or sectors

Training and development activities vary in both approach and frequency/quantity across different sectors and employee groups.

Hendry (1995) attributes these differences to different types of labour markets and points out that service sectors tend to rely on retraining and training employees (an **internal** labour market).

Manufacturing industries have instead tended to rely on the apprenticeship system, which provides a more 'portable' qualification resulting in an **external**, occupational labour market.

2.13 Evaluating training

There are a number of ways of **validating** and **evaluating** a training scheme.

KEY TERMS

VALIDATION OF TRAINING means observing the results of the course and measuring whether the training objectives have been achieved.

EVALUATION OF TRAINING means comparing the actual costs of the scheme against the assessed benefits which are being obtained. If the costs exceed the benefits, the scheme will need to be redesigned or withdrawn.

(a)   **Trainees' reactions to the experience:** course assessment sheets completed after training can ask trainees whether they thought the training programme was relevant to their work, and whether they found it useful.

(b)   **Trainee learning:** measuring what the trainees have learned on the course by means of a test at the end of it. A further test can be taken some time after the course to see if the trainee has retained the knowledge learnt.

(c)   **Changes in job behaviour following training.** This is relevant where the aim of the training was to learn a skill.

(d)   **Organisational change as a result of training:** finding out whether the training has affected the work or behaviour of other employees not on the course.

(e)   **Impact of training on the achievement of organisational goals:** seeing whether the training scheme has contributed to the achievement of the overall objectives of the organisation.

(f)   **Trainer assessment:** the trainer can complete an assessment that identifies gaps in trainee knowledge or other deficiencies.

(g)   **HR review:** human resources employees can conduct a critical review that evaluates the training using a range of information to see if the organisation's objectives for the training have been met.

2.13.1 Levels of evaluation

Kirkpatrick (1998) identified four levels at which **training can be evaluated**.

- **Reaction** – how the trainees act, enjoyment level
- **Learning** – has the knowledge been absorbed?
- **Behaviour** – have required behavioural changes taken place?
- **Results** – what benefits have resulted from the training (eg better quality, reduced costs)?

Evaluating training usually requires **measurement before and after training**. It is difficult however to establish with any certainty what changes are directly attributable to the training alone.

Exam alert

Exam questions may require you to explain how the effectiveness of a staff training event could be evaluated. Good answers would consider issues before the event, after the event and the reaction of the participants.

CASE STUDY

Whitbread pubs reported improved performance as a result of a change in the company's training scheme. Previously the company's training scheme had aimed to improve the service standards of individuals, and there were also discussions with staff on business developments. It was felt however that other companies in the same sector had overtaken Whitbread in these respects.

Whitbread therefore introduced an integrated approach to assessment of the performance of pubs. Assessment is by four criteria; training (a certain percentage of staff have to have achieved a training award), standards (suggested by working parties of staff), team meetings and customer satisfaction.

Managers are trained in training skills and they in turn train staff, using a set of structured notes to ensure a consistent training process.

Pubs that fulfil all the criteria win a team hospitality award, consisting of a plaque, a visit from a senior executive, and a party or points for goods scheme. To retain the award and achieve further points, pubs have then to pass further assessments which take place every six months.

The scheme seemed to improve standards. Significantly staff turnover was down and a survey suggested morale had improved, with a greater sense of belonging particularly by part-time staff. A major cause of these improvements may well be the involvement of staff and management in the design process.

2.14 Career management

KEY TERM

CAREER MANAGEMENT is a technique whereby the progress of individuals within an organisation from job to job is planned with organisational needs and individual capacity in mind.

CAREER MANAGEMENT is both an individual and an organisational issue.

(a)   It ensures that the organisation has a reserve of managers-in-waiting. In flat or delayered organisations this is particularly important, as the jump in responsibility from junior to senior positions is much wider than in organisations with extensive hierarchies.

(b)   It ensures people get the right training to enable them to develop the right abilities for the job.

For the organisation, career management also determines whether, as a matter of policy, the organisation will promote from **within when possible**, as opposed to hiring **outsiders**.

2.14.1 Succession planning

Large organisations are able to plan a **logical progression** for individuals through its hierarchy over time. The objective is to ensure suitable replacements (in terms of experience and ability) are available to take over positions above them as they become available.

Advantages of succession planning	Disadvantages of succession planning
Can be **cheaper** than advertising or using agencies	Large 'talent pools' make it **hard to decide** who to promote
Develops **career structures**	**Reduces 'fresh blood'** at higher levels in the organisation
Motivates employees as rewards are visible (ie promotions are seen by all)	Vacancies may occur **before** suitable replacements are ready for promotion
Maintains the organisation's **culture** as long-serving employees are promoted	**Better candidates** may be available **outside** the business
It is **logical** and **rational**	**Planning requires** resources to manage it
	Job-for-life is increasingly becoming an **outdated concept** and the best staff may leave before vacancies become available

2.14.2 Barriers to career planning/succession planning

Flatter organisation structures, the growth of **cross-functional teams** and generally **shorter periods of employment** with a particular organisation have led to reduced potential for succession planning. Individuals now tend to take increased responsibility for their own career progression, and are more likely to accept that this may involve working for a number of organisations (and/or for themselves) throughout their career.

2.15 Management development

Management development includes **general education**, **specific learning** and **wider experience**. It is essential if managers are to make the leap from functional to general management.

KEY TERM

MANAGEMENT DEVELOPMENT is the process of improving the effectiveness of an individual manager by developing the necessary skills and understanding of organisational goals.

Pedlar et al considered the **development of management** should be down to the individual concerned and that the organisation should provide a system that increases managers' capacity and willingness to take control and responsibility for their own learning.

2.15.1 Self development

KEY POINT

Self-development is now emphasised by many professional organisations such as **CIMA**. The modern view is that membership of an organisation does not ensure competence in the future. New knowledge must be learnt and skills must be maintained and developed.

Pedlar et al found several possibilities for learning. It can be **planned** (conscious), **accidental** (unconscious) and take place **at or away from work**.

Although management development is in some respects a natural process, the term is generally used to refer to a **conscious policy** within an organisation to provide a programme of individual development.

A variety of techniques could be used, either on or off the job.

- Formal education and training
- On-the-job training
- Group learning sessions
- Job rotation
- Career planning
- Counselling

Accidental learning is unplanned. For example, situations at work or socially may develop personal attributes of a manager.

The principle behind management development is that by giving an **individual** time to study the techniques of being a **good manager**, and by **counselling** them about their **achievements** in these respects, the individual will **realise their full potential**. The time required to bring a manager to this potential is *possibly* fairly short.

2.16 The transition from functional to general management

There is one particular aspect of management development and training that organisations should look at closely – **the transition from functional to general management**. To help with this transition, an organisation should have a **planned management development programme** consisting of several aspects.

(a)   Individuals should be encouraged to acquire suitable **educational qualifications** for senior management. 'High-fliers' for example might be encouraged to study for an MBA early on in their career. Senior finance managers ought to have an accountancy qualification.

(b)   **In-house training programmes** might be provided for individuals who are being groomed for senior management. Formal training in general management skills can be very helpful.

(c)   **Careful promotion procedures** should aim to ensure that only managers with the potential to do well are promoted into senior management positions.

(d)   There should be a system of **regular performance appraisal,** in which individuals are counselled by their managers on what they have done well and not so well, how to improve their performance in their current job and how to develop their skills for a more senior job.

(e)   **Opportunities to gain suitable experience** should be provided to managers who are candidates for more senior positions. There are several possibilities.

(i)   Allowing subordinates to stand in for their boss whenever the boss is away

(ii)   Using staff officer positions to groom future high fliers

(iii) Using a divisionalised organisation structure to delegate general management responsibilities further down the management hierarchy.

Question 12.2

Human resource development

Learning outcome E2(a)

Which of the following are aspects of human resource development (HRD)?

(i)   Providing formal training courses
(ii)   On-the-job training
(iii) Succession and career planning
(iv)   Job re-design

A   (i) only
B   (i) and (ii) only
C   (i), (ii) and (iii) only
D   (i), (ii), (iii) and (iv)

Section summary

Human resource development has **benefits** for both the **employee** and **employer**.

Training and development should be **carefully planned** if it is to achieve its aims.

The **method of training** or **development** chosen should **meet the needs** of the **employee** and **employer**.

However the training or development is delivered, it should be **evaluated** in order to ascertain its success.

Career and management training provide the employee with **motivation** and the employer with a **source of future managers**.

3   Appraisal

Introduction

Appraisals **review** and **reward performance** and **potential**. They are part of **performance management** and can be used to establish areas for improvement and training needs.

KEY TERM

APPRAISAL: the systematic review and assessment of an employee's performance, potential and training needs.

3.1 Why are appraisals needed?

KEY POINT

Employee appraisal can be viewed as a **control tool** as it aims to influence employee behaviour and **maximise utilisation** of the organisation's **human resource**. The process of appraisal is designed to review performance over the past period and improve it in the future.

Appraisals are needed for a number of reasons.

(a)   Managers and supervisors may obtain **random impressions** of employees' performance (perhaps from their more noticeable successes and failures), but **rarely form a coherent, complete and objective picture**.

(b)   They may have a fair idea of their employees' **shortcomings** – but may not have devoted time and attention to the matter of **improvement and development**.

(c)   **Judgements are easy to make, but less easy to justify** in detail, in writing, or to the subject's face.

(d)   **Different assessors may be applying a different set of criteria, and varying standards of objectivity and judgement**. This undermines the value of appraisal for comparison, as well as its credibility in the eyes of the appraisee.

(e)   Unless stimulated to do so, **managers rarely give their staff adequate feedback on their performance**.

3.2 The purpose of appraisal

KEY POINT

The **general purpose** of any appraisal system is to **improve efficiency**. Personnel appraisal aims to ensure individuals are performing to the best of their ability, are developing their potential and that the organisation is best utilising their abilities.

Appraisals **may include**:

(a)   **Reward review**. Measuring the extent to which an employee is deserving of a bonus or pay increase as compared with their peers.

(b)   **Performance review**, for planning and following-up training and development programmes, ie identifying training needs, validating training methods and so on.

(c)   **Potential review**, as an aid to planning career development and succession, by attempting to predict the level and type of work the individual will be capable of in the future.

The **objectives of appraisals** include the following.

(a)   Establishing the **key deliverables** an individual has to produce to enable the organisation to achieve its objectives.

(b)   Comparing the individual's **level of performance against a standard**, as a means of quality control.

(c)   Identifying the individual's **training and development needs** in the light of actual performance.

(d)   Identifying areas that **require improvement**.

(e)   Monitoring the organisation's **initial selection procedures** against subsequent performance.

(f)   **Improving communication** between different levels in the hierarchy.

3.3 An appraisal system

A **typical appraisal system** is outlined below.

Identification of criteria for assessment, perhaps based on job analysis, performance standards, person specifications and so on.

The **preparation by the subordinate's manager of an appraisal report**. In some systems both the appraisee and appraiser prepare a report. These reports are then compared.

An **appraisal interview**, for an exchange of views about the appraisal report, targets for improvement, solutions to problems and so on.

 Review of the assessment by the assessor's own superior, so that the appraisee does not feel subject to one person's prejudices. Formal appeals may be allowed, if necessary to establish the fairness of the procedure.

 The **preparation and implementation of action plans** to achieve improvements and changes agreed.

 Follow-up monitoring the progress of the action plan.

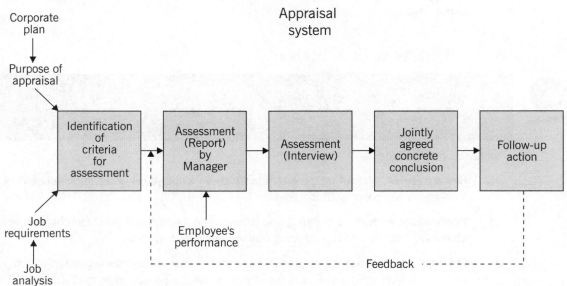

3.4 Problems of appraisal systems

Effective appraisals can be difficult to implement. Three particular difficulties are:

(a) The **formulation of desired traits and standards** against which individuals can be consistently and objectively assessed.

(b) **Recording assessments**. Managers should be encouraged to utilise a standard and understood framework, but still be allowed to express what they consider to be important, and without too much form-filling.

(c) **Getting the appraiser and appraisee together**, so that both contribute to the assessment and plans for improvement and/or development.

3.5 Appraisal techniques

The following **techniques** are often used in an appraisal system.

(a) **Overall assessment**. Managers write in narrative form their judgements about the appraisees. There will be no guaranteed consistency of the criteria and areas of assessment, however, and managers may not be able to convey clear, effective judgements in writing.

(b) **Guided assessment**. Assessors are required to comment on a number of specified characteristics and performance elements, with guidelines as to how terms such as 'application', 'integrity' and 'adaptability' are to be interpreted in the work context. This is more precise, but still rather vague.

(c)   **Grading**. Grading adds a comparative frame of reference to the general guidelines, whereby managers are asked to select one of a number of levels or degrees to which the individual in question displays the given characteristic. These are also known as **rating scales**. Numerical values may be added to ratings to give rating scores. Alternatively a less precise **graphic scale** may be used to indicate general position on a plus/minus scale.

Factor: job knowledge

High ____✓____ Average _____ Low ____

(d)   **Behavioural incident methods**. These concentrate on **employee behaviour**, which is measured against typical behaviour in each job, as defined by common **critical incidents** of successful and unsuccessful job behaviour reported by managers.

(e)   **Objectives and results-orientated schemes**. This reviews performance against specific targets and standards of performance agreed in advance. The manager becomes a counsellor. Learning and motivation theories suggest that clear and known targets are important in modifying and determining behaviour. The objectives set as part of an appraisal process should be agreed – and (again) these should be **SMART** (**S**pecific, **M**easurable, **A**chievable, **R**ealistic and **T**ime-bound).

(f)   Assessments must be related to a **common standard** (the appraisal standard), in order for comparisons to be made between individuals. On the other hand, they should also be related to meaningful performance criteria, which take account of the critical variables in each different job.

3.6 Self-appraisal

Individuals may carry out their own **self-evaluation** as a major input into the appraisal process. This has the advantage that the system is aimed at the needs of the individual. Other advantages are:

(a)   It **saves the manager time** as the employee identifies the areas of competence which are relevant to the job and their relative strengths in these competences.

(b)   It offers **increased responsibility** to the individual which may improve motivation.

(c)   This may be a way of **reconciling the goals** of both the individual and the organisation.

(d)   It may overcome the problem of needing skilled appraisers, therefore **cutting training costs** and **reducing the managerial role in appraisal**.

(e)   In giving the responsibility to an individual, the scheme may offer more **flexibility** in terms of timing, with individuals undertaking ongoing self-evaluation.

However, people are often not the best judges of their own performance. Many schemes combine the two – the manager and subordinate fill out a report and compare notes.

3.7 Upward appraisal

A notable modern trend, adopted in the UK by companies such as BP, British Airways and others, is **upward appraisal**, whereby employees are not rated by their superiors but by their subordinates. The followers appraise the leader. **Advantages of upward appraisal** include the following.

(a)   Subordinates tend to know their superior better than superiors know their subordinates.

(b)   As all subordinates rate their managers statistically, these ratings tend to be more reliable – the more subordinates the better. Instead of the biases of individual managers' ratings, the various ratings of the employees can be converted into a representative view.

(c)   Subordinates' ratings have more impact because it is unusual to receive ratings from them. It is also surprising to bosses because, despite protestations to the contrary, information often flows down organisations more smoothly and comfortably than it flows up. When it flows up it is qualitatively and quantitatively different. It is this difference that makes it valuable.

Problems with the method include fear of reprisals, vindictiveness, and extra form processing. Some bosses in strong positions might refuse to act, even if a consensus of staff suggested that they should change their ways.

3.8 Customer appraisal

In some companies part of the employee's appraisal process must take the form of **feedback from 'customers' (whether internal or external)**. This may be taken further into an influence on remuneration (at *Rank-Xerox*, 30% of a manager's annual bonus is conditional upon satisfactory levels of 'customer' feedback). This is a valuable development in that customers are the best judges of customer service, which the appraisee's boss may not see.

3.9 360 degree appraisal

Taking downwards, upwards and customer appraisals together, some organisations have instituted **360 degree appraisal** (or multi-source appraisal) by collecting feedback on an individual's performance from the following sources.

(a)   The person's immediate manager.

(b)   People who report to the appraisee, perhaps divided into groups.

(c)   Peers and co-workers. Most people interact with others within an organisation, either as members of a team or as the receivers or providers of services. They can offer useful feedback.

(d)   Customers. If sales people know what customers thought of them, they might be able to improve their technique.

(e)   The manager personally. All forms of 360 degree appraisal require people to rate themselves. Those 'who see themselves as others see them will get fewer surprises'.

Sometimes the appraisal results in a **counselling session**, especially when the result of the appraisals are conflicting. For example, an appraisee's manager may have a quite different view of the appraisee's skills than subordinates.

3.10 The appraisal report

Most appraisal systems provide for appraisals to be **recorded**. The form of the appraisal report will vary between organisations and the role involved – report forms of various lengths and complexity may be designed.

The layout of the report and factors to be included in the report should be established before the interview. The report is likely to focus on key performance issues that relate to the **job description**.

The report is likely to cover key competences. A **competence** is an observable skill or ability to complete a particular task successfully. It can include the ability to transfer skills and knowledge to new situations.

3.11 Interviews and counselling

The extent to which any **discussion** or **counselling interview** is based on the written appraisal report varies in practice.

Maier (*The Appraisal Interview*) identifies **three types of approach to appraisal interviews**.

(a)   **The tell and sell method**. The manager tells the subordinate how they have been assessed, and then tries to sell (gain acceptance of) the evaluation and the improvement plan. This requires unusual human relations skills in order to convey constructive criticism in an acceptable manner, and to motivate the appraisee.

(b)   **The tell and listen method**. The manager tells the subordinate how they have been assessed, and then invites the subordinate to respond. Moreover, this method does not assume that a change in the employee will be the sole key to improvement – the manager may receive helpful feedback about how job design, methods, environment or supervision might be improved.

(c)   **The problem-solving approach**. The manager abandons the role of critic altogether, and becomes a counsellor and helper. The discussion is centred not on the assessment, but on the employee's work problems. The employee is encouraged to think solutions through, and to make a commitment to personal improvement.

3.12 Follow-up

After the appraisal interview, the manager may complete the report, with an **overall assessment** of potential and/or the jointly-reached conclusion of the interview, with recommendations for follow-up action.

Follow-up procedures typically include the following.

(a)   **Informing the employee** of the results of the appraisal, if this has not been central to the review interview.

(b)   **Carrying out agreed actions** on training, promotion and so on.

(c)   **Monitoring the appraisee's progress** and checking that they have carried out agreed actions or improvements.

(d)   **Taking necessary steps** to help the appraisee to attain improvement objectives, by guidance, providing feedback, upgrading equipment, altering work methods and so on.

If appraisal systems operate **successfully** as feedback control systems (in other words, if they do alter employees' performance) and identify behaviours to be encouraged, then, assuming organisational success is to some measure based on individual performance, they will influence the success of strategy.

3.13 Improving the appraisal system

In theory, such appraisal schemes may seem very fair to the individual and very worthwhile for the organisation, but **in practice the appraisal system often goes wrong**.

3.13.1 Barriers to effective appraisal

Lockett (in *Effective Performance Management*) suggests that **appraisal barriers** can be identified as follows.

Appraisal barriers	Comment
Appraisal as confrontation	Many people dread appraisals, or use them 'as a sort of show down, a good sorting out or a clearing of the air.'
	• There is a lack of agreement on performance levels.
	• The feedback is subjective – in other words the manager is biased, allows personality differences to get in the way of actual performance etc.
	• The feedback is badly delivered.
	• Appraisals are 'based on yesterday's performance not on the whole year'.
	• Disagreement on long-term prospects.

Appraisal barriers	Comment
Appraisal as judgement	The appraisal 'is seen as a one-sided process in which the manager acts as judge, jury and counsel for the prosecution'. However, the process of performance management 'needs to be jointly operated in order to retain the commitment and develop the self-awareness of the individual.'
Appraisal as chat	The other extreme is that the appraisal is a friendly chat 'without ... purpose or outcome ... Many managers, embarrassed by the need to give feedback and set stretching targets, reduce the appraisal to a few mumbled "well dones!" and leave the interview with a briefcase of unresolved issues.'
Appraisal as bureaucracy	Appraisal is a form-filling exercise, to satisfy the personnel department. Its underlying purpose, improving individual and organisational performance, is forgotten.
Appraisal as unfinished business	Appraisal should be part of a continuing process of performance management.
Appraisal as annual event	Many targets set at annual appraisal meetings become irrelevant or out-of-date.

A problem with many appraisal schemes in practice is that they **reinforce hierarchy**, and are perhaps unsuitable to organisations where the relationship between management and workers is **fluid** or participatory. Upward, customer and 360° appraisals address this, but they are not widely adopted.

Appraisal systems, because they target the individual's performance, concentrate on the **lowest level of performance feedback.** They ignore the organisational and systems context of that performance. For example, if any army is badly led, no matter how brave the troops, it will be defeated. Appraisal schemes seem to regard most **organisation problems** as a function of the **personal characteristics** of its members.

3.14 Appraisal and reward

Another issue is the extent to which the appraisal system is related to the reward system.

Many employees consider that the **appraisal system** should be **linked** with the **reward system**, on the grounds that extra effort or excellent performance should be rewarded.

Although this appears to be a fair view, there are **drawbacks** to it.

(a)   **Funds available** for pay rises rarely depend on one individual's performance alone – the whole company has to do well.

(b)   **Continuous improvement** is always necessary – many businesses have 'to run to stand still'. Continuous improvement should perhaps be expected of employees as part of their work, not rewarded as extra.

(c)   In low-inflation environments, **cash pay rises are fairly small**.

(d)   **Comparisons between individuals** are hard to make, as many smaller organisations cannot afford the rigour of a job evaluation scheme.

(e)   Performance management is about a lot more than pay for *past* performance – it is often **forward looking** with regard to future performance.

3.14.1 Performance related pay

Performance Related Pay (PRP) is often introduced when other organisational or HR changes are made such as:

- The **introduction** of an **appraisal scheme**
- The **development** of **flexible working arrangements**

- The **decentralisation** of **HR** or the **responsibility** of **pay determination**
- The **harmonisation** of **working arrangements** through the organisation

Payment systems are often **modified** as a result of the introduction of PRP.

- PRP may form the **basis** of all **general pay increases**

- PRP may **replace pay increases for length of service** or **qualifications**

- PRP may be used as **additional payments above the maximum** for the grade where performance is very high.

All organisations can introduce PRP but it is often best **implemented gradually**.

By **initially introducing** it to **senior management**, they will **experience it first hand** before they apply it to their staff.

The use of PRP could be **restricted** to **specific groups** of workers to allow **adequate testing** and to **ensure sufficient safeguards are in place** before it is introduced to other workers.

3.15 Management expertise and employee empowerment

There can be **problems conducting appraisals** in organisations where **empowerment** is practised and employees are given more responsibility.

(a) Many managers **may not know enough** about the performance of individual workers to make a fair judgement.

(b) In some jobs, managers do not have the **technical expertise** to judge an employee's output.

(c) **Employees depend on other people** in the workplace/organisation to be effective – in other words, **an individual's results may not be entirely under their control**.

A person's performance is often indirectly or directly influenced by the **management style** of their line manager, who will also usually be the person conducting the appraisal.

However, given the seniority of the manager over the appraisee, the appraisee may be **reluctant** to raise issues related to their manager's management style.

Even the best objective and systematic appraisal scheme is subject to **personal** and **interpersonal problems**.

(a) Appraisal is often **defensive on the part of the appraisee**, who believes that criticism may mean a low bonus or pay rise, or a lost promotion opportunity.

(b) Appraisal is often **defensive on the part of the superior**, who cannot reconcile the role of judge and critic with the human relations aspect of interviewing and management. Managers may in any case feel uncomfortable about 'playing God' with employee's futures.

(c) The superior might show **conscious or unconscious bias** in the appraisal or may be influenced by rapport (or lack of it) with the interviewee. Systems without clearly defined standard criteria will be particularly prone to the subjectivity of the assessor's judgement.

(d) The manager and subordinate may both **be reluctant to devote time and attention to appraisal**. Their experience in the organisation may indicate that the exercise is a waste of time (especially if there is a lot of form-filling) with no relevance to the job, and no reliable follow-up action.

(e) The organisational culture may **simply not take appraisal seriously**. Interviewers are not trained or given time to prepare, appraisees are not encouraged to contribute, or the exercise is perceived as a 'nod' to Human Relations with no practical results.

3.16 Making improvements

The **appraisal scheme** should itself be **assessed** (and regularly re-assessed) according to the following general criteria for evaluating appraisal schemes.

Criteria	Comment
Relevance	• Does the system have a useful purpose, relevant to the needs of the organisation and the individual? • Is the purpose clearly expressed and widely understood by all concerned, both appraisers and appraisees? • Are the appraisal criteria relevant to the purposes of the system?
Fairness	• Is there reasonable standardisation of criteria and objectivity throughout the organisation? • Is it reasonably objective?
Serious intent	• Are the managers concerned committed to the system – or is it just something the personnel department thrusts upon them? • Who does the interviewing, and are they properly trained in interviewing and assessment techniques? • Is reasonable time and attention given to the interviews – or is it a question of 'getting them over with'? • Is there a genuine demonstrable link between performance and reward or opportunity for development?
Co-operation	• Is the appraisal a participative, problem-solving activity – or a tool of management control? • Is the appraisee given time and encouragement to prepare for the appraisal, so that they can make a constructive contribution? • Does a jointly-agreed, concrete conclusion emerge from the process? • Are appraisals held regularly?
Efficiency	• Does the system seem overly time-consuming compared to the value of its outcome? • Is it difficult and costly to administer?

Question 12.3

Performance appraisal

Learning outcome E2(vi)

Most large organisations have a performance appraisal process.

Required

Briefly describe the most common objectives of a performance appraisal system.   **(5 marks)**

Section summary

Appraisal is an important part of human resource management because it enables **employee performance** to be **measured** and **corrective action** taken if necessary. It also forms part of the **reward process**.

There are many **types of appraisal** including, **appraisal by a manager**, **self appraisal**, **upward appraisal**, **customer appraisal** and **360 degree appraisal**.

Whichever type of appraisal is used it must be **carefully conducted** and **correctly followed up**.

Chapter Roundup

✓   Good human resource practice should be followed in **all aspects** of human resource management, such as recruitment, selection and dismissal.

✓   There are a number of **legal issues** that should also be considered when **recruiting** and **dismissing** employees.

✓   **Human resource development** has **benefits** for both the **employee** and **employer**.

✓   **Training and development** should be **carefully planned** if it is to achieve its aims.

✓   The **method of training** or **development** chosen should **meet the needs** of the **employee** and **employer**.

✓   However the training or development is delivered, it should be **evaluated** in order to ascertain its success.

✓   **Career and management training** provide the employee with **motivation** and the employer with a **source of future managers**.

✓   **Appraisal** is an important part of human resource management because it enables **employee performance** to be **measured** and **corrective action** taken if necessary. It also forms part of the **reward process**.

✓   There are many **types of appraisal** including, **appraisal by a manager**, **self appraisal**, **upward appraisal**, **customer appraisal** and **360 degree appraisal**.

✓   Whichever type of appraisal is used it must be **carefully conducted** and **correctly followed up**.

Quick Quiz

1   Why should an organisation take an interest in an individual's personal development?

2   Which of the following is the final stage of recruitment before selection commences?

    A   Producing a job description
    B   Advertising the vacancy
    C   Screening candidates' CVs and selecting some for interview
    D   Interviewing candidates

3   A typing test is an example of which type of test used in the selection process?

    A   Psychological test
    B   Aptitude test
    C   Intelligence test
    D   Personality test

4   In *Kolb's* learning cycle, which process occurs after reflection?

    A   Theorising
    B   Actively experimenting
    C   Concrete experience
    D   Learning

5   Which of the following appraisal techniques requires the assessor to rate the assessee's characteristics on a scale?

    A   Guided assessment
    B   Overall assessment
    C   Behavioural incident method
    D   Grading

Answers to Quick Quiz

1   Poor personal development can cause high staff turnover, absenteeism or preoccupation with financial rewards and poor performance – self-defeating for the organisation and unhealthy for the individual.

2   C   Recruitment ends when a short list of candidates for interview have been chosen. Interviews are part of the selection process.

3   B   A typing test is an example of an aptitude test as it provides information about a candidate's abilities.

4   A   Theorising follows reflection in *Kolb's* learning cycle.

5   D   Grading requires the assessor to rate the employee's characteristics on a rating scale.

Answers to Questions

12.1 Interviews

If interview techniques are taught, it might imply that success at interview will have more to do with a candidate's ability to present themselves in an interview situation rather than their ability to do the job.

On the other hand, an interview is a test of how well a person performs under pressure, in an unfamiliar environment and with strangers. The interview might therefore reflect some of the interpersonal skills required for the job.

12.2 Human resource development

D   HRD covers all aspects of personal and management development, including formal training and on-the-job training, planning the succession into senior management positions, and career planning for individuals (particularly management recruits). Job re-design is also related to development, because the content of a job can be altered to provide better or different learning experiences.

12.3 Performance appraisal

The general purpose of an appraisal is to improve the efficiency of the organisation by ensuring individual employees are performing their role to acceptable standards and to the best of their ability. The process also considers the employees' potential to improve and to develop. Objectives of a formal performance appraisal system include the following:

- To enable a picture to be drawn up of overall staff levels and skills, strengths and weaknesses. This enables more effective HR planning

- To monitor the undertaking's initial selection procedures against the subsequent performance of recruits

- To establish what the individual has to do in a job in order that the objectives for the section or department are realised

- To assess an individual's performance including strengths and any weaknesses. This helps identify training needs

- To assess appropriate rewards (pay, bonuses etc)

- To assess potential. At the organisational level this permits career and succession planning. At the individual level it facilitates an individual development plan

Now try this question from the Exam Question Bank	Number	Level	Marks	Time
	12	Examination	30	54 mins

OBJECTIVE TEST
QUESTION AND ANSWER BANK

Each of the questions numbered **1** to **10** has only ONE correct answer. Each of these questions is worth **2 marks**.

1   Which one of the following is a not-for-profit organisation?

A   Sole traders
B   Partnerships
C   Mutual organisations
D   Public limited companies

2   If the value of a nation's currency rises in relation to those that it trades with, what will be the effect?

A   Its exports become relatively cheaper and its imports relatively more expensive
B   Its imports become relatively cheaper and its exports relatively more expensive
C   Its interest rates must rise
D   Its national income must increase

3   Which type of computer virus hides itself inside legitimate software?

A   Worms
B   Trap doors
C   Logic bombs
D   Trojans

4   Which one of the following is the cheapest method of system changeover?

A   Direct changeover
B   Parallel running
C   Pilot operation
D   Phased changeover

5   Which sourcing strategy is most likely to create a competitive advantage for the purchasing organisation?

A   Single sourcing
B   Multiple sourcing
C   Delegated sourcing
D   Parallel sourcing

6   The 5Ss are often associated with lean production. Which one of the following is not one of the 5Ss?

A   Self-discipline
B   Sanitise
C   Systemise
D   Specify

7   Industria is a manufacturing company which makes three types of cleaning product.

'Budget' uses low grade ingredients and is aimed at the cheaper end of the household market.

'Premium' uses state of the art ingredients and is aimed at the premium end of the household market.

'Professional' is a high strength version which is aimed at professional cleaners.

Which marketing strategy is Industria following?

A   Mass marketing
B   Differentiated marketing
C   Undifferentiated marketing
D   Concentrated marketing

8   Marketing activities which occur in unexpected places and take people by surprise are known as:

A   Direct marketing
B   Viral marketing
C   Guerrilla marketing
D   Interactive marketing

9   Which theorist pioneered the scientific management movement?

A   *Taylor*
B   *Weber*
C   *Schein*
D   *Herzberg*

10 Integrating new recruits into the culture, beliefs and mission of an organisation is known, according to *Harrison*, as:

A   Recruitment
B   Indoctrination
C   Dialogic learning
D   Training

Each of the questions numbered **11** to **15** require a brief written response. The response should be in note form and should not exceed 50 words. Each of these questions is worth **4 marks**.

---

11 Explain what is meant by the term political risk.

12 Describe the philosophy of lean production.

13 Distinguish quality assurance from quality control.

14 Explain why three additional Ps are sometimes added to the original four Ps of the marketing mix.

15 Explain the meaning and the thinking behind employee empowerment.

1   C   Mutuals are primarily in business to provide services to their customers. They are not owned by shareholders whom they have to pay a share of their profit to.

2   B   If a nation's currency rises in value relative to those it trades with, then the cost to customer nations of its exports will increase. Conversely, the cost of goods imported from those nations will fall. Interest rates do not have to rise. The nation's national income may fall if the rise in prices results in decreased demand for exports. On the other hand, if demand for exports remains steady, the higher price would mean an increase in national income.

3   D   Trojans, or Trojan horses, are a type of virus that hides itself in legitimate software.

4   A   Direct changeover is the cheapest because it only involves one step – the old system is switched off and the new system is switched on (although if the changeover does not go as expected additional costs may be incurred).

5   A   Single sourcing is most likely to result in a competitive advantage because it strengthens the supplier/purchaser relationship, secures confidential information, aids quality control and creates economies of scale. Under the other methods the reverse is more likely to be true.

6   D   Specify is not one of the 5Ss. The others are Structurise and Standardise.

7   B   Differentiated marketing involves selling different product versions, each aimed at different market segments.

8   C   Guerrilla marketing events occur in unexpected places and usually involve taking people by surprise.

9   A   *Taylor* pioneered the scientific management movement.

10   C   *Harrison* named the element of the induction process, where new recruits are integrated into the culture, beliefs and mission of an organisation, as dialogic learning.

11   **Political risk** is the risk of an organisation incurring losses due to non-market factors, usually related to government policy. These include financial factors such as currency controls and economic data, and stability factors such as rioting and civil war.

12   **Lean production** aims to minimise the amount of resources (including time) used in all activities of an enterprise. It involves identifying and eliminating all non-value-adding activities. Lean production involves the systematic elimination of all forms of waste.

13   **Quality assurance** focuses on the way a product or service is produced. Production procedures and standards are introduced that aim to prevent defects before the good/service is produced. **Quality control** focuses on the checking of work that has been done – finding mistakes after the event rather than eliminating them.

14   The **traditional 'four Ps'** (product, price, place, promotion) relate to both products and services. Services have characteristics that led to the addition of three extra Ps (people, processes, physical evidence) to more accurately reflect the service provision process (eg for insurance: representative, the policy setting and selling process, insurance certificate).

15   **Employee empowerment** means giving staff at all levels the authority and freedom to make decisions that affect how they do their job. The thinking behind the theory is that those who actually do the work are best positioned to make decisions relating to how their work is done.

EXAM QUESTION AND ANSWER BANK

What the examiner means

The very important table below has been prepared by CIMA to help you interpret exam questions.

Learning objectives	Verbs used	Definition
1 Knowledge What are you expected to know	• List • State • Define	• Make a list of • Express, fully or clearly, the details of/facts of • Give the exact meaning of
2 Comprehension What you are expected to understand	• Describe • Distinguish • Explain • Identify • Illustrate	• Communicate the key features of • Highlight the differences between • Make clear or intelligible/state the meaning of • Recognise, establish or select after consideration • Use an example to describe or explain something
3 Application How you are expected to apply your knowledge	• Apply • Calculate/ compute • Demonstrate • Prepare • Reconcile • Solve • Tabulate	• Put to practical use • Ascertain or reckon mathematically • Prove with certainty or to exhibit by practical means • Make or get ready for use • Make or prove consistent/compatible • Find an answer to • Arrange in a table
4 Analysis How you are expected to analyse the detail of what you have learned	• Analyse • Categorise • Compare and contrast • Construct • Discuss • Interpret • Prioritise • Produce	• Examine in detail the structure of • Place into a defined class or division • Show the similarities and/or differences between • Build up or compile • Examine in detail by argument • Translate into intelligible or familiar terms • Place in order of priority or sequence for action • Create or bring into existence
5 Evaluation How you are expected to use your learning to evaluate, make decisions or recommendations	• Advise • Evaluate • Recommend	• Counsel, inform or notify • Appraise or assess the value of • Propose a course of action

Guidance in our Practice and Revision Kit focuses on how the verbs are used in questions.

1 Country and political risk

45 mins

Learning outcome: A2(vii)

TH is a manufacturing company based in Europe. The costs of labour and raw materials have increased substantially in recent years and the board is now considering relocating all of its factories to a new country outside Europe – Starland.

Until a year ago, Starland was run by an unpopular military dictatorship, but this was overthrown in a civil war which finished six months ago. The country is now becoming a democracy and the new government is keen to establish trade links with countries around the world in order to develop its economy and new industries. To do this it is offering generous tax breaks for companies who locate their businesses in the country. This, together with very low labour costs and a plentiful supply of cheap raw materials, have led to TH considering the relocation.

Required

(a)   Explain what country and political risks are and how TH can analyse the risks involved in relocating to Starland.

(10 marks)

Note: You are not required to explain models of risk analysis.

(b)   Using a model of your choice, analyse the risks TH will face in relocating to Starland and advise the company whether the relocation should take place.

(15 marks)

(Total = 25 marks)

2 Corporate governance and corporate responsibility   36 mins

Learning outcomes: A2(i), A2(ii)

(a)   Define corporate governance and briefly explain four corporate governance issues that organisations may face.

(10 marks)

(b)   Define corporate social responsibility and briefly explain the four layers of corporate social responsibility identified by Caroll and Buchholtz.

(10 marks)

(Total = 20 marks)

3 External information

54 mins

Learning outcome: B1(i)

JM is a private company which manufactures a range of packaging materials for customers in the fresh and frozen food industries. Before his recent retirement, the company's chairman and founder was the main source of external information – he kept his 'finger on the pulse' of the industry utilising his network of personal contacts built up over a period of some twenty years. Since his retirement, the board has felt that external information has been lacking. They wish to implement a formal system to capture relevant external information.

Required

(a)   Describe the aspects of its environment that JM should gather information on and the sources that may provide it.

(22 marks)

(b)   Explain four ways the board could use the captured information.

(8 marks)

(Total = 30 marks)

4 Service level agreement; obtaining IT services 45 mins

Learning outcome: B2(v)

GDC provides a facilities management service for DS in respect of its information systems, however the directors of DS are not satisfied with GDC 's performance. The appointment of GDC was relatively rushed and although an outline contract was agreed, no detailed Service Level Agreement was produced.

Details of the contract are.

The contract can be terminated by either party with three months' notice.

GDC will provide information systems services for DS, the services to include:

- Purchase of all hardware and software
- Repair and maintenance of all equipment
- Help desk and other support services for users
- Writing and maintenance of in-house software
- Provision of management information

Price charged to be renegotiated each year but any increase must not exceed inflation, plus 10%.

Required

(a) Explain, from the point of view of DS, why it might have received poor service from GDC, even though GDC has met the requirements of the contract. (15 marks)

(b) Explain five benefits of outsourcing that DS would have enjoyed if the contract and SLA had been drafted properly. (10 marks)

(Total = 25 marks)

5 Operations strategy 54 mins

Learning outcomes: C1(ii), C1(v)

(a) Six factors that should be taken into account when devising an operations strategy are:

- Capability
- Range and location of operations
- Investment in technology
- Strategic buyer-supplier relationships
- New products/services
- Structure of operations

Briefly describe what each of the six factors identified above mean in the context of operations strategy. Illustrate your answer with examples related to a retail supermarket chain. (15 marks)

(b) Explain the concept of sustainability, including four factors that should be taken into account when considering the issue of sustainability in operations management. (15 marks)

(Total = 30 marks)

6 TQM and virtual companies   45 mins

Learning outcomes B1(iii), C2(ii)

Total Quality Management (TQM) and virtual companies are relatively new developments in operations management.

(a)   Explain the main characteristics of a Total Quality Management (TQM) programme.   (15 marks)

(b)   Define the term 'virtual company' and then explain how technological advances have enabled the widespread formation of virtual companies and supply chains.   (10 marks)

(Total = 25 marks)

7 Inventories and JIT   54 mins

Learning outcome: C2(vi)

(a)   In relation to inventory control levels, briefly explain the following.

(i)	Reorder level	(2 marks)
(ii)	Minimum level	(2 marks)
(iii)	Maximum level	(2 marks)
(iv)	Reorder quantity	(2 marks)
(v)	Average inventory	(2 marks)

(b)   Identify and explain five features of a just-in-time (JIT) production system.   (15 marks)

(c)   Identify the financial benefits of JIT.   (5 marks)

(Total = 30 marks)

8 The marketing concept   36 mins

Learning outcome: D1(i)

Explain what is meant by 'the marketing concept'. Compare this with a production orientation and a sales orientation.

(20 marks)

9 Branding   36 mins

Learning outcome: D2(xi)

(a)   Explain four benefits that branding brings to an organisation.   (8 marks)

(b)   Explain brand extension, multi-branding and family branding as branding strategies.   (6 marks)

(c)   Explain the following methods of valuing a brand.

(i)	Market approach	(2 marks)
(ii)	Cost approach	(2 marks)
(iii)	Income approach	(2 marks)

(Total = 20 marks)

10 Consumer purchasing

45 mins

Learning outcome: D1(iv)

(a)   Explain the term 'buyer behaviour' and the various stages that household consumers go through when making a purchase.

(13 marks)

(b)   Explain four influences on household consumer purchasing.

(12 marks)

(Total = 25 marks)

11 HR plan and workforce flexibility (OMIS 5/05 – amended)

54 mins

Learning outcomes: E2(viii), E2(x)

The country of Mythland contains several areas of high unemployment, one such area is where CX Beers were produced until recently. CX was an old, family-owned brewery that supplied licensed outlets, including local restaurants, with its beer. CX represented one of the last local brewers of any size, despite retaining many working practices that evolved at least a century ago. Situated on a (now) underused dockside site, the company had, over the years, invested little in plant and machinery and someone jokingly once suggested that much of the brewing equipment should rightfully be in a museum! The company was forced to cease trading last month, despite having an enthusiastic, long-serving, highly skilled workforce and a national reputation for the beer 'CX Winter Warmer' (thanks to winning several national awards). The workforce, many of whom have only ever worked for CX Beers are now facing up to the difficulty of finding alternative employment.

In a press statement the owners said that the brewery's closure was sad for the area, the local workforce and traditionally brewed beer in general. The owners blamed the situation on inefficient and expensive brewing methods, fierce competition from large rival brewers and limited geographical sales. They also mentioned a dependence on seasonal sales that made cash flow difficult (35% over the Christmas period). They concluded that they would like the CX tradition to continue by selling the company as a going concern, however unlikely this was.

It is speculated that property developers may be interested in the site as the dockland area is showing signs of regeneration as a leisure and tourism attraction (thanks to the efforts of the Mythland government). However, two of CX's managers would like to save the business and are drawing up a business plan for a management buy-out. They have three main initiatives that they feel could, in combination, save the enterprise:

- Use the site as a basis for a 'living' museum of traditionally brewed beer (with out of date brewing equipment and methods of working as an attraction)
- Produce bottled beer for sales in supermarkets
- Employ a more flexible but suitably experienced workforce

One of the managers (your former boss) has asked for your help in advising him how to draft a detailed human resource (HR) plan to inform the business plan.

Required

(a)   Explain the key stages and issues involved in preparing a HR plan for the CX buy-out.   (13 marks)

(b)   Discuss how the buy-out team can achieve workforce flexibility.   (8 marks)

(c)   Identify five benefits to the organisation and the community in re-employing previous employees.

(5 marks)

(d)   Identify two marketing opportunities available to the new organisation.   (4 marks)

(Total = 30 marks)

12 Online recruitment (OMIS 11/06 amended) 54 mins

Learning outcomes: B1(i), B2(i), B2(ii), B2(iv), E2(i), E2(ii)

B3 is a family run personnel agency. It offers a range of services to both individuals and corporate clients (mainly local medium-sized organisations). The son of the managing director (MD) is currently studying for a specialist university business degree. His course includes a 'management consultancy' module where students are required to analyse an organisation and identify a range of development options for the business. The MD's son's investigations of B3 have led to a consultancy report being produced, extracts of which include:

'B3 should maximise the opportunities offered by information technology to a greater extent. In particular:

- Opportunity 1. B3 could develop its recent successful experiment in e-cruitment (the identification of employment opportunities through the world wide web and the emailing of clients). Currently details of vacancies are collected and matched to individual client's search criteria. When a match is identified clients are emailed and, if they are interested, interviews arranged. This service is not offered by any of B3's main competitors. There is a difficulty, however, in that many companies have barred access to personal emails at work and web access to recruitment sites such as B3's site from their offices. Market research suggests that significant opportunities for m-cruitment (advertising jobs by mobile telephones) also exist. Making use of recent software developments, a text message containing a job title and some contact details could be sent out to individual clients instead of an email, so providing a more convenient and speedy service.
- Opportunity 2. Virtually all CVs are currently received in electronic form and a policy decision should be made to develop a paperless operating environment through the development of databases, so upgrading existing office technology.

Analysis of profit indicates that executive searches, corporate 'headhunting' and vacancy identification for individuals (traditional and especially e-cruitment) are all profitable activities.

Involvement in selection processes with corporate clients is unprofitable and should be discontinued. Instead B3 should identify clear guidelines for corporate clients to follow once the short-listing of candidates has occurred'.

Required

(a) Evaluate the opportunities for B3 identified in the consultancy report. (12 marks)

(b) Produce guidelines for the selection process that should be adopted by an organisation presented with a short-list of candidates. (8 marks)

(c) Briefly explain five acceptable reasons for dismissing employees. (10 marks)

(Total = 30 marks)

1 Country and political risk

(a)   **Political risk**

Political risk is the risk of an organisation incurring losses due to non-market factors. These factors are usually related to government policy such as trade rules and the tax regime. However it also relates to financial factors such as currency controls and economic data, and stability factors such as rioting and civil war.

Country risk

Country risk is more narrowly defined than political risk and usually relates to risks in the business environment (including market factors) in a specific country.

Analysing political and country risk

It is important that TH **analyses the political and country risk** of Starland before it commits to relocating all of its factories. Once it knows the risks, the organisation can decide whether or not to proceed with the relocation. If relocation does go ahead, by knowing what the risks are, TH can put into place **plans** to reduce or avoid them.

Analysis of political and country risk is notoriously difficult. Some elements of risk, such as financial factors, can be **quantified**, however some factors such as the risk of civil war are based on assumptions and guess work.

TH has the choice of employing a **third party** (such as a global credit rating agency) to carry out the risk assessment, or it can do its own research into Starland and produce its **own assessment** using news stories and market information. Some organisations may provide this information for a fee.

(b)   **Starland risk analysis**

Once TH has identified the political and country risks of Starland, it needs to weigh up the probability of the risk occurring and the consequences to its operations should the worst happen. *Jennings and Wattam* (1998) devised the following model to weigh up political risk.

Impact of risk

		Low	High
Probability of risk	**High**	A	B
	Low	C	D

Using the model, TH will classify Starland and its relocation according to the probability of risk and the impact the risk will have on the business.

The possible results and implications for the organisation are:

Situation A – High probability of risk, low impact.

TH should accept the risks it classifies in this segment but introduce a policy to manage them. However, it may have to reconsider its plans if the cost of preventing the risk is too high compared to the impact that the risk will have on it.

Situation B – High probability of risk, high impact.

The relocation to Starland is likely to fall into this category. Due to the high risk and potential impact on TH, the relocation should only go ahead if the risk can be managed and contingency plans put in place. The potential benefits of the plan must outweigh the costs of managing the risk and the potential impact.

Situation C – Low probability of risk, low impact.

To the classified in this segment, the risk must be unlikely to occur and have low potential impact. This is the ideal situation as the costs of managing the risk will be low, but this doesn't apply to TH and the proposed relocation.

Situation D – Low probability of risk, high impact.

Risks in this segment are problematic because although the probability of risk is low, the damage it can inflict on TH is high. If TH chooses to go ahead then it must take action to minimise the chance of the risk occurring and the potential impact it will have on the organisation. If this cannot be achieved in a cost-effective manner then the organisation should consider abandoning its plans.

Risk analysis of Starland

The **main risks** involved in relocating factories to Starland are **civil war** and **failure of the fledgling government**. The nation has only just recovered from a previous war and it is highly possible that if tensions rise or if the new government becomes unpopular, trouble could occur again. Therefore there is a **high probability of risk**.

By relocating all of its factories to Starland means **TH is risking its entire operation**. If civil war or governmental failure occurs, it will have a major impact on business operations. This will probably mean the factories will stop production, or may even be destroyed. Therefore there is a **high impact on the organisation**.

Advice

TH should only go ahead with the relocation if the **risks can be managed** and **contingency plans** put in place.

The company **cannot manage the risk** because **civil war** and **governmental failure** are **out of its control**. However, it could develop **contingency plans** to cover the risk of operations ceasing. This is likely to be expensive as it will mean finding **alternative locations to produce its goods**. These costs are likely to **outweigh any benefits** of moving production and therefore TH should not relocate its factories – at least not until the country is stable.

2 Corporate governance and corporate responsibility

> **Top tips.** Notice how our answers in this answer bank use headings and small paragraphs. These enable the marker to quickly identify each point that you make and award you marks. Answers that consist of large blocks of text can be unreadable, resulting in fewer marks being awarded as the marker cannot spot the points easily.
>
> Always present your answers clearly to maximise the amount of marks you can be awarded.
>
> Both parts of this question could be answered using textbook knowledge and are quite straightforward as they don't require you to apply your knowledge or analyse a scenario. Not all questions will be structured like this so make the most of it.
>
> In part (b) you did not have to use the *Caroll and Buchholtz* model to come up with points, if you did then you would indicate to the marker that you have good depth of knowledge. However you could have come up with four equally valid points of your own.

(a)　**Corporate governance**

Corporate governance is the system by which companies and other organisations are directed and controlled. In other words it consists of an organisation's internal rules which control how it functions.

A number of high profile scandals and corporate failures have identified a number of corporate governance failings that business organisations may face.

Domination by a single individual

A feature of many corporate governance scandals has been boards dominated by a single senior executive with other board members merely acting as a rubber stamp. Sometimes the single individual may bypass the board to action their own interests. The report on the UK Guinness case suggested that the Chief Executive, Ernest Saunders paid himself a substantial reward without consulting the other directors.

Lack of adequate control function

An obvious weakness is a lack of internal audit, since this is one of the most important aspects of internal control.

Another important control is the lack of adequate technical knowledge in key roles, for example in the audit committee or in senior compliance positions. A rapid turnover of staff involved in accounting or control may suggest inadequate resourcing, and will make control more difficult because of lack of continuity.

Lack of supervision

Employees who are not properly supervised can create large losses for the organisation through their own incompetence, negligence or fraudulent activity. The behaviour of Nick Leeson, the employee who caused the collapse of Barings bank was not challenged because he appeared to be successful, whereas he was using unauthorised accounts to cover up his large trading losses. Leeson was able to do this because he was in charge of both dealing and settlement, a systems weakness or lack of segregation of key roles that featured in other financial frauds.

Lack of contact with shareholders

Often, board members grow up with the company but lose touch with the interests and views of shareholders. One possible symptom of this is the payment of remuneration packages that do not appear to be warranted by results. Equally, the directors may choose to pursue their own interests and ignore the requirements of the shareholders.

(b) **Corporate social responsibility**

Corporate social responsibility is an appreciation of companies that they should show an awareness of the social and ethical effects of their actions.

There is no legal framework forcing companies to be socially responsible, however pressure is created through consumer demand for the producers of products and services to demonstrate an ethical and moral side.

Caroll and Buchholtz identified four main 'layers' of corporate social responsibility that organisations have.

Economic responsibilities

Economic responsibilities relate to an organisation's obligations to provide a source of finance to various stakeholders. These include, shareholders who demand a good return on their investment and employees who want fair pay and good employment conditions. Businesses are formed to be properly functioning economic units and so economic responsibilities form the basis of all other responsibilities.

Legal responsibilities

All organisations are required to comply with the laws of the states that they operate in, for example employment laws or companies legislation. Business have a duty to obey these legal responsibilities because laws are based on the moral values and beliefs of the people who live in the state and therefore they should uphold them.

Ethical responsibilities

Ethical responsibilities require organisations to act in a fair and just way even if the law does not compel them to do so. An example of this is paying employees above the legal minimum wage if it means they will have a better quality of life.

Philanthropic responsibilities

Philanthropic responsibilities include charitable donations, contributions to local communities and providing employees with the chances to improve their own lives. Companies are not required by anyone to make charitable donations and so on, but it is argued that they have a duty to support their local environment and employees because they obtain benefits from them.

3 External information

> **Top tips.**
>
> Your answer to part (a) should have considered a range of issues – a PEST analysis is a particularly useful tool for doing this. However you did not have to use this model as a wide range of answers could have scored well.
>
> In part (b) you should have considered a strategic approach to using the information as this reflects the level of the board within JM.

(a) **The business environment**

Some aspects of JM's **external environment** will be more important for the company than others. Just what the most important aspects are vary from organisation to organisation. The first step that should therefore be taken is for an individual or a committee to be appointed to establish (and subsequently review) what aspects of the external environment should be monitored by formal methods and procedures.

The **aspects of the environment** that might be monitored include the following.

Competitors

Information should be gathered about what competitors are doing, how successful they are and how much of a threat they are. New contracts awarded by food companies will be of interest to JM.

Suppliers

Information should be gathered about suppliers and potential suppliers, their prices, product or service quality and delivery dates etc.

Customers

An organisation should always try to be aware of the needs of its customers, to identify changes in these needs, to recognise potential market segments, and to assess the size of a potential market. Customer awareness is vital for new product development and successful selling.

Legal changes

Changes in the law might affect how an organisation operates, and any such changes should be monitored. For example, changes in data protection legislation.

Political changes

Some organisations are affected by national or local politics. If politics are important, the organisation should try to monitor political decisions at both national and local level.

Financial and economic conditions

Most organisations have to monitor developments in financial and economic conditions. For example, a company's treasury department must be aware of current money market interest rates and foreign exchange rates. The general rate of inflation is also significant for decisions about wage increases for employees.

Environmental pressures

The use of CFCs in packaging has been identified as contributing to the hole in the ozone layer. Companies such as JM therefore need to find alternative materials to use in their products.

Sources of information

(i)   **Suppliers'** price lists and brochures.

(ii)   **Published reports and accounts** (of competitors, suppliers and business customers).

(iii)   **Government** reports (often, reports on specific topics. Economic and trade reports, for example, are frequently produced by central government).

(iv)   **Government statistics**.

(v)   **External databases**, provided by specialist organisations and often available over the **Internet**. Treasury departments, for example, use external databases to obtain information about current interest rates and foreign exchange rates.

(vi)   **Newspaper** and other **media** reports.

(vii)   **Competitor** and **industry Websites**.

(b)   The board will take a **strategic approach** when using the captured information. It is likely to use the information for:

Planning

The information will help JM to formulate a plan to react to the external environment and therefore assist with, among other things, resource planning, assessing possible time-scales for implementation and the likely impact of alternative scenarios on the company.

Controlling

Once the plan is implemented, its actual performance must be controlled. Information is required to assess whether it is proceeding as planned or whether there is some unexpected deviation from plan. It may consequently be necessary to take some form of corrective action.

Performance measurement

Overall performance of the plan must be measured in order to enable its success or failure to be determined. Constant monitoring of the external factors will help the board keep the plan on course.

Decision making

The board requires information to make informed decisions. Without it they cannot react logically to the situation that faces JM.

4 Service level agreement; obtaining IT services

> **Top tips.** In part (a), think about what is in the SLA, and also what isn't. For example, there isn't a clause detailing any financial penalty for providing poor service. Part (b) requires you to think more widely about information systems service provision. Consider the general benefits of outsourcing in part (c) and apply to DS.

(a)   GDC appears to have met its **legal obligations** even though the level of service it has provided to DS has been poor. There are a number of reasons for this.

Lack of service level agreement (SLA)

DS **rushed the appointment** of GDC and did not insist on a detailed Service Level Agreement (SLA). The contract does not specify the **level of service** that GDC will provide.

For example, GDC is obligated to provide 'management information', but there is no detailed definition of what this information will entail, and no deadline for the provision of the information. (eg '...within 5 working days of month-end').

Transfer of systems control

DS handed **complete control** of its systems to GDC. The absence of expertise within DS puts it at a disadvantage when arguing its case with GDC.

For example, GDC could spend significant amounts of DS money on sub-standard hardware and software. DS would **not have the expertise to question** or challenge this purchase, resulting in poor use of DS funds and a poor level of service. However, even when purchasing sub-standard hardware GDC would not have breached the requirement of the contract to 'purchase all hardware and software'.

Transfer of systems development control

GDC is also responsible for the writing and maintenance of in-house software. **Unless GDC has a detailed understanding of DS the software written may not be suitable**. As GDC receives a set annual fee, it may be tempted to produce software as quickly and cheaply as possible. As the contract has no mention of software standards, GDC would be meeting its legal obligations.

Age of agreement

Another reason that could be contributing to DS receiving poor service is that **the agreement is now two years old**. Changes could have taken place inside DS within the past two years that an outside organisation such as GDC does not understand. The nature of management information required now may be different to that required two years ago.

Lack of financial incentive

Service levels could also be suffering because **GDC has no financial incentive to provide a good standard of service.** GDC has the right under the contract to increase the annual fee, above the rate of inflation, without any consultation and with no reference to the satisfaction of DS.

(b)   The **advantages** to DS of outsourcing are as follows.

(Any five from the following.)

Cost

Outsourcing removes uncertainty about cost, as the annual contract price is fixed in advance. If computing services are inefficient, the costs will be borne by GDC.

Stability

Successful contracts build a stable relationship over the long-term. This would encourage DS to plan for the future.

Economies of scale

Outsourcing brings the benefits of economies of scale to DS. GDC may conduct research into new technologies or agree deals with equipment suppliers that that benefit a number of its clients including DS.

Skills and knowledge

Specialist organisations, such as GDC, are able to retain skills and knowledge. DS may not have a sufficiently well-developed information systems department to offer staff opportunities for career development. Talented staff would leave to pursue their careers elsewhere.

Expertise

New skills and knowledge become available. A specialist company such as GDC can share staff with specific expertise (for example, with experience of writing in-house software) between several clients who would not otherwise benefit from them.

Flexibility

GDC can scale resources up or down depending upon demand. For instance, during a major changeover from one system to another the number of information systems staff needed may be twice as large as it will be once the new system is working satisfactorily.

5 Operations strategy

> **Top tips.** Part (a) is based on Brown's theory. When reading the question, remember that 'brief descriptions' mean basic 'book knowledge'. You are then required to apply this knowledge to a supermarket chain.
>
> Your answer to part (b) might be based on any of the five considerations mentioned in the chapter (you only needed to mention four of them), however you would still earn marks for others as long as they are relevant to operations management.

(a) **Brown identified six factors important to operations strategy**. Each of these is described below, with examples relating to a retail supermarket chain

Capability required

Any operations strategy will be influenced by what it is that the organisation 'does'.

For example, a supermarket chain sells food and other items to consumers.

Range and location of operations

The operations strategy will be affected by the scale and geographical spread of the organisation's operations.

For example, a supermarket chain with say 10 outlets in one region of a country will face different operation strategy issues than a nationwide chain.

Investment in technology

Technology will impact upon operations and therefore operations strategy as it has the potential to change the processes associated with operations.

For example, a supermarket chain that uses an electronic bar code scanning system at its checkouts which is linked to its stock/warehousing system will operate differently to a chain relying on less-automated systems.

Strategic buyer-seller relationships

Who key strategic partners are will affect operations strategy.

For example, a supermarket may have a preferred supplier for canned food items. Operations may then be designed to help facilitate this relationship. Relationships with 'buyers' (consumers) may be developed using loyalty card schemes – and operations changed based on what the scheme reveals.

New products/services

This relates to how long the business will be able to do what it is currently doing (in the same way).

A supermarket may find it also needs to offer on-line shopping and home delivery. It could also decide to move into non-traditional areas such as consumer electronics – or even consumer insurance or finance. These types of changes require changes to operations strategy.

Structure of operations

Operations strategy will also be influenced by how staff are organised and managed.

For example, will 'regional managers' have responsibility and complete control over all stores in one region – or will one national strategy apply?

Issues such as staff levels, shift patterns and human resources policies will also affect operations strategy. For example, will stores be open 24 hours – and if so how will this be staffed?

(b)   **Sustainability**

Sustainability is about ensuring a better quality of life for everyone, both now and in the future. It focuses on social progress that recognises the needs of everyone, effective protection of the environment, prudent use of natural resources and maintenance of high and stable levels of economic growth or employment.

Sustainability and operations management

Five sustainability considerations relevant to operations management are:

Sustainable for whom

This issue concerns which species (other than humans) are to be sustained, the level of world population that should be sustained and the needs of developing countries.

An operations management consideration is whether organisations should source products from developing nations or look to the tried and tested industries of developed countries.

Sustainable in what way

There are three types of sustainability relevant to operations management.

Ecological sustainability concerns the preservation of the environment so it can function as naturally as possible. The operations management issue is whether organisations should continue production processes which are harmful to the environment, or should they look for other less harmful (but possibly more expensive) alternatives?

Social sustainability is about personal growth and development. For organisations the issue is whether or not employees should be treated like robots by requiring them to perform repetitive tasks, or should they be given scope to develop their abilities and perform a wide range of production roles?

Economic sustainability is about producing goods and services that people want whilst maximising the organisation's profitability. The operations issue here is to ensure the organisation produces products and services that its customers want whilst minimising waste to maximise profit.

Sustainable for how long

The issue here is generational equity. This is about ensuring future generations can enjoy the same environmental conditions as the current generation, and that social welfare is maintained or increased.

The main operations management concern is the use of natural materials. As the world has finite resources, production levels cannot be sustained forever. Therefore organisations need to plan their use of resources carefully, especially the rate by which they use them up. They should also look for new ways of producing the products that people want, as well as looking for sustainable resources.

Sustainable at what cost

There is a balance to be found between preserving the environment and natural resources with the need to produce goods and services.

The operations management issue concerns sourcing materials which balance the need for sustainability with the need to produce goods and services. For example, organisations can look at substituting some raw materials with sustainable alternatives or look to produce products using more sustainable processes.

Sustainable by whom

Ideally the whole world will take responsibility for sustainability, but this is unlikely due to a lack of meaningful global international agreements.

The operations management issue is that individual organisations must take on responsibility for sustainability themselves rather than waiting for legal regulation.

6 TQM and virtual companies

> **Top tips.** An easy way to answer part (a) is to memorise the seven principles of TQM – if you remember what they are you should not have a problem explaining them.
>
> Hopefully part (b) will not have caught you out. We covered virtual companies in Chapter 3, but they could equally be examined as part of an operations question. Exams frequently test different syllabus areas together, so it is important that you get used to answering questions such as this.

(a)   **Total quality management**

In a nutshell, total quality management (TQM) is a management philosophy aimed at continuous improvement in all areas of operation.

A TQM initiative aims to achieve continuous improvement in quality, productivity and effectiveness. It does this by establishing management responsibility for processes as well as output

Principles of TQM

Prevention

Organisations should take measures that prevent poor quality occurring. The emphasis is on quality assurance rather than quality control.

Right first time

A culture should be developed that encourages workers to get their work right first time. This will save costly reworking and help ensure high quality output. This ultimately results in satisfied customers, repeat business and improved profitability.

Eliminate waste

The organisation should seek the most efficient and effective use of all its resources.

Continuous improvement

The Kaizen philosophy should be adopted. Organisations should seek to improve their processes continually. High quality processes mean high quality output.

Everybody's concern

Everyone in the organisation is responsible for improving processes and systems under their control.

Participation

All workers should be encouraged to share their views and the organisation should value them.

Teamwork and empowerment

Workers across departments should form team bonds so that eventually the organisation becomes one. Quality circles are useful in this regard. Workers should be empowered to make decisions as they are in the best position to decide how their work is done.

(b)   **Virtual companies**

A **virtual company** is a **collection** of **separate companies**, each with a specific expertise, who work together, sharing their expertise to compete for bigger contracts/projects than would be possible if they worked alone.

Within recent years it has become increasingly common for combinations of organisations and individuals to combine in the form of a virtual company and **virtual supply chains**. Virtual companies enable people such as executives, engineers, researchers and others, based in a number of locations, to collaborate on a particular venture.

Technology behind virtual companies

This trend has been made **possible** by the **widespread use** of **remote networking** which is now available at relatively low cost to organisations of all sizes. The collaborators are able to utilise technology to work together and present themselves as a single virtual entity to potential clients.

Virtual companies and members of virtual supply chains tend to utilise the **Internet** and related technologies such as **intranet** and **extranet**. To be successful the partners involved must do more than establish virtual links. They must provide **complimentary areas of expertise**, and develop a **close relationship** based on mutual need and trust.

A virtual company may be the best way to implement business strategies particularly strategies that require **close collaboration** with others. For example, in order to exploit a new opportunity, business partners may be required to move fast. Establishing a virtual company may enable these partners to quickly establish a united entity to pursue the opportunity. Establishing traditional 'bricks and mortar' links would take considerably longer – increasing the risk of competitors grasping the opportunity first.

7 Inventories and JIT

Top tips. Part (a) requires you to repeat text book knowledge on inventory control levels.

Part (b) is reasonably straightforward if you have studied JIT in sufficient depth. Your answer to this part may have mentioned a number of other features of a JIT system – not just the ones we mention. As long as your points are valid you will earn marks.

Part (c) requires you to think about some benefits of JIT. To answer this part you need to think a little about what you have read and apply your knowledge. In the exam you would probably only need to provide five (relevant) financial benefits to gain the full five marks.

Also, note the verb, 'identify'. If you see this verb or 'list' then you know explanation is not required.

(a)   (i)   **Reorder level**. When inventories reach this level, an order should be placed to replenish stocks. The reorder level is determined by considering the rate of consumption and the lead time (lead time is the time between placing an order with a supplier and the stock becoming available for use).

       (ii)   **Minimum level**. This is a warning level to draw management attention to the fact that inventories are approaching a dangerously low level and that outages are possible.

       (iii)   **Maximum level**. This also acts as a warning level to signal to management that stocks are reaching a potentially wasteful level.

       (iv)   **Reorder quantity**. This is the quantity of inventory which is to be ordered when inventory levels reach the reorder level. If it is set so as to minimise the total costs associated with holding and ordering inventory, then it is known as the **economic order quantity.**

       (v)   **Average inventory**. This is a calculation of the average inventory level that assumes actual levels fluctuate evenly between the minimum (or safety) inventory level and the highest possible inventory level (the amount of inventory immediately after an order is received, ie safety inventory + reorder quantity).

(b)   **JIT production systems** include the following features.

Multi-skilled workers

In a JIT production environment, production processes are shortened and simplified, however, the variety and complexity of work carried out by employees is increased. Workers must therefore be flexible and adaptable. They should be trained to operate all machines on the production line and undertake routine preventative maintenance.

Close relationships with suppliers

JIT production systems go hand-in-hand with JIT purchasing systems. These match the usage of materials with delivery of replacements from external suppliers. This means that material stocks can be kept at near-zero levels.

For JIT purchasing to be successful, the organisation must have confidence that its suppliers will deliver on time and that the materials supplied will be of very high quality. There can be no rejects or returns which would result in production delays. Therefore the company and its suppliers must build up close relationships.

Work floor layout based on workflow

Factory layouts under JIT production are designed to reduce the movement of workers and products. Traditionally machines were grouped by function (drilling, grinding and so on). A part therefore had to travel long distances, moving from one part of the factory to the other, often stopping along the way in a storage area.

Under JIT systems, material movements between operations are minimised by eliminating space between work stations and grouping machines or workers by product or component instead of by type of work performed. Products can flow from machine to machine without having to wait for the next stage of processing or returning to stores. Lead times and work in progress are therefore reduced.

An emphasis on quality

Production management within a JIT environment seeks to both eliminate scrap and defective units during production and avoid the need for reworking of units. Defects stop the production line, creating rework and possibly resulting in a failure to meet delivery dates. Quality, on the other hand, reduces costs.

Quality is assured by designing products and processes with quality in mind, introducing quality awareness programmes and statistical checks on output quality, providing continual worker training and implementing vendor quality assurance programmes to ensure that the correct product is made to the appropriate quality level on the first pass through production.

Set-up time reduction

If an organisation is able to reduce manufacturing lead time it is in a better position to respond quickly to changes in customer demand. Reducing set-up time is one way in which this can be done.

Machinery set-ups are non-value-added activities which JIT aims to reduce or even eliminate. Reducing set-up time also makes the manufacture of smaller batches more economical and worthwhile. Managers do not feel the need to spread set-up costs over as many units as possible, which then leads to high levels of inventory.

(c) JIT systems have a number of **financial benefits**.

    (i) Increase in labour productivity due to labour being multiskilled and carrying out preventative maintenance

    (ii) Reduction of investment in plant space

    (iii) Reduction in costs of storing inventory

    (iv) Reduction in risk of inventory obsolescence

    (v) Lower investment in inventory

    (vi) Reduction in costs of handling inventory

    (vii) Reduction in costs associated with scrap, defective units and reworking

    (viii) Higher revenue as a result of reduction in lost sales following failure to meet delivery dates (because of improved quality)

    (ix) Reduction in the costs of setting up production runs

    (x) Higher revenues as a result of faster response to customer demands

8 The marketing concept

> **Top tips**. With open questions such as this it is always a good idea to create a structure for your answer first by producing a bullet point plan of your headings. This will help focus your answer on the question and avoid unnecessary waffle.

The marketing concept

One definition of the **marketing concept** is 'a management orientation or outlook, that accepts that the key task of the organisation is to determine the needs, wants and values of a target market and to adapt the organisation to delivering the desired satisfaction more effectively and efficiently than its competitors'.

In other words, **customer needs** and the **market environment** are considered of **paramount importance**. Since technology, markets, the economy, social attitudes, fashions, the law and so on are all constantly changing, customer needs are likely to change too. The marketing concept is that changing needs and attitudes must be identified, and products or services adapted and developed to satisfy them.

Some organisations may be **production-oriented** and others **sales-oriented**, although it is generally accepted that most business should be **marketing-oriented** to be successful in the longer term.

If the **marketing concept** is to be **applied successfully**, it **must be shared** by all managers and supervisors in an organisation. 'Marketing' in its broader sense covers not just selling, advertising, sales promotion and pricing, but also product design and quality, after sales service, distribution, reliability of delivery dates and in many cases (such as the retailing industry) purchasing supplies. This is because the customers' needs relate to these items as well as more obvious 'marketing' factors such as sales price and how products are promoted.

Production-oriented organisations

A **production-oriented** organisation is one which believes that if it can make a **good quality product** at a **reasonable price**, then **customers will inevitably buy it** with a minimum of marketing effort. Businesses which take this view will probably concentrate on product developments and improvements, and production efficiencies to cut costs.

If there is a **lack of competition** in the market, or a **shortage of goods** to meet a basic demand, then **production orientation should be successful**. However, if there is competition and over-supply of a product, demand must be stimulated, and a production-oriented organisation will resort to the 'hard-sell' or 'product push' to 'convince' the customer of what they want.

Sales oriented organisations

A **sales-oriented** organisation is one which believes that in order to generate large volumes of output, it must invest heavily in sales promotion. This attitude implies a belief that **potential customers** are by nature **sales-resistant** and have to be persuaded to buy (or buy more). This means that the task of the business is to develop a **strong sales department**, with well-trained sales people.

Key differences

The **fundamental difference** between production, sales and marketing-oriented organisations can be summarised very briefly.

Where an organisation follows a **production** or **selling orientation**, it produces goods or services, and then expects to sell them. The nature of the organisation's business is determined by what it has chosen to produce, and there will be a reluctance to change over to producing something different.

Organisations which embrace the **marketing concept**, commit themselves to supplying what customers need. As those needs change, so too must the goods or services which are produced.

9 Branding

> **Top tips.** Questions such as this are a gift because they provide you with a ready-made structure for your answer and the mark allocations indicate how much you should write in each part. For example, part (a) requires an explanation of four benefits for a total of eight marks – therefore you only need write enough to earn two marks for each.
>
> To earn the two marks you only need to identify each benefit and write a sentence or two to justify your answer.
>
> You should follow the same principles for parts (b) and (c).

(a)   **Benefits of branding**

   The **key benefits of branding** are:

   Product differentiation

   Branding aids product differentiation as it conveys a lot of information very quickly and concisely. This helps customers to readily identify the goods or services and thereby helps to create customer loyalty to the brand. It is therefore a means of increasing or maintaining sales.

   Advertising

   Branding maximises the impact of advertising for product identification and recognition. The more similar a product is to competing goods, the more branding is necessary to create a separate product identity.

   Industry acceptance

   Branding leads to a readier acceptance of a manufacturer's goods by wholesalers and retailers. It also reduces the importance of price differentials between goods and improves product recognition.

   Market segmentation

   Branding supports market segmentation, since different brands of similar products may be developed to meet specific needs of categories of user.

(b)   **Brand extension**

   Brand extension involves the introduction of new products which 'piggy back' on the goods that are already known to the customer. The idea is to capitalise on brand loyalty which should help make the new products successful.

Multi-branding

Multi-branding is the introduction of a number of brands that all satisfy very similar product characteristics. This can be used where there is little or no brand loyalty, in order to pick up buyers who are constantly changing brands.

Family branding

This is the use of brand name power to assist all products in a range. It is often used to consolidate expensive advertising costs by putting out one message – that of the brand - rather than promoting a range of individual items.

(c) **The market approach**

The market approach generates a value on the basis of market transactions. A common method used in this form of valuation is known as relief-from-royalty which reflects the fact that owners of brands have use of the brand for free, whereas they could generate an income by licensing it. This income stream, or royalty rate, can be derived by reference to royalty or license agreements for similar assets and used to generate a value.

The cost approach

The cost approach is based on the costs incurred to build the brand. For example, costs involved in registering trademarks and promotional activities. However, it is not the most accurate method of valuation because the cost of building the brand is usually unrelated to its ability to generate revenue.

The income approach

The income approach is based on net present values. The brand's expected future earnings, or cash flows, can be used to calculate the overall economic benefit that it will generate over its life. This benefit is reduced by all expenditure relating to brand awareness that will be incurred over its life to calculate a net income figure. This income figure is then discounted at an interest rate that an investor would expect as a return based on the brand's risk profile and characteristics. This final value is the value of the brand.

10 Consumer purchasing

> **Top tips.** This answer may appear difficult to achieve, but it is just the repetition of textbook knowledge. To produce a full answer you needed to remember the stages of the consumer decision-making process and the factors which influence it. Each stage/factor is quite self-explanatory so you should have been able to write a few sentences on each without too much trouble.

(a) **Buyer behaviour**

Buyer behaviour describes the **activities** and **decision processes** relating to buying. Treating buying behaviour as a process enables organisations to distinguish between the **different buying roles** that customers sometimes assume.

Marketers make a **distinction** between **business** and **non-business (household) consumers** when considering buyer behaviour because the needs and processes used by each type of consumer are very different.

According to *Lancaster and Withey* 2003, **consumer decision making** can be broken down into five stages or steps.

Need/problem recognition

At this initial stage, the customer recognises that they have a need to fulfil or a problem to solve. This creates a motive for them to search for a solution.

Pre-purchase/ information search

The consumer then searches for products or services that meet their need or solve their problem. This may involve visiting shops, searching the internet or telephoning potential suppliers.

Evaluation of alternatives

Once they have done their research, the consumer will evaluate each of the possible solutions that they have discovered. The evaluation will determine which of the possible solutions meet their needs best, however issues such as price may also have an influence.

The purchase decision

On the basis of their evaluation, the consumer selects the product or service they want and makes the purchase.

Post-purchase evaluation

Following the purchase, the consumer evaluates the product or service to see if it does in fact meet their needs. If they are satisfied then they may purchase the product or service again out of loyalty. If they are dissatisfied then the purchasing process begins again as the need has not been fulfilled nor the problem solved.

(b)   Four influences on **household consumer purchasing** are:

(i)   **Social factors**

Social factors relate to the social groupings a consumer belongs to or aspires to, and trends in society which influence buying patterns. Examples of social factors which influence the consumer purchasing process are reference groups, families and roles or status.

Reference groups are actual or imaginary groups that influence an individual's evaluations, aspirations or behaviour. They influence a buying decision by making the individual aware of a product or brand, allowing the individual to compare their attitude with that of the group.

All **families** differ, for example in terms of socio-economic status and consumption patterns. Therefore they affect the amount of money the consumer has to spend and in what volumes purchasing needs to be made.

Roles and status influence an individual's purchasing decision because the products or services selected must be compatible with them. For example a person who sees themselves as being part of a high social class may not select an 'economy' range of food products.

(ii)   **Cultural factors**

Culture comprises the values, attitudes and beliefs in the pattern of life adopted by people, that help them integrate and communicate as members of society. It may affect a purchasing decision in many ways. For example, alcohol consumption is part of the culture of many countries in Western Europe, whereas it is frowned on in Muslim and some other countries.

(iii)   **Personal factors**

Personal factors include such things as a consumer's age, stage of family life cycle, and lifestyle. They each influence an individual's purchasing decision because the products or services they select must be compatible with them.

Individuals will buy different types of product depending on their **age**. This is particularly relevant to such products as clothes, furniture and recreation.

The **family life cycle** affects a consumer's needs and purchasing patterns. For example, a single man will have different requirements to a man who is married with children.

A **lifestyle** is an individual's way of living as identified by their activities, interests and opinions. For example vegetarians will avoid purchasing meat-based food products and those who are interested in protecting the environment will only select products which are non-polluting.

(iv)   **Psychological factors**

The process of buyer behaviour is also influenced by **four psychological factors**, motivation, perception, learning and beliefs and attitudes.

Motivation is an inner state that energises, activates, or moves, directs or channels an individual. These factors will influence a consumer's desire to purchase a particular product.

Perception is the process whereby people select, organise and interpret sensory stimuli into a meaningful and coherent picture. The way consumers view an object may vary according to their past experience, expectation, needs, interests, attitudes and beliefs.

Learning concerns the process whereby an individual's behaviour changes as a result of their experience. This may be key in a purchase decision – an individual who has had a bad experience with a product, or with the company they purchased it from, may not buy those products again.

A **belief** is a descriptive thought that a person holds about something. An **attitude** describes a person's feelings and action tendencies toward some object or idea. Both can affect a purchasing decision. For example if a person can demonstrate their beliefs through a product, or if they have an emotional attachment to it, they may be more likely to purchase it.

11 HR plan and workforce flexibility

Top tips. At all costs, avoid using this question to write everything you know about HR! Strong answers keep to the question set and are relevant to the scenario.

There is much to cover in part (a). Ensure you don't just focus on the stages involved in developing a HR plan – you are also required to describe the main issues to consider in this process.

You may have used a slightly different planning model referring to HR plans including: strategic analysis; forecasting; job analysis, recruitment and training.

In part (b), mention the different types of workforce flexibility (eg numerical, task, financial) and suggest how these could be achieved at CX.

Part (c) allows you to 'brainstorm' an answer. Make sure you plan out your answer before you start write as you may lose ideas that you generated.

You might not have realised how HR can create marketing opportunities so you might need to think laterally in Part (d).

(a)   **Human resource planning**

Human resource planning involves developing a plan to recruit, utilise, develop and retain staff.

The CX buy-out involves three main initiatives; heritage 'real ale' tours, bottling beer for sale in supermarkets and employing a flexible but experienced workforce. The HR plan associated with the buy-out must support these initiatives.

The **main issues** involved in developing a HR plan for the CX buy-out are described below.

Workable

The plan must be realistic and suitable for implementation (taking into account cost and working practices).

Impact upon culture

CX has a long history and a national reputation for traditional 'real ale' production. Although CX wishes to change, the organisation and the people that work there should preserve this feeling and reputation as it is a source of competitive advantage. Therefore, the HR plan should encourage valued ex-employees back – it should **not** be a case of 'out with the old and in with the new'.

Specific issues the plan should address include:

- Budgets, targets and standards for staffing at all levels
- How the flexibility required within the workforce will be achieved
- The retraining required and how this will be addressed
- Remuneration and reward systems
- Responsibilities and procedures for implementing, monitoring and controlling the plan

There are **four main stages involved in developing a HR plan** for the CX buy-out.

Stage 1: Conduct an audit of existing human resources

As the brewery has closed, technically there are no existing human resources. However, as the shut down only occurred a month ago, and the workforce has specialist skills, it is highly likely that most ex-employees would be available for re-employment. The buy-out team should consult HR records and speak to key ex-employees to establish the current position.

Deciding who should be offered employment is a key task. Selection should take into account existing employee skills and the potential to develop any new skills required. A key consideration for re-employment would be a willingness to be flexible rather than simply 'I want my old job back'.

Stage 2: Forecast future demand for skills/labour

Past experience should provide a reasonable estimate of staff numbers required (including seasonal fluctuations).

New activities (eg bottling) will require new skills – and increased workforce flexibility also needs to be taken into account when estimating the numbers/skill mix required. Bottling may also impact upon seasonal fluctuations. Brewery tours will require significantly different skills.

All of these factors need to be considered and addressed – within a realistic, budget.

Stage 3: Assess the external labour market and forecast supply

In this situation, the external market is somewhat blurred with the internal market (as Stage 1 of this plan included ex-employees). Supply for many positions/skills is likely to be able to be satisfied from the pool of ex-employees – but areas such as bottling and brewery tours may require specialist knowledge and skills that may need to be found from other sources. Teaching ex-employees new skills is another option.

Information relating to ex-employees will be available using CX HR records. These should provide a wide range of information including positions held, age, training undertaken and performance levels.

Stage 4: Establish a plan reconciling demand and supply

When a realistic estimate of employee numbers and skills has been established, the next step is to produce action plans that will result in the recruitment and training of a workforce that will meet the demands of CX.

The plan should ensure steps are taken to ensure all required positions and skills are accounted for. Key employees should be identified by name. There may also need to be contingencies built into the plan to allow for circumstances where expected 'first options' are unavailable.

The four steps outlined above will not run completely sequentially – in reality many aspects of the plan will span more than one stage.

(b) **Workforce flexibility**

Before the shut-down, seasonal fluctuations in sales were large – an indicator that labour flexibility has always been important.

Logic dictates that as the old CX was ultimately unsuccessful the new CX must do something different. Changes in working practices will therefore be required. This is why the CX buy-out team have identified workforce flexibility as a key aspect of their plan.

Although the introduction of brewery tours and bottled beers may help smooth seasonal fluctuations, they will also introduce the need for new skills and probably new working hours. Flexibility is therefore essential.

Types of flexibility

For CX, the **flexibility** required would include **numerical**, **task** and **financial.**

Numerical flexibility

This is key to deal with seasonal fluctuations and for different demand levels during the day and or week eg for tours.

The development of a numerically flexible workforce will involve the use of temporary and part time workers supplementing full time employees (eg *Handy's* Shamrock). Another option is the outsourcing of non-core functions.

Task or functional flexibility

This involves recruiting and developing multi-skilled staff able to perform a range of tasks. This helps reduce overall numbers and provides ready made cover in cases of absence.

At CX, an employee may for example be able to help with brewing, carry out maintenance and conduct a brewery tour all on the same day.

Financial flexibility

This is achieved most often through performance related reward system.

At CX, staff payments should be linked to output (eg litres brewed, bottles produced, feedback scores from brewery tours or achieving financial targets related to sales figures and profitability).

(c) **Five benefits of employing ex-employees** to the new organisation and local community.

Benefits to the new organisation

Knowledge and skill base

By re-employing skilled staff, CX will save money on training new employees. Their experience will be vital to keep the brewery operating, as the business grows.

Local support

The local population may get behind the new venture and offer it support by going on tours or purchasing the beer. This support may be enough to see the venture through its early stages.

Benefits to the local community

Influx of cash

The influx of cash from employment and visitors to the area will benefit other local businesses who may find their sales improve due to a knock-on effect.

Flexible working

Employees and their families may benefit from the flexible working practices on offer. Older employees can enjoy semi-retirement and younger ones can fit the job around their family commitments.

Local tradition/history

The local area will retain an important part of its history and tradition that would otherwise be lost through property development.

(d) **Marketing opportunities**

Employing local ex-employees and the other benefits to the community offer excellent PR and social marketing opportunities that may extend wider than the local area.

The diversification opportunity with the visitor centre should lead to tourism and also add more personality to CX's own beer brand. The exposure the beer is likely to receive in the local news will present CX with an opportunity to push the product further afield.

12 Online recruitment

> **Top tips**. Open-ended questions such as Part (a) are best attempted by drawing up a list of reasonable points first. Once you're happy with them you can flesh out your answer. You will need to think of wider issues when considering the opportunities in the scenario, and the chances are you would have thought of others that are not in this answer. However, you will still earn marks providing your answers are relevant, well explained and related to the scenario.
>
> Parts (b) and (c) are answerable using textbook knowledge – don't forget to present your answer clearly using headings.

(a) **Opportunity one: develop e-cruitment and m-cruitment**

The report identified a potential opportunity to expand B3's business by using the internet as a source of employment opportunities and to match them with particular clients who have registered with them. Clients would then be contacted by email or text message and interviews arranged.

The following issues should be considered.

The matching process

How will candidate details be matched to appropriate vacancies? This is likely to rely on 'keywords' but the matching criteria must be tested and refined to prevent unsuitable matches being suggested.

Speed of service

Providing the client's requirements and job specifications from the employers are held in a database, the process of matching clients to jobs would be very quick indeed. This speed would increase client satisfaction.

Communication cost

Despite many clients not being able to access personal emails and B3's website at work, they could still access them from home or Internet cafes. E-mail is far cheaper than telephone or post and a large number clients with similar needs can be contacted by a single email. This will help keep B3's costs down.

Text content

Are text messages a suitable format for this type of communication? Can sufficient detail be provided to enable an informed judgement?

Database accuracy

It is essential B3's database of vacancies and candidates is kept up-to-date. Candidates may fail to inform B3 that they're no longer looking for a new position and employers websites may not be up-to-date. There is a risk B3 would waste its (and its clients) time applying for interviews for positions that had already been filled.

Opportunity two: upgrade technology

This opportunity involves B3 adopting a paperless office through the upgrading of office technology.

The following issues should be considered.

Data security

B3 would be storing the personal details of individuals. It is important that steps are taken to protect the security and privacy of data that is held.

Data protection

As the organisation would place very high reliance on the database, system failure and complete data loss could result in its operations ceasing it. This risk can be reduced by B3 regularly backing up its data and storing it in a safe location offsite.

Practicalities

It may not be practical for all tasks to be made paperless, for example client companies may not wish to be invoiced electronically or may not have sufficient systems to process such invoices. Where agreements or contracts are made between employees, employers and B3, paper copies may still be required for signing and to give to the employee for their records.

Backup systems

In the event of a disruption to power supplies or equipment failure, B3 would struggle to continue its operations. Therefore some kind of back up paper based manual system should be available just in case.

Cost-saving

The expense of developing new software and investment in systems should create a benefit to B3 that offsets these costs. Paper, printing, filing, storage and general administration are fairly cheap and it may take sometime for B3 to recoup its investment.

File conversion

Care must be taken when converting existing paper and electronic files into the new database. In particular, it must be ensured that the source data is complete and accurate and the process of converting data includes verification and validation.

(b)   ### Selection process

Once a short-list has been created from a number of suitable applicants, the selection of the most suitable can be made using the following techniques.

Interview

The aim of interviews is to find the best candidate for a position through **direct assessment**.

The potential employer must decide the type of **interview** that is most appropriate. Where the line manager makes the decision of who to select, a one to one interview should suffice. Where the **input** of more than one person is required, a final or sequential interview can take place.

The interviewer should use a **job description** for the vacancy as well as a person specification. This will enable them to understand what is expected of a suitable candidate.

The interview should be conducted in a **location** that is quiet and comfortable to enable all parties to relax.

Candidates should be given the opportunity to talk and ask **questions** as it is important for them to learn about the organisation as much as the organisation to learn about them.

Testing

Testing candidates is a method of selection that allows the **comparison** of abilities and personality traits that would not be discovered by interviewing alone.

Testing should be set directly in **relation** to the person and job specification. This will ensure the personality and ability traits tested are required by the role.

The type of testing selected should be **relevant** to the position concerned. For example psychometric tests may not be relevant to select between candidates who have applied for a manual job making door knobs, however it would be relevant for a senior management position.

Care must be taken when **interpreting** test results since they do tend to over simplify results – the best score may not indicate the best person for the job. Results should always be considered in relation to other selection methods.

Assessment centres

Particular roles, such as those requiring **leadership**, **problem solving** or **creative abilities** may benefit from the use of assessment centres in the selection process.

The **location** of centres should be easily reached by candidates and assessors. They should provide all the **facilities** that are required by the types of assessment being carried out. Care must be taken to select assessors with the right **skills** to make meaningful judgements.

Final steps in the process

Further into the process, reference checks, medical examination and the final decision/selection should be made. The offer should be made in a formal letter.

All steps in the **process** should be **reliable**, **valid**, **fair** and **cost effective**.

(c) **Five acceptable reasons for dismissal are:**

Conduct

The employee's **behaviour breaches acceptable limits** deemed by the employer. Unacceptable conduct may or may not be laid down in the contract of employment, however most employers have rules concerning drunkenness, immorality or misconduct.

Before conduct becomes an acceptable reason for dismissal, the employee should be given **warnings** and an **opportunity to change behaviour**. However, certain misconduct may be deemed so serious that it warrants summary dismissal.

Capability

The **standard of the employee's work** is **below** that what is **expected** and after appropriate support and guidance it is clear that they are not capable of performing the role.

Before dismissing on the grounds of capability, the employer should give an employee a **reasonable chance to improve**. This can involve consulting with the employee to identify difficulties and providing training to help them.

Breach of statutory duty

It is an acceptable reason for dismissal if by continuing the employment of the employee the employer would **breach a statutory duty** (for example, a solicitor could not continue to be employed if they are struck off the professional register). The employer would be justified in terminating the employment as soon as the issue comes to light since the employer must not break the law.

Other substantial reasons

Employers are entitled to dismiss an employee where another **substantial reason** affects them adversely. Examples include **loss of trust** in an employee or even where an employee marries a direct competitor.

Redundancy

Redundancy occurs where the **business ceases**, is **relocating far away** (so the employee cannot attend work), or where the role an employee performs is to cease and they cannot be accommodated within the organisation in another role. To be an acceptable reason for dismissal, the employer must **select employees** for redundancy **fairly**, provide **reasonable notice** and consider offers of **alternative employment**.

INDEX

Note: **Key Terms** and their references are given in **bold**.

Review Form – Paper E1 Enterprise Operations (6/11)

Please help us to ensure that the CIMA learning materials we produce remain as accurate and user-friendly as possible. We cannot promise to answer every submission we receive, but we do promise that it will be read and taken into account when we up-date this Study Text.

Name: _____   Address: _____

_____

_____

How have you used this Study Text?
(Tick one box only)

☐ Home study (book only)

☐ On a course: college _____

☐ With 'correspondence' package

☐ Other _____

Why did you decide to purchase this Study Text? *(Tick one box only)*

☐ Have used BPP Texts in the past

☐ Recommendation by friend/colleague

☐ Recommendation by a lecturer at college

☐ Saw information on BPP website

☐ Saw advertising

☐ Other _____

During the past six months do you recall seeing/receiving any of the following?
(Tick as many boxes as are relevant)

☐ Our advertisement in *Financial Management*

☐ Our advertisement in *Pass*

☐ Our advertisement in *PQ*

☐ Our brochure with a letter through the post

☐ Our website www.bpp.com

Which (if any) aspects of our advertising do you find useful?
(Tick as many boxes as are relevant)

☐ Prices and publication dates of new editions

☐ Information on Text content

☐ Facility to order books off-the-page

☐ None of the above

Which BPP products have you used?

Text ☑   Success CD   ☐

Kit ☐   i-Pass   ☐

Passcard ☐   Interactive Passcard ☐

Your ratings, comments and suggestions would be appreciated on the following areas.

	Very useful	Useful	Not useful
Introductory section	☐	☐	☐
Chapter introductions	☐	☐	☐
Key terms	☐	☐	☐
Quality of explanations	☐	☐	☐
Case studies and other examples	☐	☐	☐
Exam skills and alerts	☐	☐	☐
Questions and answers in each chapter	☐	☐	☐
Fast forwards and chapter roundups	☐	☐	☐
Quick quizzes	☐	☐	☐
Question Bank	☐	☐	☐
Answer Bank	☐	☐	☐
OT Bank	☐	☐	☐
Index	☐	☐	☐

	Excellent	Good	Adequate	Poor
Overall opinion of this Study Text	☐	☐	☐	☐

Do you intend to continue using BPP products?   Yes ☐   No ☐

On the reverse of this page is space for you to write your comments about our Study Text We welcome your feedback.

The BPP Learning Media author of this edition can be e-mailed at: barrywalsh@bpp.com

Please return this form to: Adrian Sims, CIMA Publishing Director, BPP Learning Media Ltd, FREEPOST, London, W12 8BR

TELL US WHAT YOU THINK

Please note any further comments and suggestions/errors below. For example, was the text accurate, readable, concise, user-friendly and comprehensive?